9

D1582671

MEMORIES AND MEANINGS

Books by W. R. Matthews

STUDIES IN CHRISTIAN PHILOSOPHY
THE GOSPEL AND THE MODERN MIND
GOD IN CHRISTIAN THOUGHT AND EXPERIENCE
SEVEN WORDS
GABRIEL IN SEARCH OF MR. SHAW
ESSAYS IN CONSTRUCTION
THE PURPOSE OF GOD
THE HOPE OF IMMORTALITY
FOLLOWING CHRIST
STRANGERS AND PILGRIMS
ST. PAUL'S IN WARTIME
THE PROBLEM OF CHRIST IN THE 20TH CENTURY
WEEK BY WEEK
SOME CHRISTIAN WORDS
THE SEARCH FOR PERFECTION
THE LORD'S PRAYER
THE THIRTY-NINE ARTICLES
A HISTORY OF ST. PAUL'S (jt. editor)
THE YEAR THROUGH CHRISTIAN EYES
CHRIST (in series WHAT DID THEY TEACH?)
BUTLER'S SERMONS (editor)
OUR FAITH IN GOD
THE CHRISTIAN FAITH
WHAT IS MAN?
DOGMA IN HISTORY AND THOUGHT (editor)
THE PSYCHOLOGICAL APPROACH TO RELIGION
SIGNPOSTS TO GOD

MEMORIES AND MEANINGS

by

W. R. MATTHEWS

C.H., K.C.V.O., D.D., D.Lit., F.R.S.L.,
Dean Emeritus of St. Paul's

HODDER AND STOUGHTON

*Printed in Great Britain for Hodder and Stoughton Limited,
St. Paul's House, Warwick Lane, London, E.C.4, by
Northumberland Press Limited, Gateshead.*

Preface

It is a poor excuse for writing a book to allege that friends have incited one, but it is a plain statement of fact that the idea of doing so was suggested to me by some men whose opinions I respect. I can only hope that they will not regret their encouragement. The book has turned out to be much longer than I had expected, partly because my memory and my imagination when once set going proved to be strangely fertile and I have had to cut out material in order to keep the book within reasonable dimensions. One salient feature of my memories is that they record much help from many friends and, I fear, inevitably I have failed to name some of them and done scant justice to others. Another defect in this book, from my point of view, is that it tells too little about my thoughts. When I set out to write I had a plan to trace the development of my understanding and philosophy of religion. I have failed to do this and perhaps the ambition was excessive. Of course, I have changed my mind and opinions and, of course, I am more sophisticated and better informed than when I was a junior lecturer on theology and just ordained priest, but fundamentally my mind has not changed and the Christian humanist standpoint of my youth is essentially that of my old age. "Rational faith" to me is a meaningful expression and not a contradiction in terms. I shall not give up thinking, however, and so long as power to think remains I shall try to understand the meaning of faith and its relation with reason. Rational faith should be the theme of our preaching.

This book is the partial and fragmentary record of a happy life. Much of its happiness has been given by friends and companions in every stage. I am thankful, and I must acknowledge gratefully the kindness of friends in the production of this book. I thank the Publishers for their patience, Miss

Winifred Rodda for help in my retirement and in the preparation of the manuscript of *Memories and Meanings* for the press.
It is a record of experiences and thoughts up to the hour of my
ceasing to be Dean of St. Paul's; I will add only this—that the
welfare of the Cathedral and of my successor there are regular
topics of my prayers.

1969.   W. R. MATTHEWS.

The permission of Her Majesty Queen Elizabeth the Queen Mother to dedicate this book to her enables me to express in a few words my gratitude for her interest and encouragement in my Christian Ministry over more than forty years.

W. R. MATTHEWS.

Acknowledgements

Extracts from the Chronicle of Convocation of June 1938 are reproduced by permission of the Faculty Office of the Archbishop of Canterbury.

Contents

Illustrations

Key to Acknowledgements
[1] Western Morning News Co. Ltd.
[2] Associated Press
[3] Campbells Press Studio
[4] Sport & General
[5] E. N. Parkinson, A.I.P.B.
[6] Radio Times Hulton Picture Library
[7] Associated Newspapers Ltd.
[8] Topical Press Agency Ltd.
[9] Planet News Ltd.
[10] The Central Press Photos Ltd.

CHAPTER 1

Cloudy Spring

If I were asked why my life and opinions should be of interest to anyone but myself I should be at a loss for a reply, but to me, now that I have stepped aside from the highway, memories of the journey so far are fascinating and disturbing. The phrase "meaning of life" is familiar, but its precise meaning is hard to define, and philosophers may quarrel happily about "the meaning of the meaning of life" for a long time. Perhaps the question is more easily comprehended if we narrow it to the limit and ask of any one life: Has it a meaning? And, I suppose, most of us do, in fact, scrutinise our lives with the hope of finding they have some significance. That hope has led me to write this book. As I have recalled the past, and recounted some of it, I have become convinced that, though as a person I am not specially remarkable, chance, or, as I should prefer to say, Providence, led me through events of historical importance and to encounters with a number of interesting persons, and about these events and persons I formed some opinions which, I think, are worth recording.

First of all, I must try to account for my coming into the world. I was born on September 22nd, 1881, in a small and recently built house in Bushey Hill Road, Camberwell, London, and christened about a month later in All Saints' Church in that borough. My parents were Philip Walter Matthews and Alice his wife and they, together with my godparents, gave me the names of Walter Robert.

How strange are the results of dredging in one's memory for relics of infancy! I would not say that I feel no identity with the baby—but the very few vivid pictures are disconnected and moreover almost impossible to date. Yet, some of them seem to indicate an embryo disposition—not altogether a pleasing one. My earliest and most definite infant memory is of crawling up some stairs in my parents' little villa and sitting on one, while howling with grief and rage, and then pausing to reflect that some aunts would pay attention if I pretended to "hold my breath". I think the occasion must have been the christening of my brother, Hubert, and probably my rage was due to jealousy. Another memory of about the same date is, I fear, more distressing to me, though I do not accept any blame for it. I was on a beach somewhere, sitting on the sand, obviously not old enough to run or even toddle, when suddenly without any warning a violent female snatched me up in her arms and ran into the sea, swinging me backwards and forwards as if she was going to hurl me into the waves. I was terrified and, in my frenzied efforts to escape, snatched off her glasses and, I think from the fuss she made, must have broken them. I believe this fright had a mildly "traumatic" effect on me. Though I became quite a good swimmer and not, I think, in other ways more cowardly than most boys, I could never really dive; an unconquerable terror held me back from casting myself head first into water from any height, though I could screw up my courage to jump in. Whether my diagnosis of my own case is correct or not, I maintain that jokes which frighten very young children should be repressed and, since I am identifying myself with baby Walter, I will defend him from the reproaches which he could not answer then. I had no experience of the playful lady; I believe I had never met her before that day; my experience of adults was limited to about three persons who often did things which I disliked and thus I had no evidence which tended to show that it was unlikely she would throw me into the sea. Therefore it was plainly wise to do what I could to stop her. I am glad to be able to hold that my actions in a difficult emergency at so tender an age were completely logical!

These two reminiscences are of only slight interest in connection with the assessment of my qualification for a commentator on the way of the world and life's problems; but there is another, which has risen out of the unconscious only since I began recently to fix attention on my earliest years. I hope it is significant. When I was a little older, but still quite a baby, I lay awake for hours one night, wrestling with a question which had something to do with my name. Why was my name Walter? The answer in the Catechism, that it was given by my godfathers and godmothers at my baptism, did not satisfy me; and, in fact, my mother and father never understood what the question meant, which is not surprising, because I did not know myself, but I believe that, in a vague way, my infant intelligence had come upon the problem of personal identity. Babies easily become a bore and I will close the subject by remarking that, from the time when my recollection becomes clear and more or less consecutive, I am sure that I had an enquiring tendency which was beyond the normal in persistency and the cause of exasperation to my elders. I am also sure that much of it was partly habit and partly "showing off" and quite a small proportion sincere desire to know. I cannot remember a time when I was not aware that interesting things were happening and that to find out what and why was worth effort.

Camberwell, as I dimly remember it, was most unlike its present condition. The village of the early 19th century had not been obliterated and St. Giles had still something of the appearance of a country churchyard, while the Grove, along which as a schoolboy I walked or ran morning and evening, did not entirely belie its name. Deeper than the physical differences, however, are the social and psychological. When I pass through Camberwell today, I have the feeling that everything has been flattened out since I lived in it—not indeed in outward appearance, for the elongated boxes which modern architecture rejoices in have appeared here as elsewhere, but spiritually there has been a flattening. I mean that Camberwell in my childhood was a community and now it is a dormitory. In the '80s and '90s of the last century, Camberwell was a place where people dwelt and constituted a community. Degrees of culture, of income, and of public spirit were evident enough and, of course, the cause of quarrels and ill-feeling, but the diversity made for richness of content.

My maternal grandfather was, I think, what was then called a pastrycook; we should call him today a caterer on a small scale for the "gentry". I possess today some of the dinner plates which he used for the more ambitious banquets. There were wealthy city families in some of the mansions in the Grove and on the borders of Dulwich. Memories of Robert Browning lingered and my mother remembered being patted on the head

by John Ruskin. Young men reading for the Bar and recently
fledged barristers abounded, some of them destined to distinction. My father belonged to a debating society in which a young
man named Edward Clarke often spoke.

When I was born, Camberwell had already advanced in the
direction of population expansion and my parents lived in a
small, recently erected house, one of a row all of the same
pattern. All I can remember of it is that it had a tiny front
garden, with a cast-iron gate, and a brief walk to the front door,
the same being paved with coloured tiles which were slippery
and hard when you fell on them, even if you were only three
feet high. And now, having arrived at the house, we must
introduce the inhabitants: my father and mother. The first
and most fundamental thing to say about them is that they
were good. I never doubted that, though at times I thought
they were mistaken. It is my settled conviction that my greatest
good fortune, or rather I should say God's greatest mercy
towards me, is that my parents were loving and "God-fearing"
—to use a phrase then current but now seldom heard. Like
Clapham, Camberwell had undergone a kind of evangelical
conversion. The word is perhaps too strong, but at least many
earnest and relatively prosperous evangelical families had homes
there. "Camden Church", which was, I think, a "proprietary"
chapel at one time, was a centre of Anglican evangelical piety.
When I was born, Canon Melville was the incumbent and my
maternal grandmother was a faithful and, to my infant mind,
somewhat alarming attendant on his ministry. When I was a
child, I heard Melville spoken of with reverence (he had
recently died) and, in my last position, as Dean of St. Paul's,
I heard of him again. Mr. Skinner, who retired from being
Dean's Virger in 1934, told me that, in the great days when
Canon Liddon, the notable High Church preacher, was drawing large congregations under the dome of St. Paul's, the Low
Church had in Canon Melville a no less attractive divine,
indeed I think Mr. Skinner held that he was better than Liddon.
However that may be, Liddon is remembered and Melville
forgotten. When my grandmother died, I found a volume of
Melville's sermons among her books and read them. They are
pleasantly written and evidently the work of an amiable man,
but seem to skate over the difficult parts of the Christian faith.
But I am sure that, if I was given as a penance the direction

to read a sermon of either Liddon or of Melville every day, I would choose Melville.

My parents were "Godfearing" in the evangelical mode and were prominent members of the congregation in the church where I was christened. This meant that they were concerned about sin and salvation. I am sure that, from the day of my birth up to their death, each prayed for me and they prayed first of all that I would be saved, that I would have faith and, through faith, grace to live in the fear and love of God. Who can estimate the value of such prayers? Not I; but I can say that the knowledge that these prayers were going on day after day had some influence on my conduct and my thinking. And now, writing when they have been dead many years, I wish I had allowed it to have more, and I hope, and try to believe, that my father and mother pray for me still. Perhaps one of the chief characteristics of their idea of goodness was the stress on honesty and truthfulness. To deceive, or to tell a lie, was condemned as an offence against God and also as mean and cowardly. Now I come to think about it, I can see what I never saw before, that, closely allied to the Christian ideal in their minds, was the ideal of the gentleman. My parents, though very far from being of aristocratic lineage, strove to be of gentle manners and to cherish honour. To lie and cheat and make excuses was contemptible; only a coward or a badly brought up child would do such things. Perhaps there was a tinge of what is now called (erroneously) snobbishness, which could be discerned by a critical eye, though I do not think it is accurate to use the word; quite definitely, there was a touch of pride in this moral ideal: "I will not stoop to do things which mean that I compromise with other persons who have lower standards." To me, it seems that we have lost something of real value in so far as the ideal of the Christian gentleman has lost its prestige; like everything else that is noble, it has been sullied by nauseating hypocrisy, which gives the mocking cynic an easy triumph—but every victory of cynicism over goodness is a defeat of humanity.

My father was a young man when I was born and I have a clear picture of him in my mind as he was when I was nine or ten. He was a short man, who wore a moustache and rather stubby beard. His eyes were bright and expressed his emotions. He was tirelessly active and, on the whole, cheerful. He expressed his opinions freely and forcibly and I remember that he so deeply captivated my childish credulity that it was a quite painful effort to conceive that, not only were there subjects on which he had no knowledge, but, more painful still, some of his forcibly expressed opinions were totally rejected by my mother and were quite possibly mistaken. He had a quick rather than a deep intelligence. He had, too, the inestimable gift of perseverance and persistence which enabled him to carry on through great difficulties and end with the kind of success which he hoped for, an old age not wealthy but free from financial anxieties and with his children honourably settled in the world. I believe that my father had a very sketchy school education, which was oriented mainly on "commercial" subjects; he rarely referred to schooldays and I guessed that they were no source of pleasure to him in remembrance. Nor did he speak much about his occupation when he left school. I believe, but I am not sure, that for a time he "lived in" at one of the wholesale drapers' establishments which, in the 19th century, clustered round St. Paul's. I have often wondered if it ever occurred to him in his wildest dreams that his son might be Dean of the Cathedral.

My mother had, I think, the kind of education which would have qualified her to become, like two of her sisters, a "governess". She had a good knowledge of French and could read and speak the language better than her children. More important, from the point of view of my development, was the bent of her mind. She had an imagination which ranged beyond the commonplace and, though she would have laughed at the idea that she could be either a poet or a philosopher, if I have any aptitude for either of these exercises, I attribute it to her, not only in the sense that, from my early childhood she encouraged me to talk about "God, freedom and immortality" in childish parables and symbols and fostered the love of reading which has never left me, but also in the sense of inheritance. My father and mother, though very different from one another, were a devoted pair and each thought first of the other's good. I have a feeling that, without saying much, my mother set herself to complete her husband's education and to play the salutary and inoffensive critic by almost imperceptible irony. It is at least certain that Philip gave much of his leisure, which was limited, to "culture".

Modern young people, when they think of their grandparents and "greats" at all and understand that there was no radio and hardly any telephone, wonder what people did to keep boredom away. My feeling is that, in the kind of family to which I belonged as a child, there was less boredom than one would find today. People had, to a large extent, to make their own amusements and many of the occupations of their leisure were definitely cultural. In the days of my youth, nearly everyone seemed to be learning to play the piano, or some stringed instrument, or was at least ready on very slight provocation to stand up and sing a solo. Such were my parents. My mother kept up her piano-playing until arthritis snatched her piano away, and my parents were regular members of a local Choral Society, into which I was recruited when my piping treble had given place to an uncertain bass. Was there no culture as well as fun in doing our best with great musical compositions? I am sure there was, and in more than one way. Music widens the horizon of the mind; it overcomes the barriers of language and sect in subtle as well as obvious ways. For example, strong Protestants like my father and mother would not probably have read Newman's *Dream of Gerontius* or, if they had read it, would have simply rejected it as "popish"; but, when they came to sing it and were caught up in Elgar's rhythms, they had a new insight into the spiritual life and faith of many fellow-Christians. I believe that the unifying power of music has not been exploited to the full. There are untried possibilities. When we can use each other's music freely and hopefully, we shall be on the way to unity of the Spirit.

Reading was a leisure occupation in my childhood to a wider extent than at present. Certainly, I was brought up to enjoy the sound of words put together by a master and to believe that good reading was a desirable accomplishment. I am grateful to my parents for this: that they read regularly to their children. In this way at a comparatively early age I had heard a number of Dickens' novels, with occasional comments, and some of Scott.

I have not referred to my aunts, but I had a rather better than average number and have kind recollections of all. One there was, called Aunt Lizzie, who was the wife of a man who owned a chemist's shop in Worcester and had two daughters. With these cousins I shared the Dickens readings, when I spent school holidays at their home. Aunt Lizzie had introduced an innovation. She made her daughters lie flat on their backs while she read to them and of course I had to conform. I wonder how much parental reading aloud is practised now. My impression is that the habit has died out and most parents are content to let their children listen to "a book at bedtime", if they like. I am glad that I was coerced into "being read to". It was through the reading that I got the first idea of the difference between good writing and slipshod or vulgar writing.

My father joined a Shakespeare Society, consisting of friendly neighbours who met at each others' houses to read the plays. I remember that discussion arose now and then in the family circle on the interpretation of some character whose part was to be read at the next meeting. My father prided himself on his reading and took pains over it. So it came about that he knew long passages of the Plays by heart and was knowledgeable about quotations long before crossword puzzles came into fashion. I must not forget to add that he was a member too of an Essay Club, whose members prepared and read papers which were discussed. I was never invited to this club and I think I saw only one of the papers. Years later, when I was a professor and tutor, it fell to my lot to hear many undergraduates' and postgraduates' essays. I should guess that the Essay Club produced fewer imbecilities and more common sense than my college pupils. I do not agree that my father was an uneducated man. He was educating himself all his working life, qualifying himself for the duties of his various positions.

When I was born, he was a bank clerk in what became the giant Barclays Bank, largest of the British joint stock banks. In those days, it was still a "private" bank, a company of partners with unlimited liability, but it had gone some way in its long strategic movement of expansion by amalgamation. Apparently, the more important firms amalgamated, or perhaps "absorbed" is a better term, insisted that their names should be retained in the firm's title, so that the cheques bore a string of names, each of which had local history and meaning. Unless my memory is at fault, Barclays Bank Limited was then Messrs. Barclay, Bevan, Tritton, Ransome, Bouverie and Company. I am not sure that the name of Gurney was not on this roll of pecuniary credit; it is at least certain that the Gurney family was in the party. When my father retired from his final position as Chief

Inspector of the London Bankers' Clearing House, he employed his leisure in compiling a history of Barclays Bank, including all the constitutive firms, many of which were quite old. In a very small way, I helped in the research for this book and learned something thereby of local and economic history in the 18th and 19th centuries.

My father was by nature a "Protestant"; he was irked by any obstacles put in his way to express dissent when he heard speeches or sermons with which he disagreed. At one period of my childhood, this trait in his character caused me acute discomfort. Every summer, the whole family lodged for a fortnight at some seaside resort and went on Sunday to the parish church, in accordance with his view of the duty of Christian families. Not infrequently, the sermon touched on sensitive spots in his conscience—Anglo-Catholicism and the Higher Criticism were very tender spots. One occasion had an almost traumatic effect on me—at least I have never forgotten it. At a seaside place on the east coast, possibly Cromer, one Sunday morning, when I was about thirteen, the whole family, mother, father, four children and one maid, occupied a front pew. A curate of a slightly emaciated appearance and with what was then known as an 'Oxford accent', who preached, looked to me as one unlikely to have opinions which my father would pass as "sound", and my fears were enhanced when he began, "The dear saint Augustine . . ." I have no idea what the dear saint was alleged to have done or said, but to speak of any saint not mentioned in the Bible in affectionate terms was not my father's custom. I was right; after five minutes about the "dear saint", my father smelt "popery" and led his flock with no little clatter out of church. Since then, a nightmare picture of myself ascending the pulpit and the congregation incontinently rising to go has haunted me. It has never actually happened, though something uncommonly like it did at a meeting which I addressed in Sweden during the last war. I hasten to add that my father was not a fanatic and was in love and charity with clerics with whom he disagreed. As years went by, his acquaintance widened and, with it, his tolerance, though he always resented going to a parish church and being given what he could not find in the Prayer Book.

Reading through what I have written about my father, I am conscious of an omission which distorts the picture; I have not mentioned his tendency to sudden anger. Normally easy and cheerful, he could be furiously angry when he, or someone he loved, was being injured or unfairly treated. A very early memory of my childhood, when I was still in the spade and pail phase of infancy, comes to mind. We were at Eastbourne, or some seaside place of the kind, and we, mother and father and I, were walking slowly along the front ("esplanade" seems to stick in my memory); invalids and old people in bath-chairs were being pushed or pulled along by 'bath-chair men', who looked half asleep. One of them, it seems, pushed or pulled his chair over my mother's foot, causing her to cry out. My father, like a bantam fighting cock, first cursed the man and, when he received a surly reply, squared up to the culprit and was about to deliver a straight punch, when my mother caught his arm and started to persuade her belligerent husband that the man meant no harm and she was not badly hurt.

From my present detached point of view, detached by the interval of about eighty years, I can see that this incident, trivial and even ludicrous as one might think, really displays in action the characters of the two partners in this successful marriage. The impetuous action and quick reaction of my father and the contrasting sweet reasonableness of my mother. And she was like that. She generally saw both sides of a quarrel and tried to understand the motives of persons who annoyed her. Her disapproval expressed itself in gentle irony rather than strong language. Compared with her husband, she was endowed with imagination and a more subtle sense of humour. In temperament and intellect, I think I resemble her more than him. For example, when I am really angry, which is rare, instead of becoming eloquent with protest and reproof, I go pale, feel sick, and become speechless.

I really seem to have been insufferably dreamy when a boy. My father sent me once to an empty house which he had bought with instructions to look out for workmen doing some odd jobs. I went, provided with sandwiches and a writing pad. I spent a happy day writing some preposterous story and in the evening returned home. When my father asked about the workmen I assured him none had come. Unfortunately, when he expostulated vigorously with the contractors he was met by the fact that the workmen had done the whole job. I really cannot remember that my father was specially eloquent in his reproof on this occasion; perhaps he guessed that I was predestined to be the absentminded professor.

I cannot remember a time when I did not go to church, from which I deduce that I was taken by my parents at a very early age. I can hardly remember a time when I was not aware that there are different kinds of churches and that people differ on the question: Which kind of church is the best? This is connected with my earliest experience of school. Along with my mother, another maternal figure dominated my early childhood—that of Miss Batstone, who kept an infants' school in Coplestone Road, Camberwell, to which my parents had moved from the house of my birth. Miss Batstone had some at least of the technique of the kindergarten and taught her pupils knitting, among many activities which keep children quiet and develop muscular and other kinds of co-ordination. Miss Batstone lived to extreme old age and sent a message to me from her death-bed, some time after the end of the last war. She believed in loving her pupils and she had a capacity for affection which was poured out on all the children of her little school. I cannot help believing that I was a kind of favourite; I thought so when I was young and her message at the end confirms my belief. Because I was her favourite, she thought I ought to be taken to the best kind of church, so that I might at least have a glimpse of the pure Protestant worship of God, even that I might be brought into the Baptist fold and weaned away from the Church of England. I went with her, after careful consideration by my parents, to the Baptist Chapel in Rye Lane, Peckham, at that time under the ministry of a popular preacher named Ewing. Alas, I have no recollection of the service or the sermon, except that the sermon was longer and the hymns were louder than in All Saints'. And indeed there was not any very marked difference between the outward form of the services, except that the vicar wore a white surplice when he read the prayers and a black gown when he preached, while Mr. Ewing wore a black gown all the time—or was it a frock coat? I really do not remember.

All Saints' Church in Blenheim Grove, which my parents and many of their friends had helped to build, had, and still has, an extreme evangelical C. of E. colour. There I preached my first sermon after being ordained deacon and was glad to be allowed to do so, because of earlier associations and many old friends who were still faithful to it; but I had long revolted against its teaching and the long process of "liberating" myself, as it seems to me now, was a decisive phase in my mental and spiritual growth. Here again, my education and my religion were closely associated and I have never been able to understand how anyone who knows the meaning of words can believe that whether a school is "religious" or "secular" is a matter of indifference. All Saints', when I was christened in it and for several years subsequently, had a forceful vicar, T. J. Gaster, who had been a missionary in India and never failed to keep the missionary cause constantly before his congregation.

The outstanding merit of All Saints' in my days was that it was whole-heartedly evangelistic and every worshipper was urged to take some part in proclaiming the gospel. To anticipate some years, when I was confirmed at about the age of fifteen, a layman, a remarkable man named Brown, approached me with the alarming challenge, "Now that you have become a full member of the church, what are you going to do to witness for Christ? If you haven't made up your mind yet, I want you to help with the Sunday evening open-air services at the corner of Rye Lane." When I disclaimed any capacity for the role he had assigned me, he rejoined, "Well, I am sure you can read and I want you to give out the number of a hymn and read the words, so that people who haven't got hymn books can join in the singing." Reluctantly I allowed myself to be pushed on to a soapbox platform and found myself talking to a fluctuating group of hearers. The experience of evangelistic oratory, which open-air services gave me, was far more useful in my later occupation than the school debating society.

I must add a word about Mr. Brown, because he does not fit into the pattern which "progressive" religious commentators have of earnest evangelical laymen at the end of the 19th century. Mr. Brown was neither stuffy nor reactionary; I suppose, since he was superintendent of the Sunday School, that he accepted the fundamentalist theology which he heard from the pulpit, but his social and political views were radical and, to me, sometimes startling. A saying of his, arising out of a conversation on the condition of the poor, stays in my memory: "There are only two things which keep revolution from this country, religion and beer." Whether he went on to say "and both are getting weaker", or it was a comment of mine, I cannot say; but I deduced from his words that he was not altogether opposed to revolution, since he was definitely opposed to beer.

When I was small and taken to church, I cannot claim that I was ever bored, but, having the good fortune to sit in one of the churchwardens' pews at the back, I could let my imagination play about what happened in the remote chancel. In our Low Church ceremonial no surpliced choir was tolerated and no solemn entry of choir and clergy; the officiating cleric was preceded to the reading-desk by the churchwardens and, to my eyes, it seemed that they released him from the organ. That was enough to start fantasy working and I built up in my imagination a detailed picture of the house inside the organ. I remember spending some time on the location of the bathroom. When I was able to read, I found food for thought in the prayer book, which is praiseworthy, but I fear it was not always edification that I drew from its pages. Like most children, I was fascinated by words, how they were spelt, how pronounced and what they meant. Early in life, I encountered the Thirty-nine Articles of Religion, which were to plague me for most of my adult life. As an innocent and ignorant child, I was intrigued by phrases like "as the Pelagians do vainly talk". But, at a comparatively early age, I began to apprehend their meaning and it was not long—it was before I was confirmed—that I felt the magnetic attraction of the study of theology and the disturbing nature of some of the ideas of God suggested in the Articles. These feelings have lasted until today.

But it is time to give due attention to my pastors and masters. I have been told that my first conversation with Mr. Gaster was unpropitious. He was a diligent visitor and often had tea in the nursery, which was inhabited in those days by a very small me, a nurse and my infant brother Hubert. I wearied, it is alleged, of the vicar's talk and said in a loud, clear voice, "You *are* making a tea, Mr. Gaster." No doubt, I said this because it had often been said to me and I regarded it as a genial and courteous remark. Mr. Gaster was a diligent, zealous and eloquent man, but he was a fanatical believer in a rigid Calvinistic type of Protestant theology. Thus it came about that, when my mind was on the point of waking and was putting to itself questions of great moment, the sermons to which I listened with a real desire to learn were too often powerful statements of dogmas, which I had to free myself from in order to think as a boy who would be a man of the 20th century.

Mr. Gaster believed in the verbal inspiration of the whole Bible and was unfortunately persuaded that it was his duty not only to hold, but to defend by argument, the literal accuracy of every word in it. He had a lecture on Noah and the Ark, in which he dealt with the obvious difficulty of conceiving a vessel which would float on the waves of the deluge and contain two at least of every species of living being on the earth. While I was a boy, this lecture made me suspect that I was being asked to swallow sheer superstitions, but the difficulty which weighed hardest on my faith was a moral one. I really listened attentively to the lessons in church and, belonging as I did to the Scripture Union which bound its members to read some selected portion of the Bible every day, I read much of the Old Testament which is never used in public worship. At that period of my life, I possessed, or was possessed by, a vivid imagination and pictured to myself the wholesale massacres which, according to the Old Testament, were directly commanded by God and how men who, more merciful than their Creator, hesitated to carry out to the bitter end these atrocious tortures and slaughters were cast out as enemies and disobedient to God. Of course, I did not keep silence about my difficulties and, since I was a great reader of all kinds of books, I was well aware that I was not the first to recognise their force, but I hoped that some answer had been found and would be known to the clergy. I need not say that I was mistaken. The only hint of any rational reply that I received from my pastors was the allegation that the populations, massacred in holy wars decreed by Jehovah, were exceptionally wicked and deserved all they got.

A fixed idea in the circles of my youthful fellow-believers, students and their pastors was that the Pope is Antichrist and that the "Puseyites", which was the customary denigrating appellation for High Church, Anglo-Catholics and disciples of the Oxford Movement, were either dupes or Jesuits who, by hypocritical intrusion into the ministry of the Protestant Church, were working to overthrow the Church of England and undo the work of the glorious Reformation. Mr. Gaster was no less ardent in this field of controversy than in that of the authority of Scripture and he prepared two lectures on this theme which were at least equal in entertainment value to that on Noah's Ark.

So far as I was concerned, I was more ready to be convinced

that the Pope was Antichrist than that the Ark story was true, because just about that time I was being bullied at school by an older and larger boy who was a zealous propagandist for the Catholic faith. His method was simple. He would waylay me on the way home from school and jump on me from behind a tree, then, having captured me, he would twist my arm to make me say a formula confessing the Catholic faith. I am not sure what the formula was. I do not think it had a definite anathema in it, such as, "To hell with Luther", but it emphatically asserted "I am a Catholic and not a Protestant". Today, threatened with torture, I should not hesitate to say "I am a Catholic" and I should hope to get away with the statement that I am not a Calvinist. Anyone who has had his arm twisted by an expert will know that it is no joke to be laughed off and I am happy to believe that I never agreed to be a Catholic under duress. In my then state of understanding, to give way would have been a denial of what I believed. Mr. Gaster's lectures then found a sympathetic hearer, when he lectured on the subject "The Wreck of the Ritualists on the Rock of Rome", in which he elaborated the idea that the Pope is Antichrist, though I felt that perhaps a stronger case could be made for the view that he is the Man of Sin. Remember that the prevailing opinion of the religious people whom I knew and loved was that Roman Catholic worship is idolatry and that it was better to be an Atheist than a Papist. I had a hot argument with the vicar's son on this when he maintained that it is better to have no God than a false God.

My formal education, though not specifically denominational, was to some extent affected by the religious controversies of the period. The time came when the beloved Miss Batstone was considered to have taken me through the infant stage and I was transferred to a small school for children, conducted by Miss Rose of Camberwell Grove, who occupied a house by the railway tunnel. I have a clear memory of what Miss Rose looked like, but no memory of any definite utterance or action of hers. She was like an illustration to Dickens. Her small head was surrounded by ringlets of grey hair and, as I recall, she dressed always in black and shiny clothes which showed off the carefully arranged grey locks. Miss Rose was very different to Miss Batstone and, in my opinion then, a change considerably for the worse. Now, I am inclined to think that Miss Rose's impersonal discipline and Victorian insistence on behaviour like little gentlemen was good medicine, if taken in small doses.

Only one incident survives either in memory or in family records and that a trivial one. Miss Rose had one good custom. Every Monday morning, each child was required to write out what he or she could remember of the Sunday sermon. It may seem strange that Miss Rose could count on each having heard a sermon, but I have no recollection of any default, and, in the section of society to which the children belonged, church-going was the rule rather than the exception. The exercise was a salutary one from the point of view of intellectual training, though questionable from the point of view of spiritual edification. I profited by this sermon exercise, because my wandering, dreamy mind was forced to try to find what the sermon was about and put it into my own childish vocabulary. To this day, in listening to any discourse, I instinctively follow any argument there may be and summarise the main points. I am a compulsive listener to sermons and hardly ever fall asleep, even in the dreariest and most platitudinous address, unless I make myself inattentive by an act of will. One significant episode is worth recording. Miss Rose was the antithesis of Miss Batstone in her religious allegiance and, under my second schoolmistress, I was open to the dangerous influence of a "Puseyite", an adherent of the vicar of St. Giles's, Camberwell, who according to many earnest Protestants was leading his flock rapidly to Rome. Another small boy's parents took him to the chapel of an extreme Calvinist sect, whose minister was so logical that he denounced all evangelistic efforts to convert heathen or atheists on the ground that everyone who was predestined to salvation would be saved anyway and no missionary zeal could convert those who were predestined to damnation, so that to try to do so was a blasphemous implied criticism of the righteous judgment of God. This minister did not hesitate to speak his mind on all "Arminian" preachers, but he was specially eloquent on Puseyite clergy and my little Calvinist companion memorised a wonderful flourish: "Meanwhile the old man in Rome laughs in his sleeve at the nonsense of these deluded idolaters." What enormity in the parish church called forth this condemnation is now forgotten, but the words of the anathema lived at least one day longer than the Sunday in the schoolroom of Miss Rose. That she expressed her reaction forcibly I know, but her actual words are lost in oblivion.

When I left Miss Rose's Academy for the Sons and Daughters of Gentlemen, my childhood came to an end, and boyhood began when I went to Wilson's Grammar School, Camberwell; but, before we cross this bridge, I must allude to two misfortunes which adversely affected my development and my happiness. The first is a slight physical defect which showed itself almost as soon as I was able to walk. My feet were misshaped in the sense that I had gross fallen arches. Had I been born thirty years later, probably this affliction would have been speedily cured. One of my sons, when a small boy, had the same defect, but by then medical science had advanced and remedial exercises, steadily performed, removed the handicap so effectively that the boy became an Oxford cricket blue and a good all-round athlete. In my day, our good old family doctor, Bramley Taylor, prescribed almost the opposite treatment, not exercise but support and rigidity, with the result that I found myself "in irons"; a metal bar on each leg hampered my movements but relieved the pain which had been quite bad until parents and doctor were persuaded that there really was something wrong with me. I do not wish to stress this handicap or pretend that it was a great affliction. In my thirties and forties, I could walk twenty miles a day with only mild aching of ankles, but all hope of prowess in football and cricket was out, though it took me some time to accept this and my attempts in the field nearly always ended in disappointment. I may be exaggerating my failure, but my impression is that the only sporting trophy I ever gained was a half prize in a three-legged race.

A more serious and less self-centred cause of regret was the prolonged illness of my brother Hubert. Born about three years after me, he showed signs of physical weakness early in his life and, though I was never told the truth about him, he had, in fact, tuberculosis and his life was a series of hospital treatments, anxious but hopeful intervals and operations. He died on March 24th, 1902, aged eighteen. He was a patient and, on the whole, cheerful invalid and deeply loved by all in the family and by many friends.

We who live in a welfare state can hardly realise what chronic illness meant in the old days to a middle-class family living on the salary of a bank clerk. The voluntary hospitals were free and the financial strain was eased while the patient was occupying a hospital bed, but the fees of consultant doctors had to be added to the fees of the family doctor and often the patient had to be nursed and fed on a special diet at home. My mother, when she was old with her memories, said to my sister (proudly, she thinks), "There was very little money, but we've always had a servant and we've always had a holiday." I resent the smile of the superior person at this bourgeois boast; my mother was thinking of the hard work and planning, which carried the family through the years of Hubert's illness, and of my father's heavy labour when, after a hard day in Barclays Bank, he earned extra money by clerical work on audits in the evening. Though I came to disagree with my father on politics and welcome in principle the welfare state, I admire his sturdy independence, his determination to be beholden to no one and to ask for nothing but his just earnings. I am sure he would be horrified by the attitude of so many today, who think it is the duty of the state to give them grants out of the taxes for every human need. The psychological effect of chronic illness in the house is to make the members who are well feel guilty. That at least is my experience. To be well and hopeful, while Hubert was growing weaker, seemed callous. This feeling took a poignant form when I was haunted by the suspicion that I might have been guilty of causing the illness. Did some blow given in rough play start the dreadful disease, and was that blow given by me? In another mode of thinking, was Hubert's illness due to the wrath of God for some sin of mine?

I find it strange that my years at Wilson's are less clear in my memory than those of my childhood. I believe that the reason for this is the fact that we remember and cherish happy days and tend to forget those when we were miserable. Is this a truth about human beings in general, or is it true only about persons who are optimists by nature? Far be it from me to indulge in self-pity for which there are no grounds. Compared with the majority of adolescents, I was fortunate, but there were two causes which produced disturbance and occasionally misery. A Victorian adolescent in the middle classes was likely to be ill-prepared for the oncoming of puberty, but I think I was exceptionally ignorant about sex when I went to Wilson's. The evangelical preachers were hot against sin in general, but rarely descended to sin in particular and my father did not show interest in my sexual development and *mores* until a High

Church vicar, who knew something about me, wrote to him. When he became awake to his responsibility, he acted and I have no ground to complain. The concealment of sex in those circles and those days was so successful that not until I had left school for some years did I become aware of homosexuality. This was not so exceptional as contemporary sex theorists would suppose. My wife, who was at a women's residential college in the University of London, had the same experience. The awareness of sex in a religious context, though far better than irreligious enlightenment on the subject, had in my case certain perils. The teaching of the Church both High and Low seemed to focus attention on masturbation and a common theme of addresses to men and of pastoral direction of individuals was the spiritual and physical ruin which overtakes sinners of this sort. I am still indignant with the bad psychology and the bad theology with which some of my pastors and masters terrorised me, and am thankful that today pastors are acting on the principle that truth makes us free and we do wrong when we conceal or distort it.

A deeper, but connected, cause of unrest was the conflict which developed in my mind on the subject of religion. I despair of conveying to the young of this generation any clear idea of the mental agony which doubts about the faith caused to sensitive spirits of my generation. Looking back on my school days, I see one aspect which lends coherence to a commonplace story of suburban boyhood. Wilson's Grammar School, Camberwell, was founded by Edward Wilson, vicar of Camberwell, in 1618 with the charitable purpose of educating children of the village. Its story has been well told by a distinguished Old Boy, Allport. Wilson's foundation was religious and Anglican in its tradition, but it was not a Church school in the technical sense and what religious teaching there was could pass as "undenominational". In my time, the Chairman of the Governors was the Rev. F. F. Kelly, the father of a well-known President of the Royal Academy. The existence of Wilson's had not been uninterrupted, for in the early 19th century, owing to mismanagement by the Governors, the school was suspended. It had been recently restarted by the public-spirited action of a group of Camberwell people and, when I attended, a shy and apprehensive small boy, the Headmaster, who had been appointed when the restored school was reopened, was still in office and remained there the whole of my time. The Rev. Dr. Macdowell was no doubt a man of energy and foresight when he was appointed, for he accomplished a task which required both these gifts; but he was not at his best in my time, having, I now recognise, early symptoms of old age. He was an impressive figure and he had organised the School well, adding at least one original touch. Corporal punishment was not abolished, but it was confined to the last day of every term. Boys condemned to be beaten had their names entered in a black book and, on the day of doom, the Headmaster devoted some time to working through the list. It was said that there was a distinct advantage in being a late addition to the list of condemned, as it was possible that the Head's arm might be tired before he reached the end. I know of no evidence to confirm this theory.

Dr. Macdowell was not a doctor of divinity in my first years and I had some accidental acquaintance with the process of acquiring the degree. The Oxford D.D. in those days required some almost ritual performances and a payment of a fee, but no disputation or real evidence of scholarship from candidates who were M.A.s of the University. The Headmaster composed three sermons, which he preached in Camden Church, and employed two assistant masters to translate them into Latin. These were duly presented to the Regius Professor, who no doubt read them and found no heresy in them; so then, one day, the Headmaster took morning prayers arrayed in doctor's robes and a law was laid down that henceforth he must be spoken of not as Dr. Macdowell, but as "the Doctor", as though there were no others. Later in life, it amused me when Dr. A. C. Headlam, who had been a kind of headmaster to me, confided to me his plans to make the doctor's degree a real credential of scholarship.

I ought not to write too critically about Dr. Macdowell, because he was kind to me and took an interest in my future, and moreover I deceived him once in committing a sin which was on my conscience for a long time. Morning prayers and homework are the theme: the first conducted by the Headmaster, the second so absurdly heavy that no boy could do it all and survive —or so it seemed to me. Not for the first time, I surreptitiously one morning at prayers mugged up a little of the set book. The Headmaster saw what I was doing and, when prayers were over but the school still assembled, he called me up: I could not deny

My father and mother

My son Michael, killed in action May 28th, 1940

Myself, aged 2

Margaret in 1912

Dean of King's College, London

the charge and the penalty was inscription in the black book. "Did you ever do this before?" said the Head. Very rapidly, the idea passed through my mind, "If I make my eyes as wide open and round as I can, he likes me and will believe that I never did this before." I made my eyes round, or tried to, and said "Oh, no, Sir, this is the first time." I was right; he believed me. But I was not glad. I felt a cur who was frightened to tell the truth and was still too frightened to go to the Headmaster and own up. I felt too that I would probably go to hell with "all that maketh a lie". I should have been better off if I had been in the habit of going to confession; but that was not recognised as legitimate in the evangelical way of religion and a breezy talk with the curate did not appeal to me as the obvious way. I might perhaps smile at my guilty conscience over such a trivial fault, but I could not then and I ought not now. I was a little hypocrite and I did pretend to be better than I really was. And now, when I recall the incident, I ask myself, "How often have I acted the part of a Christian and of a Christian minister without complete sincerity? How often has my utterance been more spiritual than my inner thought?" I do not believe we can know ourselves sufficiently well to answer these questions with certainty and I suppose that the last judgment, so far as individuals are concerned, will be the revelation of ourselves to ourselves as we really are.

As my mind developed and I went up the school with some credit, my dissatisfaction with the religion of my parents became acute and I had some curiosity about the High Church devotion of some boys and one or two masters.

The teaching at Wilson's was, I suppose, about the level of other poorly endowed Grammar Schools in those days. I am sure that the masters were overworked and underpaid, and that applies to the Headmaster too, but I am equally sure that most of them cared for the boys and did their best for them and one of the masters was quite outstanding. Three of them were influences in my education. Mr. Wiggett was the second master who had come with Dr. Macdowell to the revived school. He was a fine teacher for stupid or lazy boys and he ruled his classes by terror, by penalties, irony, sarcasm and loud voice. Many generations of Wilsonians had trembled and perhaps even hated him; but my experience is that most of his former pupils, when they had left school, remembered him with gratitude and even affection. My first encounter with him was devastating. I had been sent to deliver a note to him. His reputation as a terror had been fully explained to me. I stood for several minutes with my hand on the door knob, trembling to hear a noise like the roar of a lion. Only the fear of what would happen to me if I failed to deliver the note persuaded me to open the door. The roar of the lion was interrupted and the black-gowned Mr. Wiggett descended on me like a bird of prey, furious at being interrupted. All ended well however. He must have seen that I was a very little and very frightened boy and he suddenly smiled and patted me on the head.

It was my good fortune to have one master who was a born teacher and a man of diverse learning—T. P. Nunn, who later became well-known as Sir Percy Nunn, Professor of Education and Director of the Institute of Education in the University of London. To him I owe more than I can estimate, chiefly because he was an indefatigable searcher for hidden talent in his pupils and thought he saw promise in me. He took me seriously and did not smile at my ambition to become a great author. He read through a long, and absurd, epic poem which I perpetrated at the age of fourteen and a half and even selected one line as good. He listened to my juvenile essays in theology and advised me to keep religion and science in separate departments of my mind. I thought at the time this was questionable advice, since all truth, I thought, must be one, and now that I can remember his later opinions I think he evaded a problem which might have led us on to dangerous ground. Percy Nunn was the greatest polymath I have ever known. His early life was unknown to me. When he dawned on my horizon, he was Science and Mathematics master for the 5th and 6th forms which, in those days and in that kind of grammar school, consisted of boys of fifteen and sixteen, with only a few of seventeen or eighteen. But Nunn was capable of teaching every subject taught in the school and many others too. He stood in at a moment's notice to take the class in Latin and, for the first time in my life, I caught the rhythm of Vergilian hexameters. Later, I discovered that he was no less adept in Anglo-Saxon verse.

On my experience with Nunn, I base my one conviction on the art of teaching, namely that there are two disqualifications—to know too little about the subject and to know too much. Nunn was a specialist in maths, but he taught me conic sections for a year without making it clear to me that a conic section is a section of a cone. No doubt I was phenomenally stupid, but Nunn knew so much that he could not conceive the possibility of such mental dimness.

I must not forget a junior master, St. Cedd, who was friendly to me when I was in the 6th form and delighted me with his irony and veiled criticism of the set-up, and also, more profitably, by his propaganda for the Anglo-Catholic form of Anglican worship which fascinated me by its romantic aura and the zeal of its disciples, without altogether convincing my reason. I had at least no hesitation in joining St. Cedd in protesting against the violent language of Mr. Kensit and his followers. It was at a meeting addressed by Mr. Kensit that I encountered vigorous religious controversy. When Mr. Kensit made what seemed to me an outrageous sweeping statement about nuns in general, St. Cedd shouted "That's a lie!", whereupon two or three muscular stewards pushed us not at all gently out of the hall and down some stone steps, which I remember were hard when you fell down them. Since then I have made it a rule to conduct my theological disputes on paper.

I have now brought myself up to my sixteenth year and my last year at the school. In my last year I was happy. I was the one and only Foundation Scholar for that year and I passed well the London Matriculation Examination which, in those days, was an extremely impersonal and stiff test for most schoolboys, who were required to pass in every subject at the same examination. I have a dim recollection that I passed in logic at that examination, as a result of private study quite independently of the school. Though I never became on any intimate terms with the Headmaster, who was a tired man and had to husband his energies, I was well-known and well thought of by many masters and was at least not unpopular with the boys. Had I been born fifty years later, there would have been no doubt about what I should do next, nor would there have been any difficulty in getting help. It is disgraceful to envy one's children and only rarely have I been tempted, but I confess that I wish I could have had the two years that my sons and my grandson had to prepare for the higher studies of the university. What should I do next? That was a question which disturbed my last year at Wilson's. As it happened, I did not go to a university, but to the City.

CHAPTER 2

City

One day, when I had been Dean of St. Paul's for a long time, I was present by invitation at the head office of the Westminster Bank in Lothbury, at the inauguration of a new system of mechanical book-keeping. I was a kind of V.I.P. and also a kind of Old Boy. At the age of seventeen, I had entered the employment of the Bank as a very junior clerk and now, to greet me on my visit so many years later, they had fished out the long compound addition sum which I had done as a test. I was glad to see that it was correct. The occasion was cheerful and friendly. I tried to convince my hearers that clerks of my generation worked much harder than they did. But I was deeply moved by the memories which the little ceremony called up, symbolising the parting of the ways in my life—the choice which made all the difference to it.

This chapter is about the years which, from one point of view, were wasted, and it was the thought that they were wasted which clouded them. How did I come to be a bank clerk? The answer is that at the age of sixteen I was incapable of making a decision for myself. I was deeply interested in many intellectual concerns, chiefly in theology and philosophy, but I could not take the step which would have opened the way to the university. I could not say, "I have a vocation to the ministry", because I was not sure that I was a Christian and, even if I might claim the title in a vague and general way, I was quite unable to assent to the Thirty-nine Articles. Most certainly my father would have moved quickly and efficiently to finance my further education if he had known to what end I was seeking a university education—that I should have no definite purpose in view seemed to him incredible. I could not blame my father's attitude. He was responsible for the future of all the family and not only of mine. In an individualist world, he had to safeguard my mother, Hubert his invalid child, and the twins, Olive and Edgar. He acted justly. Nevertheless, I was continually aware that somehow I had got mislaid. I was in the wrong place.

I will not pretend to be a martyr. My days were not filled with gloom and I was not bored by work in the bank. Among my fellow "wage slaves" there were many congenial individuals. Not a few had intellectual or artistic interests. My friend Bates, a cashier, was a learned historian, who published two scholarly works, and another talented friend was a conductor and composer. Nor did I dislike the routine of bank business. Perhaps the mechanisation of offices has made work less interesting now, but in my day it was rarely dull. The General Manager of the Westminster Bank lived at the Head Office and often after dinner would come into the bank and open one or two of the large ledgers in which the accounts were recorded. It was his custom to stare pensively at the open page and then with the one word "however" shut the book. I never heard him make any other remark.

I found the bank interesting and indeed sometimes too full of excitement, as when my two uncles were in danger of being hammered on the Stock Exchange and on days when, at the height of a Kaffir Boom, the clearing of cheques in the Clearing House grew hectic. My colleagues were friendly and cheerful and far from hostile to religion. Many of them were active members of Christian congregations: some were organists and singers. When the time came for me to say farewell, I had a happy send-off from the junior staff who gave me an inkstand with the inscription: Say what you mean and mean what you say.

Early in my 'prentice time I resolved that I would not remain half-educated. At first I thought it might be possible to take an "external" Arts degree in the University of London by private study and I embarked on a correspondence course. The help which the Correspondence College offered was excellent and I have no doubt I could have passed the examinations if I had had time to keep up the prescribed exercises. While I was still a boy, in the 'balance' department, I could do that, but when I emerged into the general office and drew an adult's pay I found that only by making myself ill and neglecting the work for which I was paid could I keep abreast. I am glad, however, that I tried and went on working at my books without the stimulus of an examination.

To read widely, as my interests guided, was possibly the best plan for me—it was probably the only one that I could have carried out. The trials of a solitary student are many; not the least in my experience is that he has few friends who sympathise with his ambition and understand why he must beware of wasting time. To one understanding friend after many years I express gratitude. He was a contemporary of my father's and not rich either in leisure or money, but he was rich in a cultivated mind and love of reading. I could talk to him and show him perhaps some verses or pass on some thought to him, sure that he would take me seriously. His name was Harnden and I never knew what was his occupation. To him I could disclose all my scepticism about religion; he was never shocked and always serenely steadfast in his faith. Through him, however, one of the most staggering blows to my Christian belief shook me. Mr. Harnden went mad, and his madness was religious. When his mind gave way, he was convinced that he had sinned against the Holy Spirit and was irretrievably damned, and so died. How intolerable that one so humble, devout, so full of courtesy and love, so near to God, as it seemed, should suffer thus. Of all the forms of the problem of evil, none is more horrifying than the spectacle of a noble mind overthrown. How to reconcile this with belief in a loving Creator? If I did not believe in life after death, I could see no hope of mitigating its sinister implications.

My failing as a student has always been lack of concentration. I have read too much—or rather too indiscriminately. About this time, I read most of Dryden's dramatic works, simply because I found a folio volume in the local library and liked the old-fashioned print. Could the reading of so many heroic couplets have sown in me the love of 18th-century literature? Could it have had some connection with the fact that my first published work was an edition of Bishop Butler's ethical writings? Reading Pepys at school had given me the idea that history was being made every day and that I was living in a centre of both history-making and history-writing. Though I never kept up writing a diary for more than a fortnight, I was continually composing one in my mind and when I read, much later, Boswell's *London Diary*, I could understand his note of caution that he must not make his life so full that he was unable to record it.

Though my reading was desultory and unsystematic, two interests were dominant in it—religion and politics. In both, I revolted against the conservative tradition. My revolt would seem little enough to "advanced" youth of the present day, but to youth of my generation it could be the cause of a real break in sympathy with one's parents. My parents were grieved by my dissent and I was grieved by their grief. I cannot tell when I began to suspect that my father was wrong in his politics, but before I left school I had adopted one liberal principle and a political hero—Home Rule for Ireland and its advocate William Ewart Gladstone. The General Election that I remember must have been the last in Gladstone's career, for in May, 1898, I got up very early to have the privilege of standing for a moment in Westminster Hall before the bier where his body lay in state. His death represented the tragedy of missed opportunity by the rejection of a great Christian statesman: so I thought then and so I think still. Many years later in Harvard, where I was giving the Noble Lectures, an American, Professor Peabody, when his colleagues were very critical of all things English, had no criticism to offer. I asked him why he seemed so lenient to my country's misdeeds. He replied, "When I was a young man I was taken to the House of Commons when Gladstone was introducing his Home Rule Bill for Ireland and I heard the old man proposing drastic changes in the constitution of Great Britain and using no argument but that they were morally right and just. There is no other country in the world where that could happen." Perhaps it is only fair to add a discordant note which was sounded by that staunch Gladstonian Liberal, Augustine Birrell. When I told him of Peabody's opinion, he said, "I can only say I have been in several Cabinets, one of them headed by Gladstone, and I do not remember ever hearing a member refer to Christian principles in the discussions."

Queen Victoria's death affected me little, except perhaps by causing wonder at the state funeral. One picture at least stays in my memory—that of King and Kaiser riding side by side behind the Queen's coffin. It is a picture which gives me no pleasure. On the Sunday morning following her death, I went to St. Edmund King and Martyr's Church in Lombard Street. I had fallen into the habit of going to City churches, partly to escape from my family's church and partly to dream about other centuries. That day I chose well. Prebendary Benham, the rector, was a historian who enlivened the columns of *The Church Times* every Friday by notes signed "Peter Lombard". He preached a large section of the great sermon by Bossuet on the death of Queen Henrietta Maria and enthralled me by the eloquence of the prose even in English.

Filial affection prompts me to add a semi-public occasion when my father lectured to the Bankers' Institute and I sat quaking in the audience. He did well and, unlike most lectures, it led to some tangible and useful results; he outlined a plan to extend the system of clearing cheques to include the metropolitan area, which was duly carried out with considerable saving of time and manpower. I never heard that the banks which profited by the innovation rewarded its author in any way. He would not approve of this last sentence. I do not suppose he thought about any reward. He was a fanatic for efficiency and the ideal of "doing the job well".

The time between my leaving school and going to University, as I now realise, was the period when I struggled to think for myself both in politics and religion. In the field of public policy, my independence was most marked—I was, in a mild degree, what was called a "pro-Boer". I do not think I ever wanted the British troops to be defeated; indeed, like most English boys then, I did not regard the defeat of Tommy Atkins as possible; but I did most earnestly hope that the war would be concluded without military victory and by agreement. The Jameson raid happened when I was only fourteen and I had no reasoned view on it, but when the South African war burst upon us I was eighteen and, looking back on the Jameson raid story, I was more than doubtful of the justice of our cause against President Krüger. I admired Lloyd George's courage in standing up against mob violence. Altogether the jingoism of the imperialist propaganda and the hysterical rejoicings over the relief of Mafeking seemed to me unworthy of a great people and symptoms of weakness. Later, when I was Dean of Exeter, I had the friendship of a remarkable and public-spirited woman, Dame Georgiana Buller, daughter of Sir Redvers Buller, who commanded the British troops. I was interested to hear her express opinions on the South African war which differed very little from my own.

I am writing these words in the house of my oldest friend, Sidney Marsh. We have quite literally known each other from the cradle, for he is only a few days older than I and we were born about a hundred yards from each other. In my *Sturm und Drang* period, we were close together in spirit, though superficially we were very different. We were both grappling with the problem: Can we be Christians in the contemporary world? I was concerned with the question: What can I believe of the Christian faith? and he with the question: How can I live the Christian life in the modern business world? His energy and ability quickly carried him upward in the insurance company which he had entered as an office boy and about the year 1908 he made his home in Walworth in a settlement which was the centre of an extremely active Scout movement and troop. By some magic of personality he persuaded some eminent men and many who were destined to become eminent to take part in his rallies and to "run with the Walworth boys" or take part in boxing matches. I suppose that some of our advanced social thinkers would now describe all these muscular Christians as "do-gooders", but why object to that? They actually did a lot of good to many boys and in many cases were actuated by love of Christ. I think I met Mr. Harold Macmillan for the first time at one of Sidney Marsh's rallies.

Neither of us found the full solution of our problem, but we came near enough, we thought, to be able to claim that our act of faith in Christ and his Church was a rational choice. Of course, I read reams of stuff which had no real importance and wasted time which a competent guide could have saved, but I really doubt whether there were many competent guides even in universities, so confused were the issues. I could see for myself that some defences of Christian faith were worthless and among them I regretfully included my hero Gladstone's *The Impregnable Rock of Holy Scripture*. I could also see for myself that some works on the negative side really missed the point. But among the futile agnostics, I do *not* include that now neglected writer Herbert Spencer. Though I agree that his massive *Synthetic Philosophy* was largely misconceived, the attempt to apply the concept of evolution in so many branches was illuminating, at least to a novice, and his *First Principles* opened up to me the problem of knowledge. No one can be expected to read a list of books, nor can I remember a tithe of my reading list. As a result of a careful study of Darwin's *Origin of Species* and many related works, I was convinced that Genesis could not be literally true and that the authority of Scripture and the nature of divine revelation would have to be investigated. The dabbling in philosophy which followed fascinated me and took me far out of my depth. It confirmed too my preference for the 18th-century writers who took pains to make themselves understood. I was troubled, however, by their conception of revelation. Among the 19th-century writers, Matthew Arnold delighted me; Rénan's *Vie de Jésus* both delighted and deeply disturbed me.

All this study was less concentrated and less confident than my description would suggest. There were bouts of depression, when much study was a weariness to the flesh and I was tempted to think that perhaps my true destiny was to be a moderately successful bank official and to marry a girl who would be a fit companion in such a career. My doubts had less effect on my conduct than one might have expected. I took part in church activities and was interested in foreign missions. A memory survives of a lecture on an African mission field, which I had prepared so thoroughly that within the allotted hour I had delivered less than a quarter of my material. My audience was well behaved, but I doubt whether they remembered any of the copious information which I provided; for my part I learned something about African ethnology and particularly of the Hausas tribes, but more useful to me was the lesson on lecturing and the danger of trying to get too much into one lecture.

I now come to an incident which I regard as a kind of divine guidance and which changed the course of my existence. Strangely, about the exact date of this experience, as also of another one which I shall describe later, I am quite unable to be precise. The experience, as it were, stands out from the normal and commonplace as though it had a timeless existence. I may add here that I am quite sure it was not a dream, and when I come to tell it there seems almost nothing to tell. Though I do not know the date, I remember the day very well. It was a summer day when the sun flooded even Bishopsgate with glory. I had been in the London office of the Swiss Banking Corporation on some routine business and, as I came down the steps at the entrance into the full light of the sun, I suddenly felt that the sun was in me. That is how I describe the experience, but of course it is a most inadequate metaphor. I was taken hold of by a power, or Spirit, which filled me with joy and peace and courage. My doubts about God were transcended. He needed me and called me. When I read C. S. Lewis's book *Surprised by Joy*, I recognised the nature of the experience. There is, however, apparently a difference. His revelation was a supernatural assurance of the Incarnation of the Son of God, mine was a supernatural assurance of the reality of the Creator God who is love. Exultant happiness carried me away. I knew and felt that God was real and that I was a child of God. It seems to me that from that moment I knew I should be refusing some kind of divine call if I did not make a break away from the routine in which I was becoming settled. I did not take this as a definite call to priesthood or to any office in the Church, but as a summons to make a choice. I could easily think of psychological causes for this experience and I do not question their validity. I was not the object of miraculous intervention. I was at the time interested in Bishop Berkeley's philosophy and I believe I had been reading his *Dialogue Between Hylas and Philonous*; certainly the refutation of materialism and the place of Mind in nature had been much in my thoughts; none the less I remain convinced that the illumination on the steps of the Swiss Bank was a gracious opening to a wider life.

This is the end of the chapter. My City life was finished. But I did not immediately become a theological student. I was by no means sure that I ought to be ordained; nor was I ready to commit myself by accepting financial help from any quarter or by applying to a bishop to be accepted as a prospective candidate. Not unreasonably, I think, I wanted to study theology before I made up my mind. With help from my father and my own savings, I could, I thought, make my way through the course in King's College, London. So the scene changes to King's College, London, where I enrolled, being a Christian by faith and a practising member of the Church of England, but far from clear whether I could honestly present myself as a candidate for Holy Orders.

CHAPTER 3

Student Days

How do we dare to say that some events in our lives were "providential"? Do not the words sound arrogant, as if we presumed to claim to be favourites of God? Yet some turning-points were so decisive and opened up such unforeseen opportunities that we do feel bound to take them as due to the grace of God. To me, my entrance as a student in King's College, London, must always appear in this light, when I consider what might have been my lot had I been accepted by another college to which I applied and, most of all, when I think of the tutors and friends who enriched my life from almost the first days up to the end of my employment and residence in the College so many years later. This book is intended by me to be a work of piety in the sense of a declaration of loyalty and love to the College to which I owe so much.

My first encounter with the institution which was to be my centre for many years was not encouraging. King's College in the Strand, when originally built in the early 19th century, was a dignified structure which happily conformed to the architectural style of its neighbour, Somerset House. Today, that nucleus of the College is more or less swallowed up in the extensions which will be completed in a few years. When I first saw the College, it still presented the outline with which it had started; the Principal lived in a wing of the College on the Embankment and near to him were students' rooms, which in my early days were, I think, occupied by medical students. In outward form the College looked much the same as it had done when the great Duke of Wellington and his fellow founders surveyed the building which they had paid for, but in fact the College was at a crisis in its history which indirectly deeply affected some students of whom I was one.

The crisis arose out of the vicissitudes of the University of

London. King's College had been founded as a kind of counterweight to University College in Gower Street, which had been established by Liberals and Secularists to provide university education and degrees untrammelled by the restrictions of Oxford and Cambridge, which were almost completely in the hands of the Established Church. This "Godless College", as its critics called it, was challenged in its turn by King's College, built on ground given by the Crown and having at its centre a chapel in which the Church of England services were sung daily. The conflicts and insults arising from this situation make amusing though not edifying reading, and even today the antagonism survives in elaborate "rags" by students contending for the possession of tribal deities: the figure of a highlander (Univ.) and that of a red lion (King's).

When University College was founded, it was hoped that it would be the University of London, but that was not the way things went. For a time, the University of London was a purely examining body, conducting examinations and granting degrees, but not concerned with teaching or research. This 19th-century conception of a modern university could not stand up against the criticism of those whose ideal of a university was a *studium generale*, a place where all learning is pursued by teachers and undergraduates. The plans for a teaching university were not easily agreed upon, largely because so many institutions of a university character had grown up independently, such as the medical schools, and it was necessary to fit them into the general scheme. But the story of the various attempts to reform the University of London is a long and rather dull one—another chapter in the story is probably about to be written. Sufficient for my narrative to establish clearly in the reader's mind that, when I became a student, one of these reconstructions was in full spate and King's College was in the process of being 'integrated' into the University, which involved a change in the government of the College. The Theological Department of King's College was not a part of the original foundation, but had become well known owing to the distinction of some of its professors and, in the case of Frederick Denison Maurice, to the scandal of his deposition by the Council of the College on the ground of heresy.

Among the new developments in the University of London was the establishment of a University Faculty of Theology and of degrees in the subject. The Faculty was constituted by the theological colleges in London, together with the Theological Department of King's College. In those days, the colleges and the students of theology in London were more numerous than they are today and most of the Christian denominations were represented by a college staffed with professors and tutors: New College (Congregational), Hackney College (Congregational), Regent's Park College (Baptist), London College of Divinity (C. of E. Evangelical), Richmond College (Methodist). Up to that date, the University of London had had no theology in its range of studies and not a few of the leading spirits in the University Senate regarded the Theological Faculty with suspicion. When one remembers the state of things not long before this in Oxford and Cambridge and the liberal tradition of the London University, their caution is comprehensible, though it was unnecessary. Prophecies of disaster based on the alleged tendency to *odium theologicum* were half serious; the idea that theology would turn out to be a "soft option" comparable to the studies of an advanced Bible class was easily accepted by our scientific colleagues. The Theological Faculty won, however, because it was a model of friendly co-operation and it set a standard for its degrees which would have been quite beyond the capacity of half the bishops in the Anglican Church.

This state of things was propitious for me and for another freshman, my friend H. M. Relton who, like me, had come from a bank and had a good background of knowledge, his father being a well-known preacher and a church historian. The authorities of King's College were on the look-out for likely candidates in the University examinations. And in the case of King's College "authorities" meant the Rev. Dr. A. C. Headlam, Principal of the College and Professor of Dogmatic Theology. He played a major part in my life and I must introduce him before we go any further.

My first impression of him was that he was formidable and my second impression that he was very "High Church". The first impression was abundantly verified, the second turned out to be an illusion based on Headlam's nervous trick of bending his knees at intervals when speaking in public. Careful observation soon convinced me that his genuflexions had no relation with the words he was uttering. He was tall and spare, his face had an austere outline which was mainly due to his long, though slender, nose. His eyes were of a cold greyish tint and, when fixed upon a delinquent or scatter-brained student, had an almost hypnotic effect. Perhaps I could sum up my impression by saying that, when I was told that he was descended from Oliver Cromwell, it seemed to me most natural and what one would have expected. Of all the physical qualities of this remarkable man, the voice lingers most persistently in memory. It was a flat north country voice and some, though not all, of his vowels had the northern ring. He always used the short "a", speaking of băth and păth, and he hardly ever elided the definite article, a habit which unconsciously I copied from him.

One of the first events in my college career was a "quiet day" conducted by the Principal for all students of theology. At the time, it seemed to me lacking in warmth, with no appeal to the emotions, leaving the hearer with no glow of love or devotion. Characteristically, it was a series of meditations on Our Lord's words to his disciples, "Be ye wise as serpents and harmless as doves", and I am ashamed to say that, either at the time of the retreat or reflecting on it later, I thought how badly the words fitted the appearance of the speaker, who had no touch of the sinuosity of serpents and was much more like a hawk than a dove. The addresses, as I recollect them, were primarily about wisdom, and harmlessness was more or less taken for granted. Was it only because of its being the prelude to a new phase of my life that I remember it, while I have totally forgotten most of the many other retreats which have moved me at the time more than Headlam's? I think not. I believe that I dimly felt what I came to be sure of after years of friendship, that there was a loving spirit in him which was partly repressed, so that emotional expressions were almost beyond his power. No doubt some psychological cause could be suggested, but I make no conjecture. The inhibition of verbal and bodily expressions of affection was, I believe, a burden to him. In the presence of small children it seemed to be suspended.

This aversion to expressions of affection was known to his fellow bishops. When he became Bishop of Gloucester, I acted as Headlam's chaplain at the service in Westminster Abbey in 1925 to commemorate the Council of Nicea, which was attended by many Eastern Patriarchs and Metropolitans, who were greeted by some Anglican bishops with kisses on both cheeks. Dr. Hensley Henson came in and asked my bishop, "Well, Headlam, have you kissed these prelates?" Headlam replied, "Not in my line," to which Henson replied with one of his off-the-cuff epigrams: "I deplore your aloofness, Headlam, because I am credibly informed that our relations with the Orthodox Church depend on the fervency of our osculations."

My own relations with Headlam, to my surprise, were good from the start. With his incredible power of work, Headlam burdened himself with reading a number of essays and with pointing out their defects to their authors one by one. By this means, he made acquaintance with every student of theology and formed an estimate of the general level of intelligence. In this test, Relton and I were among the few commended, not I think that we had better brains, but because we had practice in writing English prose. For my part, I enjoyed a facility of composition which was the consequence of all those rather futile short stories and journalistic fragments which no one had wanted. I had at least intelligence enough to guess that my performance in this essay would have its effect on my future and I gave my best. That I did not do badly was evident from the fact that Headlam actually argued with me and took seriously my amateurish dissertation on the Christian doctrine of God.

About this time, there happened a fortuitous episode which, without any design of mine, brought me to the notice of the Principal and other theological dons. I do not pride myself on the episode, though at the time I thought it was funny. It was in fact a kind of schoolboy "score". The Balfour Education Act was the centre of political controversy. At the time, the issues seemed important and perhaps one aspect of the controversy was a sign of the times—the refusal of respectable citizens to pay their rates, as a protest against what they held to be unjust law. The quarrel was largely a Church v. Chapel affair. Balfour proposed to help Church schools by public money. This infuriated the leaders of Nonconformity who, with the Anglo-Catholic party especially in mind, coined the slogan "Say 'No' to Rome on the Rates". For some time, law-abiding Protestants were in the habit of deducting part of the local rates on the ground that they went to subsidise Papist teaching in schools. They called this "passive resistance". At the height of the education controversy, a public meeting was announced at the Holborn Restaurant, in the lunch hour, to be addressed by the leading Free Church ministers. I was living then in the hostel for theological students in Mecklenburgh Square and, on the day of the meeting, I happened to pass the restaurant on my way to the hostel from the College. I saw important-looking persons going in and among them the minister of the City Temple, whom I greatly admired. On the spur of the moment, I walked in, no man hindering me, trying to look important. I was richly rewarded.

The London Free Church Ministry, in the first decade of the 20th century, was adorned by many men of renown and of spiritual and intellectual power. They were also orators of distinction. The leader and spokesman of the ministers on the Education Bill was the renowned Dr. Clifford, whose name was known throughout the land. He brought the meeting to a close with a magnificent speech, so magnificent that, though I was against his views, I could not forbear to cheer. His peroration concluded with the words, "Awake, arise, or be for ever fallen." Most stirring and appropriate. But, as I was walking out of the meeting, it occurred to me that these words are the conclusion of Satan's speech to his fellow devils in Milton's *Paradise Lost*. I thought this was rather a joke and that the "By the Way" column of the Tory evening paper the *Globe* might put in a paragraph. So I wrote one in the A.B.C. shop near the Holborn Restaurant. I cannot remember the exact words, but I think it began. "We have often found ourselves in disagreement with the leaders of Nonconformity, but we think Dr. Clifford goes a little too far . . ." The reader can complete it for himself. The paragraph duly appeared in the *Globe* and I thought it was a pleasant little squib and that would be the end of it; but the *Daily Express*, which in those days was strongly Tory, being hard up no doubt for material, gave prominence to my jest. Even that was not the end, for Dr. Clifford was unwise enough to write explaining that he had meant nothing of the kind. By that time, I began to sympathise with Dr. Clifford and to feel that I was like a small boy who had put out his tongue at a bishop. The last word of this trivial story has only recently been spoken. Reading the autobiography of P. G. Wodehouse, I discovered that he was the editor of the "By the Way" column in the *Globe* at the time. It was he who decided to print the paragraph. I suppose it is too late now to collect the 10/- which I believe was the standard rate.

Dr. Headlam was told that I was the author of the gibe at

Dr. Clifford which had tickled him. He did not like Dr. Clifford or his propaganda and no doubt the incident confirmed his view that I was a promising student. For my part, I draw only one lesson from it; read *Paradise Lost*—you never know when it will come in useful.

The principal cause of happiness in those student years was that feelings of frustration had vanished, and my mind was stretched every day by fresh challenges. I was conscious from the first week that I could stay the course and that my intelligence was capable of efforts which would take me out of the "pass" category to who could tell what achievements. Very much was given to me by the professors and tutors and they must be mentioned among the benefits which Providence bestowed in these years. The Theological Professors of King's College were, I suppose, the worst paid teachers in the country. The College had never possessed any endowment for theology and the emoluments of the professors depended almost entirely on the fees of students. Their stipends varied from year to year and, in the summer term, there was always uncertainty whether the finances would allow any additional dividend. This situation would have been impossible, but for the fact that most of the professors had livings in the country which did not demand their full time. This system has long broken down and professors of theology are full-time and supposed to be wholly occupied with teaching and research. One advantage perhaps these parochial professors had over their more fortunate successors: being parish priests in villages, they were pastors as well as scholars and never forgot that most of their students were being prepared for ordination.

Among the learned men who left an indelible impression on me, I put high on the list Alexander Nairne, Professor of Old Testament. He was one of the most accomplished scholars I have known. A poet and artist by nature, he gave a harmony and grace to every subject and, out of the stores of his reading would illustrate say a difficult passage in the Hebrew text of Job by a reference to Greek or Italian poetry. A fellow student, who loved him as I did, said of him, "When he lectures on Isaiah, I wish he would be less poetical; we might understand better what he is driving at," and I replied, "Perhaps the cold, clear light is not the best: Nairne's gold haze may be nearer the mark: one poet interpreting another." After the first world

war he retired to a fellowship in Jesus College, Cambridge, and
to a canonry of St. George's, Windsor. He published one excellent book on the Epistle to the Hebrews, *The Epistle of
Priesthood*. Would that he had written more, but he left grateful memories with many pupils.

Professor E. W. Watson was a scholar of a different type. I
think, being Professor of Church History, he may have modelled
his style on that of Edward Gibbon, who was described by
Cardinal Newman as the only first-rate ecclesiastical historian in
English. I remember verbatim, I believe, the opening sentence
of one of his lectures which ran as follows: "We now come to the
reign of Pope John XXII. It is perhaps enough to say of him that
his character was so scandalous that it is unlikely there will ever
be a John XXIII. He was in fact a retired pirate, who had invested his ill-gotten gains in the purchase of the papacy." It is
interesting to note that Professor Watson's prediction was falsi-
fied by a Pope in our own time, whose sanctity may be an atonement for the misdeeds of his predecessor. Watson had a satirical
tongue. I believe he was the author of the jest about the Pan
Anglican Conference—a vastly blown up Lambeth Conference
—that its motto should be "All was gas and gaiters" from Dickens' *Nicholas Nickleby*. He left King's College to become Regius
Professor of Church History in Oxford. He was a salutary influence in my mental life by making me think about the nature
of historical evidence.

And that same problem of historical evidence was very much
to the fore in my mind almost from the first day; it was important in the study of the Old Testament, but to me it seemed
absolutely vital in the New Testament. The Professor, H. J.
White, was a good scholar of the old school, who was engaged
for years with Bishop Wordsworth of Winchester on the text of
St. Jerome's Latin version of the New Testament, commonly
called the Vulgate. The Bishop died before the task was completed and it was carried through by White. This was a valuable
piece of work, which gave scholars the nearest approach to
Jerome's original they are likely to get. On the general subject of
the New Testament, White was conservative and dull, taking
wherever possible the traditional standpoint on such controversial questions as the authorship of the Fourth Gospel, the
authenticity of the disputed Epistles of St. Paul and the origin
of the Synoptic Gospels. Unless my memory is at fault, he did

not defend the absolutely indefensible Second Epistle of Peter. Though White on the whole referred to German New Testament criticism only to condemn and refute it, he did not ignore it and was too good a scholar to misrepresent it. What other students made of his lectures, I do not know; on my mind they left the impression that there were some open questions to which the Christian faith needed to find answers. This impression was by no means confined to the lectures on the New Testament. As my theological education advanced, it became more and more evident that intellectually Christian belief was on the defensive and much of the traditional apologetic was untenable.

I should be indeed ungrateful if I forgot Dr. Alfred Caldecott, Professor of Philosophy. In the days of which I am now writing, it would have seemed to me an absurd notion that I should succeed him and, if by some miracle I did, that I should adopt his method of teaching. Caldecott was the best-known of all the professors, having published two valuable surveys of the whole field of the Philosophy of Religion, which were accurate summaries of a large number of philosophical works, together with some critical notes. His method of lecturing was of the same type. So far from deploying a system of his own and defending it against all comers, he left his hearers to guess what his own opinions were. He did not aim at founding a "school of thought" and recruiting followers, but rather at awakening minds by asking questions and showing that more than one answer was possible. This method was exasperating to those who wanted their thinking done for them, and it led sometimes to comic exchanges. Rhetorical questions are not easily distinguished from genuine ones and Caldecott abounded in both. An ingenuous youth, I remember, fell into the trap. A lecture on "Our Knowledge of the External World" ended with the question, "If with five senses we know so much about the external world, how much should we know if we had ten senses?" To which the ingenuous youth replied, "About twice as much." But, on reflection, I wonder whether he really was an ingenuous youth. Among all the professors at that time Caldecott was the only one who had the absent-mindedness which fiction has attributed to the tribe; more than once I have had to remind him that he had a lecture to deliver in two minutes' time and he has replied, "I thought I had given it already." My affection and veneration for Alfred Caldecott has grown over the years, as I understand in retrospect what his teaching and friendship meant in my life. He was an upright and wise man. It pains me even now that, when he retired from the chair of philosophy, the Church did not make better use of him than to make him a vicar in a country parish.

For all these I wrote essays during my undergraduate years. For G. E. Newsom I think I wrote no essays, but he was one of my educators by conversation. As warden of the hostel in Mecklenburgh Square, he was available for most evenings and was a fascinating talker. He had, too, one quality which endeared him to me: he was a "seeker". Being nearer my own age, he had more understanding perhaps of the turmoil of my spirit. He had humour, public spirit and sympathy and, what was important to me, he had a philosophical background and interest. In his spare time he read through A. E. Taylor's *Elements of Metaphysics* with two or three of us. I would not agree with many conclusions in Taylor's book and, soon after he had published it, he changed his mind on fundamental questions, but it played a notable part in the education of many students. There is no comparable text book of constructive philosophy available for the present generation.

Most memorable are the essays written for Dr. Headlam. The select band of students reading for the B.D. degree were his peculiar care and he started on us early in the morning and early in the week, for we were bidden to breakfast on Mondays at eight o'clock, to be followed by reading of essays at nine. Headlam had no small talk and adhered in practice to the maxim of Bishop Butler that, prominent among the "times to be silent" are those when you have nothing to say. His silences were formidable, and we were grateful to Mrs. Headlam, who sustained a cheerful chatter over the eggs and bacon. Dr. Headlam not only originated no small talk, he had a disconcerting tendency to kill it in others. One of the minor social setbacks which I have not forgotten is quite trivial. At a larger meal in the Principal's house, I was trying to converse with my neighbours, when one of those sudden silences intervened and my voice rang out with some fatuous observation on the trams which then ran along the Embankment just beneath the Principal's house. That was embarrassing enough to a shy man, as I then was. Headlam, with the best intentions, made it worse by saying in a loud voice, "And do you consider yourself to be an authority on street traffic, Mr. Matthews?" I was covered with confusion and blushes, so that no reply, brilliant or stupid, came to my mind.

One of the essay sessions with Headlam after breakfast I happen to remember, because it included two examples of his rather rough method with promising students. The set subject for the essay was the short book by St. Athanasius *De Incarnatione*, which is a most important text in the history of Christian doctrine and for the understanding of the orthodox doctrine of the Person of Christ. The first to read his essay was a student named, I think, Brown who, from the first two sentences, showed that he had an imperfect grasp of his subject. As he proceeded, he became himself quite disheartened by his stuff and dropped the pages on the floor (I suppose by accident, but who knows). He bent down to pick his pages up and started to arrange them in their proper order. He was stopped by the icy voice of Headlam, enunciating an evident truth: "Do not trouble, Mr. Brown, to arrange the order of the pages. It will not make the smallest difference to the continuity of your thought." The unfortunate Brown was made to read all his deplorable pages all the same.

After Brown, came an essayist of a different quality, my friend Bicheno Smith, whose name indicated one side of his ancestry, gipsy, and not so clearly the other—his father was a Baptist minister. Bicheno Smith was a bright and courageous spirit; alas, he was to be granted only a few more years in this world; he was one of the victims of the great influenza epidemic of 1918–19, having come through the war unscathed. Bicheno was not awed by Athanasius and embarked upon a drastic criticism of his theology. Headlam was soon showing a sign of unease which was well-known to all who had to work with him —he was biting his fingers. Speech rapidly followed, "Mr. Smith," he said, "you are very confident in your criticisms of this Church Father; how old are you?" "One year older than Athanasius was when he wrote the book I am criticising." The retort was not only factually correct, but very much to the point, and Headlam was firmly put in his place by the twenty-four-year-old student. Was he offended? On the contrary, he was delighted and took a fatherly interest in Bicheno Smith right up to the boy's premature death.

Headlam's lectures on systematic and biblical theology were in many respects the central stream in the flood of theology in which I was so happily immersed.

His point of view was definitely Anglican, though not always in harmony with the Articles of Religion. His principle was "The Church to teach and the Bible to prove", but that did not prevent him from admitting that the causes of the formulation of Church teaching were strangely mixed and that the Bible may be used to prove many things which the Church has never agreed upon. In the opening decade of the century, theological discussion was dominated to some extent by the Liberal Protestantism of leading German scholars and among them the great Adolf Harnack stood forth like a Goliath. The simile is not altogether inappropriate, for to many orthodox minds Harnack seemed a redoubtable enemy of the people of God. Headlam, of course, was far from that fanatical standpoint and knew very well that the German theologian was a devout Christian who believed that he was carrying to their logical conclusion the principles of the Reformation. Nevertheless, I must confess that Headlam's lectures on doctrine sometimes had the form of a running fight against Adolf—and inevitably so, because Harnack was so prolific and so learned.

His two most important books were a *History of Dogma* and *What is Christianity?* Of all the German theology from the beginning of the century, these two are among the few still alive and in a sense still "kicking", because they still have the power to shock complacent believers by presenting a possible but greatly reduced version of Christianity. In brief, Harnack taught that the essence of Christianity is love of God as Father and of men as all his children. The long and complex history of Christian doctrine he held to be a long misunderstanding caused by trying to blend Greek philosophy with primitive Christianity.

These problems have changed their form and have proliferated since, but in germ the whole crisis for Christianity, of which we are now so conscious, was already there. It would be an exaggeration to say that Headlam provided the answer except in part. Even then, I was dissatisfied with some of his interpretations. Fundamentally, he differed from Harnack and the Liberal Christians, because the Church as a divinely founded institution and the witness to a tradition was a vital factor in his thinking. In the main, I agreed with him, but not always and not without reservations. At times I felt that Headlam's theological endeavour was not solely to know the truth, but partly to construct a defensible position for the Church.

The austerities of Headlam's lectures were softened for me by my discovery that R. J. Campbell of the City Temple preached on Thursdays at one p.m. and that he often dealt with theological problems in a "popular" style. Sometimes he would be dealing with the very topic on which I had heard Headlam's detached and objective comments only an hour earlier, but how differently! It was not that the two men had opposed views, or at least not always, but that they had different kinds of mind. Though not comparable with Headlam on the ground of scholarship, Campbell much excelled him in his general reading, illustrating and enforcing his message by references to poetry and fiction as well as to contemporary life. I did not exchange a word with Campbell until long afterwards, when he had become an Anglican and was Canon and Chancellor of Chichester Cathedral, but he had an influence on me through his preaching at the City Temple which helped me to carry on with the study of theology and with the training for ordination.

Campbell, at the time, was working up towards his "New Theology", which he later abandoned, and, while attracting large congregations, was not in favour either with Anglicans like Bishop Gore or with Protestant divines like Dr. P. T. Forsyth, who remarked acidly that the New Theology was like a bad photograph, over-exposed and under-developed. The stricture had some truth, as Campbell later acknowledged; but the work of alerting the intelligent laymen to the crisis of faith was necessary and, as the then Bishop of Woolwich has shown, still needs to be carried on. Indeed, when I read Bishop Robinson's book, I thought, "I have read all this before." The differences between then and now are that Robinson is a first-rate New Testament scholar and Campbell was not, and Campbell was an idealist in philosophy with a tendency to Pantheism, while Robinson, writing at a time when philosophy in England is confused, has no metaphysical foundation.

Student life in a vast and scattered university like London tends to be centred upon the individual colleges or even upon groups within the colleges. Two memorable occasions illustrate an aspect which in my day was important—that London was the intellectual centre of the nation and in it dwelt most of the leading men of the day. Today that statement would not be true, but in the years before the first world war it was. G. E. Newsom, the Warden of the hostel in Mecklenburgh Square, was a man of great charm and of imagination. He succeeded in persuading two of the most prominent writers of the day to visit the hostel and discourse without any emolument to about thirty young men who were preparing to be parsons. The two men were much in the news as protagonists of two rival forms of revolt—Bernard Shaw and Gilbert Chesterton. Newsom perceived that these two men had promise of many years of active life and what they thought was likely to be a clue to the kind of world our ministry would be exercised in. In the popular mind, Chesterton was already identified with a kind of revolutionary Christianity opposed to Socialism; and my impression is that Shaw was recognised as a critic of the so-called Christian civilisation of the established order, but not yet recognised as a kind of unorthodox prophet. Chesterton had impinged on my mind from the day when I read in the *Daily News* an article entitled "On Passing the Mustard Pot", which essayed to draw out profound principles for human life and conduct. I cannot remember what I thought of Shaw then, but probably on the whole I regarded him as a destructive critic of the Christian religion and nothing more. At any rate, I thought it generous of him to spend an evening talking to a group which could do nothing for him in return.

Chesterton arrived in a taxi, rather late, and came puffing and blowing into the room where his audience was assembled, plunging without delay into animated conversation. After some time, it was discovered that his taxi was ticking up the shillings all the time, but when I, or perhaps another student, proposed to pay it off, he would not have it, saying, "I've just had my cheque from the *Daily News*, the cabby may as well have some of it."

Chesterton's address left no impress on my memory, not even the subject, and I think I wondered whether he was quite sober, but fortunately a tough Yorkshire student named Hickelton Smith asked some question at the end, which had something to do with St. John's Gospel. Chesterton never really answered the question, but embarked upon a kind of parable in the form of a dream about St. Paul's Cathedral being pulled down in deference to "experts" and built in Knightsbridge, only to be moved under renewed pressure from "experts" to other sites and ending up about half-way up Ludgate Hill. No doubt G.K.C. used this in one of his books, but I do not know which and anyway it was irrelevant; but it was brilliantly told and evidently spontaneous.

Bernard Shaw was more memorable and more relevant and the ideas of his address appear in his prefaces. He began with enormous gusto in defiant vein, "I am glad to be here, because I know that I have the privilege of speaking to men who have decided for the rest of their lives to be conscious hypocrites. Do not imagine that I blame you for this. I am far from doing so, because I am convinced that our society can only be carried on by the employment of conscious hypocrisy. In my capacity of a member of the St. Pancras Borough Council, I share the responsibility for hypocritical words and actions for the good of the people." He then went on to describe the process of fumigating rooms in which persons with infectious diseases had lived. "The process is," Shaw alleged, "quite useless, but people believe that sulphur fumes kill microbes and go on living in houses without fear, fortunately, because there are no others to move them to." The reader can guess the rest of the discourse, if he has read the prefaces to *Major Barbara, The Doctor's Dilemma* and to other plays. Hickelton Smith was present on this occasion, too, and had the temerity to argue quite toughly with the great man on statements made by him about the criticism of the New Testament, on which Shaw's knowledge was not equal to his assurance.

The Student Christian Movement, when I joined it as an undergraduate, was in a definitely evangelical and evangelistic mood, which was shortly afterwards to be changed, largely by the influence of William Temple, to a more "liberal" type of Christian belief. My first experience of a S.C.M. conference was at the end of the Welsh Revival and was attended by numbers of Welsh students. Perhaps, at this conference, I deliberately turned my back on an experience which might have profoundly altered my whole outlook. At a meeting of the whole conference, some Welsh Revival testimonies were given by men who had taken part in the Revival as leaders of groups. They were succeeded on the platform by one who read and expounded Scripture. So far, there was nothing remarkable, but, apparently spontaneously, other readers and expounders stood up and uttered; shortly after this, prayer seemed, as it were, to break out at many places in the large gathering. Still there was nothing very remarkable or even unusual, and I was not conscious of any access of emotion; but suddenly I felt an impulse to get up and speak without any idea of what I would say. Moreover, I felt that, if I stayed a moment longer, I should be compelled to obey this impulse. I think I would have stayed but, at that critical moment, the thought occurred to me, "I am losing control of myself; it is like that time when I nearly got drunk and saved myself by leaving the company just before I was carried away from my self-possession." So I fled, as from a mortal sin. To this day, I am uncertain whether I did right; but, knowing myself better than I did then, I am fairly certain that in similar circumstances I should act in the same way.

The S.C.M. had my support all through my university career and it is relevant to mention here incidents which may have taken place when I had taken my degree and was both a very junior lecturer and a post-graduate student. The notion that violent hostility to Christianity is a recent phenomenon is of course wildly mistaken. The S.C.M. then was definitely a propaganda society and, though it fell far short of the present day Society in the publication of scholarly books, it excelled in the number of converts added to the Church in the universities. It was about this time that it adopted the slogan, "Evangelisation of the world in this generation". The opponents were neither idle nor inarticulate. H. G. Wells was a former student of the Imperial College of Science and, for some years, was the president of the Old Students' Society. He was also a prospective Socialist candidate for the representation of the University in Parliament. His influence on young scientists was considerable. Of one meeting which I addressed in the Royal College on "Why be a Christian?" I have mixed memories—of the cheerful tea with agnostics before the meeting and of the violent incursion of militant atheists, who not only shouted me down but broke up the furniture. This was one occasion when the fallacious *argumentum baculinum* proved singularly effective, because the College authorities banned all meetings of the S.C.M., on the ground that they were disorderly!

A later S.C.M. meeting at the London School of Economics is a happier memory. A discussion arising out of my address was proceeding vigorously at 10 p.m., when the College closed and was continued by an indefatigable remnant at the neighbouring café until we were turned out of that at 11.30 p.m. Argumentative tussles between Christian and non-Christian students were at least as lively as they are now; my impression is that they were more to the point, because it could be assumed then that Christians believed at least in some form of Theism and that unbelievers accepted some form of "Naturalism"; whereas now it seems a Christian may seriously assert God is dead and a scientific agnostic may hold a theory of knowledge according to which all statements, positive or negative, about the universe are unmeaning.

The end of the three years' undergraduate study and freedom came swiftly enough. I had the kind of mind which adapts itself to examinations and, when once I had mastered the anxiety which at first plagued me, I enjoyed them. A kind of auto-suggestion which I invented helped. I looked attentively round the examination hall at the other candidates and said firmly to myself, "You know as much as anyone among them and you are as clever as any of them; though you don't know as much as the examiners, you are probably cleverer." When I had pupils later, I used to pass this formula on to the more intelligent. Another advantage I had—facility in writing English. It is my conviction that many failures in examinations are due not so much to ignorance as to inability to put down known material in lucid sentences on paper. The English people as a whole do not really know their own language and have no pride in it. What is the matter with the schools?

Well, I passed the examination for the B.D. degree and, turning over such papers as survived the Blitz in 1940, I came upon Headlam's brief letter of congratulation and lived again the emotions of long ago. Characteristically, he referred to one paper on Biblical Theology, which was not so good as he had expected; but he was evidently pleased with his select pupil's performance and was sure that I ought to pursue studies further. The next step was plain enough. In that heroic age of the Faculty of Theology, no candidate could be admitted to examination for honours unless he had obtained the B.D. degree, which was a comprehensive course, including a considerable amount of Biblical Hebrew. I was deeply interested in the Philosophy of Religion and wanted above all things a chance of taking honours in that subject. I thought Headlam would contrive to make that possible, and I was right. Holding his letter in my hand recently, I reflected how cold and detached his language was. Another reflection came from the letter: how terrible his writing was. In the letter of congratulation and good wishes is a sentence which I can only suppose reads, "I hope you will not go to hell," a sentiment which no doubt is unexceptional and only too relevant to my condition, but seems unlikely in the context. It is a sidelight on his relation with me that, although later in life we were friends and colleagues, I never dared to ask him what he meant.

The time had come to make up my mind whether I should seek ordination. The choice was really wide open, for I had incurred no moral obligation, having refused all financial help from ordination funds. Some of my friends would have been disappointed if I had not been ordained, but others would have been glad. To this day, I am not sure whether my father and mother hoped I would be ordained or not. How wise of them to leave me alone to make my own decision! Of one thing I am sure: the hope of a prosperous and comfortable life had nothing to do with my choice. When I had decided to test my vocation, I supposed that I had embraced a lot of relative poverty. It is true that things did not turn out in this way and, when I had a wife and a family of three children to educate, my conception of poverty changed—but, when I chose ordination, I did not expect to have a wife and family. One of the troublesome suspicions of my motives had faded out. The question "Do you choose ordination because you want to have a life among books?" I now saw was question-begging, tacitly assuming that a life among books could not be a life dedicated to God.

The problem resolved itself into two parts—intellectual and spiritual; but, when I say that, I do not mean that intellect and spirit are opposed or in the end completely different from one another. Relatively, however, the distinction is useful and, in the case of my choice, means roughly that I had to decide whether I sincerely believed what the Church believed and whether my worship and prayer life was such as to fit me for pastoral work. I may say at once that I found the second question more difficult to answer than the first.

The Thirty-nine Articles of Religion, which are the only

legal summary of the doctrines of the Church of England, have to be assented to by every candidate for ordination, but it is certain that the majority of the clergy would not point to the Articles if they were challenged to state either the teaching of the Church or their own personal convictions. Some of the clergy seem to be content with the situation and are, I suppose, satisfied that, in the light of certain statements about the meaning of subscription, they can accept these antiquated formulas without scruple. I did not think so myself on the brink of ordination and I had scruples which I overrode. Perhaps I was wrong, but I can at least claim that I have missed no opportunity of trying to get the Articles either abolished or changed. They came near to preventing me from going forward to ordination and left me with a troubled conscience. I do not doubt that they are deterrents to many intelligent young men today. Leaving this special difficulty out of account, I found that the ethos and the tradition of the Anglican Church had become a part of me which I could not give up without a sense of desolation, but that did not prove that I was called to be a priest in the Church.

A year or two after my ordination, I coined a phrase which expressed part of my position. Supporting an effort to spread knowledge of modern critical biblical scholarship and of the origins of Christianity, I said, "There is a very good case for the Christian Faith, but unfortunately it is not the case that most people think it is." I was thinking then mainly of the belief that the verbal inerrancy of the Bible was a necessary tenet. But the dictum can be enlarged in scope. I was convinced that there is truth and reality in the Christian experience and that the doctrines and the worship of the Church were products of and expressions of this continuing experience. And I was also convinced that the creative experience of the Apostolic Church was a revelation by which all developments of faith and worship must be tested. I called myself a "Modern Churchman" or a "Liberal Churchman" and had much sympathy with Protestant liberal scholars, but I see now more clearly than I did then that I had more affinity with the Liberal Catholics, the first and proper "Modernists". It followed from this, or so I thought, that in every age the interpretation of Christianity must be adapted to the current state of knowledge. The great central doctrines of Christianity: Creation, Incarnation and Atonement had eternal validity as symbols of religious experience, but they needed to be thought out again for the modern world and, so it seemed to me, this rethinking of Christianity must be a co-operative work in which many scholars and thinkers shared. It was my hope, perhaps a presumptuous one, that I might have a part in that inspired enterprise. Free enquiry and sincere search for historical and philosophical truth, along with a veneration for the continuing revelation, was my idea. I believed then that progress towards Christian unity along these lines could be rapid and that attempts to reconcile the religious and scientific standpoints might reach at least a *modus vivendi*. Probably my thinking was less coherent than this summary might imply, but it is the nearest I can get to an accurate report on my position.

With regard to my spiritual condition, I was deeply perplexed. About half-way through my student years I wrote a poem. It was a very bad one technically, because I chose an impossible metrical pattern for my *cri de coeur*. I long ago tore it up. But it was quite literally a "cry from the heart", for it had as a refrain, "Give me back my heart, a heart that prays". The alarming verdict of my conscience was that my prayers had become cold and dull. When I had been striving to find my vocation, my prayers had been alive and thus a means of grace, but the study of theology seemed to have spoiled them. I did not know then that this experience is not uncommon. L. P. Jacks, in one of his modern parables, has the story of a man who had a remarkable religious experience; it was so remarkable that he decided to study it very seriously. For some years he researched on it from the psychological, the philosophical, the historical and the theological angles. At length, he paused to sum up the results. He found he was much better informed on many subjects and that his general education had been enriched; but, with regard to the religious experience which had started his enquiries, the one certain conclusion in his mind was that he would never have the experience again. It may be that Jesus' saying that we must become as little children if we would enter the Kingdom of Heaven applies most of all to prayer, and his prayer to our Father is a list of petitions such as a child could make.

I did not despair and to some extent the preparation for the ordination service, when all examinations and arrangements had been completed, did give me back the heart that prayed.

I am glad that there never was a serious proposal that I should be a bishop for more than one reason; but chief among them is the consciousness that, though I have persevered in prayer, I have never advanced far in the art, if that is the right word. A father in God should be pre-eminently a man of prayer and able to teach others how to pray. Unfortunately, the writings of spiritual directors have been little help to me, partly because some of the exercises are patently rules for auto-suggestion, which repels me. Intercession for others is plainly a Christian duty; but, when it consists of detailed hints or even directions to God as to what he ought to do, we seem to be approaching blasphemy. I learned my own way of meditation, on which I will not dwell now; sufficient to say that I hoped the advance made since my poem was written would be continued when I was ordained and so I decided to go forward.

But I was determined that I would have no misunderstanding. I would state my beliefs, when asked, without compromise and, if they were regarded as not fitting for an ordinand, I would take up some other occupation—perhaps journalism. It happened that my progress towards ordination was obstructed by an unexpected objection from the senior examining chaplain to the Bishop of London. Confident in the efficacy of my recently acquired B.D. degree, I was not alarmed by the examination for the diaconate, which was presided over by Archdeacon Sinclair, notable for his powerful voice. He surprised me by saying at the first session, "If anyone is caught cheating, he will be turned out." Queer, I thought, that this should be thought necessary only for ordination candidates, for I never heard this announcement anywhere else. The Archdeacon did not put me on to translate the Greek Testament in the *viva voce* and I was not surprised when the results were published and I came out top. It was, and is, the custom that the candidate who comes top in the deacon's examination should read the Gospel in the Holy Communion Service at which deacons are made and priests ordained. This was not to be my lot without controversy, for the examining chaplain recommended that I should be refused ordination on the ground that my views on the inspiration of Holy Scripture were heretical. The Bishop accepted this recommendation.

The charge of heresy was based on my answer to a question in the written examination on the narrative in the Gospel of

St. John of the Raising of Lazarus from the dead. The question was so framed as to invite an answer on the historicity of the miracle. I deliberately chose this question for two reasons, it would be my opportunity to test the acceptability of "liberal" thought on the part of the clergy and it was on a subject to which I had given thought. In my answer, I was careful to avoid making a dogmatic judgment on the miracle; I did not say that it could not have happened, but I did say that, on the historical evidence, the probability is that it did not happen—at least it cannot be regarded as an historical event. This did not mean that the description of this "sign" had no religious value. This is not the place to enter on a discussion of the character and meaning of St. John's Gospel, but I must emphasise that today the point of view which I put forward is accepted by most scholars and that, if St. John's narrative is historically true, the narrative of the other three Gospels can hardly be true.

I was inclined to go quietly and to take the examining chaplain's verdict, endorsed by the Bishop, as final and as the end of my personal dilemma; I had offered myself for ordination and had been refused. I thought perhaps it might be my duty for the sake of other liberal-minded theologians to make some protest, but I had no wish to be the centre of an acrimonious controversy. That was not Headlam's view of the matter. After biting his fingers in rage for some minutes, he said, "I will write at once to the Bishop of London." He never told me what he wrote, but I think the gist of it was that, unless I was admitted to the coming ordination of deacons forthwith, he would write to *The Times* a full account of the affair. Whatever the letter's content may have been, it was almost instantly effective and I had my first experience of ecclesiastical compromise or "finding a formula". The Bishop asked the examining chaplain to see me and try to get some assurance from me that I would not be a "ravening wolf" among the sheep. We did find a formula which I signed and in the archives at Fulham Palace perhaps the document is still extant. I kept no copy, but according to my recollection I repeated that, regarded as a purely historical problem, the Raising of Lazarus must be highly doubtful and, if confronted by the definite question, "Do you count it as an historical event?" I should be compelled to answer, "No, but I do not imply that the miracle is impossible or that further evidence might not conceivably come to light which would lead me to change my mind. I should not discuss this question in the pulpit as part of my pastoral duty and, if I did, I should make it clear that the prevailing opinion in the Church was different from mine." It is easy to dismiss all this as a face-saving operation and I fear that, in my annoyance, I suspected that was the right word for it, but looking back with far more knowledge of Bishop Winnington-Ingram I think it would be unjust. The Bishop was always acutely conscious that a bishop has imposed upon him the maintenance of the Christian faith and rooting out of errors. In my opinion, he sometimes took a too narrow view of achieving this, but his motive was good—not face-saving but faith-saving.

This chapter should culminate with my ordination, but I cannot meet the demand. My memories are confused and I think my emotions at the time must have been conflicting. The fact that there are two steps to mount, the diaconate and the priesthood, and that the services at which these steps are taken are a year apart militates against clear and distinct conceptions of what happened in the spirit of the ordinand. The best I can do is to collect such experiences and thoughts as remain from both services, without attempting to date them exactly. After all, the ordination is really one process extended over a year or more. In the Anglican tradition, the diaconate has become normally a probationary year for the full ministry of the priesthood, when the ordinand takes on the pastoral duties and privileges. In England, he also takes on restrictions. Being a priest, he cannot become a Member of Parliament or engage in trade or commerce for profit.

The ordination is preceded by a retreat. Only once have I been invited to conduct an ordination retreat, but that was enough to make me chary of criticising the retreats which I was ordered to attend at my ordination. I looked at the forty young men and some middle-aged men and wondered what I could possibly say to help them all without knowing more than two of them even by name. I have no doubt that the retreats were conducted by good and wise men, but I have to admit that nothing that was said to me has survived in memory and I threw away the opportunity of keeping a written record. At one of the retreats, if not both, the Bishop's chaplain distributed little red covered notebooks—they looked like washing books—so that we could write down memorable thoughts. At the end of the retreat I found, alas, that I had written down only one thought which, on reflection, seemed to me to be untrue—so I regretfully scratched it out. There is great spiritual benefit, I am sure, to be gained from a group with a common purpose praying together and retreat conditions with ordered services and long periods of complete silence are well adapted for this exercise. There was not enough silence in our retreats. We were talked to and talked at too much and what many of us needed was a free talk with an understanding older priest, who would listen. Confession and absolution have of course their place in any retreat and certainly in ordination retreats, but we needed too, I think, not only confessors, but listeners.

One trivial memory is worth recording—my interview with the Bishop of London during the retreat. I was walking in the Palace garden, trying to meditate, and, as I passed his study window, the Bishop, wearing his purple cassock, burst out suddenly, put his arm round my neck and said, "Well, old boy, let's have our little talk." So we did, but I cannot remember what we talked about and I was ill at ease, because I have never liked men, even bishops, embracing me without warning. It was in the evening service, the night before the ordination, that the Bishop swept away all the criticisms and hesitations, so far as I was concerned. He spoke of the ministry of the Church as the most romantic calling in the world. I thought then that the essential Winnington-Ingram came through. He gave the impression to some people that he was acting a part—and so, in a sense, he was, he had chosen the part of Christ's faithful soldier and servant and had accepted the office of a leader. It was the most glorious and adventurous thing in the world and he not only lived the part, he looked it. He was an old man then, but the fire still burned. I had occasion once, after Winnington-Ingram had retired, to say something like this to Cosmo Gordon Lang, when he was Archbishop of Canterbury. He agreed and added that no one who, like him, had known Winnington-Ingram when he became Bishop of London, could ever forget the impact he made upon all sorts of people.

I make no attempt to analyse my state of mind at the ordination. I came to it, specially to the ordination as priest, in a condition of spiritual exhaustion: as in duty bound I had examined myself and did not like what I found; but, even if I could, I would not go into detail of my critical exploration of my personality. A friend, to whom I tried to make this clear, replied, "But could you not remember some dominant feeling or thought which coloured your self-consciousness?" An interesting idea, perhaps worth trying to put to the test. I may be simply confused and talking nonsense, but after searching my memory I came to the unexpected and unwelcome conclusion that the dominant feeling, if any, was fright. When I considered in detail what I had taken on, I was terrified. The fright was on two levels. There was the natural fear of failure, that one would simply not have the mental and physical ability to stay the course. But, much more agonising, was the spiritual fear. My evangelical upbringing asserted itself here. I was undertaking a responsibility for others with regard to their eternal destiny, the "cure of souls" was not a quaint old-fashioned phrase, but a stern reality. I should be answerable to God for my flock. Moreover I was to be a witness to Christ and dedicated to preaching the gospel. Did I have the courage? Unless my memory is at fault, a recollected sin of long ago kept on troubling me. When I was about fifteen, a schoolfellow named Fletcher, of whom I was fond, was very ill and was in fact dying. I went to see him and I could tell that he suspected he would die and was afraid of death. He was the son of an editor who, I think, was an agnostic. Whether his father was in the room I do not remember; but there was someone, some adult, and I said nothing because I was frightened. I did not dare even to utter the name of Christ. That boyhood sin had troubled me, but when I grew up I forgot about it; now I thought, "I am not really braver than I was then and, what is more, I haven't the gospel to offer that I had then. With all my learning, of which I am childishly proud, what have I to say to a dying sinner?" My prayer was, I think, in effect something like this: "O God, I am frightened: I cannot do the things I am promising to do: I shall probably be careless and lazy, even if I don't abandon the job altogether. If you don't help me, I am lost."

My wife once sat next to Cardinal Griffin at lunch shortly after he had been made Archbishop of Westminster and, with perhaps undue frankness, said, "I suppose, Archbishop, when you knew that you were to be Archbishop of Westminster, you started to pray for humility." "Oh, no," he replied, "I started to pray for confidence." When she told me this, I felt he was exactly right.

CHAPTER 4

Lecturer and Curate

When I look back on my life, the years 1908 to 1914 seem to be a prelude to the real business I was called to do; but from my personal angle events happened which were to affect me profoundly—I got married, I had a son, I published my first book and I made my first contact with German theologians. When I was ordained, it was to the "title" of assistant curate in the parish church of St. Mary Abbots, Kensington. I was only a part-time curate, so that I could give a large portion of every day to study and to the light duties of a junior lecturer. I lived at the hostel in Mecklenburgh Square and helped the warden. I was very busy and very happy. The vicar of Kensington, Prebendary Pennefather, was kind to me and so was everyone else who worked in the parish, including, I remember, Lord Loreburn, the Lord Chief Justice, who sang in the voluntary choir which provided the music at the Sunday afternoon evensong. The courtly old judge always opened the door for me when I left the vestry after saying the vestry prayer. It gave comfort to a shy young man. But on the whole I felt that one year was enough in a prosperous West End parish—and it *was* prosperous. The Sunday morning service was invariably packed and the two daughter churches were full too, at the same time. A picture which does not fade is the one I used to see when, as was often the case, I stood up in my stall and intoned the words (as I hoped on G), "When the wicked man . . ." Owing to the rule that directly the service began all seats were free, these words, as if by magic, opened the floodgates to the would-be worshippers standing at the doors.

I could have gone on in Kensington and probably my life would have been easier, but I was clear that it was not the place for me. I was a radical in politics and the people in St. Mary

Abbots irresistibly reminded me of the satirical label for the C. of E., "the Conservative party at prayer". I was a "modernist" in theology, while no hint of the modern criticism of the Bible was heard in St. Mary's, and in my second sermon I had the misfortune to upset some hearer's faith. He took exception to a phrase "the Bible is a melancholy book", and evidently was so indignant that he listened to no more and thus misunderstood the whole sermon. I thought I might be more useful ministering to the uneducated. An opportunity came to serve where conditions were tough. My dear friend R. Neville Pyke, a fellow student, was now curate in the parish where I had been living, St. Peters, Regent Square; there was work and moderate pay for a second curate, the vicar liked me; so, all things working together as it seemed, I joined with Pyke in a flat and gave half my time to the parish.

At this moment, St. Peter's Church, Regent Square, is a derelict ruin and the parish has ceased to exist. An interesting history is thus ended. In the Presbyterian church in Regent Square, Edward Irving started the "Catholic Apostolic Church" and in the square the ecstatic meetings were held at which many persons "spoke with tongues". About the same time St. Peter's was a fashionable evangelical church which had a large and distinguished congregation. One fact concerning that period, which I learned from the records, is that on Good Friday there was a Communion Service with about a thousand communicants, but on Easter Day only a handful of the faithful attended. The parish, when I joined the clerical staff, was a mixed one so far as the population was concerned. Some prosperous middle-class people still lived in Mecklenburgh Square and Guildford Street, but the streets round Regent Square were filthy slums, inhabited by a motley crowd of individuals who lived from hand to mouth and were in the habit of using the banisters of the stairs for firewood, and of moonlight flitting to avoid the payment of rent. "Paradise Row" was the name of the worst block of houses. Its inhabitants often kept dwellers in the more respectable streets awake far into the night with screams which sounded like cries of "murder". So far as I know, no murder was actually committed in Paradise Row in my time, but just outside it a postman, who came to the help of a policeman who was attempting to make an arrest, was kicked to death as he lay in the gutter.

The church had not given up. In addition to the three clerics, there was a full-time paid woman worker and there were still some laymen and women who helped run clubs. The tradition of pastoral visitation was still strong and we aimed at visiting every family in the parish. I was glad that my visiting was done in the "down and out" section; my colleague, Pyke, had the outwardly respectable houses, but some of them were of a dubious character and looking back, I am astonished at the dangers that could have attended the random visits of an innocent young curate. We never quite knew the answer to the question, Where does the vicar visit? He used to keep us up to the mark by asking how many pastoral visits we had paid in the week. Of himself, he sometimes said that he had been "visiting at a distance". We thought that "visiting at a distance" was apt to occur when a parochial crisis was at hand.

A striking example will illustrate the parochial situation. Once at least in my days as an assistant curate I came into contact with a world-famous figure; Carry Nation deserved that description, for her agitation had something to do with the triumph of prohibition in the U.S.A. She was notorious for her fanatical attacks on "saloons" in America, attacks which were not confined to words. She fought for righteousness with the axe and valiantly smashed up places where intoxicants were sold, encouraging others to do the same as a Christian duty. Imagine our consternation, when we found one morning a large home-made poster on the church, announcing that Carry Nation would give an address to the Band of Hope that very same evening. The consternation was not diminished by the news that the vicar much regretted that he would be "visiting at a distance" that evening. It seemed that our zealous lady worker had, in visiting the parish, come across the formidable Carry in one of the guest houses and, with the prospect of a "scoop" for St. Peter's Band of Hope, had booked her for the parish hall. Pyke and I hoped that only a few people would hear of the meeting and we should be able to meet our American orator in peaceful obscurity. When I went to the parish hall for the meeting, it was only too plain that the news had spread. At the back of the hall, behind the exceptionally large gathering of children, I saw the landlord of the chief public house accompanied by a number of friends. He was a supporter of the church and his children were in our Sunday School. A number of others claiming to be parents of children were also present.

Carry Nation was a dangerous fanatic whose appearance frightened the children and whose speech was almost unintelligible. Pyke was in the chair and for a few minutes was able to keep some kind of order, but before long it began to dawn on the audience that Carry Nation was inciting them to riot. She had a plan. It was that the children should stand outside the local "pubs" and shout "Hell house" at the top of their voices without stopping except for breath. For some minutes, led by Carry, they practised the exercise. The adults at the back, from aloof curiosity soon changed to hostility and even the children began to understand that their parents might be inside the "Hell houses". The noise grew threatening and we could see that a move towards the platform was imminent. I said to Pyke, "The lights are going to fail. Tell them that a slight breakdown will be put right quickly." I switched off all the lights and, in the darkness, clutched Carry Nation (she was a small woman) and said to her "I must get you out of here before they can get at you." I then pushed her out of the back-door and said, "Run away as fast as you can." Meanwhile, Pyke was keeping the enraged audience in play and, when he thought we had given Carry a good start, at a sign from him I turned on the lights. I do not think all this was well-managed and of course we ought to have told the police beforehand of our fire-brand speaker. I think we did send a boy to find a policeman when the trouble started, but if he did he may well have been suspected of pulling the constabulary leg.

Pyke was not by nature the type of person described in testimonials as "good with boys" or "good with men" and he had no athletic prowess, but he was a person whom children trusted on sight and I am sure that his presence in the chair at the Carry Nation meeting was the chief safeguard against violence. He was everybody's friend.

I enjoyed my years of rough and tumble parish work, but I must admit that I was favoured by circumstances. Only half my time was given to the parish, the rest was spent in academic work of study and teaching. I lived in two worlds and never suffered the really testing hardship which is now, and was then, the lot of many parish priests. To work patiently and hopefully, year after year, in a parish which has lost any religious tradition, if it ever had one, where a faithful little band is the visible church existing in a massive environment of indifference demands heroic virtue.

There are many parishes where no man can be expected to serve for more than ten years. Only a saint could maintain a hopeful spirit much longer and, though perhaps we may have some justification for demanding saintliness from a vicar, we have no ground for expecting saintliness in the vicar's wife. Bishops too often either forget what parish life was like or never experienced its rigours and tend to discourage movement from one parish to another. Exchange of livings, which used to be a way of escape from an intolerable situation, is now discouraged by bishops who have the power of veto. No doubt there are reasons for caution in this matter, but would it not be better and more positive if the bishops took up vigorously the question, How to give the clergy more freedom of movement without destroying the parochial system? I am well aware that the "parson's freehold" would come up for discussion before any plan could get under way, but one of the conclusions which seems to emerge clearly from Leslie Paul's study of the deployment of the clergy is that the freehold must be modified if any rational deployment is to be achieved.

It would be misleading to suggest that my two worlds, that of theological study and that of pastoral duties, never met. The Bishop of London, the beloved Dr. Winnington-Ingram, was deeply concerned about the orthodoxy of his clergy and, from time to time, issued directions to the Rural Deans that the Rural Decanal Chapter should vote on resolutions defending the faith, such as one affirming belief in the miracles of the gospels. It happened that, early in my curacy at St. Peter's he required that all the Chapters should vote on a resolution affirming their adherence to the Athanasian Creed. The vicar of St. Pancras, the Rural Dean, duly summoned the meeting and nearly all the clergy in the Deanery of St. Pancras duly attended it. If I had taken to heart the trouble which I got into at the ordination examination, I would have held my tongue and I went to the meeting fully determined to do so, but the docile speeches of the Rural Dean and other local pillars of the Church made me so indignant and my vicar (R. S. Stoney), who opposed the resolution, seemed to be alone among the speakers, so that at last "the fire kindled within me and I spake with my tongue". My opening remarks I well remember, because at the time I thought them clever, though now I should consider them "brash".

At least they woke everyone up. "The Athanasian Creed," I said, "reminds me of a black beetle; for just as a black beetle is neither black nor a beetle, so the Athanasian Creed is neither a creed nor is it by St. Athanasius." The expression on the Rural Dean's face suggested that the roof might be expected to fall in at any moment. I do not remember the rest of my speech, except that I attacked the whole conception of anathemas as the answer to heretics. My vicar made a speech of sound common-sense and, to our surprise, was supported by an evangelical vicar whose parish was next door to St. Peter's. To this day, I have not made up my mind as to how much of his speech was spoken with his tongue in his cheek, to use a most inappropriate metaphor. "The objection that weighs with me," he said, "is not theological, but tactical. I mean the Athanasian Creed fails in tact. Anathemas are not tactful. If I were to go up to a stranger in the street and say, 'My friend, you are damned,' I should probably be telling him the truth, but it would not be the best way to present the Gospel to him—not tactful." He went on to argue that the Athanasian Creed was —like the Coronation Oath against Transubstantiation—unpleasant, but perhaps useful, if said only once in every reign!

My studies went on with many interruptions and I began to think about writing on the subject of the Philosophy of Religion. It seemed to me at the time that the scope of the subject needed definition and, in fact, that any serious work on it must begin with a study of the History of Philosophy and the Nature of Religion—a daunting programme! By degrees, the duties of my lectureship were increased and I found myself dealing with Ethics as well as Logic. Fortunately, the University prescribed set books on Ethics and in three years I lectured on Butler, Aristotle, Plato and Herbert Spencer, all on an elementary level, but the attempt to explain the thought of these great thinkers taught me much. Incidentally, one of the minor things I learned was to treat one's text with respect. Spencer's *Data of Ethics* was in my opinion not worthy to rank with the other set books and I spent too long in destructive criticism, until a charming Irish boy said to me, "If Spencer writes such rot, couldn't we take him as read?" Butler's *Sermons on Human Nature,* together with the *Dissertation on Virtue* attached to the *Analogy* were among the set books. An edition which brought together in one handy volume all Butler's ethical writings with an introduction and careful analyses would, I thought, be useful to the student of Ethical Theory and to the general reader. A friend who was a lecturer in the English department, Guthkelch, who had edited some of Swift's works, introduced me to George Bell and Sons, who accepted my proposal and offered £20 for the copyright. I have never sold another copyright and I sometimes regret that I sold this one, for the book is still reprinted, but I have no grievance. I was unknown, and there was no certainty that my book would be the kind of thing to appeal to students. Moreover Messrs. Bell and Sons have presented me with the library editions of the two magnificent issues of Webster's *Second* and *Third New International Dictionary.* Turning over my copy of this first literary venture, I note that, though I had been working on it for at least two years, it was published in 1914. The shadow of the war was creeping up and I reflect with sadness that Guthkelch was an early victim. Unfit for military service, he laboured beyond the limit of his strength to carry on the work of others who had joined up and fell dead while lecturing in King's College. As my chronicle proceeds, it becomes tinged with melancholy as one after another dear companions are taken away; yet I am thankful that I knew men like Guthkelch and can still feel grateful to them.

Greatly daring, I ventured to submit an article to Dr. Headlam, who was then editing the *Church Quarterly Review,* on the philosophy of Nietzsche. I was learning German, and Nietzsche was a relatively easy author to read, though not so easy to understand. The article was accepted and even paid for, which surprised me. It is of no interest now, except that it was my first full-scale appearance in a "learned" periodical. It is, I think, readable—and unfair. Nietzsche is treated as the "Antichrist" which, at one time, he claimed to be and his ethics of power are refuted, not ineptly. When I went to Germany and could read more in that language, I understood better why he is so important in the history of thought and religion— but I still believe that, in essentials, my essay was right and said what needed then to be said.

Before the first world war, I visited Germany three times,

and every time the central aim of my visit was in Marburg on the Lahn, which had a University famous in the time of the Reformation and, in the 19th and 20th centuries, the home of many eminent professors of theology. I learned the language, though very imperfectly, in Marburg and I wandered about the country with a friend older and more expert in German than I, Clement Rogers, of whom we shall hear again. One of these visits made Marburg to me a noble city for better reasons even than eminence of learning. There I became engaged to be married: it was on what would have been a bank holiday in England, on August 2nd, 1911, in the hilly woodland which looks down on the town. This is not a romantic novel and I have no intention to unpack my heart for the amusement or even edification of readers. I will say quite simply what really sums up the matter: I thank God that I married Margaret Bryan and I cannot bear to think what my life would have been without her.

I have sometimes said that the first words that I spoke to my future wife were, "I ask the honorary secretary to read the minutes of the last meeting." I can at least claim that they are symbolically true, for at one time we were respectively Secretary and President of the London University Union Society and we became acquainted because of our shared ambition to do something to make the University a social reality as well as an examining institution. The reader may see in Bloomsbury now, near to the Senate building, the impressive premises of the present Union Society. The little group of students and young graduates to which Margaret and I belonged was its humble, and now forgotten, ancestor.

When I first knew her, she was a science student in the Royal Holloway College, one of the first women's colleges. At that time, the College was very Victorian, both in the comfort which it offered to its pupils and in the discipline which it imposed upon them. To visit a student in the College, a man had to pass severe tests. One of Margaret's fellow students was Ivy Compton-Burnett, the novelist. I must have seen her in one of my visits, but I have no remembrance of meeting her. When we became engaged, Margaret was science mistress in a Girls' High School and was doing part-time chemical research at the Imperial College of Science, Kensington. In the enthusiasm of becoming engaged, I learned by heart the chemical formula

of the substance on which she was working, but it escapes me
now; I believe that it had some connection with aniline dyes.
The news of our engagement was received with scant applause
and some foreboding. My friends and patrons in the academic
field regarded it as youthful folly which might spoil my career,
while all Margaret's friends agreed in wondering how she could
possibly adapt herself to the life of a parson's spouse. She was,
in fact, very unlike the typical clergy wife or daughter and she
never made any effort to be conventional. She had been affected
to some extent by the influence of H. G. Wells, though she
was highly critical of him and his views on marriage. I tried to
interest her in the theology which took so much of my attention and persuaded her to read Dr. Strong's *Manual of Theology*, which was highly regarded in episcopal circles, but alas,
she never got to the end and, I am afraid, thought what she did
read was most unconvincing. She was never, I think, an orthodox churchwoman, but she was deeply religious. She helped
me in ways that a more docile believer would not have found
possible.

We did not worry overmuch about whether our marriage was
thought suitable, but we had to be concerned with the practical
question how we were to live. My income from King's College
was not much more than £200 and it was imperative that I
should increase the income by paid work on Sundays. The
problem was solved when I was appointed assistant chaplain
at the Magdalen Hospital in Streatham, a post involving only
the Sunday services which were open to the public. After some
anxious months, we were married in Reading on July 9th,
1912. Then began three years full of peace and hope. The
Magdalen Hospital was an interesting 18th-century institution,
which had associations with the Foundling Hospital and with
Dr. Johnson. The most sensational episodes in its story are
connected with the Rev. Dr. Dodd who, in Dr. Johnson's time,
drew large congregations to the Magdalen Hospital. It seems
to have been quite the thing for fashionable persons to go to
the Magdalen Chapel in the Blackfriars Bridge Road to hear
the Magdalens sing and the great Dr. Dodd preach. The story
ends with the hanging of Dr. Dodd for forgery. It can be read
in detail in more than one book. Perhaps its only genuine
historical value is the evidence it gives of the criminal justice
of the period and the fact that Dr. Dodd preached, in Newgate

jail on the Sunday before his execution, a sermon written for
him by Dr. Johnson. It was the occasion of one of the Doctor's
best known and most questionable remarks. When some inquisi-
tive person, who suspected that Johnson was the author, said
to him that Dr. Dodd's last sermon was much better than any
previous sermons by him, Dr. Johnson replied, "Depend upon
it, Sir, when a man knows he is to be hanged in a fortnight,
it concentrates his mind wonderfully." Most men, one might
think, would be affected in precisely the opposite manner.

Apart from historical and literary associations, the old chaplain, Mr. Watkins, and his family, together with some friendly
and cultivated persons who formed the Sunday morning congregation, made life very easy and happy for the young cleric
and his wife who had come to live among them: and when
our firstborn son Michael was added our cup of blessing seemed
almost too full, though our income was not quite £300. We
had a solidly-built Victorian villa in Drewstead Road, just
opposite the hospital, with a garden in which a fig tree grew,
and a gardener who came once a week and not only kept the
garden tidy and sometimes bright, but instructed me from
time to time on the real meaning of some Old Testament
prophecies. The biblical scholar applied his learning to practical
affairs, for when he had a troublesome boil he followed scrip-
tural guidance and made himself a plaster of figs from our
garden—and the boil vanished as if by magic. When Michael
came, we were able not only to have a nurse for the month
but to employ one to look after the baby. I must add, to get
the record clear, that my father and mother had moved to a
commodious house and garden not far away in Dulwich and
that their financial situation was much improved. I mention
this, because we did not have the anxiety, which haunted young
married couples in those pre-Welfare State days, about what
would happen if some catastrophe or illness struck the parents.

We were indeed happy—happier perhaps than we knew,
for we had not known real fear or near despair. The first
holiday of our wedded life we spent in Germany, partly in
Marburg which we loved because of its associations. We
tramped about too in the Hartz Mountains and in the tiny
principalities which still had a limited separate existence. In
Wernigerode, I remember, we had an experience which, with
the fatuous optimism of really happy people, we took to be

a good omen—I cannot think why. It was a curious coincidence, though. We went to *Schloss* chapel at which the Prince of Wernigerode was present and his Lutheran chaplain preached. We were both, I think, delighted that our German had improved so much that we understood the sermon perfectly. The coincidence was that, on our honeymoon in Yorkshire on the corresponding Sunday in the previous year, the vicar of the church had quoted the well-known passage from Bede's *History* comparing human lives to a bird flying in from the darkness into a lighted hall and through it into the dark at the other side. And now, exactly one year later, in a foreign land and a foreign tongue, the preacher quoted at length the same simile from Bede's *History*. I recall these trivial but cheerful things, because it is hard to be clear about the profound difference that the world war made to millions of homes in many lands. *"Nie kehrst du wieder goldene Zeit,"* we used to sing with the German students in Marburg and our *goldene Zeit*, Margaret's and mine, was the years between our marriage and the coming of war. We saw a way we believed to a useful, happy and peaceful life, full of work, but of work which we loved to do. For me, the ambition of my life was that I should be a professor and perhaps be mentioned in learned works on theology and philosophy. I thought that this was a possible achievement if I worked hard. I had begun to publish articles and soon my first book would be at the printers. My little son, I determined, should have all the advantages of education which I had missed, if I could possibly secure them for him. He was born in our little house and was baptised in the name of Michael Harrington by the professor who had succeeded Dr. Headlam as Dean of the College—Dr. Alfred Caldecott. The baby howled at the top of his voice throughout. Whether this had any significance except that Dr. Caldecott was not accustomed to handling babies, I cannot say.

The outbreak of war and the end of our "golden time" came when we were having a wonderful holiday in Doonside, near Aberdeen, as guests of Sir Alexander and Lady McRobert. Lady McRobert had been my wife's friend at college and was herself expecting a baby. In the lovely highland country and the brilliant weather of that year of destiny, we hardly gave a thought to the menace of war. We could not seriously believe that the civilised world would tear itself in pieces in a world war. Yet the war came on August 4th, 1914, and it was to happen that my new son and the three sons of Lady McRobert should die in a second war fighting the Germans for whom we felt, at that time, admiration and affection.

When war was certain, I had to get to London without delay. The rail journey from Aberdeen was protracted and disturbing. The train was held up by the mobilisation of soldiers and I arrived at Euston about 2 a.m., when no trains or bus or cab seemed to be moving, and I set out to walk all the way to Dulwich, where I was to sleep at my father's house. The night was warm and fine. My way took me past Buckingham Palace and my impression is that there was a considerable crowd assembled even then. When I arrived in Dulwich, I found my father almost in a state of collapse, having arrived home from Lombard Street only a short time before I got there. He said to me, "My boy, tomorrow morning every bank in this country will be bankrupt." He was Chief Inspector of the Bankers' Clearing House and *ex officio* Secretary of the Committee of London Clearing Bankers, which had been wrestling for the day and most of the night with the problems of wartime finance. It is a matter of history that the immediate problem was solved —or postponed—by a "moratorium" severely restricting the drawing of money out of the banks. My father always insisted that the credit for this financial policy ought to go to Rufus Isaacs, whose clearness of mind and decisive action carried the day, when the City pundits were at a loss. I am convinced that this is true, because my father, who was a stubborn Tory, would never have gone out of his way to commend an eminent Liberal unless facts compelled him to.

During my long train ride on this inauspicious day, I had pondered, like thousands of others, on the probable consequences for my family. I knew enough about Germany and the Germans to be sure that the optimistic predictions of a short war and speedy victory were nonsensical and I expected that many young men would be needed in the forces, causing the student population to fall perhaps to such a low level as to cause colleges to cease to function; all of these things happened, but in my gloomiest moments I did not expect the sustained slaughter for over three years which so profoundly changed Europe and the Europeans.

The events which I had foreseen duly took place, but not

quite as soon as I expected. I think it was about this time that I remembered my former military training as a volunteer in the First Surrey Rifles. I had been hopeless at marching, owing to my dropped arches, but in a modest way I had been a fairly useful rifle shooter. I went to the recruiting officer, chiefly to placate my conscience, because I felt that inevitably young men would consult me on whether they ought to join up and also that in many cases I should think that they ought; but it has always seemed to me most distasteful to advise a man to risk his life if one has not offered to do it oneself. The recruiting officer looked at my feet and then at my clerical collar and told me to run away.

To put a long story in a word, King's College, London, almost ceased to exist after the first year of the war and theological students seemed to vanish more rapidly than the others. The College could not afford to pay the teaching staff. Some academic work continued under the Dean and senior professors. I was the junior lecturer. I was young and active. Clearly I must find some other employment. We must give up our little house and store our furniture and, picking up our baby, move back to a curacy, or perhaps, if the signs were favourable, to work across the ocean.

CHAPTER 5

My Parish and Zeppelins

The world crisis of 1914 was reflected in various dimensions in innumerable families. Our little home was more fortunate than most. Though it was evident from the first that the junior lecturers at King's College would soon have neither pupils nor pay, there was some interval of time to prepare for the lean years. The prospects of making ends meet were good. I was not wanted as an army chaplain, but I could go back to the status of assistant curate and my wife could teach science in a school. There was a gleam of light, however, from another quarter. The post of Principal of the Anglican College in the University of Sydney, Australia, was vacant and, by the kind offices of two of my professorial friends, my name was put forward to the committee in England which was selecting a short list for the governing body in Australia. The English committee, of which William Temple was chairman, put forward my name alone and, for a time, we thought our problem was solved. We were mistaken. The Australian governing body rejected me. I recently turned up the testimonials which my good friends wrote for me and I can only suppose the Australians never read the testimonials, or else did not believe them. The only hint I had of their reasons was that I probably would not be able to cope with the exceptionally tough Australian undergraduates. They may have been right, and I certainly am thankful that I was not appointed, but I still feel a trifle hurt about the "tough undergraduates"—I never had any difficulty with students of all kinds in London, including wild engineers and temperamental medicals.

Prebendary Pennefather kindly welcomed me back on his staff of curates in Kensington, on a full-time basis, and Margaret took a post as teacher of chemistry in a boys' grammar school.

We moved to a house near the church, where we had three rooms and a share of the garden. The baby was a problem, but we found a kind and reliable lady help who looked after him by day. Unfortunately he seemed to sleep most of the day and wake most of the night, protesting shrilly if his mother would not take him out of his cot. Though the work was hard when combined with sleepless nights, she enjoyed it and certainly made her mark at the school. She sent a boy who had been insolent to the headmaster with a note asking that he should be caned. When the headmaster refused to cane the boy, she refused to teach him. For some time after the war was over, boys would come and tell her how they were getting on. They admired her forthright manner.

For some months we carried on, not unhappily but troubled by the menace of war. Then, to my great surprise, a friend whom I knew as a fellow member of an ancient clerical dining club suggested that he should propose me as his successor in the vicarage of Christ Church, Crouch End. The friend was C. J. Sharp, who had been offered the nomination to the parish church of Ealing which he intended to accept, but wanted first to make sure that his successor in Crouch End would carry on the work on the liberal principles which he had adopted. He was, in fact, the most consistent liberal I have ever known— liberal in religion, in politics and in his dealings with people. Free thought, free speech and free enterprise were his watchwords; perhaps it was not surprising that he feared the consequences to his flock if a dogmatic Anglo-Catholic or Evangelical filled his place. I must add that, to me, his most attractive characteristic was his enthusiasm for sound learning for all, laity as well as clergy. A vigorous literary and debating society was one of the chief parochial institutions.

In my then state of mind and feeling, this was exactly the rare kind of parish where I could feel at home. But I was astonished, for though I knew Sharp liked me, I had always suspected that he regarded me as a shy, shrinking individual without initiative. I also felt that my name would be quite unacceptable to the Bishop of London who had the power to nominate. Sharp, however, was confident. He had me to preach in the church on several Sundays and managed to convince leading members of the Parochial Church Council that I was the man to minister to "such an intelligent congregation" as theirs. Though P.C.C.s had no legal status in those days, the Crouch End Council included two lawyers who were skilled in making cases and representations. They had an interview with the Bishop, who rejected my name as impossible—"too young, and never heard of him". He proceeded to nominate others whom the P.C.C. set itself to frighten off by grim forecasts of the financial position. They were in a strong position, because the endowment of the living was only £62 per annum and anything beyond that depended on the congregation. They said, in effect and perhaps straight out, "You may think, my Lord, that you have the appointment to a good living, but if we don't like the man you nominate it will cease to be a good living."

Of course, I was not in on these transactions and had in fact almost written off the prospect as most unlikely. I heard the most fantastic rumours of unfortunate priests who had been frightened away. One, who I think must have been mythical, was alleged to have eleven children and a cow which he would bring with him, presumably to feed the eleven children. The one possible candidate of whom I am certain was my old friend and tutor, Dr. Caldecott, who wanted to retire from academic work after a lifetime of diligent and distinguished scholarly labour. He needed a quiet living in the country, where he could have peace and leisure to think and write. To ask him to take charge of a large urban parish in wartime and one moreover which appeared to be a landmark for Zeppelins would have been irresponsible folly.

The last act of this comedy opened with an invitation from the Bishop to lunch at London House, St. James's Square. The only other guest was the editor of *The Times*, whose presence so overawed me that I spoke only when spoken to. After lunch the editor soon withdrew and the Bishop, with his accustomed camaraderie, drew me into his study and said: "You aren't at all the kind of man I thought you must be. When those dear people from Crouch End kept on saying that they were 'such an intelligent congregation' and that you were the only candidate up to their standard, I thought you must be one of those self-advertising, self-confident young men, who had succeeded in imposing himself on these good folk; but now I can see that you are quite a different chap." These words led up to the offer of the living of Christ Church, Crouch End. Though, of course, I had suspected that the Bishop wanted to have a look at me as a possible vicar of an important parish in his diocese, I had in fact ceased to expect a definite offer and was speaking the simple truth when I asked for time to consider and take advice before I replied. The Bishop was a trifle impatient and remarked that I should be foolish not to accept, but I was not sure. I had hoped that I might proceed along the academic career, and my loftiest ambition was to become a professor. I do not think the Bishop understood my dilemma, but he allowed me the week to decide and consult. The opinions of friends were on the side of acceptance and the prospect of independent work and a permanent home for wife and child turned the scale; and soon I was inducted as vicar by the Bishop of Willesden. Margaret had to disengage herself as quickly as possible from teaching chemistry and I from the duties of a curate of Kensington Parish Church. We found nothing but help and goodwill in those whom our unexpected departure must have inconvenienced. One other auspicious event cheered our move; I persuaded my friend and former fellow curate, Neville Pyke, to accept the post of assistant curate. He had recently married and wanted to take his wife to an environment more cheerful and hopeful than Regent Square.

It was perhaps a warning that my lot was henceforth to be amid war's tumults that, on the first night when I slept in my new parish, sleep was abruptly cut short by the sound of guns and bombs. I was a guest in the house of Mr. Davies, one of the sidesmen of the church, whose house was on a hill. That night I saw an unforgettable spectacle. It all passed so rapidly, like a vivid dream, that I could not swear to the details of my story. I saw, as I believe, the bringing down of a Zeppelin in flames somewhere in the neighbourhood of Potter's Bar, and I think I heard a great noise, as it were a mixture of shouts of triumph and relief from myriads of spectators and cries of agony from the large crew of the airship who were being burned alive. Part of this picture may be "such stuff as dreams are made on"; could I have heard that great cry of mingled joy and agony? I do not know; but the picture remains and symbolised for me the whole war period: fear, relief, joy in victory and the intolerable pain of all the defeated and injured. In my dream, if it was partly a dream, I ended by feeling sorry for the German lads who had been so eager to destroy and were being themselves destroyed.

The coming of war was the occasion of a spiritual crisis for most thoughtful believers and my own experience was in no respect notably different from that of many others. The most immediately urgent crisis was personal, in that it arose from the question, What ought I to do? I was now in a position of relative comfort and security and, though I had been told by authority both of Church and State that my duty was to stay where I was, I still felt uncertain. Pyke had the same searching of conscience as I and together we placed ourselves in the hands of the Bishop of London to decide for us what we ought to do. In the strain on manpower that soon developed, it really was hard to justify the employment of two young and fairly able-bodied clerics in one prosperous parish of 6,000 persons. We never reached a solution which set my conscience at rest, but we certainly were not idle and, in addition to the parish duties, worked with the Y.M.C.A. and the organisation for the reception of the wounded.

A spiritual and moral problem demanded some action from the moment when I took over the responsibilities of vicar: the question, "Ought I to volunteer and fight?" was haunting, and torturing, many young men. In my opinion, conscription ought to have been enacted from the day war was declared. My adhesion to the Liberal Party was strained severely by its obstinate refusal to face the situation. As it was, the voluntary enlistment, and the Kitchener appeal for recruits, worked in a "dysgenic" direction, selecting the adventurous, patriotic, courageous and idealistic types for destruction. The doctrine of pacifism in Christian history has strong advocates and, to the plain man, many words attributed to Christ in the New Testament seem to condemn all warfare as contrary to the will of God. It happened that, among the Free Church ministers in the Hornsey area, there were some who were pacifists in principle, but the one who stood out as the avowed preacher of pacifism in its absolute form was the minister of the great Congregational church, Park Chapel, which was in my parish and with which Christ Church was in friendly rivalry. The Rev. G. E. Darlaston, the minister, had my sincere admiration. Depending, as he did, for his livelihood on the support of the congregation, he preached the gospel as he understood it without compromise; he offended some of his people and some came to Christ Church to swell my congregation, but the majority of those who disagreed stayed with him. I record this because it seemed to me to redound to the honour of both the minister and people.

For my part, I worked out an answer which still appears to me to be valid. It is not original and is not a complete answer to all difficulties. The main point is that the Christian Church has become inextricably bound to civilisation. It might have developed on other lines. It might have been a purely "Eschatological" community with no interest in the present world and quite aloof from secular society, its eyes fixed unwavering on the "life of the world to come". The Church may have been like that in some places in its early days, but, largely under the leadership of St. Paul, it chose to seek a *modus vivendi* with the Roman Empire and thereafter worked out the idea of a Christian Empire and later of a Christian Civilisation. No man has a right to accept the protection and the amenities of civilised life unless he is prepared to uphold and defend the State and its institutions when they are attacked by an enemy. To opt out of civilisation is not really possible, unless one becomes an ascetic of the most extreme kind. The precepts of the Sermon on the Mount, which are often quoted in support of absolute pacifism, can be understood only in relation to the Kingdom of God and it is the duty of every Christian to pray and work for that Kingdom by guiding his conduct towards the realisation of a society in which the Sermon on the Mount will be the obviously reasonable law. I hope and believe that I never urged a man to join the forces in war, though I certainly tried to clear up the thoughts of some men so that they might make their own decisions. There were pulpit orators in those days who spoke like recruiting officers and stoked the fires of hate. At least one used my pulpit for his diatribe; I shuddered and I hope I made it clear to my people that I did not say "Amen".

At this time, when religious perplexities were rife, a movement was started in the Church of England called "The National Mission of Repentance and Hope". It has been well described by the late Canon Roger Lloyd in his monumental work *The Church of England 1900-1965*. His careful study convinces me that the Mission was more important, and had more good results, than I had supposed. Without in any way disputing his summing up, I must own that, seen from my particular corner, the Mission made very little impact, after a preparation which absorbed much energy. To me it seems that the Mission had some connection with the famous slogan, "Business as Usual", which doped the intelligence of the public and nearly lost us the war. In a large proportion of the population, the idea that the war would be quite short was propagated by individuals with various motives and so it was thought that hostilities would be a brief interruption to the normal activities. Another foolish and optimistic delusion was that the people in the homeland would suffer no more than they had done in the South African War.

Certainly, some excellent material for the Mission was produced, which could have been the basis for a religious revival with a sound theological framework, but when the Mission came most people were busily employed in war work and interested in subjects other than the Mission thought they ought to be interested in. For example, much attention was paid, and justly, to the Christian ideal of society; I think the creation of a "Christian Sociology" was first attempted in the Mission, but at the time people at large wanted light on matters of individual life and death. Is there a Father in Heaven who cares for us his children? Is there life after death? Shall I meet my boy in Heaven? One of the very sound purposes of the Mission was to propagate the conception of collective responsibility; to convince the ordinary man that the guilt of causing the war was not confined to the Kaiser, or to the German General Staff, or to the German people, but that we all had some share in it. Sound doctrine: but difficult to present to congregations without absurd exaggeration. The son of my old vicar, Prebendary Pennefather, told me that he wanted to put a notice in the pulpit for the preacher's eye: "N.B. This congregation did not start the war." I knew what he meant. The guilt so widely spread seemed unreal. I could not but feel that most of the congregation in St. Mary Abbots were more stupid than wicked and the congregation at Crouch End were neither stupid nor wicked, and had done what they could to prevent war.

My P.C.C. had no hesitation about the National Mission— almost unanimously it disliked the idea. Why they felt so strongly against it I never discovered, but I think the word "mission" had for them disagreeable overtones. There was an animated, but completely amicable, discussion because I felt that we ought to have some part in the movement in which the archbishops and bishops were summoning us all to join. I carried the motion, but only by giving assurances. One of the speakers used a significant phrase: "We don't want the dancing dervish type of missioner here." They shrank from the emotional appeal which could have been implied in the word "mission". In the end, a well-known Broad Church preacher, Archdeacon Bevan, vicar of St. Luke's, Chelsea, and I changed pulpits on the allotted Sunday and everyone was satisfied. This kind of "general post" among the clergy caused by the Mission was most inconvenient and many parishes would have been happy to pray for the objects of the Mission, led by their parish priests, who had ample material provided by the organising committee. Indirectly, I believe that the Mission did good by preparing the minds of some laymen for the "Life and Liberty" Movement, which brought some element of self-government into the Church of England.

Mr. Sharp had organised the parish so well that I had really nothing to do but keep the activities going. He had learned from the Free Churches that keen laymen and laywomen will often be the best leaders if given responsibility. His principle was that, though the vicar must know all that is going on in the work of the church, he will do well not to attempt to run the whole set-up. Find people you can trust—and then trust them. Though the war caused anxiety and grievous losses, the parish work went on almost without a hitch and, though some families moved out into the country to avoid Zeppelins and later aeroplane bombs, the congregations were good. It will shock some readers when I say that this continued cohesion of the parish was, in my opinion, partly due to the fact that the system of "pew rents" prevailed. I am aware of the arguments against the system and agree that in many parishes they are unanswerable; but in a parish like Christ Church no one was so poor as to be unable to pay £1 a year for a seat and there were free seats for those who objected in principle. The system of pew rents had the advantage of giving people a propriety feeling ("my church" meant something): it kept families together and strangers were welcomed and shown into seats by sidesmen. So far from banishing friendliness from the church, when properly organised the pew rent system fosters it. But I suppose such comments are now too late and we are not likely to see a revival of this time-honoured custom.

One of the objects which Pyke and I had very much at heart was to make the agony of war an opportunity of drawing together the members of all the Christian groups in our neighbourhood. Today the proposition that in adversity followers of Christ

should join in prayer and should not allow differences of de-
nomination to stand in the way is accepted by most believers; it
was not so in 1914, when the memory of the controversy over
denominational schools was still fresh. We thought we would
be more likely to succeed if we invited all who wished to join
in prayer to meet not in a church but in our spacious church
hall. In a way, the initiative was met by an encouraging response, though we were dismayed to note that there was strong
opposition to the meeting, even in our own nominally liberal
and tolerant congregation. We had some difficulty in getting the
agreement of the P.C.C. to the use of the church hall for our
prayer meeting. The leading Free Church ministers took part
and the hall was full. I do not doubt that the meeting was blessed
by God. But regarded as a move towards Christian unity, it was
a failure and, I fear, increased the sense of alienation in some
hearts. We had in fact underestimated the difference between
modes of worship and prayer.

The meeting began, after a brief speech of welcome by me
from the chair, with a prayer by a venerable retired Methodist
minister. He was evidently a most holy and dedicated man, but
a touch of the farcical came into the proceedings, at least to
me. He began by calling attention to me in an embarrassing
manner. I was young to be the vicar of that parish and I looked
younger than I was. After dwelling on my apparent defects at
depressing length, he prayed. "Nevertheless, may he be a burning and shining light." I could not help thinking that "nevertheless" was the key word. I wished he would get on to the war.
But, alas, he began with an obvious "howler". "O Lord," he
prayed, "Thou seest that the world is upside down, but we know
that Thou canst turn it downside up." It has been one of my
trials in my vocation as a minister of the Gospel that ludicrous
ideas are apt to occur to me even in solemn moments, and so it
was then. There is no difference between "upside down" and
"downside up", so our Methodist friend was really praying for
the continuance of the *status quo*. I had to hold on tight to my
chair to resist the impulse to point this out. There followed some
inspiring singing of hymns and a noble address by the Presbyterian minister; but on the whole the general feeling was that
fellowship in worship had suffered a setback and undoubtedly
my own flock's verdict was "Never again".

Another effort towards Christian co-operation had more success. It originated from my wife's friendship with some of the women doctors at the Royal Free Hospital. One of the consequences of the war was great concern for the decline of sexual morality and, in connection with that, the ignorance of girls on this vital matter. There was an outcry for sex education on one side and deep suspicion of attempts to provide it on the other. My wife organised a public meeting for women only on the subject of sex instruction and, having secured an eminent woman doctor to speak from the scientific and medical point of view, asked the Mothers' Union to provide a speaker on the religious principles involved. The wife of the Bishop of Willesden was in the chair. For the time and place, this was a pioneering achievement. The hall was packed and the press were excluded. I was not present of course, but I had ample evidence that the address of the doctor made a deep impression on all who heard it and changed many women's minds on the matter. The Mothers' Union was not quite equal to the occasion, because, I think, they had not understood the purpose of the meeting and the expectations of the audience. Perhaps it was too much to expect a first-rate well-informed speech to match that of the eminent doctor, but the one given was unfortunately quite out of harmony with the detached and rational state of mind which we were trying to promote.

Shortly afterwards we had another disagreement with the Mothers' Union and severed our connection with it. We instituted a weekly celebration of the Holy Communion on Monday afternoons at 3 p.m. for the numerous mothers who could not attend on Sunday. The Mothers' Union had the impertinence to forbid me to call it a Mothers' Union service on the ground that it was held after midday and fell under the category of "Evening Communion" which, in those days, was supposed to be the sign of "Evangelicals" or "Low Church". To my request for the authority on which their objection was based I had no reply. Not until later in my career, when I was Dean of Exeter, did I become reconciled to the Mothers' Union, after seeing the good side of the organisation and the self-sacrifice of many of its members.

Christ Church was a happy parish and the history of happy parishes is apt to be dull reading to outsiders. There were no quarrels or controversies, though there was plenty of discussion. The P.C.C. had real power over the finances and consequently had a real sense of responsibility. I can remember only one little breeze—trivial perhaps but characteristic. In preparation for the National Mission I bought, on my own initiative, a lot of hymn pamphlets issued by the S.P.C.K. They had in them the "Corn Law Hymn" by Ebenezer Elliott, which has the well-known lines,

> "When wilt Thou save the people?
> O God of mercy, when?
> The people, Lord, the people,
> Not thrones and crowns but men."

The conservatives on the P.C.C. moved that these pamphlets be not paid for out of church funds. I learnt from the discussion that, in the recent General Election, this hymn had been sung as a regular feature at local Liberal Party meetings. After a lively debate, in which I pointed out that the Archbishop of Canterbury had written a commendatory foreword, we reached a compromise: it was ordered, on the motion of an eminent solicitor, that the third line should read, "Not thrones alone but men". So my pocket was relieved, and Tory sensitivity respected, while only the verse suffered.

I would gladly linger over this period of my life and recall many friends and small happenings. One event to me is no triviality, for a night of wakeful anxiety is among my more vivid memories. The whole family was gathered more or less under the stairs. My wife was nursing our baby, recently christened Barbara, I was reading Hardy's *Dynasts* and little Michael was holding on to his mother. A bomb, which I think must have come from a Zeppelin, exploded fairly near and the house was shaken. A dialogue, the memory of which still wrings my heart, ensued. The little boy, trying hard to be brave, said, "But you aren't frightened, Mummy, are you, *you* aren't frightened?" My lion-hearted wife laughed and said, "Oh no, not nearly as frightened as I would be by a cow." The German bomb missed the boy then, but another German bomb did not miss him twenty-four years later, when he was killed at Dunkirk on the bridge of H.M.S. *Greyhound*.

Crouch End was a happy place for us chiefly because there were so many pleasant people there. I can only pluck, as it were, one or two samples out of the bag. As I write, the news of the death of Sir Idris Bell means the loss of one who was a true friend and, as everyone knows, a great scholar. He had not then attained the high distinction of F.B.A. and Keeper of the Manuscripts of the British Museum, but we all knew that he would reach the summit in his branch of learning. He was a regular attendant at the meetings of the Literary Society and contributed papers which, such was his courtesy, we were all able to understand. His father, Charles Bell, was a learned man, too. When I knew him, he had retired from the occupation of pharmaceutical chemist and devoted his leisure to the study of English poetry. His wide reading and his remarkable memory, together with his independent opinions, made his conversation a delight. Many other exceptional men crowd into my mind, men who held responsible positions, such as the General Manager of the Guardian Insurance Company and two or three literary physicians. It was really, as it claimed to be, an "intelligent congregation". Let me make it clear that I did not collect or attract it; I found it there, collected by my predecessor. The most that I can claim is that, in the short time during which I was vicar, I did not drive them away.

Two inheritances from the Sharp period were of great value. One, a matter of administration, appealed to the businessmen who constituted a large proportion of our parish; the finances were dealt with like the affairs of a public limited company. A firm of chartered accountants, who were paid a proper fee, audited all the accounts and signed a statement that they had satisfied themselves that all money subscribed and collected had been given to the objects for which they were intended. The other inheritance was a fine musical tradition with a good organ, a keen and competent choir and a first-rate organist. Dr. Walker Robson was a good musician who composed several well-known anthems, including one for which the words were taken from one of my books. Perhaps his most exceptional gift was his ability to enlist and inspire amateur singers. He seemed equally good with boys and adults. He could make singing in church to the glory of God really exciting. Naturally he had an "artistic temperament" and was apt to take offence over what seemed to ordinary persons trifles, but this was only one aspect of his personality and was connected with his dedication to the cause of music.

We kept in touch when I had left Crouch End for King's College and he had left as a consequence of an unfortunate conflict with the vicar. The words which he set to music are a prayer which was printed in a book entitled *Seven Words* which I wrote in Exeter and which was based on my Good Friday addresses in the Cathedral:

"Thou hast a work for me to do; O Lord, shew it to me: Thou hast a place for me to fill; give me grace to fill it to Thy glory: Thou hast given me a soul to make; make Thou it for me, and build me into Thy spiritual temple, for Jesus' sake."

For reasons which I do not comprehend, the anthem was popular in Free Churches but rarely heard in Anglican Churches and never in St. Paul's. It is still sung, however, at Christ Church, Crouch End.

The parish, like all other well-ordered parishes, did not lack eccentrics but, looking back, I think they were all kindly or perhaps "holy" eccentrics. One had an eccentricity which I remember gratefully. Miss Peachey was an old lady who lived in a large house. A formidable old lady, she spoke her mind with all the assurance that is apt to be conferred by a large private income. She was indeed the only private individual I have known whose bank was the Bank of England and who paid her household accounts by drafts on the Governor and Company of the Bank of England. Her pleasing habit was that, when I or Neville Pyke preached a sermon of which she approved, she paid £5 into the preacher's banking account without saying anything. Other eccentrics were individuals who chose air raid alerts as occasions to consult me on moral problems. One poor girl in great distress asked for guidance on the question whether she ought to pay a surgeon to take off her brother's leg. The answer was easy—to get the best available medical opinion, but when on her behalf I rang up the likely doctors in the vicinity they had all gone to ground and emerged to answer their calls only when the all clear signal sounded. Another knotty problem presented in similar circumstances was the question whether a Christian woman could marry a man who played ping-pong on Sunday. After a short period of silent meditation, I replied quite definitely that she could and thereby, I hope, made two persons happy.

To a parish priest, the duty of preaching week by week is a

great opportunity and, to a conscientious man, a constant anxiety. In Crouch End, the people expected well-prepared and intelligent sermons and we in Christ Church were stimulated, perhaps unduly, by the knowledge that our performances in the pulpit were compared with those of Mr. Darlaston of the Congregational Church, who was a really learned and eloquent divine who had studied theology under Harnack, the most famous Protestant scholar of the time. Two sermons have survived from those that were delivered towards the end of my ministry in the parish. They were carefully prepared, for they are written out in full and their subjects are revealing. At evensong on Sunday, March 18th, 1917, I preached on "Christian Liberty", evidently moved by the Russian revolution. I read the glowing words today with a wry smile.

"Who has not felt his soul stirred in the last week by the news from Russia? The future may be doubtful and difficult, but we cannot be wrong when we rejoice at the sight of a great nation rising in its majesty and throwing off the shackles which have long restrained it, moving its mighty limbs and crying, 'Begone anachronisms and away with antiquated oppressions'. The soul of the Russian people will express itself; it will add its own contribution freely to the human treasury. May God bless Russia and keep her free."

If I could have foreseen that the Russian revolution prepared the way for Stalin, I might well have expressed my feelings in the second sermon, preached at evensong on Sunday, July 15th, 1917, on "The Religion of Despair". But the inspiration of that discourse was not an historical event, but an essay by Bertrand Russell, entitled *A Free Man's Worship*. Perhaps the essay is so well-known that I need say no more than that it is a brilliantly written pessimistic summing-up of the nature of the universe, as disclosed by science, involving the almost certain destruction of the human race and its values. Any "worship", any ideal of human life, must be built not on any hope but on "the firm foundations of unyielding despair". The sermon tried to get too much into half an hour, but it did make the real reply of Christianity to Russell—it is to bring Kierkegaard to confront him. There is a form of fundamental Christian faith which begins with a despair of the world, of life and of oneself. Full salvation is granted only to those who cry for it out of the deep.

I refer to these sermons to illustrate the kind of teaching we were able to give and the level of understanding on which we could count. Where would I find such a congregation now? Not in many places, and not in so many places as then, for I can think of several churches in London where in 1915 intelligent sermons on great subjects were eagerly listened to by large congregations. As one example, I will mention the Rev. Duncan Jones of St. Mary, Primrose Hill, with whom I often changed pulpits, though our forms of service differed considerably. Duncan Jones became Dean of Chichester about the same time as I became Dean of Exeter. I record it as my opinion that in all denominations, and particularly in the Church of England, the standard of preaching has declined and that is partly due to a decline in the intelligence of congregations. The causes and consequences of this are complex.

The end of our happy experience in Christ Church, Crouch End, was near, though we had no premonition of its coming. In the calendar of my life, December 27th, 1917, must always stand out as a sudden and momentous turning-point. I had been summoned to a meeting of the Council of King's College for the afternoon of that day, for the purpose of electing a Dean of King's College and a Professor of the Philosophy of Religion to succeed my old tutor, Dr. A. Caldecott. I was a member of the Council as elected, with others, to represent the teaching staff of the Theological department of King's College. I imagined that the Rev. C. Legg, the chaplain, would be elected as Dean and had decided to vote for him if I was present. But I was uncertain whether I should go to the meeting, because my brother, who was a temporary naval officer, was at the end of leave on that day and I was determined to say goodbye to him. I was not thinking of my future then in terms of academic advancement, but rather in terms of parochial work. The war was, I thought, near its end and I had plans which Pyke and I had worked out for what I believed could be a forward movement in our parish; we had the ambition to make Christ Church a centre of liberal Anglican teaching and a pioneering parish in the movement towards co-operation and brotherhood with the Free Churches.

I was in the College at the opening of the Council, which was presided over by Dr. Burge, the Bishop of Southwark, in the absence of the Bishop of London. Dr. Caldecott said to me,

"Perhaps it would be better if you did not stay for the main business. It could be embarrassing to you if the Council discussed some of our senior colleagues." I was so stupid that I never thought, "That means they will be discussing me." It simply did not occur to me that anyone would regard me as a possible candidate. I knew that Dr. Whitney, the Church historian, had been mentioned in many quarters and, if the Council wanted a distinguished and well-known scholar for Dean, he seemed an obvious choice. So without hesitation I went off, met my brother, had tea with him and saw him off in his train. I nearly went home straightaway, but I thought I might as well look in at the College first and hear the Council's decision. When I arrived, I was met by someone, I forget who it was, who said, "You have been elected Dean." I laughed at what I thought was a leg-pull, but soon was convinced by the Secretary of the College that it was sober truth and that the Bishop of Southwark was pleased at the decision. If the Bishop had been an advocate of my cause, I fear he must have been disappointed at my reaction. I was full not of joy, but of consternation. I had never considered or imagined the situation in which I suddenly found myself. I had no prepared reply. I kept my head sufficiently to stammer out my surprise and my need for time to reflect. That night neither my wife nor I slept much and in the morning a postcard came from my friend Clement Rogers, who, I thought, was most favourably disposed towards me; on it were scribbled the words, "If you accept, we shall all resign."

CHAPTER 6

My Further Education - Dean and Professor

How much Clement Rogers' postcard influenced me, when I decided to accept the office of Dean, I cannot tell, but I suspect that without the emotional reaction to that challenge I would have chosen the easier path and refused. I am at least certain that I said in most unclerical words, "I'm damned if I let myself be pushed round by these persons", and sent my telegram accepting without delay. And, having done that, I wrote to the Bishop of London to forestall any approaches to him by the objectors to persuade him to try to veto the appointment. But I could not hide from myself that I was really frightened and might have been misled into an act of presumptuous folly. I wrote also to Dr. Caldecott, who had shown signs of changing his mind about my appointment, to say that I had accepted, relying on his unswerving support. The more I thought about the decision the more obvious it appeared that here and now was a crisis which would profoundly affect the rest of my life and that of my family. Could I regard this as a "vocation" in the proper sense of a call by God to undertake a special service for the Kingdom of God? I have never felt the clear assurance which some Christians have had that they were guided by God at every step. To me decisions of great moment have always been the outcome of anxious reflection and I have always assumed that, when an opportunity was offered which I had not sought and was not patently beyond my capacities, I had some reason to believe that it was a vocation. Quite certainly, I had not sought this appointment; the possibility that I should be considered for it had never crossed my mind. I remembered a remark of Dr. Headlam to my wife about me, "He has never been fully extended yet." How did I know that I was not able to do well in such a responsible post? Was it not a fulfilment of some of Dr. Headlam's hopes that a student of the University of London and of King's College should rise to authority, and did I not owe it to the College and to all its students that I should do all I could for our *Alma Mater*? With such thoughts I gathered confidence, but at heart I was a frightened man and, in retrospect, I see more clearly than I did at the time that Margaret's courage and belief in me supported me all through.

I did not become Dean of King's College until February, 1918. The intervening time was occupied by leave-taking in Crouch End and provision for residence elsewhere—the College had no house to offer because the Warden's House in Vincent Square, which I was to live in, was occupied by the War Office as a hospital. We left Crouch End with regret and were overwhelmed by the kindness of all the parish and by gifts which I felt we had done so little to deserve. I still think of Christ Church as "my" parish church. The appointment of my successor as vicar concerned me deeply and I feared the parish might have to endure a long interregnum like that which had preceded my own appointment. I need not have been anxious. The Bishop of London, when asked to receive a deputation from the Parochial Church Council, wrote to me, "Don't let those dear people who form your so intelligent congregation come again; just tell me whom they want." That was easy, for to my joy everyone wanted my friend and curate, Neville Pyke, and the Bishop promptly nominated him, breaking an unwritten rule that bishops, for some unknown reason, dislike appointing curates to be vicars of parishes where they are. Everyone was happy.

Except me. I had to prepare myself for the task which I had accepted. I was Professor of the Philosophy of Religion and, though I had published essays and papers which Dr. Barnes, afterwards the famous Bishop of Birmingham, considered sufficient evidence of my competence, I had no lectures prepared and the syllabus of the University for the newly-established Divinity degree called for a two-year course of lectures not only on Theism as a philosophy, but on the elements of Comparative Religion. I could not give all my attention to this study because the defection of some professors who had objected to my appointment caused vacancies which it might soon be urgent to fill. Not all the threatened resignations occurred. Clement Rogers, to my great relief, changed his mind about my fitness for the office of Dean and became a strong ally. He filled the vacant chair of Pastoral Theology and was a well-loved and remembered figure in the College for all the rest of my time there. Popular apologetics, in his opinion, formed a part of the subject of Pastoral Theology, and he practised what he preached by joining the Hyde Park orators on Sunday afternoons. His little volumes entitled *Question Time in Hyde Park* were a mine of sensible and well-informed answers to popular objections to the Christian faith. Professor H. J. White, whose chair was that of New Testament Exegesis, was among those who deplored and protested against my election as Dean; but he did not resign, feeling that it was his duty to help the College in its ill-fortune. I was grateful for his loyalty, which made my reconstruction of the teaching staff much easier; when, shortly afterwards, he was appointed Dean of Christ Church, Oxford, the difficult transition period was almost over. Another scholar who came to my assistance was my old friend of student days H. Maurice Relton, whose steps had been parallel to mine and who, like me, was about to become a D.D. of the University. His special interest was Systematic and Historical Theology, which embraces a large measure of biblical material, and he was a brilliant lecturer.

The time between the Armistice on November 11th, 1918, and the return of the students to the College was for me one of suspense and acute discomfort. For a while my wife and family lived in a country lodging, while I had a room in the College in the Strand, where I was joined by the demobilised former chaplain, Freddy Marsh, later fellow of Selwyn College, Cambridge, and Professor of Hebrew. He had been gassed and invalided out of the army. Though he had escaped the worst disability, his respiration was permanently affected and he was subject to attacks of complete speechlessness. More than once he returned late at night to College in a speechless condition and we found the College night porter hard to persuade that it was due to German gas and not English liquor. Marsh and I took the opportunity of these days of comparative leisure to draw up a list of "ancient customs" for the hostel in Vincent Square, of which he had been sub-warden. Plato would have approved, I think, of our little deception: did he not base his ideal republic on a magnificent fiction? At any rate, I can testify that these "ancient customs" worked well when the troops returned and I never heard any question about their authenticity.

The terrible epidemic of influenza which followed the great

war and killed more victims than all the fighting found us, my wife, myself, two very small children and a children's nurse, inhabiting a furnished house in Streatham, not far from the house we had lived in when first married. The nurse, by the way, was the daughter of a lion tamer. She stayed with us until the children were all at boarding schools and then married and lived in Canada. In both wars we were blessed by having staunch supporters at home.

Among the victims of the epidemic was my friend Bicheno Smith, the writer of an essay referred to in a previous chapter, who had come safely through the war as a chaplain at the front. Plague conditions prevailed for a short time. Doctors were unable to visit all the patients who needed them and would not think of visiting anyone whose temperature was lower than 102°. In the street where we lived, the milkman was the source of information and every morning reported the number of dead on his rounds. Every adult in our company had influenza, but fortunately not all at the same time. My own experience leads me to think that the type of influenza then raging, though of short duration, had exceptionally enervating after-effects. It was an effective damper on the hopeful exuberance of the peace and I think probably warped the good sense and good will of the nation.

All through this period when I had time to think of public affairs I was out of sympathy with the Lloyd George policy and disturbed by the "Hang the Kaiser" slogan. The making of the Treaty of Versailles was an error which I knew made another war only too probable. My wife cordially agreed with this and we both came into conflict with my father whose implacability, though not uncommon, was quite unreasonable—and he was a kindly man who sincerely tried to live a Christian life. At this time too the decline and disruption of the Liberal Party seemed a disaster which could have been avoided if personal ambitions and resentments had been subordinated to the public good.

I have been writing, on the whole, as though King's College, London, was entirely devoted to Theology, but of course this is far from being the case. Though the Theological Department is governed by the Council of King's College and the other faculties are governed by the University of London, for many purposes King's College is one entity and three officials are officials of the whole College—the Principal, the Dean and the Secretary. In the constitution, which came into force shortly before the 1914 war, the relations between Principal and Dean, Council and University delegacy were carefully defined and, by the skill of Dr. Headlam, all interests, particularly the Church interest, were guarded. The first lay Principal of King's College was appointed by the Crown on the resignation of Dr. Headlam, who became Regius Professor of Divinity in Oxford. Dr. Ronald Burrows was an admirable choice. A Christian Socialist in politics, a classical scholar of note, and the husband of a Bishop's daughter, it seemed that under his direction progress and traditional values would be assured. Dr. Burrows had kept the College in being and active during the war by public lectures on subjects of general interest, particularly in post-war reconstruction. Venizelos was one of the lecturers and President Masaryk in exile became a Professor of Political Philosophy. I listened with deep interest to his exposition of the principle of democratic self-determination as applied to the fragments of the Austrian Empire and I remember wondering whether the small states which he wished to endow with sovereign independence would be viable. Someone about this date, I think, coined the verb "to Balkanise"; it expresses what I thought, though my knowledge of the facts, historical, ethnographic and economic, was so slight that I had no qualifications to form any opinion; but I noticed that this defect did not deter many others from expressing quite violent convictions.

Ronald Burrows had vision and, undaunted by the war, made plans for the future of King's College as a centre of learning and of social idealism. He was a member of the Council which had elected me Dean of the College. Though I do not know how he voted, it is unlikely that the Council would have elected me if he had expressed strong opposition. It was a misfortune that, almost immediately I took office, I had a controversy with him. It was about a minor matter and, what was worse, about money. Today principals and bursars deal with large sums and would doubtless scorn to quarrel about the cost of lighting lecture rooms, but both Burrows and I were compelled to worry about such things, and I more than he. I really did not know how the salaries of the very depleted teaching staff were to be paid. Burrows demanded that my side of the College should double its annual payment for heat and light, basing his demand on the amount of space used by my department. I countered by calling in time to redress the balance of space and pointed out that theologians used space for about half the time which science students used it. The argument was not ended by agreement and Burrows evidently resented my obstinacy. Finally Lord Hambledon, a great benefactor of the College and prominent on both governing bodies, was called in to adjudicate and, to my great relief, came down on my side. Why was I so obstinate? I think because I felt that it was important to show from the start that I was not going to be a "yes man" and intended to stand up for the rights of the Council. I never had another dispute of this kind during my whole time as a Dean. One good thing came out of this storm in a teacup, I came to know the Secretary, S. T. Shovelton, and to trust him. He was a dominant factor in my life for fourteen years and a close friend up to the summer of 1967. I took my old comrade's burial service on July 4th. He was a man of great ability, who devoted all his knowledge and skill to the service of the College. A mathematician, he had been a fellow of Merton College, Oxford, and came to King's College originally to teach, but before long was appointed Secretary of the College and was more than fully occupied with administration. From time to time he amused himself and many readers of *The New Statesman* by ingenious mathematical puzzles and paradoxes.

I ought to have reflected more deeply than I did on the demands of my new vocation—the teaching of Theology and the education of candidates for ordination. It was partly my fault that I shirked a drastic criticism of the traditional system and, in particular, I know that I should have given more thought to the spiritual development of the students. I was not without excuse, for the pressure of events almost compelled me to live "from hand to mouth", or at least from day to day. The first duty, as I saw it, was to keep the College from collapsing and there was real danger that the College which I was responsible for—the Theological Department of King's College, London—would be unable to carry on because of poverty, or fail to hold its place in the University of London because of its inability to attract students or to persuade teachers of real eminence to become professors. A fear which haunted me was that bishops would tacitly "boycott" King's College when considering candidates for ordination. I knew that the story of my election "over the heads", as it was expressed, of far better and more orthodox scholars was current in episcopal circles.

As it happened, external events which neither the bishops nor I had foreseen changed the whole situation. The first was the decision of the U.S.A. to utilise the period of demobilisation and repatriation of the forces in Europe to give the troops, or those deemed suitable for the privilege, an opportunity of a brief course in an English or Scottish university. This admirable plan worked well enough and helped to keep a large number of impatient warriors more or less interested. In my recollection, it was a happy interlude. The business of allotting students to colleges was perhaps a trifle haphazard and I never discovered why the authorities supposed that King's College was the proper centre for Mormons. Some slight difficulties arose, too, with members of the U.S. forces who wanted to combine Theology with some other subject. One man was determined to study both Theology and Metallurgy; the connection appeared to be that the ingenuous youth intended to preach the gospel in South America and had the bright idea that on his missionary journeys he could look for gold mines. We provided short courses for our guests on religion in England and some history connected with it, which seemed to interest them, and we were sorry to say goodbye; but I do not think we made any deep impression, because so far as I remember I never had a letter or visit from any student after they had left these shores.

Of vastly more importance was the action of the Government on the problem of the ex-service men and the universities. The pressure for demobilisation became dangerous and caused riots of soldiers who feared that they would miss the market unless they were released without delay. So far as students who had been in college at the outbreak of war were concerned, no great difficulties arose. It was obviously just that they should be subsidised by a grateful country and should have the way made easy to their degrees. Those who did not come back because they had died in the war were lamentably many and among them were the brightest boys: their names are recorded on the memorial tablets at the entrance to the College Chapel. Among those who came back, two I record with special joy. A V.C. was among my former pupils. Mellish was the first chaplain to be awarded the decoration in the first world war. I think I taught him Logic, but claim no part in the education of a hero. The second returning student came to see me when I was overwhelmed with interviews and I simply do not remember his name. If he is still alive, perhaps he may repair this lacuna in my story. I remembered him well enough then as a cheerful muscular Christian who had only just left school. He had enlisted as a private at the first opportunity and I had heard of his becoming an officer practically on the field of battle. In a desperate emergency he had displayed powers of leadership. When he came to see me at the end of the war, he was a Brigadier General and covered with decorations. He wanted my advice on whether it was his duty to respond still to the call to the Christian ministry which he believed he had received, and he had to make up his mind at once. The army wanted to keep him as a regular officer and could not wait for an answer. I wonder if I was guided to do right on this occasion. I could see that he was attracted to the career which he had so gloriously begun and I wondered how much of his sense of vocation had lasted. "Do you still read the Greek Testament?" I asked. "There is no sector of the British front," he answered, "on which I have not read the Greek Testament, and on no sector have I been able to make head or tail of it." I sensed that he hoped for a word from me which would relieve him of the feeling that he was dedicated to the priesthood. I said the word. I thought then that his happiest life would be in the army in which he might almost be said to have grown up and I was confident he would be a Christian soldier. I record this individual case as one instance, which happened to impress itself on my memory, of the kind of personal problem which came up every day. I can only pray that my mistakes in dealing with them may be forgiven.

The Government's plan for giving grants to all ex-service men who were accepted by universities for a degree course was a stroke of fortune for King's College and also for diocesan funds, which were relieved of expenditure for one generation of ordinands and of course temporarily lost the power of the purse in the selection of approved candidates. The suspicion in orthodox circles of the Theology taught at King's was greatly reduced by the accession of Bishop Gore to the teachers of Theology. This is one event in my administration which I remember with satisfaction.

The very evening of the day on which Charles Gore's resignation of the Bishopric of Oxford was made public I wrote a letter to him suggesting that he should come to London and lecture in King's College. I had no personal knowledge of Gore and he had none of me, except perhaps that I was a member of the Modern Churchmen's Union and an adherent, up to a point, of Dr. Rashdall's theological and philosophical thought. My plea for help was based on the special need of London for Christian scholars whose words carried weight with educated people. I prayed hard that it would be effective. Gore did not reject the proposal out of hand. He came to see me and the College: he met some of my colleagues and, to me most memorable of all, he came to meals at the warden's house of King's College in Vincent Square, Westminster, where he talked to my wife and my small children, who were intrigued by his beard, his deep voice and the contortions of his body when his mind was wrestling with some problem.

The access of Gore was a strength in many ways. His presence on the staff of lecturers—and for some years on the governing body—made a difference which on the whole was, in my opinion, an improvement, not that the professors and lecturers were unreasonable or stupid. They were almost too reasonable, in one sense. Being both intelligent and eminently articulate, arguments were almost too well sustained. I remember saying once that, if three of my colleagues, Dr. Box, Professor Jenkins and Dr. Relton, ever agreed, I should immediately resign. Bishop Gore had an influence which made for brevity in discussion. I formed the opinion that he was, by temperament, pessimistic. I had expected that a man so notable as a pioneer of Christian Socialism would be all for adventure and reform, but this was not his attitude in practical affairs. To call him obstructive would be quite unfair. He did not generally so much oppose new policies as prepare us for disappointment. In any situation where more than one event was possible, he expected the worst. This may have been a characteristic acquired by years of experience and I knew him only in his old age. He was on cordial terms with the professors of many subjects whom he met at lunch and he lectured most effectively to the large audiences of students of all faculties, for whom the College by its statutes is bound to provide a weekly lecture on religion. The prestige of bishops was probably greater then than now and Gore had been a public figure for a long time, so that we ought to have expected the influx of reporters and press photographers which happened when he began to lecture. They were a nuisance for a short time, but they soon faded out and they produced one admirable drawing of Gore expounding the history of Christian doctrine.

I most gratefully remember that he wrote on my behalf when I was a candidate for the office of Chaplain to Gray's Inn—all the more so because, much to my disappointment, the very good proposal that he should be Master of the Temple was rejected by the two Inns of Inner and Middle Temple, owing to the opposition of one or two extreme Protestant Benchers. Gore said nothing about his regret that this notable pulpit was not to be his, though he must have felt, as so many did, that it would have been a perfect answer to the question what he should do in the vigorous years of his retirement. All that he said to me, when I was appointed by another Inn of Court to be their preacher, was "Ah, yes, you are the kind of man they like," which I took to be a statement of truth, but no eulogy. And that reminds me that Gore could be not only uncomfortably perceptive but almost cynical in his judgments of character. A touch of cynicism coloured his conversation about a mission on which he went to the Patriarchs and Archbishops of the Orthodox Eastern Church on behalf of the Archbishop of Canterbury. He was not encouraged by this experience and summed up his findings in a sentence: "Well, perhaps the Eastern Church beats us by being certainly in the Apostolic Succession, but we beat them by having more Apostolic morals." He also gave me a piece of advice that, if I ever had to interview an Eastern Patriarch or Archbishop, to make quite sure that the great man's secretary was not present because the secretary was most probably a spy in the employ of an enemy or rival. That advice was given long ago and I have never had occasion to test it in practice. No doubt it is now out of date.

On May 14th, 1920, Ronald Burrows the Principal of King's, who had worked so hard to prepare for the peace, died after an illness which had more or less incapacitated him for a year. It was one of those personal calamities which seem to frustrate or hold up many good designs and to waste faculties which had been cultivated for the service of mankind. All who knew her lamented that Mrs. Burrows, who had been the Principal's lively support, would no longer be there to be hostess to cheerful, and often polyglot, parties. Who would succeed to the office?

It was a crucial question, for the building up of the whole College and the operation of its unique constitution, one might almost say its "amphibian" constitution, called for a man of exceptional quality. Of all the professors and heads of departments in the College, I had the most reason for apprehension; if the Crown nominated an atheist or an anti-clerical zealot, a dangerous clash between the two sides of the College and the two governing bodies could hardly be avoided. The Crown no doubt took advice and sounded opinion; probably my opinion was asked for, but I do not remember it and quite certainly I did not suggest the name of Ernest Barker, because I knew nothing about him but that he had written useful books on Greek philosophy. When I heard that he was a Congregationalist in religion, I was only half reassured.

My first meeting with Barker cleared all my doubts away. I need not attempt a character sketch of one who became one of my most trusted friends, for he has written one of the most attractive autobiographies in English, telling us of his childhood and of his career in the academic and educational world and of the many men whom he had known. When Barker first visited the College after his appointment, I think I was the first, after the Secretary, to meet him. It was a private meeting. I saw a man who looked like a scholar and not like a senior civil servant, for which I was glad. He spoke with a marked but pleasant Lancashire accent and the first sentence he uttered was, "I'm a man of no dignity." This was in fact untrue, because he had the natural dignity of the simple scholar who has a pride in learning. It was, however, quite true in the sense that he never stood upon his dignity, the least pompous of men. His Lancashire accent somehow lent weight to his speech, and I suspect that he made no attempt to discard it. I do not know, however, whether he was actually aware of his accent, for once, when he had read a lesson from the Bible at a College service, I said to him, "I wish I had just a touch of your accent, it sounds so much more impressive than mine," and his reply seemed to indicate that he did not know what I was talking about. Much later in our association, I heard him use his accent to excellent effect in an embarrassing situation. He was in the chair at a public lecture in the College hall, given by Dr. L. P. Jacks, the well-known author and liberal theologian, who had gone on well over the hour and the audience, as 7 p.m. approached, was wondering whether they would get any dinner. It had been a very good lecture and Jacks was a very eminent man; the chair man's problem was to say something warm—and short. Barker was equal to the occasion; in a rather heightened Lancashire accent he said, "We have been listening to a great teacher of men. The only way in which we can properly receive his message is with a solemn hōōsh." Hush would have sounded trivial—hōōsh made it just right.

Many years later, I was able to quote Barker's words with reference to himself. When Peterhouse in Cambridge entertained him on the occasion of his retirement from the chair of Political Philosophy, a representative of each of the five colleges with which he had been closely associated was invited to lunch and I had the good fortune to be the guest from King's College, London. We were asked to contribute short appreciations of Ernest Barker and I felt I could not do better than say of him: "We have been listening for many years to Ernest Barker, a great teacher of men and it may be that the best tribute we can pay to his learning and wisdom is to receive his message with a solemn hōōsh."

Barker and I were closely associated in the administration of the College in a period when student behaviour was a matter of deep concern. The student population of the years 1919-1923 or 4 was not at all like that of the years 1945-1950. The slaughter and the agony of the first world war was, in some respects, more grievous than that of the second world war, but the mood of the immediate post-war students was far more hopeful. The young men, and many no longer young, who came back from the first war, were conscious that they had done well and believed that the future was bright. Many of them, too, had grown up suddenly, had become self-reliant, had acquired skills and had lived close to all kinds and classes of fellow citizens. The discipline of universities, such as it was, stemmed from the public schools and, in some modern universities, was almost non-existent. In London the discipline had to be administered by the colleges, which varied considerably in their care for students, while the central government located in the Senate House had neither the knowledge nor the power to cope with undergraduate unrest.

In contrast with the present day, the university disorders of the 1920s had little or no political meaning. They were, on the whole, exceptionally well organised "rags", some of which got out of hand. A typical example which happened in my time was the successful hoax of the visit of "Lloyd George" to the London School of Economics, when the Director (Sir William Beveridge), the professors and students assembled to receive the Prime Minister who was supposed to be coming to lunch. An impressive car drove up and a figure dashed out of it—a man with abundant flowing locks, but not Lloyd George. Detected, of course, at once when he opened his mouth to speak, somehow he made his escape, no one ever told me how.

A "rag" of more importance, with which Barker and I were deeply concerned, was the deplorable capture of "Pussyfoot" Johnson, the well-known American agitator for Prohibition. A public meeting in a hall near to King's College was attacked in due military form with pioneers, advance guard and assault group, directed I believe by a youthful ex-major. Johnson was seized on the platform and carried triumphantly out into the Strand. So far, all was good humoured, but, tragically, brawling in London streets cannot be confined to university students. Others who have different aims and standards join in. This happened; stones began to fly, thrown by who knows who? Pussyfoot Johnson was struck and, as a consequence, completely lost the sight of one eye. We believed that the stone was thrown by a hooligan who was not a member of the University, but we could not prove it and there was no doubt that the mêlée was started by students. I am glad to record the generous and Christian behaviour of the victim who put us to shame by forgiving his assailants and making no claim for punishment of culprits or compensation for injury. The lesson of this sad affair as it applies to student demonstrations in cities has not even yet been properly grasped and applied.

Much nearer home, so far as Barker and I were concerned, were the incidents which I call the women student riots. King's College had always been exclusively masculine, except that the Council had set up a separate establishment, King's College Women's Department, in Kensington at which some of the professors and lecturers lectured to women students. The Women's Department had its own Principal, a distinguished writer on Philosophy, Hilda Oakeley. The war brought this Victorian arrangement to an end and women students appeared in the College almost without discussion or question. But that did not mean that all was happy. Some of us felt that the character of the College had been changed for the worse and all felt that the feminine influx made the already over-crowded laboratories and lecture rooms almost intolerable. Perhaps, inevitably, the women students themselves did not help much. The Principal was alarmed at the aggressive behaviour of some girls, who had what he regarded as bad manners, and quite rightly proposed to speak to a meeting of women students on "Manners". Somehow this was interpreted as meaning that he intended to expel all, or at least a large number, of women students. I suspected that some mischievous young men spread the rumour abroad and, when the time came for the Principal to leave his study for the meeting which he had called, there were about 200 men students blocking his path. In this emergency he telephoned me to clear the way for him. I went and surveyed the terrain and, having talked to one or two men, returned to my room and telephoned to Barker that I feared I could clear a way for him neither by persuasion nor force. This awkward crisis of authority was dangerous for a few days, but was resolved partly by the diplomacy of the President of the Students' Union, Ivison Macadam, who enjoyed showing his skill in calming storms which perhaps he had had some part in stirring up. It was announced that the Principal would address the whole College on "Manners" and that he and I alone would represent the College authority.

I confess that I went to that meeting in considerable trepidation, because one of my theological students had told me there was a plot of some bolder spirits to seize the Principal, and perhaps me too, and carry us out on to the Embankment. I have never seen a hall more packed than King's College hall was that afternoon. I need not have been apprehensive. Once more, Barker met the crisis by his Lancashire accent and his "undignified" dignity. He rose amid a menacing silence to speak to young men and women who looked hostile. He began, "Such manners as I have been able to acquire have been gained by the sweat of my brow." He went on to elaborate the text by a moving but unsentimental account of his early life and struggles. The women student riots mark the time when Barker, from being rather unpopular, became more and more attached to the College and the College to him.

But how could anyone write about women students at K.C.L.

without paying a tribute to the Hon. Eleanor Plumer, whose death has been announced since I began to write this chapter? She was the daughter of the famous Field Marshal, who is considered by many authorities to have been the best British commander in the first world war. She inherited in no small measure her father's qualities and these were displayed triumphantly on the occasion of a really momentous "rag", when King's College was invaded by barbarian hordes from University College, who drove into the quad in moving vans and surged into King's seeking to capture "Reggie", the red lion, which was the College mascot. They were met by deluges from hoses situated on upper stories. I shall not soon forget the shock I had when, looking out of my window, I saw about a dozen youths struggling just in front of a parapet, which suddenly collapsed precipitating most of the combatants into a stony courtyard on a lower level. It seemed that serious damage to the troops was inevitable and it would be surprising if no one was killed. The only serious injury, however, was a broken arm and, when I was satisfied about that, it occurred to me to ask, "Where are the women?" There were none. Miss Plumer had evidently received advance intelligence of the planned attack and had taken measures to keep the girls out. We had some women students in the Faculty of Theology, and we had a tutor for them, Miss Evelyn Hippisley, but I never found out what magic these two ladies used to keep their flocks so quiet.

The General Strike in 1926 was an important historical event, the significance of which can be better judged today than was possible to those who had to take action when it burst upon an unprepared nation. To compare it with a college "rag" would be ridiculous and flippant, but in my memories somehow it ranks with students' activities naturally enough, I suppose, because the Principal and I had to give some kind of direction. Neither of us was prepared to go "all out" for a strike-breaking crusade against the unions, and neither of us was oblivious of the danger of a complete breakdown of social order and a lapse into anarchy and starvation. For my part, I thought the one man who spoke the Christian truth and pointed towards reconciliation was the Archbishop of Canterbury, Randall Davidson. We agreed to leave the choice of action to individuals' consciences, while urging all to "keep quiet" and abstain from violent action and violent speech. The task of maintaining the supply of food, we urged, was in the interests of the whole community. The students in the Theological faculty from the first day undertook to meet the milk trains at Waterloo Station and elsewhere when needed. It happened strangely that the only actual fighting that I saw in the strike was at Waterloo; but it was not between students and strikers but between students of London University and undergraduates from Cambridge who tried to "muscle in" on milk delivery.

Some of my pupils had more exciting occupations, such as bus-driving in districts where violence was threatened. At the time, one could not help being alarmed at the dangerous things which were being done by amateurs. One cheerful youth told me with glee that he had the job of driving a train to and from Peterborough and London. I asked him if he was sure he could do it. He replied that there was really no difficulty: you simply had to know what handle to pull, that he knew how to start the train and had no doubt that he would master the art of stopping it before he reached Peterborough. It is amazing that there were no serious disasters. The experience of carrying on skilled work during the strike was no doubt good for students who were expecting to become parish priests. One might hope that they would learn to respect and sympathise with craftsmen and wage-earners. That was not, however, the result for those students who talked to me about their feelings. While grateful for some friendly exchanges with workmen on strike, they were impressed most of all by the varied meanings of the word "skilled". In their opinion, for what it was worth, most of the "skills" could be acquired by any intelligent man in a week or two.

The story of "what I did in the General Strike" shall end on a royal note. I was an honorary chaplain to King George V, an honour for which Dr. Burge suggested my name. It fell to my lot to be preacher at the Chapel Royal, St. James's Palace, and in Buckingham Palace on the Sunday morning after the strike was called off. The King and Queen attended the service at Buckingham Palace and naturally I said something about the great event of the previous week. In those days, it was the custom, when the court was at Buckingham Palace, for the preacher at the end of the service to walk straight out of the Chapel, without taking off his robes, up a few stairs to a landing on which the King and Queen were standing, accompanied by the ladies and gentlemen in waiting; thereupon the King and Queen engaged him in conversation for about ten minutes. Those who had the honour of being H.M.'s chaplains were used to original turns of speech in his conversation. Some thought that he spoke recklessly; my own opinion was that he sometimes spoke with his tongue in his cheek to see what you would say. After some words of agreement with my all too cautious sermon, he said, "I'll tell you what I think about this strike. I call it a piece of damned impertinence. If we're going to have a revolution, let's do the thing properly. You can't have a revolution unless you start by shooting the bobbies. Now they didn't shoot a single bobby; when I saw that, I knew it wouldn't work." Hoping that I should not be shot down for another piece of "damned impertinence", I ventured to say, "I think, Sir, next time they had better ask you to direct the strike." He laughed and said, "'Pon my soul, I think I'd do it better than these fellows." Queen Mary, justly thinking that the conversation was getting unduly hilarious, wound it up by remarking, "We ought to be deeply thankful that there was no shooting. When people are killed in disputes, such bitterness is left and goes on for a long time."

I ventured to report this conversation to a colleague at King's College, Miss Ingram, who was a left-wing Republican and under the impression that George V was shaking in his shoes with fright. She was delighted and apparently suddenly converted to Royalism. "That's the best thing I've heard for a long time," she cried. "Good old George: that's the spirit."

But my work as Dean of King's must be judged in the light of the main responsibility of the post, which was to serve the students of Theology and promote research in the subject while keeping steadily in mind the needs of those who were preparing for ordination in the Church of England. I suppose all dedicated teachers, when they look back, are conscious of failures and shortcomings, but cheered by thoughts of pupils who, as we say, "do us credit". In retrospective mood I have sometimes begun a list of bishops, deans, professors and even some distinguished scientists, physicians and engineers who attended my lectures, but how, after all, do I know that I had any real part in their achievements? They may have succeeded not because of my ministrations, but in spite of them. Ever since I ceased to be a professor, I have been meeting former K.C. students, sometimes when I preached for them. Some have proudly and lovingly referred to their student notes of my lectures and said, "I still read them; you answered the questions years ago." My heart warms by reason of these old students' kindness, but at the same time it sinks, because of the only too plain indication that the old student had never thought it necessary to read anything else on the subject. Should I not have done better to follow the example of my own predecessor and tutor, Dr. Alfred Caldecott, who used to exasperate me so by never answering any question and leaving you to think it out for yourself?

The theological faculty of King's College is not a theological college but exists side by side with other faculties of Language, Literature, History, Science and Medicine. In the theological colleges, as they had developed since the Oxford Movement, a different purpose was served—that of isolating theological students from worldly studies. In my opinion the isolated theological colleges, though often wonderful schools of spiritual life, had, on the whole, been mistakenly aloof from the world. Be this as it may, Theology in K.C.L. could not be isolated; its teachers met, in the Senior Common Room, teachers of all other faculties and its students mixed freely in the Union Society and elsewhere with students of History, Engineering, Medicine and all the gamut of university disciplines. Even the most stupid theologian became aware that the search for truth had many sides and took many forms. The room in which I normally lectured was in my time uncomfortably close to a chemical laboratory, which now and then emitted penetrating odours of H_2SO_4. I remember saying to a restive audience of theologians: "Perhaps these fumes are a device of Satan to prevent you from attending to my words of wisdom, but it is equally likely that they are meant by Providence to remind us that we must always take account of scientific method and truth." Because it lived close to philosophers, historians and chemists, Theology at King's was taught with freedom for discussion and dissent. I did not make this spirit; I found it there when I was a student. For example, it was not thought remarkable when a friend of mine, aged about twenty, stood up at the end of a lecture by the learned and formidable Dr. Headlam and argued that the lecture was tainted by the heresy of Apollinarianism.

I was always conscious that the course of theological studies at King's College was open to criticism, but it was not until I came into contact with the Scottish Presbyterian ministers and the Scottish universities that I understood the difference between the intellectual level of the average parish minister in Scotland and the average parish priest in England. It seemed to me too that the university professors of theology north of the border were on the whole more effective than their counterparts in the south. Archbishop Cosmo Gordon Lang, who knew both sides of the picture intimately, I am sure agreed with my judgment, for once when I had been meeting Scottish professors I said, rather impertinently, that we had nothing to equal them. Dr. Lang replied, "Sometimes, when I preside over a meeting of the diocesan bishops in England, I think to myself, 'Would that the Scottish professors could all become bishops. How they would raise the level of our discussions.'" One of the causes of the difference is that Scotland, a much smaller country, has had four universities, while England has had only two, with the consequence that first-rate university education was adapted to the needs of poor men in one and to the tastes of rich men in the other. We have swung in England to the other extreme and I have lost count of the new universities which spring up on every side, but at the time of which I am writing these were not even dreamed of. To judge the education of theological students fairly, the limitations of poverty must always be reckoned with. The College itself was poor with practically no endowments and no grants from public funds and it attracted few sons of even moderately prosperous parents. Further, the meagre funds available for assisting ordinands were administered by men who assumed as a self-evident principle that all the bright boys were to be helped to go to Oxford or Cambridge and other colleges could have the remnant. The situation has changed now, but not so much as might have been hoped. For example, the number of professors of theological subjects who were students in the University of London is small—fewer I think than when I left King's College in 1932.

. In the circumstances, it seemed necessary to carry on the evening lectures in Theology, which were a burden on the staff and of course on students too. They were, however, not only a necessary evil but a means of grace to many. It was possible to pass the examinations for the diploma in Theology, A.K.C. (Associate of King's College), by keeping a course of four years in the evening, followed by one year of full-time

study. In a way, I rejoice that this course has been abolished
as no longer needed, but I regret it too. Some of the Lord's
elect have entered the ministry by this road. I doubt whether
there is a much better test of a vocation than persisting in four
years of study while earning one's living and working full-time
in a secular job. Certainly some of my best students were in the
evening classes when I first met them. One in particular I hold
in affectionate memory—Harold Smith, a youth with a strong
Cockney accent, who entered for the evening course and proved
to be not only a glutton for study but an almost miraculous
absorber of knowledge. He was for years a kind of maid of all
work in the theological faculty; there was no department of
the subject, including Hebrew, which he was not able and
willing to teach. His special line of scholarship was the History
of Religion or, as it was then called, Comparative Religions.
In order to equip himself for this, he learned Sanscrit. When
he was appointed professor of the subject in Manchester University, we were all very glad, but we never found anyone else
to take his place. Alas, his tenure of the Manchester chair was
not long; he collapsed and died while lecturing to his students.
He said himself that he owed his start on the academic career
in which he was happy to the evening classes in Theology at
King's College. The students of today, for whom I have great
regard and good hope, sometimes think their grants are too
small and that they have a claim on the Church or on the
nation for more subsidy. I wonder how many have a sense of
vocation like that of the men in the old evening course.

Obviously enough, the course at King's for ordination candidates was too short. For men who had passed the London matric
or similar examination, two years was the normal duration of
the course and, for those who had no qualifying certificate and
no Greek, a "preliminary year" was prescribed. I began my
teaching career by explaining Logic to the "preliminary year".
The plague of poverty hindered the lengthening of the course,
but it was achieved and, before I left the College, the Central
Advisory Council of Training for the Ministry had laid down
regulations for the examining of ordination candidates and had
instituted an examination for all colleges. The King's College
diploma of A.K.C. in Theology was accepted by C.A.C.T.M.,
which appointed an external examiner to keep watch on the
standard. All this was not achieved without a good measure

of argument which sometimes was not completely free from asperity. A manoeuvre of mine, which at the time seemed to me to be neither funny nor impertinent, now strikes me as both. I was striving to get the King's College diploma accepted as a qualifying degree for ordination, while most of the other members were doubtful how to vote, and the chairman, the then Bishop of Manchester, was evidently against me. One of my points on which I felt strongly was that we had the Philosophy of Religion as a principal subject in our course, but C.A.C.T.M.'s General Ordination Examination had no tincture of Philosophy. Somewhat superciliously, the Bishop said the subject was vague and of little use to clergy in their parishes, to which I replied, "My Lord, the only way I can make my case for the Philosophy of Religion is to give a brief outline of the lectures which I give on the syllabus of the London University examination." I began, as was my custom, to discourse on some important definitions of religion and on the different points of view which they represented. For how long I went on, I cannot say, nor whether the restiveness of my audience signified agreement, but I certainly persuaded the bishop that there is a subject called Philosophy of Religion.

On the whole, the institution of C.A.C.T.M. was a useful reform, because it secured some approach to a common policy in the matter of ordination. No regulation can take away from a bishop the power and responsibility of ordaining, and their conformity to standards of intellectual and moral qualifications in their acceptance of candidates is voluntary, but I can testify that the situation has improved since the old days when some bishops accepted men with what seemed to me undue optimism. Strangely, it was one of the most learned and mentally alive bishops who was most unpredictable in his judgments.

But there is a problem behind all the subsidiary questions. Do we know what kind of ministers we need and, supposing that finance did not cramp our planning, what would be our ideal clerical education? That was a query which was never far off. And it was, of course, not an exclusively Anglican problem. So far as I could discover, all the Churches had similar difficulties. When I was most deeply involved in the training of clergy, there was an inter-denominational conference of men, principals of theological colleges and professors of theology, who were in daily contact with theological students, presided over by William Temple, then Archbishop of York. It emerged that we were all worried and conscious that we were not doing all that we ought, but there were marked differences in our approaches, in our presuppositions.

The difference between mine and the distinguished representatives of Free Church colleges was clear. The dominant thought of my Free Church colleagues was the prophetic ministry. To discover and develop the prophetic gift in students was, it seemed to them, the main duty of teachers in theological colleges. I do not think this is so marked a characteristic today. At the time of which I am writing, there were many powerful preachers and there were many congregations which hung upon their words, and also the trend of biblical scholarship was to fasten on the prophetic writings of the Old Testament as the creative centre of the Hebrew religion and the principal *praeparatio evangelica*, the priestly literature being counted as on a lower level. After listening to exponents of this point of view for some hours, I fear I reacted too strongly against it by saying that my experience of dealing with theological students was different. I found that I did not lack young men who thought they were prophets, but most of them needed to be persuaded that they were not prophets but, if they worked hard, might become tolerable parish priests. I exaggerated, but I had a valid point, for is it not absurd and even irreverent to imagine that a man may prophesy to order and turn on the tap, as it were, at 11 a.m. and 6.30 p.m. every Sunday? I was really arguing against myself in these reflections, for I was well aware that my own preaching and lecturing too often took the form of discussions about problems in religion, as if the Church of Christ was a fellowship of students of Comparative Religion. I was sure, however, that the minister had no justification for existing unless he was convinced that there is a divine revelation in Scripture and the pastoral office of the Church is for a large part the explanation and application of revelation. But what is revelation? On that question I lectured in Liverpool and the lectures were published. Though I do not retract anything in the book, I would not claim that it provides a complete answer to the questions which the idea of revelation poses when we think it out. It is at least clear that whether or not you believe there is a revelation will determine the kind of education you would think suitable for the clergy.

It was on my visit to the U.S.A. to give the Noble lectures in Harvard that another question struck me as urgent. In the U.S.A., I came across men with degrees in Divinity who could not read the Greek Testament. That astounded me and I still think that a B.D. who knows no Greek is a kind of contradiction in terms, but I had to admit that there was a case for substituting psychological, sociological and philosophical study of religion for linguistic scholarship. Is not the unwelcome truth that a fully equipped Christian minister would be at home in both fields, in Biblical and Systematic Theology and in the culture of the modern scientific society, and that no one is capable of meeting these demands? I confess that many of the students who passed through King's in my time were not adequately educated and that I was inadequately educated myself, but we were at least aware of the tension between faith and knowledge. Walter Bageot's libellous comment on the public schools of the 19th century was that, though it could not be claimed that they succeeded in teaching their pupils Greek and Latin, they left on their minds the indelible impression that there were such languages. Doubtless we did not give our theological students any deep knowledge of science and its methods, but it would have been impossible to spend even one term in the theological faculty without being confronted with the reality of scientific research and the tension between it and orthodox belief.

One defect in the training of ordinands could not be remedied. Most men, when they have finished their university examinations, before they feel ready to be ordained, need a period of quiet study and thought in which they can deepen their spiritual life and finally dedicate their lives to the priesthood. I never had this period myself and I have always regretted it; and, when I was responsible for ordinands, I was sorry that only a few of my students had this advantage. Shortage of money and the pressure of vicars eagerly looking for curates combined to prevent them, and even the minority who were allowed to have some terms at a theological college did not profit by them as much as one expected, because too often they were lectured to on subjects which they had heard more adequately expounded by university professors. I am afraid the result sometimes was not training in contemplation but holy boredom. Not until long after I had left was this defect removed

by the addition of a year after the final examinations in King's
College at a provincial branch of King's, where the time of
quiet reflection was adapted to the course at King's College
and the University of London. This really creative innovation
was conceived and carried through by Eric Abbott, when Dean
of the College, to whom I and all lovers of K.C.L. owe lasting
gratitude.

CHAPTER 7

My Further Education Continued

Whatever the effects of my labours to educate my pupils during the years 1918 to 1932, it is certain that my pupils and my colleagues in various groups educated me. I must try to record some of my debts. The greatest debt cannot ever be estimated —to my students, undergraduates and postgraduates. It was they who compelled me, by their willingness to learn, to tackle subjects and problems which mental laziness would have otherwise caused me to pass over and it was they who helped me by their questions to clear my thoughts and I hope to express them lucidly. In this field I owe so much to students who must be nameless but are not forgotten by me. My love and thanks to them.

The University of London and specially its Faculty of Theology was for fourteen years the world in which I lived—King's College was my home in that world. *Ex officio* I was a member of the Senate—or rather I was elected by the Council of King's College to represent the theological side of the College. The proceedings of University senates have the quality of being often intensely interesting to a small circle of academic persons and dismally boring and even unintelligible to everyone else. London was no exception; but I can say that, when I first took my seat, the proceedings were vastly more lively than they were when I resigned from it in 1960. At the earlier date, there were frequently debates on matters of principle, but at the later date the business was so well organised and prepared by committees that page after page of numbered resolutions were passed without a word of explanation or criticism. The development of the Senate was an object lesson of the way in which government by free discussion merges almost imperceptibly into government by caucus and bureaucrats.

As in duty bound, I begin with the members of the University

Faculty of Theology. I count it one of my special pieces of good fortune that it was a kind of foretaste in miniature of the British Council of Churches. At the time, there were colleges connected with the University representing all the larger "Free Churches". New College and Hackney College in Hampstead were Independent or Congregational, Regent's Park College was Baptist, Richmond College Wesleyan; the Anglican point of view was maintained by the London College of Divinity which was Evangelical in allegiance. King's College was Anglican without qualification. In passing, it is worth recording that the normal situation with regard to endowments was reversed in London. Some of the Non-Conformist "academies" of the 18th century had accumulated some property which was available as endowment in the 20th. When war came in 1914, one at least of the Colleges made a useful profit. It had endowments for the maintenance of candidates for the Ministry which piled up when there were hardly any students to support.

The principals and many of the tutors in the Colleges included in their number some really eminent men. Perhaps the one who is best remembered today is P. T. Forsyth of Hackney College. His books are still reprinted and, what is more, referred to by contemporary theologians, I think with good reason. Though his thought did not move on lines that were easy for me to accept, I saw then and I see more clearly now that Forsyth was an important man and his teaching has to be taken into account in any estimate of Christian theology in the 20th century. In a moment of reckless dogmatism, I once said that everything of value in the writings of Karl Barth had been said earlier and more clearly by Forsyth. There was a grain of truth in this hasty remark. Biblical theology and the effort to construct a system of evangelical doctrine on the basis of the biblical revelation had a powerful advocate in Forsyth who, like Barth, was a cultivator of humanist culture as his book *Christ on Parnassus* proves. I might have learned more from Forsyth if I had been personally more attracted by him. He had a sharp tongue which he used to combat what he held to be heresy. I never cease from surprise at the way my memory retains snatches of quite unremarkable talk. Perhaps these sporadic reminiscences are given to help me to present my colleagues as real human beings. Well then: Forsyth asked me to dine at Hackney College with evident doubt about its quality: "Glad to see you, if you can come," he said, "a cut off the joint—but be prepared for either a whole burnt offering or a bloody sacrifice."

The Principal of New College, Hampstead, was Dr. A. E. Garvie, to whom I was no stranger, for when a student I had diligently followed his lectures on Comparative Religions for three terms. I think he was a little astonished at my appearance as a full-blown member of the Theological Faculty and a professor so soon after my brief spell on the students' benches in his lecture room. But he never said so and he never would have betrayed surprise, even if he had felt it. He was a remarkable man in more than one respect. He was a linguist of genius. Beside the three sacred tongues, Hebrew, Greek and Latin in which he was more than proficient, he knew German like a native and at least two other European tongues. In the early stages of the Ecumenical Movement, during the "Faith and Order" conferences and negotiations, Garvie's linguistic facility was most useful and I have been told (I was never on any of these most important committees) that Garvie could preside over an argumentative committee with perfect ease in English, German and French.

When Bishop Gore joined the teaching staff at King's, one of my hopes was that his presence in the Faculty meetings would help me to hold my own with my distinguished Free Church colleagues. He did more than that. Gore and Garvie knew each other already and loved each other. I learned that what I had suspected was true, that there is a fellowship in the Spirit which is deeper than a fellowship in belief. Gore and Garvie were almost at opposite extremes in theology within our group, one a leader of the Anglo-Catholic movement in the Church of England, the other a Protestant divine learned in the wisdom of German liberal theology. Yet I am sure they were nearer together than either of them was to anyone in the faculty of his own theological colour. They were united in spirit by their total commitment to Christ. It was touching to see these two old men chaffing one another like schoolboys and to hear Garvie's story about himself and Gore making a joint propagandist tour in the U.S.A. during the 1914 war. They came together to a city where an enterprising bookseller had bought up a lot of Gore's books and advertised them with a large placard, "St. Paul's Epistle to the Romans (damaged) by Bishop

Gore." "I couldn't agree more," said Garvie. It was said of Burke that "he spoke pamphlets"; it might have been said of Garvie that, when he lectured, he spoke treatises. After the German fashion, he would dictate sections to the students and illustrate and elaborate these texts with comments and references. I have heard it said that Garvie once quite literally spoke a treatise, because some enterprising student took down a complete course of Garvie's lectures and published them under his own name. The transcript, apparently, of any public utterance is the copyright of the reporter and not of the speaker.

Of all my friends and colleagues in the University faculty of Theology, Wheeler Robinson was much the closest. He and I were associated as joint editors of the Library of Constructive Theology, which included in its list some books which had considerable influence between the wars. Wheeler Robinson was a distinguished Hebrew scholar and the author of at least one first-rate book, an introduction to the religion of the Hebrews. When I first met him, he was Principal of Regent's Park College, the Baptist training college for ministers. In those days, it justified its name by its geographical situation and occupied a magnificent mansion built by a city magnate. The interior decoration was sumptuous and pagan. The incongruity of the building with the Puritan tradition of the Baptists impressed me every time I spoke in their hall or chapel and I remember beginning one speech by saying, "Having in mind your traditions and the purpose of this College, I must assume that the charming young creatures depicted on the ceiling and walls of this sumptuous apartment are cherubs, but I must own that to my Anglican eyes they look uncommonly like cupids." The Principal frequently invited me to speak to his students and I am glad to record that my friend Dr. Payne, who recently laid down the office of Secretary to the Baptist Union, had been one of my pupils at King's and later was a student and lecturer at Regent's Park. The College moved from London to Oxford, thus achieving Robinson's ambition for it, and is now housed in a sober and suitably collegiate edifice next door to a Dominican Priory—far removed from any suggestion of cupids.

The Library of Constructive Theology was projected by the fertile mind of Sir James Marchant, whose original scheme was that William Temple should be associated with a distinguished Free Church scholar. I was the substitute for Temple when he discovered that he could not himself act as editor. I believe that he suggested me as his substitute and that I owe him a debt of gratitude for this opportunity of enlarging my education. We started the series with a winner—H. R. Mackintosh on *The Christian Experience of Forgiveness*, and almost all of the books in the Library before 1939 were useful and some brilliant. Among those in which I was the editor chiefly concerned, I am specially proud of Evelyn Underhill's on *Worship*, F. R. Barry's *Relevance of Christianity* and Oliver Quick's on *Sacraments*. With regard to the last of these, I believe I did some good by clearing up a few passages which were obscure; and with regard to the first, I profited much by the friendship of a cultivated and most Christian lady who at my suggestion was elected an honorary Fellow of King's College, London—the only woman theological Fellow. Only one of the books which Wheeler Robinson and I planned was a disappointment, but that was one on which we had built great expectations, Grensted on *The Incarnation*. Our friend had been captivated by the Oxford Group Movement and, instead of a lucid theological treatise on the central doctrine of the Faith, was "guided" as he believed by the Holy Spirit to give us a long sermon which touched only incidentally on the elucidation of the doctrine.

The coming of war, for some reason which escapes me, brought the series into less favourable conditions. Perhaps constructive theology was "out" and destructive theology was "in": some Christian writers were expounding the dogma that "God is dead"; by which they appeared to mean that the idea of God was unintelligible. The chief reason, however, was that the underlying philosophy had changed during the war; when we started the Library of Constructive Theology, the prevailing philosophy was a species of idealism which, in a general way, was Hegelian in spirit. An Italian thinker Benedetto Croce was a prolific writer on philosophy who propounded an idealism of a modernised Hegelian type, which laid stress on the conception of "forms" of the Spirit and of a dialectical development through history. The question whether religion was a "form of the spirit" like art and philosophy was for a time debated in philosophical circles and, in my Boyle Lectures, *Studies in Christian Philosophy*, I ventured on a modest contribution aimed at the conclusion that Croce and Hegel were

wrong in holding philosophy to be the highest and most conclusive "form of the spirit" and that religion, when dialectically
developed, was the legitimate claimant to supremacy. Holding
these views, it was natural for me to look on religious experience as the guiding idea for constructive theology and the titles
of our volumes indicated our presupposition, thus my own
book was called *God in Christian Thought and Experience*.
Misunderstanding is almost unavoidable in such discussions and
I do not complain that some readers took "experience" in a
purely psychological sense, as did James in his famous *Varieties
of Religious Experience*. Wheeler Robinson and I, though
deeply interested in psychology, thought we were writing
theology.

The learned Christian scholars of whom I have been writing
were confident and hopeful. They believed that the once formidable conflict between Religion and Science had been, at least
in principle, resolved and that the limits of scientific knowledge
had been defined, though they would agree that the new science
of psychology—or rather the new psychology—might suggest
some problems for Christian faith. In the main too, the field
of biblical criticism offered prospects of peaceful progress. The
general outline of the religion of the Hebrews and the insight
of the Old Testament Prophets was not hard to reconcile with
a liberal version of Christian orthodoxy. The question, "Who
was Jesus?" or the validity of the Gospels as testimonies to
his person and teaching was not indeed laid to rest, but the
"Synoptic Problem" had been solved by agreement on the
sources and inter-relation of the first three Gospels, while the
Fourth Gospel, which remained a puzzle with regard to its
reliability as an historical narrative, was better understood
than before as a mystical interpretation of the Incarnation. For
my part, I shared the confidence of my seniors, except perhaps
that Albert Schweitzer's *Quest of the Historical Jesus* disturbed
me, as it disturbs me still. How, I wondered, could such a
dedicated Christian life as his be inspired by the personality
of a deluded fanatic such as Schweitzer's interpretation of Jesus
and his beliefs presented to his readers? When Otto's *Idea of
the Holy* came out, my somewhat rationalistic approach to the
understanding of religion received a shock, because it was
evident that the book was of first-rate importance and brought
out an incontrovertible element in religious experience, while

apparently leading to an irrational God. In one respect I shared
in the illusions of my companions. In those days, we felt no
anxiety about world war. We had fought the war to end war
and the League of Nations was the guardian of Peace. We
thought, or at least I thought, that the League of Nations was
the triumphant creation of Liberal Christian idealism.

Most of these scholars were members of a group which had
no publicity, but indirectly contributed not a little to the "spirit
of the age"—at least in its religious aspect. The London Society
for the Study of Religion was a private, though not a secret,
society. Admission to it was far from easy and, by a paradox,
the smaller the religious group to which one belonged, the
better one's chance of election. This was because an attempt
was made to get a more or less even representation of points
of view. Jewish (orthodox and liberal), Roman Catholic, Anglican, Free Church and Unitarian, with one or two Agnostics
of various kinds, were brought together to form as it were a
composite photograph of the current theological scene. The
attempt to represent all opinions tended to misrepresent the
true balance, for there were many individuals who would have
been most welcome, but for whom there was no vacancy because they were Anglicans or Roman Catholics, while Unitarians
nearly always had a speedy initiation. When I was elected owing
to the advocacy of my friend and tutor Dr. Caldecott, I was
the youngest member and considerably overawed by the company in which I found myself, but I was aware that an opportunity of making contact with first-rate minds and fine spirits
was offered and, whether I made the best use of it or no, the
Society and particularly two or three of its members left an
indelible impression on me. I must recall some of these men.

If there is one individual whose figure stands in my memory
as the symbol of the L.S.S.R., it is that of Baron von Hügel. His
biography has been written by Michael de la Bedoyère and his
writings have been widely read. I will confine myself to my own
experience of him. It began with an embarrassing encounter.
My mentor and friend G. E. Newsom, who did much to launch
me into the little world of scholarly ecclesiastics and laymen,
took the opportunity of an evening party in the Senior Common
Room at King's College to introduce me to "the Baron", and
no doubt with the most generous intentions made a little ceremony of it when a number of guests were spectators. Von

Hügel was a venerable and formidable person and carried with him a kind of aura both of learning and sanctity; for that I was prepared, but I was not prepared for his deafness, though I knew he was deaf, but I did not know that he was stone deaf and could only be made to hear by speaking into a very large hearing-aid about the size of a cigar box. When I was presented to him, von Hügel said nothing, but handed to me his cigar box hearing-aid with the obvious purpose of listening to words of wisdom from one who had been described to him as a promising young man. Possibly I stammered out a few disjointed syllables, but my recollection is that I became completely tongue-tied. Anyway I looked an utter fool and the matter was made worse by the fact that my fiancée, to whom I had recently become engaged, was present at her first party of theological pundits.

Von Hügel's influence and his deafness determined to some extent the proceedings of the Society. Since he was unable to follow any discussion or indeed to hear the paper which was being discussed, it was the custom that the reader of the paper should send it to the Baron some days before the meeting so that he could prepare his comments in advance. On the evening when the paper was read, the Baron's comments were read after a brief interval and started the discussion. This system in fact conduced to animated and relevant speeches because the Baron had a generous mind and a very wide range of interests together with a definite point of view. When it was my turn to read the paper, I was impressed by the attention which he gave to all my propositions; though disagreeing with many, he left the pleasing impression on my mind that they were all worth considering.

The master work of this great man is the *Mystical Element in Religion,* studied with special reference to the life and letters of St. Catherine of Genoa. Many who have read this work will agree that the style of writing seemed often to make difficult concepts more obscure, but will affirm that it is one of the books which made a difference to their lives as well as their thought. I am sure that he really struggled hard to be understood. George Newsom used to tell with amusement of a visit which he once paid to von Hügel's house in Vicarage Gate, Kensington, on some urgent business. The great man emerged from his study with reluctance, having been disturbed in literary composition, and remarked in anguished tones: "How difficult it seems to be to get people to understand what labour and sweat of mind goes into turning out these beautifully lucid sentences." I suppose that he still thought partly in German, though his English vocabulary was extensive. Popular addresses by von Hügel were sometimes superb and inimitable. Homely illustrations and slang words in unexpected contexts were employed to convey spiritual and moral ideas. To say the least it was impossible to let one's attention wander when he was talking.

When I knew von Hügel, he was involved in the controversy about Modernism in the Roman Catholic Church. The movement was coming to the surface and the general public in England were beginning to notice that scholars and priests were being censured and some excommunicated. The centre of the storm was the Abbé Alfred Loisy, who was an eminent New Testament scholar. He came into prominence by a short book *L'Evangile et L'Eglise*, which was ostensibly at least a refutation of the famous Protestant scholar Adolf Harnack and specially of the book *Das Wesen des Christentums*, translated into English under the title *What is Christianity?* Loisy differed from Harnack fundamentally on the connection of the Gospel and the Church. Harnack, and the Liberal Protestants in general, looked for the genuine, original gospel as preached by Jesus of Nazareth, freed from the complexities and corruptions of tradition and legend. They sought for the "Historical Jesus" and Harnack held that the answer to the question, "What is the essence of Christianity?" was, "It is the simple message that God is the Father of all men and they are all brothers." To this Loisy replied that we could know nothing about the Historical Jesus apart from the Church. The Church gives us the Gospels and is the bearer of the tradition. The concept of a communal and developing experience, in which the figure of Christ was the centre, was latent in Loisy's writings and was also implicit in the Idealist philosophy of religion. Unfortunately the Roman Church, or at least the Curia, did not welcome the defence provided by the champion. *Non tali auxilio, nec defensoribus istis* was the official reaction and perhaps this was not really surprising because Loisy and some of his followers were at least as drastic in their criticism of the New Testament as Harnack. I confess that, when these events were taking place,

I did not understand the issues which were being decided. In the quarrel between Loisy and Harnack, I was inclined to the Protestant "Jesus of History" school of thought and had little interest in the Roman Church. Today I know that the condemnation of Modernism was a disaster from which the whole Church is now suffering. If arguments had been used and not anathemas and if the Curia and the Pope had "reasoned together" with the Modernists, the present crisis in the Roman Church would have been avoided.

Von Hügel was not excommunicated, though he was deeply involved in the problems of his friends. One of these friends, George Tyrrell, I met but foolishly failed to cultivate his acquaintance. He was an Anglican priest who had become a Jesuit; being a prolific writer on theology, his modernist views were not concealed and the sentence fell upon him. No doubt he was urged by friends and by his own remembered affections for the Anglican worship to return to the Church of his baptism, but he resolutely remained under excommunication until his death, I suppose to maintain his claim that he was not lawfully excommunicated. In my opinion, Tyrrell was the best writer and the most impressive person among the English Modernists. His book *Christianity at the Cross Roads* was prophetic at the time of its publication because he was among the first to think constructively about the Apocalyptic element in the Gospels and Schweitzer's interpretation of them. Von Hügel had reason for anxiety and grief in the misfortunes of his friends and the setback to freedom of scholarship caused by their persecution, but additional trouble came to him through misunderstandings of his motives. Loisy's *Memoirs* are sometimes sad reading. That he felt bitter is natural enough, but that he blamed von Hügel for lack of support in the controversy is tragic, and I do not doubt von Hügel was deeply hurt. He was thinking of the wider issue. He never retracted any of his writings and that he should stand by his critical writings on the Bible without incurring the censure of the ecclesiastical authorities did something to keep open a door for the future.

Certainly von Hügel had a profound influence on me, but one not easy to define. He led me to see something of the power of mysticism and of its link with institutional religion as well as with Theology and Philosophy. But was he himself a mystic?

In a general way of course he was. I suspect all religion, except the merely conventional kind, touches on mystical experience because it is a more or less conscious love of God; but, if we mean by "mystic" one who has attained the "unitive" state, the ecstatic union with God in which the finite self is as it were lost in God, then the number of mystics is small. It has been my privilege to know personally four writers who have made memorable contributions to our knowledge of mysticism. I cannot say that I know any one of them achieved the unitive state. My predecessor at St. Paul's, Dr. W. R. Inge, was a pioneer of the study in England and wrote a standard work on Plotinus, the mystical pagan who had so extraordinary an influence on Christian piety: he was one who responded to the words of mystical devotion and knew at least partially what thirst the mystics were seeking to satisfy; but, though he did not deserve the title "gloomy Dean", no one I think ever called him "the joyous Dean". So I would say of von Hügel, who seemed to labour and groan in the conflict of his spirit. I admired his fortitude, his faith hardly won, and his obedience. How carefully he kept all the laws of his Church! For example, on the occasions when we joined in the Lord's Prayer, or even in silent prayer, he would withdraw into another room to pray by himself in order to keep the regulation against worshipping with heretics. I feel that he sometimes wore the laws and customs of Church discipline like a hair shirt as a kind of penance.

Rudolf Otto, who wrote a masterly book on *Mysticism, Eastern and Western*, was oppressed by the tragic sense of life. Evelyn Underhill in my recollection seemed full of a quiet joy. Perhaps she was very near to the unitive state. But as I write these words, I know that, if she is looking over my shoulder, she is objecting to any hint that she could be higher in the knowledge of God than her loved spiritual guide. And the last observation on this topic shall be about these two lay mystics. Baron von Hügel and Dr. Evelyn Underhill were probably the two most powerful personal spiritual directors for educated persons in their generation.

Many other members of the L.S.S.R. I could happily hold in remembrance, among them Dr. Edwyn Bevan and Professor Burkitt, but time would fail and I mention only one more. Strange that the two who had the deepest influence on me were one a Roman Catholic and the other a Jew! Yet so it is and

I do not hesitate to own it. Claude Montefiore was not perhaps so potent an intellectual element in my experience as von Hügel, but he was more attractive to me as a person and I not only felt a deep affection for him but recognised some affinity in the way in which our minds worked. I think he must have felt something of the same, because on his deathbed he specially asked that I should minister to him and pray with him. This was a privilege which embarrassed me, because he was deaf and one had to shout to make him hear and it was difficult to me to pray in a manner which would imply no Christian belief. It was a surprise to me that the belief in Jesus Christ as mediator had so permeated my imagination that only by a sustained effort could I pray like a Jew. The Lord's Prayer of course is not a specifically Christian prayer and could be spoken by a Jew without a qualm, but I realised that for my part I could not believe I had a Father in Heaven unless I believed that he was revealed in Jesus Christ.

Another factor in my mental condition was, as I discovered, that I thought of Claude Montefiore as a "real" Christian, though of course I never told him so. He was an excellent scholar in biblical studies and in the Rabbinic learning and also a man of wide general culture. His book on the Synoptic Gospels had real value and was read with profit by intelligent Christians not less than Jews. He had prepared for the book by a careful study of German New Testament criticism and it still remains a useful record of the scholarship of the late 19th century and the early 20th. The most interesting contribution is Montefiore's estimate of the character and teaching of Jesus. With considerable courage, he totally rejected the traditional Jewish controversial estimate of Jesus and claimed him as one of the chief glories of Hebrew prophecy—indeed that he should be acknowledged as the greatest of the prophets. This did not imply, as Montefiore was careful to make clear, any approach to Christian orthodoxy. The doctrine of the Incarnation remained for him a tragic error which had no basis in the teaching of the historical Jesus. Most worthy of note is Montefiore's judgment on the meaning of the Love of God as proclaimed by Jesus. The Prophets and Psalmists at their highest level of inspiration had dwelt upon the love of God and his mercy towards sinners who turned to him in repentance. In this Jesus was carrying on the prophetic message; but, Montefiore insisted,

in one most vital respect Jesus surpassed the most exalted
teaching of the Prophets: whereas they had in their widest hope
included all men, asserting that God's love embraces them and
that he is gracious to all who call upon him, Jesus' gospel is
that of the seeking love of God which does not wait until the
sinner turns but goes out in search of the lost.

Montefiore's Jewish "righteousness" governed all his activities. "My station and its duties" had a very inclusive application
in his personal activities. I was once seriously consulted by him
on a problem of conduct arising out of his situation as a land-
owner. He was the "squire" of a country parish near to
Southampton, to whose university he was a generous benefactor. His question was a simple one: he was an annual sub-
scriber to the funds of the parish church, as that was evidently
what any decent squire would do, but did I think that he
ought to subscribe to the diocesan fund? After a brief interval
for reflection on my friend's scrupulous conscience, I replied,
"No, but don't tell the Bishop I said so." His "liberal" Judaistic
faith was inconsistent with the aspirations of Zionism and, like
many other old Jewish families, his children were brought up
to think that Britain was their native land. I remember once
when I was talking in a club about the anti-Semitic danger
and the hope that Zionism might be one of the answers, a
very English-looking member fiercely disclaimed all interest
in the plan. He was a Jew and proud of it, he said, but his
great grandfather fought under Nelson at Trafalgar and he was
as exclusively English as I was.

A matter which perplexed me for years was the nature of
religion in general and whether the great religions of the world
would develop and perhaps draw together. A dictum of Rudolf
Otto impressed me as posing this question: "None of the great
religions of the world must be allowed to die until it has spoken
its last and highest word." Montefiore alone, I thought, among
the members of the L.S.S.R. had clear ideas on this important
matter. He knew what he hoped for Judaism; it was that the
Liberal Jewish point of view would prevail and the historical
elements—the Mosaic Law, the ceremonial law and the belief
about the Messiah—would be remembered as great traditions
but transcended by a more spiritual creed which would be
Ethical Theism. He looked for the convergence of the mono-
theistic religions, Judaism, Christianity and Islam to the Shema,

the Lord our God is one and he is just and merciful. Though I could not agree with his prediction or with his hope, it seemed to me that he was right in regarding religion—all living religions—as dynamic and therefore as changing, as having a future and as growing towards fulfilment. I had tried to advocate such a view when discussing the relation between religion and philosophy in my *Studies in Christian Philosophy*, but no one took much notice of it and in my opinion the Christian theologians were too much concerned with what Christianity had been in the past and too little with what it would have to be in the future. Undoubtedly my contact with Claude Montefiore was a principal factor in my zeal against anti-Semitism and I will add here the name of another learned Jew who helped me to understand the qualities in some Jews which tend to antagonise their Gentile neighbours. Some years before the war, I had a small part in helping Dr. Oswald Schwarz, an eminent Vienna psychologist, to become naturalised in England. He knew many English doctors and spoke the language fluently. When he started to practise in England, he told me that his adjustment to the English environment was the most difficult psychological exercise he had ever attempted, even though he was not only aware of the problem but knew theoretically how to solve it. He added, "How long do you suppose a family from Poland, which does not even know that there is a problem, will take to accommodate its behaviour to the new social environment? Not less than three generations."

Another institution to which I owe much assistance in my continued education is the Honourable and Learned Society of Gray's Inn and I count my appointment first as chaplain and then as preacher there as one of the most fortunate events in my life. It came about largely because some good friends, among them Ernest Barker and Bishop Gore, knew that I had been seeking a pulpit from which I might preach on Sunday and some additional income which would enable me to pay my children's school fees. Gray's Inn was already well known to me, for I had often been a member of the congregation in undergraduate days, when I was attracted partly by the charming little 15th-century chapel and partly by the scholarly sermons of Canon Fletcher. I think it would be hard to overestimate the benefits which I derived from my ten years' incumbency of the Gray's Inn post. Though I was working hard in the College, at one time lecturing ten times a week as well as administering the Theological Faculty, I felt that to proclaim the gospel was an aspect of the ministry to which I was called and I earnestly desired to have a pulpit and a congregation, so that I might attempt to present a version of Christianity which was thought out in the light of modern knowledge to a group of educated people. When I was appointed, I soon found that there was a danger that my work with my lectures and pupils might suffer because of my engagements on Sundays but also that there was a possibility that, if I was intelligent, I might contrive that my two occupations would help one another. Thus I made a rule that I would never think about my sermon for Sunday before lunchtime on Saturday. I am afraid that this was clean contrary to the advice which I gave to the students who were hoping to be ordained. To them I advocated the plan of thinking about their sermons for a week before they were preached—but then I saw no likelihood that they would become professors.

The congregation was often quite alarmingly distinguished. The Masters of the Bench had seats in the chancel at the foot of the pulpit and two of them invariably read the lessons. One of the Benchers was Dean of the Chapel, which meant that he could choose the hymns and anthems. I cannot remember that he ever chose the subject of my sermon, though it would not have surprised me if he had—perhaps I should hardly have noticed it, because it would have been done with such perfect courtesy. The plain truth was that I was hired by the Masters of the Bench to preach and conduct services as required and could have been sacked at any time with three months' notice.

On one occasion, I believe, I did run some slight risk of eviction. F. E. Smith was Lord Chancellor and a Bencher of Gray's Inn. He had made the headlines with a brilliant, provocative and, in my view, pernicious speech to the University of St. Andrews on the subject of ambition, in which he said, "Still there are glittering prizes for the sharp sword" and much more to the same effect. He was speaking to the generation of undergraduates which came up soon after the end of the first world war and I really shuddered to think that the idealism of youth should be directed to egotistic conflict for selfish rewards. I owed the Lord Chancellor gratitude for having supported my candidature, but I felt all the more it was my duty to protest. So I did and I will not say that I did not enjoy the drama of denouncing the doctrine of the Inn's favourite son in the Inn's Chapel, but I did not want to be a martyr. I learnt afterwards that the Benchers who were present at the service held an informal meeting to discuss what should be done about the sermon. They decided that nothing should be done and that it was really an honour to Gray's Inn that the views I held should be heard in the Chapel.

I am indebted to the Masters of the Bench who were in office while I was chaplain on many counts and not least because they took me and my wife into the social life of the Inn so far as that was possible. I could dine in the hall whenever I liked and lunch too. Memories of pleasant meals with Benchers, their ladies and distinguished guests crowd in on me. The Treasurer and Under Treasurer seemed to take pains to put me in the vicinity of notable visitors. For example, the only long conversation I ever had with Lloyd George was at the luncheon table one Sunday. I had wondered why many men of ability found him attractive and persuasive. How he did it I do not know, but he conveyed to me the impression that he was eager to hear my opinion and gave my words full attention, while all the time I knew with my reason that almost certainly he would forget our conversation five minutes after it finished. One of the Benchers made a tart remark when Lloyd George was out of hearing, "Did you notice in Chapel? Very typical; he and Megan arrived too late for the General Confession but in good time for the Absolution."

In the early days of my association with the Inn, I took Professor Merriman of Harvard as my guest to a garden party in the walks—the famous walks where Elizabeth I used to walk with Francis Bacon, it is said. He met at the party many notables of the English Bench and Bar, most of them Gray's Inn men but some from other Inns of Court, and as we came away he said, "This afternoon I have walked in the pages of Thackeray." I hasten to add that this is quite inapplicable to the present Benchers, but it was not inapt to those of the former generation and peculiarly apt to the Dean of the Chapel in my day, Sir Lewis Coward, K.C., President of the Court of Railways and Canals (I know this because it fell to me to translate his title into Latin to be inscribed on his commemorative tablet on the wall of the hall). He was the son of a Prebendary of St.

Paul's and Commissary to the Dean and Chapter. I little thought that a few years later I should be his Dean and concerned with appointing his successor. He was a Victorian and proud of it. If I laugh about him, it does not mean that I did not love him and enjoy his company. A conversation between him and our organist is recorded—or perhaps reconstructed, for I was not present. Mr. Long was a good musician and played the organ well. He also trained the little choir consisting of three men and three boys more than adequately. He had leave of absence for some months to visit India, where he gave recitals and did some examining. When he returned, he had lost the habit of tempering the organ's power to the size of the Chapel and almost deafened the congregation. Sir Lewis Coward summoned Mr. Long to his presence and addressed him as follows, "Mr. Long, sir, you must abate your noise on that organ. Why, last Sunday you nearly blew the Benchers out of their seats: this must cease, sir." To which Mr. Long replied, "Sir Lewis, I will not be spoken to as if I did not know my business. Why, recently I have been playing before crowned heads in India." To which Sir Lewis replied indignantly, "And do you venture, sir, to compare the Benchers of Gray's Inn to a lot of damned black-faced rajas?" I do not defend the sentiments or the language, but remark that the Dean of the Chapel and the Organist remained on the best of terms.

Two Gray's Inn Benchers must be mentioned together— Lord Merrivale (formerly Sir Henry Duke), President of the Divorce and Admiralty division, and Tim Healy, at one time Governor General of Ireland. Merrivale was a man who had risen to the top of his profession by sheer ability, hard work and personal integrity. The son of a Devon farmer, he retained throughout his life a touch of the enchanting Devonian speech. One of his judicial colleagues told me his method in cross-examination was unique. He overawed the witness. He seemed to embody the majesty of the law and the spirit of equity. Sometimes he extracted truth from a reluctant witness by the impression of his moral ascendancy. In important cross-examinations, I was told, he tried to think of one decisive question and to lead up to it by subtle suggestions, so that he could put the master question with shattering effect.

Tim Healy was not often in Gray's Inn, but in one summer term, when he had left Ireland finally to its own devices, he dined there almost every evening and by good fortune I was free on several of those evenings and heard his conversation in a small group of men as clever as himself—I wish I could remember one-tenth of his talk. These two Benchers were prominent at a dinner when a large number of men who had played considerable parts in the history of Ireland were present, Lord Merrivale presiding as Treasurer, and Tim Healy, who at the time was Governor General of Ireland, as the principal guest. A pleasing custom of the Inn was that speeches at dinner were barred, but lively talk was expected. On this memorable occasion, however, the Treasurer, apparently *motu proprio*, without consulting anyone, delivered from the chair a speech in honour of Tim Healy and touching upon the state of Ireland, discreetly as I thought. I was seated opposite Healy and could see that he was disturbed by this unexpected emergency —not ruffled, but taken aback—and in his delicate situation as Governor General he might well hesitate to speak without careful preparation. I wondered how he would meet the crisis. Would he just say nothing? He said in fact a number of words, but they were patently not his words. He slowly took up the elegant menu card and said, "With your permission, Mr. Treasurer, I will address you in the French language." He then read the menu very slowly from soup to savoury and adding in English, "May good digestion wait on appetite" sat down. This surely was the perfect reply, for without any formal refusal of the chairman's invitation to speak he conveyed a mild protest, while at the same time avoiding any utterance which could embarrass himself or anyone else.

Though, in the technical sense, my office as preacher did not include a "cure of souls" I was to some degree responsible for the spiritual life of the Inn. On the whole, I would say that the high court judges are not only men of the highest integrity, but the majority of them are men of personal religion. I know of judges who pray constantly for the grace of God in their judicial work. It would surprise many who see the judge in a difficult case, or presiding over a trial for murder, sitting still like a statue and speaking only in impersonal, unemotional tones, if they could know his thoughts and feelings. Three at least of the judges I have known were praying every day for the prisoners whom they were trying—and I have no doubt that all after their various manners sought spiritual help. Many of the leading men in the law take part in the work of the Church quietly and without any self-assertion. Lord Atkin, among the Gray's Inn lawyers, played a great part in drawing up the constitution of the Church in Wales after it had been dis-established and no small part of the success of the impoverished Church, which so far from being destroyed experienced an upsurge of new life, is due to the devoted service of eminent laymen, among whom lawyers were prominent.

When I was appointed preacher, I thought my congregation though small would be weighty so far as mental capacity was concerned. I was right of course, but the consequences were not exactly what I had expected. I was deeply concerned with the problems of faith and the presentation of the gospel to the modern mind and I imagined that they would have much the same feeling. But on the whole they did not. They did not want to dig up the foundations, though they were ready to listen to attempts at putting, as they would have said, old truths in new clothes. My formula for sermons was picturesquely des-cribed by an acute fellow priest who heard me often: it was first of all to cause my hearers to tremble for the safety of the ark and wonder whether I was about to abandon it and then with varying success to reassure them as to its safety. I was convinced that there was an "ark", if that is taken as the symbol of a revelation of God. The Christian faith, as represented in the Church's creeds and worship was, I firmly believed, a system of symbols which were the products of a long corporate spiritual experience, guided as I would believe by the Holy Spirit. The development of knowledge, however, had rendered some of the accepted interpretations of these symbols obsolete and even unintelligible. This fact, I thought, must be admitted and acted upon, not however by discarding the Faith, but by a sustained effort to understand it more deeply and perhaps find new and more intelligible words to express the spiritual content. One might say that, in my own thinking and in my teaching of my theological students, I was always trembling for the ark and in quest of a means of preserving its essential meaning. I have not changed in any fundamental respect since then.

I am not surprised that my beloved Benchers had limited enthusiasm for theological speculation, and I record with grati-tude that they were kindly critics and most of them first-rate judges of clear English prose discourse. Two learned ladies were

I think my most formidable critics—both were amateur theologians and no less accustomed to sit in judgment on intellectual exercises than the judges of the High Court. Miss Grey, High Mistress of St. Paul's School for Girls, and Miss Faithfull, Headmistress of Cheltenham College for Young Women, were of the tradition of "Miss Beale and Miss Buss", the almost legendary pioneers of public school education for girls and the opening of universities to women. Both were convinced, practising churchwomen and, I think, advocates of the ordination of women, a subject on which I had expressed what was then a definitely minority view on the eligibility of women for the priesthood. The thought that one or both of these ladies might be in the congregation has more than once made me look up my references and "prune my words". Before I pass on from the enchantment of Gray's Inn I must acknowledge the educational value of the conversations with guests at the Inn's hospitable table.

Ramsay MacDonald I had of course seen at a distance and had joined in a small discussion group at which he read a paper, but I had never exchanged a word with him. I found him personally attractive. He had a beautiful speaking voice and a romantic handsomeness not often bestowed on politicians. The dinner at which I had him as a neighbour took place at a time when he was in opposition and in serious trouble with his followers in the House of Commons. I thought it tactful to remark on the confusion of the political situation, to which he replied by saying that he had become a recluse and was not well informed on current affairs because he was collecting material for a life of John Knox. This seemed to be a dead end and I tried another opening. Arnold Bennett had recently published his novel *Lord Raingo* and it was thought by many that the central character had some resemblance to a well-known peer who was a newspaper owner. I asked Ramsay what he thought. He gave a fantastic answer. "There are some books that I hang outside my window for a time to clean them before I open them and I haven't opened *Lord Raingo* yet." The obvious significance of this is that Ramsay thought me an impertinent nonentity and wanted no talk with me, but I do not think that can be the explanation, because he went on to speak of other authors whom he admired and about advice he had given to certain publishers.

Stephen Leacock was by profession a professor of Political Philosophy in one of the older Canadian universities and the author of a book on justice which was regarded with respect by fellow philosophers. But, beside his vocation to philosophy, he had another vocation to promote innocent merriment—or perhaps it was all one vocation, for he helped us to laugh at ourselves. Unlike some other humorists I have known, who were funny in print but dull in conversation, Stephen Leacock was excellent company, but I cannot remember any bright spots in the gentle genial glow of his talk, except an exclamation when we at the high table followed the Treasurer out of hall into the so-called "Pension Room" where the Benchers and their guests took dessert. Leacock, perhaps a trifle awed by the learned society—if not by its learning at least by the amplitude of its hospitality—said "What? more eating and drinking? When does it end?" "Not yet," I said. "You really ought to write another chapter in the *Arcadian Adventures with the Idle Rich*." In the event, he went one better and wrote *My Discovery of Britain*, in which Gray's Inn figured at some length, and I was able to alarm some of the Benchers by telling them that they were described in a chapter headed "Is England Going Dry?"

H. G. Wells, in my opinion, was a man of genius and, when I had an evening next to him in hall, I began quite sincerely by thanking him for many hours of pleasure enjoyed in reading his writings. He replied in his squeaky voice, "Ah, but you don't like my ideas." (He was advocating "trial marriages" at the time.) "You are afraid of them." At this challenge, a riposte flashed into my mind which had never occurred to me before. "No," I said. "Not frightened, because I am sure evolution will beat you." Elaborating the idea, I said, "No doubt you know many couples who are living together on the trial marriage principle; tell me how many of them do you know who have more than one child?" He could not think of any. "You see then," I said, "natural selection will eliminate those who have a tendency to enter into trial marriages." Of course, I see now that the argument is open to objections. For example, Wells might have pointed out that the trial marriage pairs had not had time enough so far to produce more than one child. But he did not, and I suspected that in fact he did not know more than two or three participants in trial marriages. But Wells was a fascinating talker and though, on the whole, anti-Christian, always seemed to me to be a "seeker" in spirit; for me it was a lively and profitable evening.

From these relatively commonplace details of my experience, I pass to an experience which continued for nearly fourteen years and was quite certainly a major factor in my further education, though on looking back I feel that the purpose with which the movement was inaugurated and sustained was only partly achieved, largely because of the timidity of the Archbishops and bishops. I refer to the Archbishops' Commission on Doctrine in the Church of England, which was set up in 1922 and published its Report in 1938, its deliberations having stretched almost from the first world war to the second. That I was selected by the archbishops to serve on this Commission was a welcome sign that, in spite of some doubts about the wisdom of my appointment as Dean of King's College and Professor, my reputation as a theologian was tolerably good. The first chairman was Dr. Burge, my old supporter, who had become Bishop of Oxford, and no doubt he put forward my name. Young theologians were at a premium in those days, because it was recognised that the Commission must have time to produce its Report and might reasonably hope to have some of its members surviving at the end of its deliberations, even if only to be excommunicated. As it happened, several members died and, to my deep regret, Dr. Burge was soon taken from us. William Temple, Archbishop of York, was appointed in his place.

From the beginning, all its members were conscious that they were in a position of great responsibility and that, if the Commission succeeded, it might prove a turning-point in the history of Anglicanism—and not of Anglicanism only. The purpose, as defined by the archbishops and steadily kept in mind by Archbishop Temple, was not to produce a "body of divinity" for the guidance of the Church; it was primarily to define the permissible limits of teaching in the Church of England. Controversy between High and Low Church had been fierce at times in the past, but now the conflict had become complicated by the rise of the Modernists who presented, as it were, a Catholic version of broad church theology, though neither party would have accepted that statement. From the bishops' point of view, the Commission had an immediate practical purpose. They were charged with the duty, as clearly stated in the office for the Consecration of Bishops, of "banishing and driving away all erroneous and strange doctrine", and they were confronted with the situation that there was no agreement on what was banned by the words "erroneous and strange". It was not an unreasonable hope that the Commission would give a clear guidance on the permissible variations of interpretation and where original thought and modern criticism should rightly be restrained by the bishops as guardians of the Faith.

The Report is now in print and I wish everyone who cares for religious truth would read it. I believe that the Commission almost succeeded and that its influence on opinion would have made for unity and concord if the archbishops and bishops had adopted and propagated the Report. Some of the members of the Commission, and I among them, hoped that one of the early results would be the drastic revision of the Thirty-nine Articles of Religion, but, alas, the opportunity was lost, the war came and new situations arose so that we are still saddled with an out-of-date and misleading doctrinal document to represent the teaching of the Church of England. One of the more encouraging developments of recent months is that the archbishops have appointed another Commission on Doctrine. I hope it will not rest until it has produced a statement of our version of the Christian Faith which modern educated persons can regard with respect or else, if after really earnest work and prayer they are unable to agree on one, let them give advice on how to live without special Articles of our own, relying only on the creeds of the Universal Church.

It is clear that one of the dominant purposes of the archbishops in setting up the Commission was a practical one. The conflicting currents in the Church of England had become violent. The extremes on either side aimed at purging their opposites from the Church and both agreed that the majority who were attached to the middle way and hoped that they were both Catholic and Reformed were feeble compromisers. The expressed aim of the Commission was to formulate the limits within which disagreements were tolerable. The members included theologians of all hues except the orange of Fundamentalist Protestantism. Most welcome to me was the inclusion of professors of philosophy—all laymen: A. E. Taylor, Professor in Edinburgh; Clement C. J. Webb, Nolloth Professor, Oxford;

Professor W. H. Moberly of Birmingham; and Will Spens, a chemist who was Master of Corpus Christi College, Cambridge. One wonders whether a comparable number of Anglican lay philosophers could be gathered today to serve on a doctrinal commission.

One wonders too, perhaps even more, whether a chairman could be found who could do anything like what William Temple did for the Commission. I was not among the "fans" of William Temple, but I always admired his ability and his wonderful power of clear thinking and effortless oratory. No one could doubt his profoundly sincere commitment to the cause of Christ and the Church. At the time when Cosmo Gordon Lang was Archbishop of Canterbury and Temple of York, I said, only half in jest, that the country would make a good bargain if it exchanged its Prime Minister and Chancellor for the two archbishops. I think perhaps my slight reservation may have been due to his loud and hearty laugh which grated on my ears, though to most ears it was, I suppose, like the sound of the trumpet. At least I may say that William Temple was a living refutation of a line of Pope's which had sometimes comforted me: "The loud laugh which speaks the empty mind". In Temple's presence that was palpably absurd.

William Temple had a prodigious memory, and was endowed too with a mind clear, probing and comprehensive. These qualities were most valuable to the Commission and Temple exercised them without stint for our benefit. Often, after a prolonged discussion in which several points of view had been advocated and could be adopted without patent heresy, he would take the documents which were relevant and work on them late into the night, coming back the following morning with a statement which we all could accept. I once said to him, after a brilliant piece of drafting from his pen, "If you had been at the Council of Nicaea, we need never have lost the Arians." I meant simply that he could have avoided the sharp break of excommunication for heresy by getting the conflicting doctrines more clearly expressed. Temple did not seem pleased with what I intended as congratulation.

The Doctrinal Commission was not only a means of my further education; it was an occasion of much happiness to me. The method of work by means of memoranda, circulated among members, and residential conferences of the whole Commission

provided for me, at least once in the year, several days of friendly
talk with men whose writings I had read and with opportunities
of leisurely discussion. Though we were profoundly serious
about the work in hand, my recollection is that our days were
filled with prayer and laughter. A frivolous picture comes into
my mind. I was sitting next to the Bishop of Ripon, one of the
brighter bishops, and we were reading a learned memorandum
in a full session. What it was about is now unknown I suppose
to anyone. I remember only the final words "Religious and
Septuagintal". The Bishop made only one comment; he pointed
out that the last phrase was a perfect end line for a limerick
and challenged me to compose one. I am ashamed to divulge
that I spent some time on this task and even more ashamed
of the feeble result:

> An old man who passed under a lintel
> Was knocked on the head by a quintal;
> His language, though terse
> And not couched in verse,
> Was religious and septuagintal.

Among the eminent men whom I was so glad to meet I think
Professor A. E. Taylor came first in order of preference. I had
studied his book on metaphysics and was indebted to it for
much enlightenment—as I thought then and still think, though
the fashion now in "with-it" philosophers is to condemn metaphysics as pseudo problems with meaningless answers. I nearly
opened my first conversation with the Professor by handing
my suitcase to him under the impression that he was a "gyp"
or porter at St. John's College, Cambridge, where members were
assembling for the first residential conference. Having avoided
that gaffe, I found myself that same evening with a group of
other members in Taylor's room, listening to him discoursing
almost without an interval for hours on the most varied subjects ranging, I remember, from the doctrine of the Holy
Trinity, through the poems of Ovid, to methods of brewing
beer. I will not deny that the copiousness of some contributions
to our discussions was sometimes hard to take and, when Taylor
was launched on a philosophical disquisition to be followed by
Rawlinson with a theologian's exposition, there was not much
time left for anyone else on that particular day. But after all,
when you have twenty learned men all most articulate and given

to dialectic, what can you expect? I for one am grateful for all that I learned by listening and for the skill of our chairman, who guided the flood of talk and memoranda towards a coherent Report.

Why cannot that Report which eventually came out of our labours be republished and, with some amendments, be accepted as sufficient for the present day? If we could answer this question, we should have a welcome light on our contemporary situation. I am one of the three survivors of the Commission which drew up the Report and I speak only for myself, but I am fairly certain that Bishop F. R. Barry would agree that somehow the times have left our findings behind. When I read the Report now, I have ambivalent feelings. I am still of the opinion that we did a good job and that the prayers which were offered by us and by many others that the Holy Spirit would guide us were answered. I wish with all my heart that our statement on Doctrine of the Church could be read by all educated persons—particularly by schoolmasters and schoolmistresses. But there remains the need for something more. Somehow the world of learning and scholarship has changed— not necessarily "moved on"—but changed since we wrote. The New Testament, it can be said, does not look quite the same now. Qumran, the Scrolls and their implications are a new factor. No doubt some weight must be allowed to this, but I do not think it is the dominant one. The plain fact is that theology is in sad straits because so many theologians do not believe in God.

The philosophers who belonged to our Commission were among the most respected professors of the period and they were all Anglican Christians believing in God, holding some version of ethical monotheism and affirming the metaphysical dogma that God the Creator is the sustainer of all that exists. In the main the prevailing philosophy of the universities allowed at least a primary importance to religion. Some of the Idealist thinkers at the time were in general agreement that religion, or the religious experience, was an eternal form of the Absolute. Today British philosophers, on the whole, are in revolt from metaphysics altogether and hold that metaphysical statements are unmeaning. Thus the traditional philosophical introduction to Christian theology is ruled out of court.

There are two possible policies which would logically be

consistent with the acceptance of this abdication of every claim that reason can throw any light on the ultimate nature of being and the universe. One is to give up the quest for understanding and accept the melancholy conclusion that the Riddle of the Universe is not only insoluble but nonsensical; the other is to turn to the "Revelations" which have played so remarkable a part in human history. Reality surely may be found in transcendent experiences rather than in intellectual speculation. Was not Jerome right when he said "It has not pleased the Lord to save his people by dialectic"? Though we did not understand the full significance of our findings, we had given some thought to the authority of Revelation. Just about the time when we published our Report, Karl Barth, the great Protestant systematic theologian, was writing the opening treatises of his massive exposition of biblical revelation, which totally rejected natural theology and gave no reason for believing that Revelation was true.

Looking back now, it seems to me that the whole episode of the Archbishops' Commission on Doctrine is an instance of the wonderful resources of the Anglican Church and the maddening ineffectiveness of its employment of them. To point to any advantage to the Church caused by the long exertions of so many busy and learned men would be difficult, and that there has been any at all a matter of faith rather than sight; but to me it was not barren. In estimating my debt to it, I include the friendship of one man whom I might never have met elsewhere, Wilfred Knox, brother of the famous Ronnie Knox. Wilfred was an Anglo-Catholic, a member of an Anglican Franciscan brotherhood and later a Fellow of Pembroke College, Cambridge, the author of two scholarly works on St. Paul. We differed in almost every respect, parentage, education, Churchmanship, temperament, yet by one of those strange affinities we were kindred spirits. I was always glad when I sat next to him and we could exchange comments. We laughed at the same things and detested the same things. Where he left me behind was the inner life of prayer. I learnt from him specially that a man could be a humorist and a sceptic and, at the same time, a saint who lived by faith. I wish I had met him earlier and known him longer.

I was not deeply involved in the 1928 revision of the Book of Common Prayer. I am no liturgiologist and I fear I was inclined to agree with an outrageous dictum of Dr. Headlam's, who wrote that the study of liturgiology and of Hebrew seemed to sap the intelligence. I am sure that this is not true of Hebrew. What study I was able to give to the text of the proposed revised Book of Common Prayer led me to agree with Archbishop Brillioth, the Lutheran Primate of Sweden, that the 1928 Book liturgy of the Eucharist was the finest liturgy in Christendom. I had nothing to do with the debates in Convocation on the Revision nor with the double rejection of the Book by the House of Commons. Though I was a modernist in theology, I found no particular difficulty in the symbolism of the Prayer Book and I found much to admire and love in its language. Certainly none of the new prayers in the 1928 Book was worthy to be compared with Cranmer's. Two things however troubled me deeply. The first was the movement which defeated the new Book. The loud voiced protests, which undoubtedly had their effect on the Commons vote, came from the two extreme parties in the Church. There was an unholy alliance between the extreme Protestants and the extreme Anglo-Catholics—the former because they feared the Mass and the latter because they feared they might be prevented from saying the Latin Mass in their churches. When the 1928 Book became legal, the chaos in episcopal regulation would, it was hoped, be halted and excuses for "supplementing" or "supplanting" the Holy Communion by the Roman liturgy would be abolished. Allied with this was my feeling of dismay at the optimism of the bishops. When the discussion on the Prayer Book was at its hottest, the Bishop of London, Dr. Winnington-Ingram, summoned a meeting of his clergy in the church of St. Martin-in-the-Fields. The church was packed and feeling ran high, largely in favour of the Revised Book. Two opposition speeches followed a conciliatory address from the chair by the Bishop. The Evangelical spoke as one who honestly felt that an attempt was being made to undo the blessed work of the reformers. One had heard all that he said before many times, but he was courteous and out to convince us by argument. The Anglo-Catholic speech came from a priest whom I knew and admired for his zeal and his wit—Maurice Child. He, like many other Anglo-Catholic extremists, while holding theoretically that episcopacy is of the essence of the Church, spoke very freely about the shortcomings of the bishops with whom he had to do. His speech shocked me by its insolent discourtesy. The only passage of his diatribe that I remember was a pointed interpretation of the parable of the Good Shepherd, applied to Anglican bishops in general and to Dr. Winnington-Ingram in particular, whom he designated as one of the false shepherds who had climbed into the fold by "some other way" and were misleading, or abandoning, the flock. Though not holding that bishops are so much the essence of the Church that there could be no valid ministry without them, I hold that they are of the *bene esse* of the Church and "fathers in God"; moreover, the bishop in this case was a Christian pastor who had inspired many people to live Christian lives and for whom I, with many others, had real affection. It affronted my sense of fitness to hear fanatical young priests laughing and applauding insolent sarcasms against their Father in God and I made a note that, on the first opportunity, I would tell him of my indignation. It happened that the opportunity occurred the next day and I advanced resolutely through a crowd of clerics who surrounded him. He forestalled me and my speech was never delivered. He said, "We had a wonderful meeting yesterday. I knew they were all behind me. The diocese is united: all enthusiastically on my side." The crowning irony of the situation was that the disorder in the London diocese was one of the facts which weighed against the 1928 Prayer Book in the debate in the House of Commons.

In this chapter about my further education, I have not sufficiently kept in mind the daily round of teaching and administration by which I suppose my mind was exercised and formed. One lesson, the topic touched upon by the Psalmist "Put not your trust in princes", stayed in my memory as a cautionary tale. The University of London, as I have already observed, was always under criticism and the object of reforming zeal. The reorganisation of the University which Haldane had proposed was taken in hand after the war by the eminent Oxford historian H. A. L. Fisher, who was President of the Board of Education in the Coalition Government. The idea of concentration by bringing more colleges into Bloomsbury in the vicinity of the new Senate House and the old University College was attractive and Fisher wholeheartedly supported it. One day, almost without warning, we at King's College received a letter from the Vice Chancellor to the effect that the Senate had decided to move King's College and would like to begin on preparation for building a new college in Bloomsbury without delay. Like most of my colleagues at King's College, I disliked the idea because of historical associations and also because I feared that the consequences of a move next door to University College might be a take-over campaign. But, as the head of the theological department of King's and the servant of the Council of the College, I had the responsibility of seeing that the Council could carry out the terms of the Charter and of the Act of Parliament constituting the King's College set-up, which secured the existence of a theological department in which the professors and tutors were members of the Church of England and prepared students for the ministry of that Church. Under the existing constitution, these rights were safeguarded by the fact that the land on which the College was built was held by the Corporation of King's College on a grant from the Crown in perpetuity so long as it was a college in which the doctrine and worship of the Church of England was taught and observed. The danger that we should be absorbed into the University and lose our independence was obvious.

An interview with Mr. Fisher was full of interest; his conversation was stimulating and his manner sympathetic. He seemed to understand my difficulty and assured me that, if the Council agreed to move, he could assure it that the Universities Grants Commission would finance the Council's part of the work in the theological department. I pointed out that up to that time it had been assumed that the U.G.C. could not subsidise denominational colleges. Fisher assured me that this would no longer be an obstacle and called on a senior civil servant who was with him at the interview to confirm his assurance. It was almost absurd to imagine that these two responsible authorities could be mistaken on a matter of principle and still more that they were deliberately misleading me. But to be quite safe, I decided to try an experiment. If the Grants Commission could finance King's College theological department in a new college which was working on precisely the same principles and constitution as the old one, there could be no principle which precluded the Commissioners from assisting the department at once. I therefore wrote to the secretary of the Commission, applying for grants to increase the salaries of theological professors. I had no written reply, but the secretary asked me to see him. He spoke at some length on the reasons why my

application could not be successful and why to go further with
it would be not only a waste of time but unwise in the interests
of King's College. None of this was new to me of course, but I
asked him if there was any possibility of the policy being
changed for example to facilitate the reorganisation of London
University. He emphatically assured me that any change of
policy in this matter was quite out of the question. I thanked
him for making the situation so clear to me, particularly because
it convinced me that assurances given to me by the President
of the Board of Education were baseless and I must advise the
Council of King's College to put no faith in them. He said,
"You are a very clever young man." I do not feel ashamed of
laughing over this and thinking just once I really was clever.
At the time, I summed it all up in the words of the Psalmist,
"We are escaped like a bird out of the snare of the fowler."

To round off this story, a gratuitous legal opinion came to
me from my learned friend Lord Justice Atkin. After the Sunday
morning service in Gray's Inn Chapel, I walked down Chancery
Lane with him and told him we had to answer a letter from
the University, knowing that he was a member of the Court.
He said "Yes, I was present when the letter was passed by the
Court and I thought it would be interesting if you in King's
College simply acknowledged receipt of the letter and asked on
what legal authority the University claimed to be acting." I
could not persuade the Council to be quite so terse in its reply,
but in effect the question was the answer. And so far as I know
it was never answered. The idea of moving King's College
faded out and it remains in the Strand to this day. But no
attempt to preserve valued possessions is ever completely
successful. The precious object changes, for all our pains to
keep it as it was. King's College, as I write, is in process of
being enlarged and already the entrance, which so many have
passed through and remembered all the rest of their lives, has
been swallowed up. The College is in danger of being blown
out beyond all recognition. The importance of limitation in
beloved institutions is overlooked and foolish Old Boys may be
infected by the modern superstition that to be big is the same
thing as being great. When I was Dean, I agreed with Ernest
Barker, who held that expansion in numbers beyond a certain
limit, even if space were available, would change the ethos of
the College. I have the same opinion now.

When the year 1932 dawned, I had no suspicion that it would be my last year in the academic world. I was very busy and very happy. My ambition did not reach beyond the office of Professor, which still seems to me one of the most honourable titles one can bear. Two objects of endeavour kept me going— to make the Theological Faculty of King's College renowned as a great centre of Christian thought and, for myself, that I might write at least one book on Christian theology which would help in the necessary work of expressing the Christian faith in the symbols and thought-forms of the 20th century. Perhaps stronger even than these aspirations was to give my three clever children the best possible education.

The curse of university life, from the standpoint of the dons, is the proliferation of committees which steal time and energy from the proper activities of teaching and research. I was on at least twelve committees which were active, and at the end of my time as Professor and Dean I was chairman of four of them. I do not say that I was bored by this committee work; most of it was interesting and necessary, but it was exhausting. In the latter part of my deanship, the College realised that to provide me with adequate secretarial assistance was really an economy and that I needed more than just a shorthand typist. What a relief it was when I had educated women who could take some of the correspondence and replies to questions off my shoulders. I should mention too in this connection that my dear friend Richard Hanson, as Chaplain of the College, was indefatigable in matters concerning applications for entry to the College and in interviewing. I am convinced that intelligent and devoted secretaries have made the successes of many eminent persons and saved from disgrace still more stupid ones. Two of my secretaries stand out in my list of those to whom I owe gratitude. Miss Sandbach Marshall was a pupil who took the B.D. degree and was engaged in post-graduate study. She came to my assistance for an almost nominal emolument and not only presided over the secretarial work of typists and kept the minutes of the meetings of the Professorial Board, but collaborated with me in the translation of Schleiermacher's *Christliche Glaube* into English.

H. R. Mackintosh, the eminent Edinburgh Professor of Theology, gathered a small group of theological teachers to co-operate with him in producing an English version of

Schleiermacher's massive work on dogmatic theology. Schleiermacher was a German professor, a member of the Romantic movement and a popular preacher in Berlin—all qualities which encouraged copiousness of utterance. As a preacher he was lucid enough, but in the book we were translating he was writing as a professor in the full Teutonic academic style, with sentences which might be a page long and a method of exposition which needed understanding if one wanted to comprehend his argument. I could not have completed my allotted portion, which was the vital one—the doctrine of the Being of God— in time but for Miss Sandbach Marshall's co-operation. We would translate several pages literally and then the difficulties really began. What we had was apparently nonsense. Only by concentrated labour did we get something which made sense in English and indeed I wondered sometimes whether what we found was Schleiermacher's sense or ours. Years later, in 1939, when I was lecturing in Marburg, the Professor of Church History, Siegfried, told me that he always read Schleiermacher in our translation because he found the English version much easier to understand than the German text. None of our team was paid a penny for this hard labour. We did not expect any profit, except perhaps the honour of having some part in a scholarly enterprise, but we did not get much of that because no sooner was our translation published than Schleiermacher fell out of fashion as the great Protestant theologian, even in Scotland, and his place was taken by Karl Barth.

Miss Sandbach Marshall was one of those women, more numerous then than they are today, who did not need to earn their living and studied theology primarily because the subject interested them. At King's in my time, there were several. I remember one young woman who consulted me on how she could become a really cultured person by studying for a degree in the University. After considering many possibilities, we came to the conclusion that theology, studied in a liberal and comprehensive spirit, can be for some the answer to the question, What shall I do to become a really educated person? Miss Sandbach Marshall was devoted to Rudolf Otto and his "numinous" religion. She kept in touch with Marburg and the worship which Otto directed in the little chapel (Michelschen), well known to many English and Scottish students in those days. The sudden death of Otto and the swift oncoming of the world war shattered so many things precious in her eyes. She remained in London and died during the war. I deeply regret that I was so much occupied with the defence and preservation of St. Paul's that I did not search her out.

Miss Grace Stewart Somerville was the perfect professional secretary, as well as a loyal friend. She had been with Julian Huxley and was the daughter of an eminent Scottish divine— a staunch Presbyterian, so she knew how to write to theologians and to professors and soon learned how to converse with bishops. Her competence carried me through the last years of my time at King's College, by seeing that I was at the right place at the right time, with the right papers and a notion of what the meeting was about. She was with me when the letter came from Ramsay MacDonald, the Prime Minister, informing me that he wished to recommend me to the King for appointment to the Deanery of Exeter. Once more in my life an unexpected choice was presented to me. I do not think I was aware that the Deanery was vacant. I certainly had never considered the possibility that I might be Dean of Exeter, a city which I knew very little about. My wife and I realised that the question was not simply whether we were attracted by the place but whether it was possible and right that we should leave the university world, in which we had a recognised place and on the whole were happy in our relations with students, and start on a different line altogether.

I have the privilege of quoting from a letter which Miss Somerville has written in response to a request that she would write something about her memories of our work together at King's:

"I clearly remember a meeting of the Theological Faculty Board, with yourself in the chair. A heated argument arose on whether Procedure A or Procedure B be adopted. You took no part and the temperature rose. In a slight lull, you roused yourself and said serenely, 'Well, I think we are all agreed' and gave Procedure C, of which no mention had been made. All murmured contentedly, 'Yes, yes, that's just what I meant.' Calm was restored."

In our perplexity, a blunt word from Miss Somerville had no little weight. "I shall hate to lose you from the College, but I think if you stay here much longer you will burst."

CHAPTER 8

Changing Course

The choice which Margaret and I had to make went deeper than questions of expediency or convenience. Beyond the consideration of our personal happiness and mundane concern about cost of living in new and unfamiliar circumstances lay the fact that, if we chose to leave King's College to go to Exeter, we should change direction. I think we were both convinced that we were fulfilling a vocation and certainly I was happy, though perhaps overworked. I am not confident that Margaret was so happy, because the conditions of my work during term time kept me very busy and she used to complain that only in the vacations did we really have any family life. We had to make up our minds in a short time while our current affairs went on just as usual; my lectures and my correspondence did not cease conveniently while I pondered on the future. I suppose everyone has experienced the curious psychological process in which one is horribly perplexed and undecided; things flit through one's memory, one seems to be day-dreaming most of the time when one ought to be pursuing an orderly train of thought: and then, without knowing quite why, one is aware that the choice has been made—almost as if it had made itself. Of course, if one has been praying for guidance, it is reasonable to believe that this is it, but I know that something like this can happen to persons who do not consciously pray for guidance.

Should we change course and go to Exeter? We reflected that the new direction would not be so different from the old as we had feared. In those days, it was quite widely recognised that deans ought to be scholars and there were notable examples at the time, among them Dr. Inge of St. Paul's, Dr. Hastings Rashdall of Carlisle, and Dr. Hensley Henson of Durham. With regard to my experience of cathedral services and organisation, I felt (mistakenly as it happened) that I was sufficiently informed because I was at the time one of the two Canons Theologian attached to Liverpool Cathedral—my colleague in this office was my friend Dr. Grensted, whom I had worked with on many bodies including the Commission on Doctrine. In fact, however, Liverpool Cathedral was so atypical as to be a misleading model. It was half-built and, instead of being an old building with hoary traditions and historical associations, it was a great venture of faith carried forward towards completion by the enthusiasm, and co-operation of remarkable men, clerical and lay.

It was the duty of the Canons Theologian to lecture in the Cathedral when called on by the Bishop once or twice a year. To me, Dr. David, the very forward-looking Bishop of Liverpool, assigned lecturing to the junior clergy, specially the deacons and the newly ordained priests. I enjoyed this, but my audiences did not always show marked appreciation of my efforts. Some of the fledgling priests thought me a heretic and others a man of no learning. The Bishop was not to be ignored however. To those who would not attend my lectures, he wrote a note saying, "If you do not go to Dr. Matthews' lectures, I must ask you to come and consult with me on how you can be helped to serve God with your mind." Nearly all chose my lectures as the lesser of two evils.

On the last occasion when I functioned as canon, the junior clergy staged what I can only suppose was a kind of good-humoured protest. There were four or five lectures, each one followed by questions. At the end of each lecture, a member of the audience, a different one every time, asked, "Do you believe in a personal devil?", a question totally irrelevant to the theme of my lecture, which I declined to answer until, at the last lecture I replied: "The anxiety of Liverpool clergy to be assured of the existence of the devil is strange. I think the well-known theologian Mr. Punch throws some light on the subject. Some years ago, I remember, he had a picture of a small girl being severely reproved by her mother for rudeness to Nurse. 'You know who puts these wicked thoughts into your mind,' says the mother; 'Well,' says the child, 'Satan may have told me to scratch, but spitting was quite my own idea.' I always wonder how much is really my own idea." I was relieved when laughter, not often heard in the Lady Chapel, closed the incident.

Liverpool Cathedral, though no model for ancient foundations, was then an exciting place. While Dwelly was Dean, there was always enthusiasm in the air and many young men and women were around, busy with many kinds of enterprise. Liverpool, being somewhat "orange" in ecclesiastical allegiance, did not take kindly to the wearing of gorgeous colours by its clergy; Dwelly dressed them in sober black and white, but put lay officials, vergers, sidesmen, servers, beadles and many other functionaries in most of the colours of the rainbow. In those days, the gospel was diligently preached. Dwelly and the residentiary canon, Charles Raven, had built up a great congregation for a people's service on Sunday evenings at 8 p.m., which consisted of congregational singing of hymns and address, followed by prayer. Raven had recently left Liverpool to return to Cambridge, but he often came back to Liverpool and proved the truth of what I had come to believe: that a man who had a struggle with doubts and difficulties and was thinking all the time on the problems could often be the most powerful preacher, just because his mind was never at rest. Raven spoke to modern men where they were—perplexed but seeking—in words which they understood.

My happiness in Liverpool Cathedral was somewhat disturbed by a circumstance on which I will not dwell because I never understood its cause. But it must be touched upon, because it had no small part in my reflections on my own future. This troublesome circumstance was the disagreement, or rather the almost intolerable tension, between Dr. David, the Bishop of Liverpool, and Mr. Dwelly who had just been appointed the first Dean of the unfinished Cathedral, to the building and establishment of which both had given devoted leadership. I admired and loved both these men and was naturally embarrassed because each would talk freely with me, while for years they were not on speaking terms with each other. I know it is almost unbelievable, but I must repeat that to this day I do not know the cause of this quarrel or what it was about. One fact, however, was only too evident—that the disagreement of these two good men was a weakness in the Cathedral's witness to the Christian faith and, if only they had been able to go forward in brotherly unity as in old days, the Church and the City of Liverpool would have had reason to be thankful for the Cathedral even more than it has now. The lesson, I hope, was

not entirely lost on me; at least I can claim that, in the two
Cathedrals in which I have been Dean, I have lived at peace
with the Bishops—I might even say "in brotherly union and
concord".

Ironically, when I went to Exeter, my experience at Liverpool, so far from impressing people in that diocese, seemed to
alarm them. One of the Prebendaries, when I was duly installed
there, spread the terrible rumour that I wanted to disturb the
centuries-old customs of Exeter by "Liverpudlian Innovations".

Perhaps the question of my mental and spiritual fitness was
the most difficult to answer, as it was certainly the most important. The reader may remember that, in my student days, I
lamented the loss of "a heart that prayed". That sense of loss
was never wholly overcome. As Dean of the College, I was not
negligent in attendance at services. On every morning during
term, I was present at the Holy Communion service in the
Hostel Chapel and at morning prayer in the College Chapel.
I did not feel bored by the constant round of corporate worship.
From a child, I had actually enjoyed church services, and even
at periods when I was theoretically an agnostic I did not cease
to join in public worship. Of course, I did not call myself an
agnostic after I was ordained and I never ceased intellectually
to believe in God. But I lived with men who were men of
prayer in a sense that I could only faintly comprehend: men
of whom it was truly said that they had a wonderful "prayer
life". My failure to advance further was partly due to a perfectly
justifiable scruple. Though prayer is not always intercessory,
we begin by asking something from God and, when instinctively we turn to Him in times of anxiety, fear and depression,
we hope that He will give us what we think we need. Even if
we say "Thy will be done", does not the fact that we are praying
indicate that we are afraid that God's will may be sadly mis-
informed unless we respectfully represent to Him our views
of the situation? Of course I know there are answers to this
kind of talk and I am very sure the mind of God is beyond
our understanding, but when I come to pray for other people,
and also for myself, I think, "God knows better than I what
is good for me and for my friend and God loves me and my
friend more than we love each other. Is not the only logical
thing to leave the issue in God's hands?" So my prayer of
intercession really is a kind of thinking about my friend, or

whoever is the subject of my concern, in the presence of God.

Immanuel Kant had a curious scruple about private prayer. He thought that any rational man would be ashamed to be seen praying alone. The great philosopher, who had such a profound influence in modern Christian theology, was at variance with the teaching of Jesus on prayer, which has little to say in favour of public prayer, but much on that which is solitary and unseen. No Christian today would, I suppose, agree with Kant on this point, but there is something to be said about private prayer. Sometimes I have thought that men of much prayer have apparently deteriorated in character, instead of improving as a result of their devotions. We can all see by looking into ourselves how this might be. Some auto-suggestion enters into prayer and some methods of training in prayer are calculated to encourage auto-suggestion. I do not condemn auto-suggestion as such; on the contrary, I think that we might profitably use it to help moral development so long as we know what we are doing. Meditation in various forms is closely allied with prayer, and mystics like Evelyn Underhill have opened the "mystic way" to many ordinary people. I will not say that I have no mystical experience, but my progress in the way has been pitifully limited and I think it is because my intellect is restless. Too often, when I have tried to meditate on God and his attributes in order to attain personal communion with Him, or with "the Absolute" as I have sometimes expressed my purpose, my discursive intelligence turns over the idea, all kinds of interesting questions arise and I engage in a kind of internal dialogue with myself so that, at the end of my so-called meditation, I have had an interesting time and perhaps have understood some theological notion better than before—but how much more? Meditation for me is largely thinking about God and myself while trying to remember that he is present. Hegel's saying, I think in reply to his landlady who was distressed that such a well-behaved professor did not go to church, *"Das denken ist auch Gottesdienst"*, has sometimes comforted me, but after all I did not neglect *Gottesdienst* and the quality of my *denken* was open to question. I concluded that my inner life was shallow and prayed that it might be deepened in my ministry at Exeter.

No one of average intelligence who kept in touch with the drift of the times, and particularly of the culture of the western world, could miss the truth that religion was passing through a

King's College hostel in Vincent Square

With a group of senior students of the theological faculty in 1931

Procession leaving Exeter Cathedral after the Thanksgiving Service to commemorate its 800th anniversary. Sunday, June 25th, 1933

critical period in which many things which had been taken as foundation certainties were shaken or almost destroyed. If he was a seeker by nature, he could not accept the idea of "sacrifice of the intellect" as a religious duty and every doctrine of the faith of his fathers appeared to be questionable. When I had adjusted myself in part to the situation by admitting that faith is a kind of tension between belief and doubt or, perhaps better, the constant overcoming of unbelief, I often rallied my spirits by dwelling on a sentence in one of Thomas Carlyle's essays to the effect that the time has come when we must learn to regard many things which we had taken to be actual facts as eternal truths. At the crossroads where I was standing, I looked back to reassure myself that I had a gospel to preach.

A list of published works was evidence that I had been think-ing and, as it seemed to me, that I had something rational and important to say. The first really considerable contribution was the publication of my Boyle lectures in 1921 by Macmillan, which I ventured to submit successfully to the University of London as a thesis for the degree of Doctor of Divinity. The lectureship's title appealed to me. What a romantic privilege to write under the aegis and endowment of Robert Boyle, who is described on his monument as "The Father of Chemistry and the Uncle of the Earl of Cork"! The 16th-century scientific pioneer who had given his name to a "law of nature" and endowed a lectureship to maintain the reasonableness of religion was, I thought, an admirable figurehead for my little voyage on the turbulent sea of theological controversy. *Studies in Christian Philosophy* had a good reception, though Macmillan's did not express any very great hopes for it and I believe it was only the strong advocacy of my friend, Dr. Relton's father, who "read" my MSS for the publisher, that turned the scale in my favour. A second and revised edition, which included a reply to some very cogent criticism by Dr. F. R. Tennant, appeared in 1928 and the book remained in print up to the outbreak of war. That Tennant took so much notice of my thesis is a happy memory and I have another bond of union with him— neither of us was invited to give the Gifford Lectures which are supposed to be devoted to the defence and exposition of "natural religion" or "rational belief". I say nothing about my own eligibility for the lectureship, except that I have written quite a lot on the subject; of Tennant, any critic of sufficient learning to have a right to an opinion would say he was the outstanding author of the day in the field of English philosophical theology. At least both Tennant and I could claim that we wrote about the subject of which Lord Gifford founded his lecture to advance the study, while some of the Gifford Lectures were almost irrelevant and at least one Gifford lecturer explicitly denied that there was such a subject and held that time spent on lecturing on it was not only wasted but promoted a dangerous illusion.

I have read my book again forty-eight years later and, on the whole, I am not ashamed of it. Faults of style and possible objections too lightly skated over are there and I feel the whole book is written by a man who has read a lot but is, so to speak, "rather young for his age"—trying to write like a professor and doctor but rather overdoing it. The touch of pomposity is not absent, and pedantry, which may pass in an academic thesis, ought to have been purged out of the published book. It was quite unnecessary to quote St. John in Greek and a modern scholar in German—particularly when there was a "howler" in the German.

No doubt the book is "outmoded", a fate which it shares with most of the writings of Plato and not a little of Aristotle. The habit of using this word as a "dismissive" expression is, in my opinion, a sign of philosophical decadence. I suppose it is a consequence of the fact that modern philosophy in English-speaking nations has, on the whole, lost the conception of Eternal Truth and thus is forced to concentrate attention on contemporary truth, truth that is not outmoded. But unfortunately, if there is no such thing as eternal truth, there cannot be any sense in "contemporary" truth; so at least it seems to me, and thus I do not understand in what sense modern philosophy claims to be true even when it is not yet "outmoded".

I have no retractions to make concerning the substance of this book though, if I were writing now, I should probably choose somewhat different questions to study. The discussion of the relation between religion and philosophy still seems to me both important and on the right lines. The contention that Hegel's triad of art, religion and philosophy, the three "forms" of the Spirit, should be revised so as to make religion the synthesis of art and philosophy still seems plausible. If anyone reads my book now, I would ask him to note carefully that I regard all three "forms" as growing towards fuller expression. Philosophy and religion have more to reveal of their content and perhaps when that process is nearer its end they will be seen to be one.

This first attempt at writing on the philosophy of religion at length brings out, I think, a tendency which I can see now prevailed throughout my development. My religion was predominantly intellectual. From the time as far back as I can remember, when I lay awake wondering what made me different from anyone else and similar questions, my hope in my religious experience has been to know not only the answers but what—or who—is behind all this confused show of passing existence. Salvation to me has always been a kind of enlightenment. I fear that my ministry has often been less useful than it might have been, because I did not feel deeply in my spirit the need of a sinner for the assurance of forgiveness. When I ought to have been answering his question, What must I do to be saved? I have been offering to him reasons for believing in the existence of God. I must add, however, that the intellectual believer has one safeguard against boredom, for if one begins to think about God the subject proves to be inexhaustible. It can be a step towards that supreme duty which is so hard to fulfil—that of loving God.

In 1925 Macmillan's published a "popular" book called in England *The Gospel and the Modern Mind* and in America *God and This Troubled World*. It was a somewhat expanded version of a course of sermons preached in St. Bartholomew's, Madison Avenue, New York, in August, 1924, intended for the edification of students at the summer vacation course of Columbia University. How far they achieved their purpose, I cannot tell. The first Sunday was a disturbing experience, because I had not been forewarned about the possible reaction of my congregation. No sooner had I entered the clergy vestry at the end of the service, when some of its members followed me in a state of excitement which might have indicated either approval or detestation. An emotional lady seemed to be determined either to assault or embrace me, while repeating the words, "My, doctor, that was a crackerjack!" It was with relief that I gathered the word indicated enthusiastic approval. A more severe trial of nerve was in store, however. In the course of my talks on *Substitutes for Christianity*, Bernard Shaw's religion of the Life Force and his attack on what he called "Crosstianity" naturally had a prominent share of attention and, no less naturally, I had to explain the teaching which I was criticising. *The Herald Tribune* was good enough to take an interest in my sermons and sent a reporter who evidently took down my exposition of Shaw and did not stay to hear my refutation. When I opened my newspaper on Monday, I read headlines which to my horror I found applied to me: "Famous English Divine finds Apostles Disagreeing: Latest Phase of Modernist Controversy: What Will Bishops Do?" I had scarcely taken in the meaning of these words when the telephone rang and a voice said, "I guess you would like press cutting coverage from all over the United States", to which I replied, "I never want to see another American paper as long as I live."

The disaster was mitigated by the fact that no bishops were apparently reading the daily press at the time and for once I applauded the habit of all the senior clergy and ministers to vanish from the cities during the summer months. Floods of letters came—so many that I gave up the attempt even to read them all and my wife said she was no theologian. I tried to deal with one very impressive document from a society in Los Angeles, which stated my damnation, and that of all other believers in organic evolution, was certain, but I made the mistake of trying to be ironical and simply confused my hearers. One lesson I have learned by many years of public speaking: it is, never be ironical in a foreign country and even in your own country try it only on carefully selected audiences.

The other adventures in this our first visit to the U.S.A. are out of place in a chapter devoted to theological studies but it would be ungracious not to say how friends sprang up all around in St. Bartholomew's Church, which we always remembered with affection and specially Mr. Lane, to whom I dedicated the book.

Liverpool Lectures gave me opportunities to think out loud on the problems of theology, and the Theological Lecture Society printed some of these essays. In the twenties, I published booklets on *The Idea of Revelation, The Psychological Approach to Religion* (1923), *Is God a Person?* and a long paper in a composite volume edited by Sir James Marchant on the doctrine of the Incarnation. The volume was entitled *The Future of Christianity* and I thought my task was to take account of the new tendencies in Philosophy, particularly Bergson and the Italian Idealists, Croce and Gentile. This brief work caused me much anxiety and I fear that it contributed very little to the enlightenment of the public. Nor did the experts pay much attention to it, for the philosophy which was in fashion when I wrote soon fell out of fashion and today its once famous exponents are "outmoded". I continue however not only to believe in the Incarnation, but also that the "outmoded" Bergson, Croce and Gentile have something still to say to us. After the war I returned to the subject and my Maurice Lectures, *The Problem of Christ in the Twentieth Century* (1949) are an expansion of the original essay. In the twenties the conviction grew steadily that a rational doctrine of Revelation, and of Incarnation as the culmination of Revelation, was needed and that the lack of them constituted a threat to the future of the Church.

When I was transplanted from London to Exeter my mind needed some leisure to bring order and proportion into my thinking. The constant demand on the attention involved in academical work was relaxed in Exeter and for a brief period I had mental peace.

CHAPTER 9

Exeter: Paradisal Interlude

In retrospect, the three years which I spent in Exeter as Dean of the Cathedral stand out as happy beyond all others and, for that reason, they are clear in memory as it were with a light of their own. Margaret felt this even more deeply than I and never ceased in the urban scenes of Ludgate Hill to long for the peace of Exeter and its friendly spirit. I think from the outset we both fell in love with the Cathedral and still to me its interior is dearer than almost any other. But really one should not compare buildings which are so different in style as Exeter and St. Paul's. Margaret was quite right when she said, trying to do justice to Wren, "This is a magnificent building, but it is a temple to a different God—the God of mathematics." I wonder what God Exeter Cathedral is built for. Could one say, without being pagan, "to the God of Springtime"? When I go into Exeter Cathedral, if the sun is shining, I always think of a wood in spring when the buds are on the point of bursting. The arches of the long unbroken roof, partly interrupted by the choir screen with the organ on it, somehow suggest the joyful mystery of life. But, though we were drawn by the beauty of the Cathedral and its setting in the historic city, we could not help some anxiety and some regret. The only time in my life when I left a position gladly was when I retired from the service of the Westminster Bank. That was opening a door to freedom and to spiritual and intellectual adventure; all the other changes have meant an end to part of one's life and to part of oneself. Most of all, I felt this when the students and staff of King's College, including professors and college porters, said goodbye to me with such overwhelming expressions of affection and with presents which came from men and women who were none of them rich and most of them chronically "hard up". I felt ashamed that I had not done more for the College, and perhaps a little that I was deserting it.

Another emotion was fear that enthusiastic students might cause my violent end. One evening in the autumn term in 1931, a visitor might have seen a disorderly triumphant procession of young men carrying me on their shoulders along the Strand. I hoped I looked happy, but I did not feel it, and when finally they carried me back into the College, up some stone stairs to a balcony where, for a few agonising moments, I was acclaimed by the company I prayed hard that they would put me back on my feet.

Among messages of goodwill on my new appointment, I was glad to have a stringent comment from Dr. Graham Wallas of the London School of Economics, with whom I had skirmished in the Senate on the subject of professors of theology in the University. He wished me well and warned me to remember that I was one of the few persons in England who could tell the truth without fear of consequences. "Be sure that you use this privilege well," he enjoined. He meant, of course, that the Letters Patent issued on October 30th, 1931, gave to me the deanery of Exeter and all its rights and privileges "for the term of his natural life" and that, so long as I committed no criminal offence and avoided the bankruptcy court, no one could touch me. Fortunately, my conscience never compelled me to take advantage of this immunity.

To hand over to someone else an institution for which one has been responsible is not easy, at least I have not found it so. I have remained "committed" to some extent to all the institutions which I have served in a responsible capacity. My close friend Richard Hanson was to follow me in the office of dean. I could not help thinking of the possible difficulties which might arise. I would have done better no doubt to restrict myself to my own problems.

The deanery at Exeter was the problem there. My predecessor Dr. Gamble had employed nine members on his domestic staff and, when one looked into the matter, it was clear that to conduct the deanery on the same lines as his would require at least seven full-time domestic workers. We had evidently to cut down the deanery and it was plain that the only way to do this was to cut off the 18th-century wing and make it a separate house. My friend, the architect of King's College hostel, produced a plan which I submitted to the Chapter. The number of "consents" which were required was formidable for, beside the Chapter, the Bishop and the Ecclesiastical Commissioners had to agree. Fortunately for me, the secretary of the Commissioners at that time was a former schoolfellow, Sir Sidney Downing, and that we had this youthful connection emboldened me to seek his advice. I took no step which he had not approved. Without that approval, the whole scheme would have foundered, because the lawyer who was the Chapter clerk held very strongly that the plan which I was proposing to the Chapter was *ultra vires*. A dramatic and painful meeting of the Chapter, however, settled the controversy. The Chapter clerk stated his case fully, but I was able in reply to read a telegram received that morning from the secretary of the Ecclesiastical Commissioners which pronounced that the plan submitted by me was perfectly legal and, in his opinion, most desirable.

The alteration to the deanery was not considerable and the wing, thus cut off, provided an excellent dwelling for one of the priest vicars. My satisfaction was complete when my friend and former pupil Marcus Knight and his wife were the first occupants. As I write, they are almost on the same spot—now in the deanery. A superstitious comment on this transaction is in place here. The famous deanery ghost of a mediaeval nun is alleged to have been annoyed by these changes, and persons sensitive to psychic phenomena claim that the deanery is less uncanny than it used to be. The financing of this building operation and reconstruction was provided partly by a loan from the Commissioners, secured on the income of the dean and repaid over twenty years, and partly by about £800 from my own savings. I comforted myself by the reflection that I was providing for the rest of our lives. We little thought that in three years' time a similar situation would confront us at St. Paul's. I mention these details not as ground for complaint, but to remove the popular illusion that deans of cathedrals have no financial anxieties.

The salient feature of our entry to our new life in Exeter, as we saw it, was the thoroughly friendly and Christian spirit of all the persons concerned, and particularly of the four residentiary canons who composed the Chapter. A long time after I had left Exeter, I learned why this kind of co-operation was so marked from the first. When the Crown appointed me dean,

I was an unknown quantity. I doubt if any member of the Chapter had heard of me. It appeared that I was much younger than any of them and that my background was different from theirs. Instead of combining in advance to keep the strange intruder in his place, they did the opposite. They held a meeting before I was installed, to agree on how I should be received. They recognised that I might have new ideas which were not attractive to them, some ideas perhaps derived from Liverpool and some inspired by "Modernism", and they resolved to do all they could to back me and to pray for me. This spirit of charity and fellowship prevailed and, perhaps even more than the beauty of the Cathedral and the ancient city, made the three years in Exeter golden in our memories.

The installation enchanted me. Though the day was early January and cloudy, fitful watery sunlight shone on the ceremonies at the entrance to the close. I was thrilled by the civic procession of the mayor preceded by the cap of maintenance, recalling mediaeval times, and the sheriff with aldermen. I managed to say my piece with a loud voice and throughout the service in the Cathedral, relying on the dean's virger, made no outstanding mistake. One interesting item in the proceedings deserves to be recorded because it would be a pity of it were ever given up. Though appointed by Letters Patent from the Crown, I was also elected to the office by the Greater Chapter, consisting of the canons and prebendaries. The election was twofold —first to prebendary and then to dean. This custom goes back, of course, to pre-Reformation times and is continued in spite of a special act of parliament which took away the right of election after the Chapter had won a law suit in the House of Lords.

The installation was the installation of an innocent, in the sense of an ignorant and guileless individual, and I think the bishop and the diocesan registrar got me to sign a document which had no authority. In St. Mary Major Church, which is only a few yards from the Cathedral, a curious ceremony was held to which I was summoned by the registrar. At the ceremony the registrar read a legal document which might be taken to mean that I admitted the bishop had some right in the Cathedral other than those laid down in the statutes. The document was, I am convinced, concocted by Mr. Michelmore, the registrar, and was quite out of order, because it ended with the words "God save the King"—a thing which no ecclesiastical document is likely to do. Whether I signed the document or not I cannot remember and it does not matter, for it was out of order; I am almost certain that I never paid the three guineas which the lawyers demanded for this otiose service.

The installation brought me into contact with the succentor and the master of the choir school, Mr. Llewellyn, and Mr. Langhorne, and with Miss Geraldine Longridge. With all of these I was to have almost daily contact and it was important, I thought, that I should be on good terms with them. One of the first topics which concerned them was a humiliating one. I was too short. Compared with all the other Cathedral clergy, with canons, prebendaries and minor canons, I was such a pigmy that I could not wear any of the copes in the place. Miss Longridge was called in to do an emergency operation to prevent me from looking ridiculous. I think it was then that I asked the question, "What is a chasuble?" which was passed round as an indication of my Protestant bigotry, my ignorance or my flippancy, according to taste. I was not really ignorant, but I thought I would indicate where my interests lay. At the beginning of my ministry in Exeter, I thought it was evident that the worship of the Cathedral was beautifully ordered and interferences with its settled course would be harmful at least until I had much more experience. I thought too that probably the Cathedral, like many others, was too inward-looking and too little concerned with the Kingdom of God in this troubled world—as it was then the world of the great slump and the unemployed in England. I never cared very much what was worn in church and it seemed to me that the vestiarian controversy which breaks out from time to time in the Anglican Communion is a childish waste of time. I believe that, in the three years of my ministry there, by the grace of God I did have some slight influence in widening the horizons of the faithful.

The lack of a secretary soon made me feel that chaos was imminent. King's College had provided a first-rate one and thereby ruined any aptitude I might have had to keep my correspondence in order. This practical problem was wonderfully solved by Miss Longridge, who lived in the Close and worked for the Cathedral. She became my voluntary secretary and I am understating the facts if I say that without her help, both with correspondence and typing as well as driver of my car, I could not have done half of what I did.

The Bishop of Exeter Lord William Cecil and his wife Lady
Florence were most kind in their welcome to one who, I am
sure, had come to them as a complete surprise. They invited us
to stay with them at Barton Place (where they lived, on the
outskirts of Exeter) for the installation and included in their
hospitality Dr. Headlam Bishop of Gloucester, who remarked
characteristically, "I felt I must come to see you on the last day
when you are a reasonable human being. My experience is that,
when a man is installed as dean of a cathedral, he becomes pre-
judiced and pigheaded." The beginning of our happy and
friendly association with Bishop Cecil and his wife was not without its alarming moments, which were, however, mostly endured
by my wife. Dr. Headlam and I were out at tea-time on the
day before the installation and she had a tête-à-tête session with
the Bishop, who seemed to be putting her through some kind of
test. As they sat down, he threw some powder on the fire, which
caused its flames to turn bright green. "Nice colour," said the
Bishop. "Yes, copper sulphate," said my wife, feeling that she
had vindicated the genuineness of her B.Sc. degree. Shortly
after, when crumpets had appeared, two rats came out of holes
in the floor and advanced towards the Bishop who tossed pieces
of crumpet to them. My wife fortunately had no fear of animals,
though she drew the line at rats. Feeling that she must betray no
weakness, she continued eating crumpets, making no reference
to the rats. The Bishop himself drew her attention to them,
remarking that they were intelligent and could be friendly
animals, to which she agreed. From that time onward, the
Bishop and she were on excellent terms. He had inherited from
his father, the Conservative Prime Minister, an interest in
science, though not his father's experimental curiosity. He was
a regular reader of *Nature* and frequently quoted it in sermons
—not always happily. He had, however, one quality of the
great scientific pioneers; he was always ready to learn and to
change his mind when good reason showed him wrong. Once he
made great play in an address with an article in *Nature*, but
misunderstood it and was both amused and grateful when my
wife convinced him that the article in question concluded the
very opposite of what he had supposed.

William Cecil was a great eccentric and the affectionate
nickname that his fellow bishops bestowed on him, "Love in a
Mist", was appropriate enough. I could fill this chapter with

amusing stories about his absent-mindedness, all of them true, but that would miss the essential truth about the man. The essential truth is that he was a great Christian and a great bishop. A cleverly written book by an American woman, who spent a year or two in the University College while I was living in the deanery, purported to give an outsider's view of Exeter, including its bishop and his wife. The title *With Malice Towards Some* was apt enough, though I would not accuse the author of ill-will. It is a startling instance of the facility with which intelligent strangers may observe carefully a society and get it quite out of focus. In the American's book, the class-structure is stressed to the point that it is the clue to the whole situation. That the bishop was a Cecil and his wife on the same social level had some influence no doubt, but the fundamental reason they were loved and respected was that they were devoted servants of Christ and his church in Exeter. Though he and Winnington-Ingram, Bishop of London, were different from one another in most things, they were alike in this—they could say some very silly things and one could easily laugh at them; but they could sometimes speak like prophets and make one feel that they were closer to God than most men. Twice at least I heard William Cecil when he looked and spoke like a prophet. Both times were in a secular setting. He spoke at a meeting in the civic hall to support the League of Nations. One or two competent political speeches were received with tepid applause. Then came the Bishop with his large head and flowing beard, looking and sounding like one who had really glimpsed the future and felt the terrible consequences if civilisation failed to understand the signs of the times and the call to work for peace. The other time was outside the Cathedral late in the evening of the Sunday which ended the 800th Anniversary Festival. He stood on a platform on the Cathedral green, at the foot of the floodlit church walls. I was able to hear only a part of what he was saying, because the crowd was great, but I shall not forget the scene—the picture of the father in God encouraging and blessing his flock.

Of the members of the Cathedral foundation in my time there, only two are still living as I write these words: E. Hall, formerly Archdeacon of Totnes, and Sir Thomas Armstrong, organist, now on the point of retiring from the office of Principal of the Royal Academy of Music. Of all the periods of my life,

the three years in Exeter was most fertile in friendships. They
endured after I had left for London and in my memory they
still endure. I could not omit their names, though I dare not
embark upon the rich chapter of their various kindness. Surtees,
Bishop of Crediton; Thompson, Archdeacon of Exeter and his
wife; McLaren, the student and scholarly preacher; Leake, the
Archdeacon of Totnes; and to them I will add the name of a
mayor of Exeter and of his wife who is still active in the life of
the city—Major Kenneth Gatey, M.C.

The Cathedral had twenty-six "prebendaries" who were members of the Greater Chapter and took their turns on Sunday
afternoons. Most of them were vicars of parishes in the diocese
and we saw them infrequently, but some lived in Exeter. All
were friendly though not all, as I shall record, thought I was
a good dean. Among them we knew Prebendary E. Reid and his
wife. They did not agree with my theology or my policy, but
they were kind and diligent Christians. I have heard the prebendary described as a "holy man" by plain straight-forward
people and I think they were right. I am glad that his daughter,
Margaret Hunter, now lives in South Devon and is my friend
whom I visit whenever I return for a few days to my beloved
county.

The mayor is the link in my narrative to the event which
spread over a large part of the three years—the 800th Anniversary of the Cathedral and the celebrations to be held in connection with it. The Friends of Exeter Cathedral were a progressive
body which had almost reached a thousand members. I was
promptly enrolled as No. 1,000. Owing to the illness and death
of my predecessor and the length of the vacancy before I was
installed, nothing had been arranged and, since the date of the
anniversary was St. Peter's Day, 1933, preparations had to be
speeded up if anything worthy of the City and Cathedral were
to be done. I confess that my recollection of the way in which we
overcame the difficulties is confused. First came the urgent need
to get settled in the deanery with a study and a secretary. For a
time we lived in an hotel at ruinous expense, and then we had
a bedroom in the deanery but no front door. Breakfast was the
only meal we could provide for ourselves and the children when
they came home from school. Strangely, in the deanery there is
a private chapel, and it happened there was a gas fire which
actually functioned in it. I used to toast sausages at the fire and

I am sure we were thankful enough to atone for any sacrilege involved.

During this nomadic period, the Bishop wandered in one Sunday evening, while I was at Evensong and my wife in bed with a heavy cold. Finding no front door, he walked in and explored the house until he found the one occupied room with my wife in it. Without a word of explanation, he sat down by her bed and began a conversation on the food values of shellfish.

When the workmen were out of the house, plans for the celebration of the 800th Anniversary were taken in hand. My impression is that, before my arrival in Exeter, nothing more than the ordinary Festival of the Friends of the Cathedral on St. Peter's Day had been envisaged. To me, it seemed the opportunity should be seized to express memorably our love and pride in our Cathedral and city and inspire all our citizens with local patriotism. Already I had been made aware of the feeling in civic circles of pride in the long history of the city and how the mayor and sheriff quite naturally, when they took up office, had a dignity based on the consciousness that they were in a long line of succession reaching back beyond the Norman Conquest. A large and influential committee, representing the city and the county, set to work with enthusiasm. Of all the persons who contributed so much to the festival, only two can be mentioned here. The University College of the South West had on its teaching staff Mr. Arnold Riley, who was an enthusiast and an expert in amateur drama and in religious drama. Perhaps recklessly we decided, without consulting the Bishop, to present religious drama in the Cathedral and that, in the festival year, we would do this twice. In the coming Lent we would perform Masefield's *Good Friday* and in the week of the festival, June 25th to July 2nd, we would produce a new drama on the subject of St. Peter, to whom the Cathedral was dedicated. Mr. Gordon Bottomley, who had published some much admired verse dramas, was suggested by Mr. Riley and, to our great pleasure agreed to write a dramatic poem with the title *The Acts of St. Peter*.

The rehearsals of Masefield's drama were a wonderful experience for me. Arnold Riley recruited actors from all over the city. The Archdeacon of Exeter played the Centurion, the master of the Choir School was King Herod, the chief C.I.D. officer had an important part, as did the proprietor of one of the large

furniture stores. Staff and students from the two colleges were
among the actors and I, wearing a long white beard, was Joseph
of Arimathea. We were a happy team and a religious one. We
joined in a corporate Communion service and began our rehearsals with prayer. A disturbing incident proved that I was
not only a very amateur actor but, what was more important, a
very amateur dean. I had omitted to ask the Bishop's consent
or indeed, I fear, to inform him of our plans. When the performance was advertised, he expressed in public his disapproval and
the Methodists, to my surprise, agreed, holding that drama was
a violation of the sanctity of the House of God. In this emergency, I wrote to the Bishop a kind of open letter, imploring
him not to condemn our well-meant effort until he had seen
the play. He saw the play and changed his mind, proclaiming
with due publicity that it was the best sermon he had ever heard
and urging everyone to see it. For my part, I gained a juster
opinion on Masefield as a dramatic poet and comprehended
that the apparently irrelevant poem spoken by a blind beggar,
holding up, as I had thought, the action, so far from being a
blunder is a master stroke which contributes not a little to the
emotional tone of the whole play.

Mr. St. John Ervine, the famous playwright, and his wife
were members of the Friends and stout supporters of the festival.
He wrote on Exeter and its Cathedral; he favourably reviewed
our dramatic attempts and both became such friends that St.
John admitted to me without hesitation that Margaret and I
were partially reproduced on the stage in *Robert's Wife*, but
he did not say in what characters. One fragment of dialogue in
Robert's Wife, however, which raised a laugh, he did "lift"
from our luncheon table. We were discussing the meaning of
"progress" and Margaret said, "That's easy: formerly people
couldn't read, now they read *The Daily Express*." He was kind
enough to invite us to a lunch at the Garrick Club to mark the
first night of *Robert's Wife*. At that time he was disturbed, because he had just discovered that "Jumbo Parsons", then Bishop
of Southwark, was married to a woman doctor like the bishop in
his play.

In the 1930s, and more particularly in provincial areas, the
ecumenical idea was in embryo and the old frustrating clash
between church and chapel was a fact of life which one had to
recognise. My own principles, as well as my experience in

London, led me to hope for real unity with all Christians in social work and, so far as possible, in public worship. An attempt to further these aims produced a reaction in the Anglican clergy of the diocese of Exeter which really shook my belief in the Church of England as a Christian body. I thought a course of public lectures in the Cathedral by well-known scholars of different denominations would be a step towards mutual understanding. At the time, the Kingdom of God and the teaching of the New Testament on it were at the centre of theological discussion. Why not have a course of lectures in the Cathedral on this fundamental idea in Christian belief by experts?

A series of lectures was agreed to by the Chapter to be equally distributed among Anglican and Free Church divines. Two revered friends, Dr. Wheeler Robinson and Dr. Scott Lidgett, generously agreed to lecture and we sent out notices to the clergy, expecting that many would be glad to come to the whole course, leaving church and chapel behind for an hour. The result was widely different. A majority of the clergy signed a protest against this use of the Cathedral and appealed to the Bishop to intervene. I must regretfully say that he disappointed me on this occasion. He pointed out that our Free Church friends had not subscribed to the Thirty-nine Articles and that disqualified them from preaching in church. When I reported this to Dr. Scott Lidgett, he was amused and said, "Bring out the Thirty-nine Articles and I will sign them on the spot: I expect I agree with them better than either the Bishop or you." The lectures were delivered as planned; the Cathedral was full for all and packed for those given by Free Church scholars. The lectures were reported in full by the local papers. I started something then which unfortunately was not followed up when I left. Reflecting on this incident, I read a significance in it which was only dimly apparent at the time. Why did the majority of the clergy protest? Not, I think, chiefly on the alleged ground of principle, but really because they did not want to think critically about religion. They were content with what they had been taught at their theological colleges. Because they did not dare to think then, the crisis of belief in the Church now is unavoidable.

The festival was a brilliant success. The weather was perfect. The opening ceremonies: a civic luncheon presided over by my friend the mayor, Major Kenneth Gatey, M.C., followed by a procession of the mayors and portreeves of all the corporations

Leaving St. Paul's after preaching my first sermon as Dean

Dean and Chapter of St. Paul's, 1934. Left to right, Canons H. R. L. (Dick) Sheppard, S. A. Alexander, J. K. Mozley and Archdeacon E. N. Sharpe

The St. Paul's Watch, Second World War. From a drawing by Sir Muirhead
Bone

of the south west, and Evensong in the Cathedral were pictur-
esque and historical. Never before had so many Devon and Corn-
wall corporations joined together in the Mother Church of the
south west, and the maces carried before the mayors and portreeves, representing ships and oars, were a revelation to most
spectators. Both Archbishops preached during the festival and
everyone who had promised to preach, or conduct, or play music,
or produce, or act in the festival drama, *The Acts of St. Peter,*
kept his or her word and, it seemed to me, was at the top of his
or her form. For the first time in history, the Cathedral was
floodlit and such was the renown of the electrical floodlighting
that the gas company asked to have a go. We had in Exeter an
opportunity of comparing the two types of floodlighting, which
very few cities have had. For my part, I thought that, though
the electric light seemed more dramatic, the softer light of gas
brought out the romantic magical charm of our Cathedral.

All this was achieved by wonderful co-operation of voluntary
workers and first-rate direction. I can remember only one
anxious moment when catastrophe was possible. Mr. Gordon
Bottomley had finished his dramatic poem with admirable
punctuality and was staying at the deanery, where one evening
he would read the play to a select audience of five or six persons
who were most responsible for producing it. Bottomley, like
other poets whom I have known, read his own poetry in a kind
of sing-song, intoxicated, I suppose, by the rhythm. As the reading proceeded, I became more and more worried at its length
and I could see from Riley's expression that he was in despair.
I wished the end would come. But for another reason I wished
it would not come, for my wife was fast asleep, lulled by the
voice of the poet. When he lifted his eyes from his manuscripts,
he could not fail to see her. By good fortune, she woke at the
moment the voice ceased and so many comments came from
listeners that it was not noticed. And the length of the play was
in fact easily regulated, because it was a series of episodes in the
life of St. Peter, some of them legendary, strung together by
a chorus. Though of course the drama of Masefield's *Good
Friday* could not be expected in this looser kind of composition,
it had the advantage of employing many members in the chorus
as well as actors on the stage. Bottomley's play has been performed elsewhere, but I am sorry to say it has not been repeated
in Exeter.

When the festival was over, I felt that we could happily spend the rest of our working lives in Exeter and, though there were moments when I felt like an exile from the centre of things in London, there were many other moments when I felt that we had found our home. My wife had that feeling perhaps more strongly. She had no wish to be at the centre of things and she loved her garden, her friends in the Close and the countryside. She was seriously ill for some months and not really fit to deal with a change in our lives so soon. I think it was about this time that a foreboding of change began to take shape. I knew that Dr. Inge was intending to retire and he made no secret of the fact that I was one of the possible successors to St. Paul's deanery whom he would welcome, but there was no probability that his advice would be accepted and Ramsay MacDonald was the Prime Minister. The "centre of things", I thought, might well become a most uncomfortable and taxing situation.

In 1933 after the festival, Margaret and I had a holiday in Germany, as we often did. We travelled to Nuremberg on the day before Hitler shot Rohm and, on our first day, were greeted by enormous placards announcing the murder. We moved over the frontier into Austria and there, in a cosmopolitan hotel, listened, in the company of hotel guests, to the speech of Hitler on the radio, defending his action, in which he said, "For forty-eight hours I represented the justice of the German Reich." At one point his voice became hoarse and, remembering the cry "Danton's blood is choking you", which confounded Robespierre when defending himself in the French Assembly, I said to an English-speaking Italian Jew who was sitting next to me, "The blood of Rohm is choking him." He was terrified and whispered, "For God's sake keep silent. The hotel keeper is a Nazi and I think there are Austrian police in the house." I think it was the next morning that, walking on one of the hills, I met a young man who told me he was a former Communist schoolmaster from Vienna who was making his way *"über die grüne Grenze"* into Germany to support Hitler in his crusade to unite all Germans and create a Teutonic cultural unit. He had been converted by *Mein Kampf*. I read *Mein Kampf* myself and, though I was not converted, I was convinced that those who laughed at the book as propagandist nonsense were grievously mistaken. The British "sense of humour", of which we are proud, can be a curse. I am fairly certain that, if our political leaders had entertained the idea that Hitler meant quite seriously what he wrote, we might have avoided the war altogether or at least entered it with more chance of a quick victory.

The three years in Exeter had not been barren from the point of view of authorship. The book *God in Christian Thought and Experience* was well received and was soon reprinted. Though I made no drastic changes, each time some amendments and short additions were made which demanded attention. The *Guardian*, a Church weekly of long standing, invited me to contribute articles under the title "Essays in Construction". I was glad to have the opportunity to attempt a "popular" restatement of the Christian Faith in the light of modern scholarship, intelligible to anyone of secondary school education, because I was acutely aware of the confusion in so many minds. I confess too that the very modest remuneration which the *Guardian* was able to afford was welcome in the struggle to keep the deanery going and to educate three children. The need which the "Essays in Construction" were intended to meet still exists, but its form has changed, owing to new fashions in philosophy and, to some extent, advances in New Testament scholarship. My friend, Canon Freddy Hood, cheered me last year by telling me that, when "Essays in Construction" were published in book form, he found them helpful.

On Good Friday, 1931, I preached the Three Hours' addresses in Exeter Cathedral and expanded them so that they made a fair-sized book. The first time that I took a Three Hours' service was when I was Dean of King's College and the place was Wells Cathedral. The occasion was made memorable to me by the presence of Dr. Randall Davidson, Archbishop of Canterbury, who was staying at the deanery and went out of his way to encourage me. The Dean of Wells, Armitage Robinson, who invited me, had eccentric habits which went far to turn night into day and it was regarded as worth noting that he attended the service during the Third Hour from 2 to 3 p.m. A penalty of writing a book on the Seven Words is that the author cannot get away from his book. So at least I have found it. I have said all that I have to say in the book *Seven Words*, which still is being reprinted.

At Exeter I wrote my only essay in satire, but it will be admitted that my one arrow was aimed at a lofty target—Bernard Shaw and his satirical book *The Black Girl and Her Search for*

God. I never doubted that Shaw was a genius, but I thought his *Black Girl* was an unfair attack on the Christian faith, based upon a misrepresentation. My satirical tract was entitled *The Adventures of Gabriel in His Search for Mr. Shaw, a Modest Companion for the Black Girl.* I wrote it after dinner in seven days. I had a lucky turn in finding an artist, Ruth Wood of Exeter Art College, to illustrate my *jeu d'esprit* with the right touch of fantasy and an excellent caricature of Mr. Shaw's features. The book went into five impressions and I added in later impressions a preface on the model of Shaw's own publications. Mr. St. John Ervine in his *Life of Bernard Shaw* says some kind things about my book, but thinks that I go too far in the Epilogue. If any reader thinks it worth while to judge for himself, he will not find it easy to get a copy. The War killed the book in 1939. Mr. Shaw is reported to have said, "It's a pity the Dean is so frivolous when I am so serious." Since then, I have kept my essays in satire for private circulation only.

A venture into journalism in the shape of the Cathedral *Bulletin* was a success in the sense that it was widely read, but a failure from the point of view of profit. My good friend Sir James Owen, the owner and editor of the *Express and Echo* (which I must say was a much more interesting and independent paper under his direction than it is now, when it is owned by a combine), did me the honour of quoting verbatim all that I wrote in the *Bulletin*, which cost sixpence, while the *Express and Echo* sold for one penny. But the main purpose of the *Bulletin* was achieved—publicity for the Cathedral. When I left Exeter, I had in mind to liven the *Bulletin* by getting Ruth Wood to do caricatures of local worthies to accompany "profiles" which I intended to write. Looking back over thirty years of experience of Cathedral and municipal relations, I am inclined to think it was fortunate I was called away before I could put the plan into operation.

The time has come to bring down the curtain on this idyll. The letter from Ramsey MacDonald offering me nomination to St. Paul's came and, after some heart-searching, both Margaret's and mine, I accepted. I suppose I always really intended to and it would be hypocritical to deny that I was thrilled by the challenge to hold a unique post in the Church and to be one of a line of scholars and divines who had added lustre to the Anglican ministry. I remember thinking too that no one would

expect me to be a bishop now, which I thought a piece of good
fortune. The farewell to Exeter was heart-rending. Though I
had been dean only for three years and one month, I was loaded
with generous and nostalgic gifts and with expressions of affection beyond all that I could possibly deserve. My drive up to
London to take up a coveted appointment was not a triumphant
and joyful journey, as might have been imagined. Miss Longridge, who drove the car, told me that I wept all the way to
Honiton; then I stopped the car and, leaning on a gate, contem-
plated the beloved landscape for some time and then, having
regained composure, resumed the journey to London and the
future. I remember only that, when I thought of the deanery
where we had been so happy, and on which I had spent so much,
I was sad.

APPENDIX

William Exon

A shaggy head, a woolly mind,
The Cecil temper—and behind?
Ah yes! I wonder what you'd find!
A humble soul, perplext and kind?

W.R.M., Exeter

*Hymn for the Festival of the 800th
Anniversary of the Cathedral*

Thou hast builded this House for Thy glory, O Lord,
  By the thoughts and the labours of men;
On its stones benediction and peace have been poured,
And the beauty which flows from the God they adored
  Be with us now—as with them.
    No walls can encompass Thy measureless might,
      In Thee is no time and no place;
    But Thou comest to us in the rays of Thy light,
      And the beauty which shines in Thy face.

Thou hast builded this House for Thy worship, my King,
  And its arches spring up to Thy praise;
Here Thy children in gladness their offerings bring,
Here unceasing they songs of Jerusalem sing;
  My heart with them I would raise.

Thou needest no worship nor service of earth,
   Who dwellest alone and complete;
But, O Father, accept from the sons of new birth
   The tribute they lay at Thy feet.

Thou hast builded this House, O my Hero Divine,
   For Thy people, Thy scattering flock;
Where Thou callest by name all the sheep that are Thine,
And Thou givest Thy heavenly bread and new wine,
   Setting their feet on Thy rock.
     I belong to Thy wonderful household, O God,
        Keep me ever by grace in Thy fold;
     O comfort me still with Thy staff and Thy rod,
        Till the gates everlasting unfold.

Thou art building a City, O Spirit of Might,
   Through the endless procession of years;
And wherever men labour for justice and right,
Wherever they struggle from darkness to light,
   Thy glorious city appears.
     We are citizens true of Thy Kingdom sublime,
        Let us serve it with mind and with will;
     O Lord, through our lives in the hazards of time
        Thy purpose eternal fulfil.

W.R.M., Exeter

A Prayer for Light

O God, Who clothest Thyself with light as with
a garment, and makest the outgoings of the
morning and evening to praise Thee, mercifully
grant that, as by Thy created light we
perceive the wonders of Thy universe, so by
the uncreated light of Thy Spirit we may
discern the adorable majesty of Thy Being,
and that our hearts and minds being illumined
by His Presence, we may walk in Thy paths
without stumbling until at last all shadows
flee away and in Thy Perfect Light we see
light, Who with the Son and the Holy Spirit
art God for everlasting.   Amen.

W.R.M., Exeter

CHAPTER 10

Dean of St. Paul's

By the time of my public installation as Dean of St. Paul's, Margaret and I had endured once more some of the harassments inseparable in those days from a removal from one deanery to another. Once more the problems of "fixtures" and of valuation of curtains and carpets were discussed *ad nauseam* and it happened unfortunately that the wife of my successor at Exeter was a specially determined bargain-seeker. In St. Paul's the cost of decoration and repairs and of electric wiring fell upon the incoming dean and as the last straw it was proposed by the Chapter treasurer that the "pension" allotted to Dr. Inge by the Chapter, possibly illegally, should be deducted from my income so long as he lived. Fortunately a compromise was agreed on this, but the agitation left in our minds by these material anxieties deprived the installation of much glamour. In my memory, it has nothing like the glow of the Exeter installation. And yet the service itself was warm enough. I had indeed something of the feeling of a home-coming, for the Cathedral was full of King's College friends. I think I was personally popular there and I had not been forgotten in three years, but there was something more in the demonstration of interest and good will towards me personally. I represented a kind of "break through". A man who belonged to neither Oxford nor Cambridge had been appointed to an ecclesiastical post traditionally associated with scholarship. Perhaps today that does not seem remarkable, but then it did and in fact the prejudice was powerful enough to be an "accepted" principle in many quarters. The installation in St. Paul's had been protested against by the senior canon, Alexander, on the ground that my London degrees did not qualify me to hold the office of Dean of St. Paul's, even though I had Letters Patent from the Crown appointing me "for the term of my natural life". The knowledge that my appointment could have some importance in the development of the prestige of London University degrees, and perhaps of "modern" universities as well, weighed with me when I accepted the nomination to St. Paul's.

None of the canons was unknown to me and one was in a sense my own choice, for, when I was approached on the subject of St. Paul's, I had said that I would feel happy if H. R. L. Sheppard, popularly known as Dick Sheppard, would be appointed to the vacant canonry. Dick, who in a short time became my close friend, was almost a complete stranger and at first he was most reluctant to come to St. Paul's. He had been Dean of Canterbury, but resigned owing to illness. He was a victim of asthma which incapacitated him from time to time. His name is almost forgotten now, but not by those who were alive and adult at the end of the first world war. He was one of the three chaplains: G. A. Studdert Kennedy, Tubby Clayton and Dick Sheppard, who made deep impressions on the minds of troops and of the post-war generation. All of them were men of ability and of popular gifts: they were also completely dedicated Christians. At the time when I began to know Dick Sheppard intimately, he was involved in promoting the Peace Pledge Union which was destined to cause a lot of trouble and searching of conscience, its purpose being to enrol every available individual among its members who entered into a solemn covenant that they would take no part in any war. It was in fact the organisation of extreme pacifists.

When I persuaded Dick to come to St. Paul's, I was thinking primarily of his great work in St. Martin-in-the-Fields, where he had taken over an empty and inactive church at the end of the first world war and made it the centre of a live religious fellowship and vigorous social service in the name of Christ. He had, too, the distinction of being a pioneer of evangelism on the wireless. I thought that if I could persuade Dick to come there might be "ructions", but nobody would be able to say that St. Paul's was "dead".

And that this was being said was borne in upon me by two events which happened immediately my appointment became public. I was summoned to call on the Archbishop of Canterbury, Cosmo Gordon Lang, and on the Prime Minister, Mr. Ramsay MacDonald. Both of these authorities (Church and

State, one might say) indicated that they expected me to bring, or cause to be brought, new life into the Cathedral. Beyond the fact that I had a great responsibility and that the Archbishop had prayed for me, little of this interview remains in my memory, except that he gave me his blessing, which sent me away encouraged. Of the Prime Minister's interview I have vivid recollections. I was shown into the Cabinet room at No. 10, Downing Street, where I found the Prime Minister sitting alone. I always admired the beauty of his speaking voice and the dignity of his appearance. Compared with the Conservative and Liberal leaders, Ramsay looked and spoke like the genuine aristocrat. He stood up and addressed me with the words, "I am a layman, from the crown of my head to the soles of my feet, but I realise the importance of religion in the national life and the service it can render in counteracting the forces of disruption which are more menacing than many people recognise." The rest of his speech was most embarrassing to me, because he criticised my friend and predecessor Dr. Inge, as it seemed to me, unfairly. He seemed to deplore particularly the dean's weekly essays in *The Evening Standard*, which I think he called "the yellow press". Why "yellow" should be a denigrating epithet when applied to newspapers is a semantic puzzle which I left for leisurely consideration. My immediate need was to think of words to express my disagreement and I had at least three points which I intended to make. I never made them and I have wondered whether I failed to take my opportunity through shyness; but I really do not see how I could have asserted my right of reply, for Mr. Baldwin was abruptly shown into the room, evidently with some urgent business, and I was rapidly shown out. I cannot remember that I uttered a single word on this, to me, momentous occasion. I am writing these words on the day after the monument to Ramsay MacDonald was dedicated in Westminster Abbey and I was glad that I had some small part in this too long delayed tribute to a man who in my opinion was a great patriotic statesman.

The first sermon that I preached as Dean of St. Paul's was on Advent Sunday, 1934. Some thought about my style of preaching led me to conclude that I must avoid any appearance of trying to speak on the level of Dr. Inge, chiefly because I had neither the learning nor the wit to compare with his; but also because I hoped that, with Dick Sheppard on our side, we might make St. Paul's a place where ordinary people could hear the gospel. My text on this Advent Sunday was "Owe no man anything but to love one another" and the *British Weekly*, which was kind enough to report my first appearance in the St. Paul's pulpit as dean, remarked very truly that it could have been preached by any curate. The Bishop of London was, I think, pleasantly surprised by my preaching. He and Dr. Inge had not been on good terms with one another and I suppose it would have been difficult to find in the whole Anglican communion two clerics less congenial with each other. Dr. Winnington-Ingram, as I found when I was ordained, had a deep mistrust of Modernism and I was not only a member of the Modern Churchmen's Union, but the president elect of that heretical body. He must have thought that I was an inferior version of Dr. Inge. My illustrious predecessor was a great man and a great Christian, but he was a somewhat imperfect churchman in the sense that he was not always careful to observe times and seasons. Preaching, as was his duty on the great festivals, it was complained sometimes that his sermon had little relevance to the festival. A story was current that a former canon, Simpson, who had a resonant voice, interrupted a decanal discourse on Christmas Day by replying to a rhetorical question, "Perhaps you are wondering when I am coming to the subject of our festival?" with a hearty "We are".

He invented a label for me which soothed his apprehensions—Orthodox Modernist. I used to think that this was almost a contradiction in terms and an unworthy compromise, but now I have come to accept the label as not far out. The Christian faith to me has always been a system and I have never supposed that individual doctrines can be properly understood in isolation from its other main affirmations. That genial atheist, Thomas Hobbes, stated a truth very coarsely and with hostile intent when he compared "our most holy religion" with "a nauseous pill or potion which must be swallowed whole or not at all". Or to speak the language of reverence, the Christian faith is the expression and creation of a revelatory spiritual experience of which we have record in the New Testament and in the tradition of the Church. This experience and body of teaching needs to be grasped and understood by every generation and, as knowledge grows, interpretation of the revelation must change and develop. The criticism of Modernists that they had no gospel to preach was, I am convinced, true only of a few. The Bishop's chaplain, who was with him in St. Paul's on my first Easter Day, told me that, after I had been preaching for ten minutes, the Bishop bent forward and whispered "Why, this is the gorspel!" in the slightly Cockney accent which he had acquired.

I was delighted that my first sermon on a "special" occasion was at a service in St. Paul's to commemorate the 150th anniversary of the death of Samuel Johnson and shortly afterwards I was elected President of the Dr. Johnson Society of London. To be so near to the house in Gough Square where the lexicographer had "tugged at the oar" so valiantly meant something to me which went just a little way towards reconciling me, but not my wife, to the loss of our home in Exeter. Perhaps too the thought of Fleet Street and Johnson suggested a way of making use of the deanery in a pastoral way. We had decided that we must live in the deanery as a place where we could offer modest hospitality. To camp out in a corner of the vast mansion would seem to be a faint-hearted refusal to "have a go". Incredible as it seems now, up to the outbreak of war we had five maids and a man and the whole house could not have been maintained on the scale demanded with fewer. When our three children were at home and one or two guests staying with us, we felt that the deanery was just the right size. A hospitable gesture was the institution of a weekly sherry party for junior workers in Fleet Street. Every Thursday, we were "at home" and, with the help of Dick Sheppard and C. B. Mortlock who knew many young journalists, we collected quite a lively and mixed group. We laid in sherry by the barrel!

Some queer people appeared among the guests and, as the years passed, the ideological conflicts on the Continent were reflected in the company in our drawing-room. Among them Ernst Toller, the Communist playwright, who had led a *putsch* and was now a refugee in England, stands out in memory. He was a charming and highly intelligent man, who seemed to be caught up in a fateful destiny which ended in a tragic death in America. When I knew him, he was a cheerful young man who in exile set himself to the task of writing a book on the common people of west European countries. He made a study of the English common people largely by listening to conversations in public houses. When I asked him if there was much difference between common people in England and in Germany or France, he said there was one significant distinctive mark of public house conversation—two topics which were subjects of violent argument in other countries, politics and religion, were never mentioned in English public houses. He thought that the cause of this silence was due not to stupidity but to politeness and a dislike of hurting other people's feelings. I think Toller must have frequented waterside taverns, for he added that in a London bar in the evening you would almost always find a man telling a yarn of highly improbable adventures to an audience of straight-faced men who were waiting to tell their own stories.

To finish the account of our Thursday symposia, I must record that many young men and young women became our friends—some, all too soon to be engulfed in the war, the shadow of which grew darker with every month. The changes in public emotions and affairs were reflected naturally enough in the minds of intelligent and young workers and the propagandists did not leave us alone. I think it must have been as early as 1936 that the Nazis began to appear from time to time among our sherry party guests. They were charming and well-mannered young men, I suppose from the schools which Hitler designed on the pattern of English public schools for the training of future leaders. Our English guests, too, were affected by the shadow. They reacted against the propaganda. One memorable afternoon I had to try to separate two men who had come to blows in my drawing-room, a German National Socialist and an eminent young journalist who wrote a column in *The Daily Express* as William Hickey and is now a well-known Labour Member of Parliament, Mr. Tom Driberg.

The first New Year's Eve at St. Paul's was described as "traditional" by some and "barbarous" by others. I agreed with the latter. The Cathedral was locked and guarded; no gleam of light came from the towering church. Around midnight, an unruly crowd, alleged to be Scottish and certainly consisting of many persons who had drunk too much Scotch whisky assembled and shouted, sang and danced with appropriate tumult. Dick Sheppard and I mixed with the crowd and wondered what could be done about it. As I pushed open the door of the courtyard in front of the deanery, a tipsy woman greeted me with hospitable noises and pressed me to take a swig out of a whisky bottle which she was waving in the air. We thought that we ought to do something about this custom. Not that we wanted to damp down cheerfulness or spoil a long-established party, but that we thought it was definitely unChristian to bolt and bar the Cathedral against any who might want to pray and give thanks to God.

The following year we drastically changed the proceedings. In the Cathedral we had a service and outside we had a Salvation Army band. It was characteristic of Dick Sheppard that he gave me the safe and easy job inside, while he stood on a platform outside facing the mob; he pointed out incontrovertibly that he had more experience of dealing with mobs. The mob on that night was beyond even his power to charm and he was howled down, narrowly escaping being knocked out by empty bottles. The police stopped the outside service altogether and insisted that admission to the Watch Night service should be by ticket only. Today New Year's Eve at St. Paul's is more orderly and, to me, by comparison with the old days, rather dull. But some tradition of disorder still hangs about. It was at a Watch Night service in the late fifties that, when I had concluded it from the pulpit, a loud voice from the west door began another address to the congregation which filled dome and nave. It took six policemen to overcome him and, from my vantage point in the pulpit, I could see how to cope with rioters—turn them face down. He fought hard, but in the end the forces of order prevailed. It seemed that the police had been tactless in their approach: they had called him "Paddy", whereas they ought to have called him "Jock".

One relatively minor change in the order of services in St. Paul's, on which my heart was set, nearly led to my resignation a few years after my coming. The tradition of St. Paul's which I inherited was strictly in accord with the Prayer Book. The Sunday morning service consisted of Morning Prayer, Litany, Holy Communion, all sung and with a sermon as part of the Communion. Shortly before my time, the Litany had been dropped on Sunday mornings, but it seemed to me that it would be much better to have a break between Morning Prayer and the Holy Communion, having the sermon at the end of Morning Prayer. It is incredible today that this slight change should be regarded as revolutionary. Nearly every English cathedral has now adopted it. But my Chapter did not like it, or at least I could not get a majority for it and without the Chapter's agreement I could do nothing. The reason I felt strongly on this detail was that I had evidence of deplorable effects of our custom in the tourist season. In the large congregations during the summer months, I could see that not a few strangers unfamiliar with Anglican liturgy went up with the communicants to the altar, without knowing what they were doing, and beyond all dispute in those months the Prayer of Consecration which should be the most solemn and peaceful part of the service was disturbed by an exodus of persons who had just realised that they were confronted with a mystery. St. Paul has some stern words about those who eat the Eucharistic bread and drink of the cup "without discerning the Lord's body". In the event, the Chapter withdrew its opposition, but only because they were convinced that I would have resigned if they did not. My dear but argumentative friend, Canon Kenneth Mozley, had received a note from me to the effect that I would resign and make my reasons public. In reply he delivered a note at the deanery in person and fortunately the door was opened by my wife, to whom he said, "The Dean has some nonsensical stuff about resigning. Of course, no one could resign on such grounds." She replied, "That's just where you are wrong. He won't stay where everything he wants to do is obstructed and I'll see that he tells everyone why he is resigning." The point which I was concerned with was not to keep non-conformists away from the Communion in St. Paul's. So far as I was concerned, they were more than welcome if their conscience was clear. What shocked me was that the blessed sacrament should be received carelessly and unheedingly as a quaint part of a tourist attraction.

In Exeter I had no criticism to make of the daily round of Cathedral services which became a part of my life, but in St. Paul's the full choral service of Mattins every morning at 10 o'clock, lasting forty-five minutes, was it seemed at odds with the activity of the City which was all around. To a busy man, and we were busy, the idea seemed clear that the Kingdom of God might be better served if the Morning Prayers were said and the clergy's presumably important labours not daily interrupted. In winter months, the congregations at weekday Mattins were almost non-existent—two or three very often. One November morning, as I sat in my stall at Mattins, I saw only one solitary individual in the Cathedral—the only person there who was not paid to be present. There came into my mind the outline of a music hall type song, *The Man Who Went to Mattins at St. Paul's*. In an indiscreet moment, I repeated the jingle to some students and other irresponsible persons like my dear colleague, Professor Sam Hooke, and they will expect to have the correct text. Let me say that I did not compose the song during the service and that Greta Garbo's demand for solitude was well-known at the time, though no doubt forgotten now.

Every morning when the bell so loudly calls,
On the stones my lonely footstep gently falls
  Through the empty, echoing aisles,
  And the chairs that stretch for miles,
Walks the Man who goes to Mattins at St. Paul's.

There is emptiness in benches and in stalls,
Through a wilderness the choir slowly crawls,
  And, if Garbo wants a rest,
  I really think she'd best
Join the Man who goes to Mattins at St. Paul's.

O, I love to be within these ancient walls,
And, if solitary worship sometimes palls,
  I won't resign my place
  As the world's church-going ace,
I'm the Man who goes to Mattins at St. Paul's.

So could there be a tablet that recalls
My claim to be remembered in these halls?
  And just write upon the stone
  These moving words alone,
"He never missed a Mattins at St. Paul's."

I did succeed in getting the custom changed by having Mattins said on Wednesdays and Fridays and the choir singing on those days at 1 p.m., when a congregation was able to attend by cutting short the lunch hour.

State services and services of national importance often happen in St. Paul's and the Cathedral is surely an unsurpassed setting for such acts of worship. My first state service was on May 6th, 1935, which took the form of a Thanksgiving for the Silver

Jubilee of King George V. I was told, and can easily believe it, that he was surprised and moved by the affection which the people of this land and of the Empire showed towards him; and I can also cite another report from "reliable sources" that, if he had chosen the kind of religious service which appealed to him, he would have had a "popular" service of prayer, Bible-reading and hymns in the Albert Hall. He was certainly a regular reader of the Bible. I cannot remember whether he made the remark to me or I heard it from another chaplain, it is at least quite in character: "A wonderful book, but there are some very queer things in it."

State services are so carefully prepared that mistakes or hitches are rare, but it so happened that my first state service was marred by a breakdown which probably was not noticed by most, but was only too evident to the King and Queen and the royal family. At the end, the invariable arrangement is that the Royal personages leave first, passing down the whole length of the Nave, escorted by the Dean and Chapter. In the case where the Monarch is present in state, the Lord Mayor walks in front, holding aloft the famous pearl sword. On this occasion, however, the twenty-six prebendaries stole a march on the royal party, and with amazement we saw these venerable clergymen, all wearing copes, file out of their stalls and process across the path which the King must take to the west door. King George was an impatient man. I wonder if anyone guessed what he was saying to me as we passed down the Cathedral: "A wonderful service. The Queen and I are most grateful. Just one thing wrong with it—too many parsons getting in the way."

I did not fall entirely out of favour, however, for shortly afterwards I was created K.C.V.O., an order which is given, so it is said, to those who have rendered personal service to the Monarch. A serious illness prevented me from attending the investiture at Buckingham Palace and it was some time later when I had recovered that the King graciously invested me alone. The irregularity of the proceeding no doubt was the cause of an error on the part of the gentleman in attendance who, when I was kneeling before the King, handed him the sword to give me the accolade, and it was only because I protested before the sword touched my shoulder that I did not become a genuine knight. Of course, the King knew perfectly well that a priest cannot be a knight. When the brief ceremony

was over, he referred to the last time we had met and elaborated
a little on the parade of the prebendaries. "Too many parsons:
I didn't know there were so many damn parsons in England: it
was worse than a levee." Most unlike my usual form, I thought
of what seemed an apt reply: "I look forward, Sire, to the day
of your Golden Jubilee, when we shall try to be quite perfect
in our service."

In that illness, which for a time was dangerous, the Bishop
of London came to see me every day while anxiety lasted and
on every visit he brought to Margaret and me love and hope.
One day, when the sun was shining, he insisted on taking her
for a walk in the City. Wearing his purple cassock, he escorted
her on his arm through the streets, greeting people and being
greeted, blessing many who knelt on the path as he passed.
Sentimental, embarrassing, even superstitious? I can think of
many denigratory words which could be applied, but the only
word I would allow as just is "romantic". Winnington-Ingram
was a romantic and his was a romantic faith. He felt he was
leading an army of the Lord: he was glad and proud to be a
bishop, a father in God; he did not think he was "dressed up"
in his purple: his garments proclaimed his office, and above
all he loved all who were members of his flock. Sometimes I
laughed at him, but I hope never unkindly, never with a
priggish sense of intellectual superiority.

The years 1935 and 1936 saw the funerals of two war leaders,
Jellicoe and Beatty, whose tombs are side by side near to that
of Nelson. At one, probably that of Jellicoe, two slight grounds
for hope flickered. Two German admirals were present: sign
of peace? The Prince of Wales was every inch a king when
the Germans were presented to him: a favourable omen for
the reign of Edward VIII?

With the abdication I had nothing to do and have no comment to contribute on the event. My impression is that everyone
concerned in it was actuated by a sincere wish to do what was
just and in the interest of the country. It happened that I had
an appointment with the Archbishop of Canterbury at Lambeth
Palace on the morning after his broadcast address which was so
unpopular with a large section of the public and thought to be
unduly censorious by many who, on the whole, agreed with the
abdication policy. When I saw him, he was reading letters commenting on his broadcast. One of them described it as "the voice

of Christian England". That, I am convinced, was what the
Archbishop tried to be. Well aware of the probable reaction to
his words, he said what he believed it was his duty to say. Of
all the archbishops I have known, I would say that he had the
most moral courage. A widespread misconception of his character
was that he was a somewhat pompous prelate on good terms with
"the world". His gift of smooth and elegant discourse and his
dignity in public life perhaps misled superficial observers. He
was a complex personality—one of his former chaplains explained to me that there were at least five distinct selves in his
composition: I have forgotten most of them, but I remember
the first—a great prelate and ecclesiastical statesman—and I
remember the last and central self—a humble and loving pastor.

No one wants to hear the details of other people's illnesses and
I have no satisfaction in recalling my own. The years from
1935 onwards were punctuated by periods when I was out of
action. I collapsed in Cambridge and was told by a kind young
doctor there so often not to be frightened that I was quite
alarmed. In the illness which followed, I met for the first time
the ear, nose and throat surgeon, Frank Ormerod, who saved
my voice and, no doubt, my life, more than once—a beloved
physician if ever there was one. It was said that he was fetched
out of a night club and brought to the deanery. From that date,
he played a part in every year of my life until 1967, when I
had the sad privilege of presiding over the memorial "meeting"
for him held in the Senate House of the University of London.
He and Mrs. Ormerod were full of the compassion of Christ
and of good works but, strangely, I never discovered whether
they called themselves Christian believers and the meeting took
the form of a series of appreciations by colleagues, interspersed
with music. No one protested when, at the end, I could not help
expressing my feelings in a prayer of thanksgiving for his life,
addressed to God.

I have confused memories of lying in bed in the deanery with
many grapes on the bedside table and waking up to find them all
eaten up by mice—or perhaps rats. Another night, I seem to
remember, I was left with a bottle of whisky by the bed and an
injunction to drink as much as I could before morning. And
when that illness was over, I distinctly remember a very kind
nurse advising me never to go out of doors without a hat and
never to allow myself to be pushed into doing anything that I

did not feel strong enough to do. I am afraid I have not always remembered these admonitions.

Shortly afterwards, I had trouble with my throat and it was a moot point whether I should have an operation which would probably have put an end to my public speaking and to my time as Dean of St. Paul's. Before deciding, Ormerod called in his own teacher in Laryngology who, he said, had looked down more throats than any other man in the country. The upshot of this consultation was that I should be absolutely and completely silent for six weeks. Obviously I could not live in the deanery or be with my wife and keep a vow of unbroken silence. Miss Longridge, my secretary, found a room for me by the sea on the coast of south Devon which in winter was almost deserted. She cooked meals and looked after letters, so that I was not disturbed by people who would speak to me. When I stepped into the train at Paddington, I resolved that, from that moment, I would utter no word. I carried in my pocket a tablet on which I had written, "Sorry, I have lost my voice". All went well until the train, having left Exeter, was running along the Exe estuary on which the sun was pouring golden light. A lady, who was the only other passenger in the compartment, said "Doesn't it look lovely today?" I produced my tablet and she charmingly expressed her sympathy. But, alas, shortly afterwards my suitcase, which I had placed carelessly on the seat, fell off on to my foot. I regret to record that I said, "Damn!" She looked at me with a questioning glance. I saw no possibility of explaining in less than a hundred words. She looked steadily out of the window until we stopped at Newton Abbot and, as it seemed to me, rather hurriedly got off without a word. That year for the whole of Lent I was more silent than a Trappist monk.

The result of my long silence was that no operation was performed, that I gained a stone in weight and that enforced silence was very restful. The events in the year 1936 have left few impressions on my memory and I seem to have "surfaced" when the abdication was an historical fact, and I was staying with my Exeter friend Lord Mamhead in his castle, apparently convalescent. He was pessimistic about the monarchy and believed that the new King and Queen would have no hold on the nation's affection. I violently disagreed with him and I was in fact delighted that the Duchess of York would be queen. From the day when, as Chaplain to George V, I met her, I had been devoted to her and was certain that she had the courage, intelligence and sheer goodness to give George VI just the help he needed. And, as I well knew, he needed help. Called to assume a position which he had never expected, handicapped by a serious difficulty of speech and hating the thought that he was taking the place of his elder brother, I am sure that George VI was supported by a stern sense of duty and by the Christian faith which he shared with his wife. At this point in my story, an anecdote illustrating a lighter side of royal conversation may be pardoned. At the time when the Spanish civil war was in its early stage, it may be remembered, Mr. Attlee went to visit the Republican forces. One Sunday I was at Sandringham, where most of the royal family were at lunch and I was placed opposite the Queen at a round table and next to Queen Mary, the Queen Mother. No doubt just to see what I would say, the Queen asked, "Now, Mr. Dean, if you were in Spain with Mr. Attlee and everyone was making the Communist salute, like this, what would you do?" I replied, "I think, Ma'am, I should remember Mr. Pickwick's advice and shout with the largest crowd." She laughed. But the other Queen did not. She said, "I suppose that you have some principles and I hope you would stick to them." There could be no reply. Dr. Johnson's words on a somewhat similar occasion came into my mind. "Sir, one does not bandy words with one's sovereign." But more memorable and more characteristic are the talks which I had with Queen Elizabeth on religion, about which I will say only that she was both a believer and a seeker, with a faith that gave her courage and loving kindness, together with a lively and questioning intelligence.

Perhaps without indiscretion I may recount the opening of a long conversation which took us into deep waters. After lunch at Sandringham one Sunday, she said, "You are coming for a walk with me this afternoon; I want to ask you a question." The question was fired at me without delay. "When I go to church, we seem to be always saying that Jesus is God, or at least divine: do you really believe that and, if so, what exactly do you mean by it?" As may be imagined, one afternoon was not enough to deal with such problems. I remember that I began by trying to explain what St. John's Gospel had to say on the subject and how it was related to the synoptic gospels. From there, the discussion went on to writers on religion who made no claim to orthodoxy—Mr. Middleton Murry for example and Professor Whitehead. With this background of personal knowledge, I never doubted that for the King and Queen the Coronation Service was far more than a state ceremonial, it had for them a sacramental meaning. I hope that I too went to the Coronation Service on that May morning (May 12th, 1937) in a spirit of prayer and I know that, during the anointing and crowning of the royal couple, I prayed most heartily for them both.

So near in our human nature is the solemn to the absurd, that wise men distrust stories which have no hint of the ridiculous. It was present with me in the Abbey that day. My old-fashioned doctor prescribed wine for patients recovering from illness and had strictly ordered me to drink two glasses of sherry at lunchtime. Any lunch for those allotted seats in the Abbey at the Coronation had to be brought in one's pocket, so with my small packet I included a medicine bottle full of sherry and carried it in the pocket of my cassock. We had quite a prominent seat in the row at the south side of the High Altar. As we walked in, I found to my horror that the cork had come out of the bottle and had soaked not only my handkerchief but my cassock. My wife, as always, was equal to the emergency and, as she swept in, handed bottle and handkerchief to an astonished Gold Stick in waiting. I followed in her train, but could not help feeling that it was unfortunate that, reeking of sherry, I was placed next to the head of the Salvation Army, General Evangeline Booth. She made no comment; perhaps she was tactful. We had at least one bond of union on that memorable afternoon. We were the first out of the Abbey. The breakdown of arrangements to empty the Abbey was long remembered as the perfect example of how not to organise a retreat. Three hours after the service was over, eminent persons were still marooned in the Abbey. The Salvation Army had everything laid on and in five minutes Evangeline was in her car. Five minutes later I was in a minor canon's car, having cunningly arranged that he should be just round the corner, and at 5 p.m. I was preaching at Evensong in St. Paul's.

The Coronation Service is too long, but it is one of the wonders of the world and, to the contemplative mind, full of instruction about history, kingship and corporate worship. The symbolic and beautiful scenes were unforgettable and public, but one little scene was almost private to me and Margaret. From our seats we could see behind the High Altar and, when the rites were all accomplished and there was a pause while the final procession of the King and Queen out of the Abbey was being marshalled, we saw the Queen sitting on a table, laughing lightheartedly with one of the page-boys who held up her train. Later I ventured to say that she seemed to be quite well after the strain of the day. She said things had worked out differently from what had been anticipated. A maid attended her with smelling salts in case she should feel faint. "It was she who fainted," said the Queen, "and I revived her."

During the whole of this period, the B.B.C. made great use of St. Paul's. A monthly Empire Service for the whole Commonwealth became established and we had many proofs of its value in promoting a Christian family spirit in many remote and sometimes lonely stations. At Coronation time the service itself was of course transmitted and, as I shall note later, was much discussed in Germany. Dick Sheppard had much to do with all these activities. It was he who found a way round the Chapter's opposition to what I may call the humanisation of Christmas. Crib, tree, and children's play were all, in the opinion of some members of the Chapter, beneath the dignity of St. Paul's. "All very well perhaps for provincial cathedrals, but would never do here." St. Paul's was in danger of being stifled by its Victorian dignity. Dick was on the most friendly terms with the royal family and particularly with George V. He suggested to the King that a present of large Christmas trees from Windsor Park to the Dean and Chapter for the decoration of the Cathedral would be a gracious act. It was done and the Chapter never had the courage to reject the royal gift. With it seemed to go the acceptance of the crib; so, largely owing to Dick, the ice melted and now Christmas at St. Paul's is joyful and the trees every year are laden with gifts for children in need. My decision that Dick Sheppard was the colleague I needed to make up for my own deficiencies was justified and for five years we were comrades in a reform movement for St. Paul's.

On Sunday, October 31st, 1937, he died early in the morning, alone in his house in Amen Court. To me, this was a traumatic experience, not chiefly because I loved him, but because of the circumstances of his death. The news was given to me at the 8 a.m. Celebration of Holy Communion and it fell upon my wife and myself to find someone to take charge of the house. I will not dwell upon the details of this painful situation. Enough has been written about them in Mr. Ellis Roberts' biography. The pathos of the situation was almost unbearable. Dick was loved, I suppose, by more people than any other public man of his time, but there was no one with him at the end. The popular regard for Dick was manifest in his funeral. The body, which rested in the Church of St. Martin-in-the-Fields, was carried through silent crowds to St. Paul's, where the service was attended by a congregation which filled every available corner. The burial was in the Garth in the precincts of Canterbury, where he had been Dean; once more silent crowds mourned his passing. He was a remarkable and most lovable person, endowed with a gift of holding the attention of masses of ordinary folk and of gaining the affection, and indeed the devotion, of individuals. The leader of the Peace Pledge Union and a militant pacifist, he was *persona grata* at the Guards Club. In the imagination of the multitude, Sheppard stood as a kind of symbol of renunciation of war and the determination that peace should never again be broken.

CHAPTER 11

On the Brink

The death of Dick Sheppard in my picture of the years 1934-39 is the dividing line between confident hopefulness and growing apprehension. My thoughts in those years were both agonising and confused. My regret that I could not take the absolute paci-fist view and must refuse to adhere to the policy of the Peace Pledge Union was due partly of course to my friendship, but also partly to the conviction which grew stronger as the situation developed. I propose to give a brief account of the history of my opinions and of the view of the Christian judgment on war which I worked out. The first world war had left me with my liberal principles shaken but intact. In a sense, they were elab-orated and made more explicit by the experience. With very many other Liberals, I regarded the League of Nations as the fruit of victory which could be counted as the lasting good which had come by means of the sacrifice and suffering of so many "unknown warriors" and workers. Again, with many other Chris-tians, I believed that the League of Nations was the creation of the Christian conscience which opened the way towards a peaceful comity of nations based on ideals of mutual help and the maintenance of justice. I really believed that the 1914 war could be the "war to end war" and that for a Christian it was a plain duty to support the League, because it was conson-ant with the prayer, "Thy Kingdom come on earth". Even now, with "all passion spent", I am unable to write on the failure of this faith and hope without bitter pain and resentment. I do not accept the view that the Hitler war was fated, or predestined, or a historical necessity, or caused by economic forces, or by demons; it was chiefly due to stupidity and mental slothfulness and to the reckless making of promises with no intention of keeping them. No doubt there was much conscious wickedness;

but, if the sincere idealists had done what they had engaged
to do, the evil ambitions of the wreckers could have been contained. I will add that the Treaty of Versailles was a prelude to
ultimate breakdown.

I was not without grave doubts. While still Dean of Exeter,
where I was president of the local branch of the League of
Nations Union, I presided over a large public meeting under the
auspices of the League, which was a part of a nation-wide drive
to add members and spread understanding of the aims and
constitution of the League. Unfortunately, in my opinion, the
drive was called a "Peace Ballot" with the consequence that
many voters thought they were simply agreeing that peace was
preferable to war and, moreover, that a vote for peace in this
sense was a real safeguard against war. The Exeter meeting was
a revelation of the mental confusion which prevailed.

At the time, there were three quite distinct answers to the
problem of world peace before the public and being actively
advocated. It was my business as chairman to put the issues
clearly before the meeting and to point out where the League
of Nations solution differed from the other two. As everyone
now knows, the essential principle of the League of Nations
was that every member nation entered into a covenant to resist,
by force if necessary, any attack or aggressive action, against any
other member. It was a pact of mutual security. In *The Daily
Express* at that time a policy of aloofness from the affairs of
Europe was strongly advocated. Defend the British Empire, but
enter into no agreement to repel aggression elsewhere. And the
third policy was the pacifist, with which I was soon to have close
acquaintance, namely the view that war is always wrong and
violence must be completely renounced even to defend the
country from invasion. The fact which had to be grasped before
any vote could be a valid choice was that the League of Nations
policy was inconsistent with either of the other views. It contradicted pacifism, because it held that in defined circumstances
it was a duty to fight against aggression, and it contradicted iso-
lationism because it called for resistance by the members of the
League to attacks on any fellow member. I laboured this logical
platitude by saying it all twice over. It was not enough. At the
end a charming old gentleman, who looked very wise and
sounded educated, addressed us at some length. He said that he
agreed with all that had been said. The League of Nations, in

his opinion, was the one hope of the civilised world and deserved our unswerving support. He was in hearty agreement with those who urged that we as a nation should mind our own business and keep aloof from the troubles of other nations. Above all, he felt most strongly that war was the greatest of all evils and no Christian could in any circumstances take part in it. The old gentleman's oration was received with rapturous applause and no one seemed to perceive any flaw in the argument. I ought to have stood up and cried, "You haven't understood the words you are using. This soothing speech is dangerous nonsense." But my courage failed when I looked at the happy faces of the applauding audience. Even if I could persuade them for a moment to look at the grim reality, would it not be just about as useful as going into a nursery and breaking up the children's toys?

The fear that whispered in Exeter became very audible in London. I could see that the League was to a large extent a soporific, and many who claimed to support it never intended to carry out its obligations. A climax came, so far as I was concerned, on the eve of the war. When the danger of war was desperate, a public meeting at the Albert Hall was organised to rally the League's forces which were near despair. Monsieur Cot, who was the French Minister for Aviation, was the principal speaker and I was invited to give the closing address. My mind was full of the idea that a lot depended on the adherence of citizens to the obligations of the League and that this resolute adherence should be known to potential aggressors. Thus I devoted my speech to insisting that the meeting should declare its readiness to resist aggression if necessary with force. What else was the point of the meeting? The reaction of the meeting was disconcerting. It was enthusiastically against aggression and condemned it in the strongest terms, but a considerable proportion were pacifists who had decided they would never take part in war. Letters from irate supporters of the League of Nations Union denounced me as a warmonger, when I had simply advocated strict adhesion to the official policy of the League.

I suppose the pathetic illusion that strong words and unanimous resolutions will by themselves cure rampant evils will never be quite rooted out and perhaps a cleric is of all men well qualified to understand how it arises. He ought to know the temptation to confuse good words with good deeds and the insidious gratification which creeps on him when he thinks he has preached a good sermon. And, I will add, if he is an Anglican, he has almost certainly become inured to assenting publicly to formulas about which he is extremely doubtful.

But I had a deeper trouble. What did I really believe about the Christian's duty in war? It was evident that, if war came and Dr. Sheppard's Peace Pledge Union increased in numbers, as it showed signs of doing, there would be a clash with the Government on the ground of the Union's interference with recruiting; but even more urgently I had to be prepared to advise troubled boys and parents, and my own children, on this question of conscience. In the first world war, of course, the problem had been no less acute and I had given some thought to it, but it had never caused me sleepless nights as it did in 1936-37 and onwards.

The conclusion which I reached is at least a rough approximation which is workable up to a point. Two propositions appear to be really beyond question. The first is that violence and war are condemned by the teaching of Christ as we have it in the Gospels, and if the Sermon on the Mount is a revelation of the mind of Christ it should be impossible to imagine Him taking part in armed conflict and still more to imagine Him leading a "holy war" with scientific weapons. But on the other hand, I cannot reject the argument that the duty of a citizen in a civilised state is to defend the state when it is threatened by foes. I have grown up in the community and if I am better than a savage it is due to the civilisation of which I am a member. Can I accept the benefits and refuse the duty? If the state can be defended only by "organised murder", shall I opt out on the plea that I have a nobler moral standard? If the "organised murderers" are defending my family, shall I refuse to take my share of the danger—and perhaps too of the guilt? These two propositions are in my opinion both irrefutable and contradictory.

The way out of this dilemma has been most clearly stated by A. N. Whitehead in his *Adventures of Ideas*. He argues that the gospels, and specially the Sermon on the Mount, state the absolute and unqualified good which is summed up in the new Laws for the Kingdom of God and that this was possible because in the thought of Jesus the consequences of actions did not come into the reckoning. The writers of the New Testament did not believe that this present world-order would last much longer.

They expected the Kingdom would come with power any day. The life lived in accordance with the Sermon on the Mount would be the perfect life in the perfect city. Here and now, however, we have to reckon on the coming of many tomorrows and to be anxious about what we (and still more our children) will eat. The Christian life *in via*, in this world, must be at best an approximation to the absolute good, and the tension in the Christian life is between the ideal and the possible.

Following on this consideration, one may understand what happened in the early years of Christian history. Before the infant Church two possible lines of development seemed to open out. It might stand aloof from the civilised world, a small apocalyptic group looking for the Coming of the Lord in glory — a sect of Judaism; on the other hand it might choose to live in this world even though not "of it". It might seek a *modus vivendi* with the Greco-Roman world. As we know, the Church on the whole chose to be part of history, though never to be only a part of history. Always when compromise threatened to make the Church wholly "worldly", she remembered that her life was eternal and her consummation in the future. So it seemed to me that peace and justice must be the aim of a Christian citizen and the civilised state was an ordinance of God. The authority of the state was not, so I thought, unlimited and occasions might arise when it was the duty of a Christian to disobey; but he must be prepared for martyrdom and fully assured that his protest was actuated by unselfish love.

In William Temple's earlier ministry, when he was the prophet and hero of the Student Christian Movement, he had considered these problems and for a time was attracted by the idea of a "martyr nation", of a nation which renounced war even in defence and disbanded all its forces. Something of the same kind was in the minds of the leaders of the Peace Pledge Union and Dick was working out, in consultation with some prominent lay pacifists, a strategy of non-violent resistance. The idea of a martyr nation always seemed to me invalid. A nation is not a single responsible being. Phrases like "the mind of the nation", "the national will", and so on, are really metaphor. The actual situation is that the national mind or will is a sum of millions of individual minds or wills. A government which chose, on behalf of the nation, a martyr's crown without the consent of every individual citizen would be a tyranny — and a nation has no head even to wear a martyr's crown. I feared that the Peace Pledge Union would actually increase the probability of war by giving the impression abroad that Britain would never fight. The resolution of the Oxford Union declaring it would not fight for king and country had a most deplorable effect on Germans who do not comprehend the frivolous approach to momentous problems which is an aspect of the English "sense of humour". The question, "Would Britain fight in any circumstances short of actual invasion of the homeland?" was anxiously canvassed. A trivial event in my recollections typifies the whole process of disillusionment. An interesting and well-informed German with whom I played some games of chess in Switzerland one day said, "I am cheerful today. I have read in the newspaper that Britain has added a powerful cruiser to her navy." "Why should that make you glad?" "Don't you see that the question is, Will Britain really resist aggression and has she power enough to halt it?"

Like everyone else in those years, I vacillated between hope and despair, but in retrospect I can sense that the hope slowly became implausible. A turning-point came in some off-the-record remarks of Mr. Baldwin to a deputation of which I was a member, headed by that great and noble man, Dr. George Bell, Bishop of Chichester. We had presented a plan of economic appeasement, the details of which are now completely irrelevant. When Mr. Baldwin, who was accompanied by one of his colleagues in the Government, had passed round copies of a considered reply to our memorandum, politely dismissing it, he talked freely and his words scared me so much that I remember some of them verbatim. He said, "I know some of you think that I ought to speak more roughly to Hitler than I do, but have you reflected that the reply to a stiff letter might be not a stiff reply but a bomb on your breakfast tables? We are living in a time when there is no Christian public opinion in Europe to which we can appeal. The peace of the world lies in the hands of three dictators. For all I know they may be insane, and unlimited power drives men mad. To communicate with them is almost impossible. Stalin is unapproachable, Hitler will talk, but who can rely on what he says?" I forget what he had to say about Mussolini; but it was certainly not reassuring. I had read *Mein Kampf* in the unexpurgated German version and it did not seem to me to be either absurd or insincere. Though I had no sympathy with the theories of racial superiority or the *Führerprinzip*, I knew that they were taken seriously by many German intellectuals and had a respectable background in German philosophy from Hegel onwards.

An old friend from my student days, Amy Buller, was active in efforts to understand what was happening in Germany and to keep communication open between the younger intellectuals in England and Germany. Her book *Darkness over Germany*, which appeared just about the date of the outbreak of war, is the best study I know of the rise and growth of the Nazi Party in the middle classes of Germany and of the "idealists" among the youth leaders. She came to know personally some of them without compromising or concealing her opposition to their cause, and hoped to serve the cause of peace by promoting such friendly encounters. Whether any tangible good would have rewarded her efforts is hard to say—the time was shorter than she hoped—but she proved to persons like me, who had only a smattering of German, that Nazi idealists existed. Perhaps, if more of the people in power here had understood this, they would not have blundered so tragically over Hess. Amy Buller's description of Nazi rallies and her psychological analysis of the mass emotion are historical documents in the estimation of those who want to know the "feeling" of momentous events. I think she probably understood the Hitler psychology as well as anyone and she may have been right when she argued that he ought to have been invited to England in 1938, after the Munich agreement, so that his imagination might have been given something to feed on when he thought of England and her potentialities. Perhaps this was not really feasible in the conditions, but one had only to read *Mein Kampf* to see how well aware Hitler was of the tenacity of Britain when engaged in war and the danger of taking the left-wing pacifists at their word.

Somewhat later, Winston Churchill appeared over my horizon. Politically he was out in the cold and anyone who prophesied that he would be the next Prime Minister would have seemed absurd. The policy of "appeasement" is now regarded as a kind of cowardice, or even treason, and left-wing politicians have adopted "appease" as a term of abuse. This is not how they appeared to those who were in touch with affairs at the time.

The left-wing was the pacifist lobby. It opposed the expenditure on arms and certainly had no love for Churchill. He, however, was not to be kept down. To communicate his anxieties and get them talked about, he invited selected persons to luncheon and spoke his mind. I had the honour to be invited until I unwittingly expressed disagreement with one of his beliefs. He had drawn a grim picture of the situation, of the build-up of German military power and of the Nazi plan for European conquest. It happened that Margaret and I had just returned from a motor tour over a large part of France and we had a general impression of things run down, as it were tied together with string, and it seemed to me that everyone I spoke to was either a Communist or of the opinion that Hitler could not be much worse than their own politicians. When I hinted a certain disquiet on the morale of France, Churchill, wagging his finger at me, growled out, "Mr Dean, at this moment the one thing which stands between you and destruction is the great French army." When the "great French army" broke, a year or two later, I was not in a position to say "I told you so," and I hope I never would have done so. Was not a mark of Winston's magnanimity the fact that, when events proved how true his warnings had been, he never reminded us of them? Passing out of the luncheon room, I happened to go down the stairs with Wilson Harris, the editor of *The Spectator*, which used to print some of my outpourings, and Kingsley Martin, the editor of *The New Statesman*. To each I said, "Is Winston right?" Neither gave an intelligible reply. It was amusing to read their confident comments in their next issues.

The tension of life at that time cannot have been so great as it seems in memory, because in 1938 Margaret and I spent some weeks in the U.S.A. and, what is perhaps more remarkable, we went by the German boat, the *Bremen*. The occasion was to receive an honorary degree from the University of Columbia and to preach at a few mission services in Harvard on the invitation of my friend, Dr. Willard Sperry. We were glad to be in new scenes and to have new occupations for a while in an interlude when London, St. Paul's and the threat of war seemed farther off. Not that we could forget altogether, for the good friends whom we met in Harvard, Washington and New York were involved in the world crisis, emotionally at least, as deeply as we were. The German Ambassador in Washington was not a Nazi and belonged to a family (Blankenhorn) which my wife and I had known and in whose house Barbara, our daughter, had stayed. It was a mistake on my part, I think, to visit the German Ambassador, because it shocked some of England's staunchest American supporters. In fact, however, the welcome to us at the German Embassy was warmer than that in the British. The Ambassador emphasised that he himself was from the district of Strasbourg and for a century his family had alternated between French and German nationality more than once. He was not only a pleasant but a clever man.

The conferring of the degree and the hospitality of that eminent university president, Nicholas Murray Butler, is a happy memory, though it had its moments of tension. The record of the University has it that the degree *Sanctae Theologiae Doctor* was conferred on me on October 18th, 1938, *in camera*. Why *in camera* I know not, for the proceedings took place in a large assembly in which I listened to an eloquent, and largely fictitious, account of my virtues and, having been invested with the doctor's gown and hood, was immediately called upon to deliver a lecture on the English Bible. It was during this sojourn in the U.S.A. that I had the privilege of being, for a week, chaplain to Harvard University and occupied the charming quarters (bachelor) attached to that office. The office was no sinecure, for it required me to preach a short sermon every morning and to interview any members of the University who cared to call on me. I had several most interesting visitors, but I am inclined to think that most of them were activated more by curiosity about me than anxiety about their own spiritual state.

On the night of November 9–10th, 1938, an event happened in Germany which dashed many hopes and opened many eyes —an organised *pogrom* throughout the Reich against the Jews. Even then, some optimists clung to the belief that this atrocity was, as the Nazi propaganda alleged, an excessive reaction to the murder of a German diplomat, but I think for the most part we began to have some glimpse of the evil which was stretching out to grasp control of Europe. It was time we went back. But our passage was booked on the *Bremen* and the strong Jewish element in New York hit back at Germany by organising a demonstration on the water front, which aimed at deterring all passengers from boarding its boats. Pickets took up positions near the gangways and crowds expressed hostile feelings against the few travellers who presented themselves. We had not money enough to take passage by another line, even if we could wait to find one. We were unpopular but unmolested and inwardly we were squirming at the thought we were taken to be supporters of the *pogrom*. Paradoxically the homeward trip on the almost empty *Bremen* was in some respects the most pleasant we ever had. Three state rooms were at our disposal and hothouse fruit on our table; the Atlantic was calm, the ship was lovely and strangely enough none of the officers and men who talked to us, so far as I remember, said anything at all about Hitler. When we arrived at Southampton, signs of war in preparation were apparent and a British aeroplane hovered about our ship.

Back in London, anxieties multiplied. Some sentences which I wrote shortly after the Armistice describe our plight. "From the time of the Munich meeting the Dean and Chapter had been anxiously considering the steps which should be taken to place the Cathedral in a condition of defence. It would be difficult to convey to the reader the feeling of perplexity which oppressed us. Everyone agreed that the attack from the air would be far more formidable than in the previous war, but no one seemed to have any clear idea of its probable intensity and character. Perhaps one example—a relatively trivial one— will illustrate the state of affairs. At the time of "Munich" we were most anxious to find out what the authorities wanted us to do about closing the Cathedral in the event of air raids. In the 1914–18 war it had been regarded as a shelter and people caught in the streets had been encouraged to take refuge in it. Was this to be the policy again, or was the Cathedral a dangerous structure? We could get no ruling. Mr. Godfrey Allen, the Surveyor to the Fabric, and I interviewed all the departments we could think of. At last we came upon a harassed man in a small office who was then in charge of the City's A.R.P. He said: "I don't think it matters much what you do. If there is an air-raid tonight, we expect 30,000 casualties." After that we ceased to worry. Fortunately for London and St. Paul's, the testing time was staved off for a year and since that day I have never joined in the condemnation of what Mr. Chamberlain did at Munich. (*St. Paul's Cathedral in War time*, by W. R. M.)

The Chapter, in my opinion, shared to some extent the optimism of the City of London, or perhaps the more accurate word is "incredulity". It was so hard to believe that all the threats of the German dictator were not bluff and that he was capable of launching a world war. But Godfrey Allen was thinking hard about the war and the protection of our great church; the Headmaster of the Choir School too had prepared the way to moving it to Truro Cathedral at short notice. The final decisions were postponed until April 29th, 1939, but we were well in advance of the rest of the City of London and the government departments such as the General Post Office. If we had delayed as long as they did, St. Paul's would have been destroyed.

It is almost ironical to note that in the year 1938, when history was being made all around me, I contributed a paper on *What is an Historical Event?* to the Aristotelian Society's proceedings. The paper and, so far as I remember, the animated discussion in which Dr. C. E. M. Joad took part was decently academic and abstract, showing few signs of awareness that we were involved in an historical event which could sweep us all away. For my part, however, I was not content to be swept away without comment and a letter signed only by me appeared in *The Times* of June 2nd. It was headed *A German-Czech Plebiscite? The Search for a Principle: Self-determination.* The heading devised by the editor accurately states the gist of the letter and there is no need to quote the text. Though misconceived, it was not unreasonable. But it assumed that the alleged wrongs of the Sudeten Germans were the real issue and that, if an equitable settlement could be found, the danger of war would be greatly diminished. As things were, my letter, if it had any effect at all, played into the hands of the Nazis and tended to embarrass the harassed Czechs. I do not feel guilty, however, for surely if there is a possible way of reasonable agreement a wise man will do all he can to keep it open. One unexpected consequence of my letter was a eulogistic paragraph in the *Frankfurter Zeitung*, which did me no good, and a personal enquiry at the deanery by von Ribbentrop when I was ill. This did not cure me of the habit of writing to *The Times* for, in the following year as you shall hear, I tried again to have a hand in the direction of world events.

The tensions of these two years distracted one's mind from events which in normal circumstances would have seemed memorable.

On June 3rd, 1938, I found myself involved in an ecclesiastical controversy which harmonised ill with the rumours of secular war which troubled most men's minds. The Archbishops' Commission on Doctrine in the Church of England, after fifteen years' work, had submitted its Report and it had been published, perhaps rather prematurely, so that all members of the Convocations should have opportunity to study it before it came up for discussion. To me this occasion was full of hope; because, if the bishops could be persuaded to take it seriously, the terrible burden of subscription to the Articles of Religion might be removed. It seemed to me quite reasonable to proceed without delay to a revision. Very soon, however, the dogmatists of both parties raised the alarm and, proclaiming their anxiety about the probable disturbance of the sensitive consciences of the laity, organised a mass petition of the clergy to archbishops and bishops to pass over the Report with soothing words. More than 8,000 clergy signed, a third of the number in England and Wales. I think the bishops of the two upper houses of Convocation (Canterbury and York) must have been intimidated by the petition because, although several bishops had been members of the Commission and the Archbishop of York had presided over it, the resolution passed by the bishops was aimed at avoiding trouble rather than at reform. The note of enthusiasm was lacking: —

1. That this House welcomes the Report of the Commission of Doctrine, published under the title *Doctrine in the Church of England*, as a survey of the currents of thought and belief within the Church, a statement of the agreement and disagreement actually existing, and a contribution to understanding and appreciation of one another on the part of those who differ;
2. Recognises that the Report neither is nor claims to be a declaration of the doctrine of the Church—a purpose lying outside the Commission's term of reference, and one for which no Commission appointed as this was could be competent:
3. Desires that the Report may be widely studied in that spirit of open-minded devotion to truth and readiness to learn from every tradition of Christian thought which is characteristic of the Report itself.
4. Further, inasmuch as many have misunderstood the

function of the Commission, as explained above, this House, while recognising the reality of the problems which scholars and theologians are handling and desiring to maintain in the Church the fullest freedom of enquiry which is compatible with spiritual fellowship, thinks it well to state that the doctrine of the Church of England is now, as it has been in past time, the doctrine set forth in the Creeds, in the Prayer Book, and in the Articles of Religion.*

The promoters of the petition, however, were not content with this. Their concern for the faith of the laity urged them to ask for more, and they put forward a motion in the lower house of the Canterbury Convocation which would be, by implication, a condemnation of some parts of the Report and definitely prevent attempts to liberalise the Articles and the meaning of assent to them. So at least I interpreted their proposition which ran:

That this House humbly requests their Lordships of the Upper House to add to its Resolutions in relation to the Archbishops' Commission on Doctrine the further clause:

That the Church of England holds and teaches the Nicene Creed in that sense only in which it has ever been held throughout the history of the Church, and that her ministers cannot rightly claim a liberty to set aside by private interpretation the historic meaning of those clauses which state the events of the earthly life of our Lord Jesus Christ†

After some consultation, I came to the conclusion that an explicit statement of the need to revise the Articles was the most candid and probably in the end the most effective answer. Canon A. C. Deane, who was a well-known and popular expositor of the New Testament with a gift for explaining the Christian faith to educated laymen, agreed to second my motion. He had also the qualification that, though he agreed with me on the revision of the Articles, he had a reputation for orthodoxy of which I could not boast. We proposed an amendment:

* *Chronicle of Convocation,* June, 1938.
† Ibid.

That all words after "That" be omitted and the following words substituted: "the time has now arrived when the Church should take in hand the revision of the Thirty-nine Articles in the light of the Report of the Archbishops' Commission on Doctrine."*

The debate on our amendment was lively and kept to the point. I have heard many debates in Convocation since that one, but few so good. Everyone who spoke on that occasion was aware that we were talking about matters of moment and, I will add, that we spoke and voted under the judgment of God.

The immediate result was that our amendment was defeated. The *Chronicle of Convocation* does not give the figures. It says "by a large majority". No one troubled to count.

Reading my speech thirty years later, I do not want to alter a word and I quote the record of it here because I do not think I could put my opinion better. I have found the notes of the speech which somehow survived. They consist of a dozen words on a single sheet of paper.

He could not help feeling that, notwithstanding all the grace and humour with which the proposer of the Resolution had spoken, he had hardly reached the height of his argument. The House was dealing that morning with one of the most important questions that were ever likely to come before it, a question which, as Mr. Merritt had well said, touched the foundation of the Christian faith. He would like to be allowed to commiserate with Mr. Merritt on his ill fortune in having a Balaam to second him.

He did not wish to belittle the impressiveness of the Petition and the number of signatures which had been appended to it. He had the most profound respect for the Anglican clergy, who were in many respects the salt of the earth, but it seemed to him that they had one failing, i.e. an irrepressible tendency to sign on the dotted line. That was a propensity which had been exploited by a very admirable parish priest who had signed the Petition and he said to him: "I suppose you like the Thirty-nine Articles very much," to which the parish priest replied: "Oh, I had no idea that it had anything to do with them." But indeed the present would be a

* Ibid.

very inappropriate time to speak ill of the Thirty-nine Articles. He imagined that those who had brought forward the Petition had in mind the fact that at this time a great anniversary in connection with the Reformation was being celebrated, and no doubt it seemed to them an appropriate moment to extol the virtues of that great monument of the Protestant Reformation, the Thirty-nine Articles.

The question had been raised as to how people who held the opinions which he held could assent to the Thirty-nine Articles. He could do so with a certain degree of equanimity in view of the interpretation of the nature of the assent which was given in the Clerical Subscription Act, which he took to be that the assent was given to the general sense of the Articles and not to their particular interpretation. The general sense of the Articles seemed to him to be wholly admirable, consisting as it did, in his opinion, in the repudiation of mediaeval and papal superstitions and standing as a monument of the acceptance of new knowledge and the application of new knowledge to the interpretation and understanding of the Christian faith.

It seemed to him that the addition which he proposed to the Resolution which had been sent down from the Upper House was not only far more relevant to what that Resolution contained but also far more relevant to the situation in which the Church of England found itself in the world. It was undoubtedly true that people were asking: "What then does the Church stand for?" It was undoubtedly true that a good part of the influence of the clergy was weakened because no intelligible answer could be given to that question, but who in his senses, when so questioned, referred the enquirer to the Thirty-nine Articles? He had heard many sermons in which clergymen had told him that the Church taught this or that, usually things as to which he was extremely doubtful whether the Church taught anything of the kind, but never on such occasions had he heard a clergyman say: "I know that the Church teaches this, because the Thirty-nine Articles say so." No one, he thought, when faced with the enquiry: "What is this Christianity in which you believe?" would think of saying: "Go and read the Thirty-nine Articles." Why was that? It was not, he thought, because the Thirty-nine Articles were untrue. It was not because they were couched in unintelligible language, though often in very ambiguous language. It was, he thought, because they did not speak about matters with which the clergy were concerned; they did not deal with subjects from the angle from which the clergy approached them. As Canon Barry had said, they seemed to be almost intolerably irrelevant. If he was to have something that expressed his faith, he thought it ought to be something that he could pronounce with an uplifting heart, that he could wave within the sight of the world as a banner. Whose heart was uplifted when he read the Thirty-nine Articles? Who could march to convert the world with them emblazoned upon his standard?

It was, he thought, of enormous importance that there should be some clear and concise statement of the Christian faith as it was believed by the Church of England, and he could see no reason why such a statement should not be produced. It might be said that the Doctrinal Report expressed or seemed to tolerate views which were repudiated by many members of the Church of England, but the salient fact remained that the agreement of men of very different standpoints upon what he himself considered to be the fundamentals of the Christian faith was the most remarkable achievement of the Doctrinal Commission. He very much regretted that the Upper House, with that pusillanimity which so often characterised it, seemed to have intended to give the Doctrinal Report a decent burial with musical honours. He believed that that was a false policy for the Church to adopt. Now was the time to express the opinion that advantage should be taken of the unexpected measure of agreement which had been expressed, surely not without the guidance of the Holy Spirit.

No doubt the process of revising the Thirty-nine Articles would be long and difficult, but should the Church shrink from a difficult enterprise if it was clearly the will of God for this generation? He believed himself, and he urged upon his brethren, that the courageous act was to support his Amendment and to say that, much as the House reverenced and respected the Thirty-nine Articles, the time had come for a revision of them in the light of new knowledge and for a new statement of the everlasting Gospel.*

* Ibid.

The debate on the motion continued for some time and is worth reading in the pages of the Chronicle. I made another speech in which I touched on some of the implications of the motion before the house, particularly on the phrase "traditional interpretation of the Nicene Creed", following a learned and instructive discourse by the Church historian, Dr. J. B. Kidd. The concluding words of my speech were not inapt:

> I fear the Resolution, like so many others, has been produced by people who are afraid. They have heard that there are some who are falling away from the Church because they do not quite understand what the Doctrinal Commission's Report really means. They have perhaps not also heard that there are other people who are falling away from the Church because they are convinced that the Church thinks more of tradition than it thinks of the living Word of God in these days and the needs of these days. I believe it would be a mistake for the House to send forth a Resolution the governing word of which is "tradition".*

The Resolution was pressed to a division in a house which had become very thin and carried by thirty-four votes to fifteen.

The resignation of the old Bishop of London, Winnington-Ingram, was overdue and some of his most devoted friends were sad that he waited so long, but to the end his personality was romantic and his blessing valued. His successor was presented with a difficult task in repairing the administrative defects in the diocese of London and bringing some semblance of law and order into the public services of the Church. The "Romanising" of the Anglican Church was a widespread suspicion and, in the case of some young priests, was not wholly unfounded. It was alleged that the rejection of the Revised Prayer Book by the House of Commons had been brought about by popular resentment of "Papist" proceedings in the diocese of London. Feeling in the 'thirties on this matter was stronger than we can easily understand. The situation has changed with startling rapidity and today, I suppose largely because of the Ecumenical Movement and the Second Vatican Council, it can be said that now there is an Anglicanising movement in the Roman Church as well as a Romanising movement

* Ibid, page 485.

in the C. of E. Or may it not be that the spirit of brotherhood in Christ is drawing us together?

Geoffrey Fisher was nominated for the bishopric of London by the Crown and thus I found myself presiding over his election by the Greater Chapter of St. Paul's. This was an experience which was to be repeated several times. As I have more important things to deal with in this chapter, I will defer my comments on the subject, simply remarking that my first election of a bishop confirmed my growing feeling that perhaps the time had come to disestablish the Church. That Fisher was an excellent choice I had no doubt. He had been a good Bishop of Chester and a good headmaster. On the whole, I am against the appointment of headmasters to bishoprics, which I believe should go as a rule to men who have been effective parish priests, but there are exceptions to such rules and Fisher, I believe, was one to this rule. With characteristic humility before he accepted the nomination, he wrote to me asking what qualities a Bishop of London should possess. I replied "toughness" of body, mind and spirit. I do not repent of my reply, but perhaps I might substitute "resilience"—the capacity to bear innumerable burdens with cheerfulness, and disappointments without feeling defeated.

A gleam of hope that friendship with Germany might be possible and that I might do something to promote it came to me unexpectedly in connection with the death of the famous theologian, Rudolf Otto, which occurred in 1938. I was invited to take part in his *Gedächtnisfeier*, his memorial solemnity, in the University of Marburg. I eagerly accepted, because I had admiration and affection for him since he stayed with us when he gave public university lectures in King's College, London, and I was Dean. My old love of the place, too, and memories of my engagement to my wife on the banks of the Lahn disposed me to go. Otto had great influence on the religious thought of the 20th century. Chiefly through his book *The Idea of the Holy*, which was a study of the nature of religious experience, Otto caused a fundamental rethinking of theological concepts which is still going on. His other writings on mysticism and on the idea of the Kingdom of God were also centres of controversy and in the opinion of many, including me, valuable contributions to the understanding of religion. In Germany, Otto's writings were widely read but his point of view was, I think, more congenial to the minds of English and American theologians than to his own countrymen. One reason for this perhaps is that Otto wrote with expert knowledge of other religions than his own and looked for truth in spiritual experience of many kinds. The sentence already quoted might stand as a guideline to his thought: "None of the great religions of the world must be allowed to die until it has spoken its last and highest word." I would put Rudolf Otto very high among the teachers who by their thought and personal character have helped me. We corresponded at intervals particularly on one subject which was near his heart—to compose a Book of Common Prayer for the German people.

My connection with this began in a conversation which took place in London the evening before Otto returned to Marburg, after giving his lectures on *Mysticism Eastern and Western*. He had not been in England for thirty-five years, though he lectured in English with no manuscript except one sheet of notepaper. While staying with us, he had moved about the country and formed a judgment on its condition. I asked him "what he thought of England now". I have often thought about his answer: "England is still the most religious country in Europe." I was surprised and implored him to say what he meant. His answer could be summarily stated as "that England is the one country in Europe in which large sections of the population are guided in public and private affairs by Christian principles." So far as I remember, he did not include Scotland in his verdict—and this has some bearing on the next stage of the conversation. I said, "Supposing you to be right in your estimate of the religion of the nation, to what causes would you attribute its relative soundness?" He replied, "Very largely to the Book of Common Prayer." I can remember verbatim his elaboration of this idea. "Last Sunday evening, I was in Canterbury Cathedral at Evensong. The congregation of over a thousand people was a mixture of all kinds of citizens: tradesmen with their wives, soldiers with their girls and so on through a long range of occupations—a cross section of the population. And these people had thoughts given to them which they could never have conceived by themselves in language which they could not have chosen themselves but which stays in their minds like a song." He deplored the failure of Luther to produce a Book of Common Prayer and the tendency of evangelical religion to fade away in the absence of ministers. The Roman Catholic shepherds in mountains know what to do—they set the youngest among them to lead in the recitation of the Rosary. Robinson Crusoe on his desert island read the service for the day. So the Book of Common Prayer can carry a Christian who can read through years when there is no preacher and no visible church organisation to support him. No doubt Otto's opinions are only partly represented by these fragments of conversation and are open to criticism, but the point which concerns us is that he devoted much of his time to the project of the Common Prayer alongside the experiments in corporate worship which he conducted in the little church of St. Michael (*Michelschen*) in Marburg. Occasionally he sent me drafts of services which he had composed with the aim of evoking the sense of the "Numinous", which was the directive idea in all his work both theoretical and practical.

I think I am right in saying that the last of these draft services which I received was for some anniversary of the Führer—perhaps of his inauguration. I remember that it disturbed me and I probably tore it up without commenting on it. That Otto ended his life by suicide appears to be established fact, though only recently have I been aware of it. That I should have been invited to speak at his Commemoration without being informed of my friend's manner of death is hard to believe and I am willing to admit the possibility that I was informed, or that it was common knowledge and I have simply forgotten. No trick of memory can be ruled out as impossible in the circumstances. The onset of war disturbed the balance of many minds—why not of mine? If he did kill himself, I could imagine how he came to do it. Otto took his "sense of the numinous" very seriously and his philosophy was definitely anti-rationalist. He believed that the "Irrational" was an element in the being of God. Thus in estimating persons he would look for the numinous individual. My opinion is that Otto thought he himself had a numinous quality and his influence on some persons seemed to corroborate the idea. Hitler certainly thought he had numinous powers and convinced millions that he was right. A great disillusionment about the Führer and the movement could have overthrown Otto's mind and the stepping up of anti-semitic measures culminating in the *pogrom* of November, 1938, may have been the final blow. It is significant that one of the first things I noticed as a change in Marburg when I arrived was the wrecked and ruined synagogue.

I had been in Marburg as a student just before the first world war and now it seemed all too likely I was back there just before the second. Every incident in that week is impressed on my mind. I was apparently regarded as a guest not only of the University but of the Reich—at least everything was under control. A car and chauffeur were at my disposal and I was under the protection and guidance of the Professor of Hebrew and the Old Testament, who was a delightful man of the great German academic tradition. He was a Liberal and no Nazi, but he had to guard his tongue and his two children were enthusiastic members of the *Hitler Jugend*. The girl, aged about seventeen, was taking charge of the children of a working-class woman who was in hospital, getting them off to school and putting them to bed at night. She was evidently enjoying every moment of her *Arbeitsdienst*. The boy had his eleventh birthday while I was there and to pass into a higher grade in the organisation had to spend a night alone sleeping in the woods. He came to breakfast bursting with pride. In the brief period of my stay there were marches and parades of youth of all ages. No one could see these bright upstanding and enthusiastic boys and girls without a feeling of joy at the spec-tacle, and of admiration for the skill and dedication that had gone to the building up of the *Hitler Jugend*; but to anyone who believed, as I did, that the ideals which it served were warped and cruel and that the children who composed the human material were being trained for destruction, its beauty was tragic. In parenthesis, let me add that, while this shining picture of embattled youth was still fresh in memory, I spent two nights in Cirencester, where it was the custom of youth in the evening and into the night to walk up and down the high street and howl like dogs. Sleepless in my hotel bedroom, I had a waking nightmare of the coming encounter between pre-pared and disciplined German and ignorant and untrained British youths.

I had written my speech about Otto in English and the kind wife of one of the professors translated it into beautiful German, including a familiar quotation from Tennyson into the same metre as the original. I was glad to have two or three days to improve my pronunciation and to learn "the drill" of the commemoration ceremony. I was prepared to refuse to say "Heil Hitler", but no one expected me to. In 1912, Marburg had been a town full of music and laughter—sometimes arrogant songs and laughter, but joyful. In 1939, it was a silent town. I heard no singing and no laughter in the streets. There was hardly any talking and I found out why. Walking in the town with my Professor-guide, I happened to speak of Ernst Toller and his drama. The Professor went pale and looked apprehensively around to see if anyone had overheard. Silence in public was safer. On my first evening, I wandered about the streets looking for some amusement. The best I could discover was a meeting in the parish church to protest against religious persecution. Much had been reported in England about the troubles of the Church in its relation to the Nazi Government and I thought at first that by a providential circumstance I had stumbled on persecution in practice, or at least a protest against it. So far from that being the case, the meeting was a protest against the Russian Communist and atheistic tyranny and a service of prayer for all its victims. What looked like a substantial collection was taken up for the relief of Christian refugees. I ventured to tell Professor Siegfried, who held the chair of Ecclesiastical History, my experience. He was, I think, genuinely surprised that I had expected to find signs of persecution and advised me, if I wanted to understand what was happening in Germany, to read what happened in England in the reign of Elizabeth and with the only partially successful Elizabethan settlement.

The hospitality of the University and of the theological faculty was gracious and traditional, but the rifts in the faculty could not be concealed. The rector, appointed by the Government, was a Nazi no doubt, but a courteous and cultured host. The majority of the professors with whom I came into contact were liberal in outlook and supporters, at least in secret, of the League of Nations, but a few were suspected of being paid to tell tales of their colleagues. I noticed that men who talked freely to me when we were alone became constrained in company. Another observation I record because it may have some bearing on the German character. Interest in the recent coronation of George VI was at least as great as in America. I was cross-examined on the service and copies of *The Illustrated London News* with pictures of the ceremonies were treasured

in more than one professorial home. Of all the conversations
with distinguished scholars in which I was privileged to take
part, only one fragment remains in memory. With my mentor
I was passing the chief post office and, displayed in the window,
was a greatly enlarged copy of a stamp issued to honour Hitler's
birthday. At the foot of the stamp were printed these words:
Um ein Folk zu retten muss man heroisch denken, and above
them a representation of Hitler thinking heroically, which
meant looking very ill-tempered and with folded arms. I do not
remember whether I had seen Charlie Chaplin's brilliant
mockery of the Führer, but I certainly thought he looked absurd
and remarked that, if a politician posed in this manner in
England, everyone would roar with laughter. "I know they
would," said my companion, "but are you quite sure they would
be right?" The question struck a cold shiver into my heart
then and now, when I reflect on the proofs we were forced to
accept that Hitler was no laughing matter, the shiver returns.
Once more the sense of humour which we prize can be a danger.
It is a fallacy to believe that because a man or a movement
strikes us as funny it is harmless and even if you meet defeat
with a laugh you are still defeated.

One other privilege was mine—I saw a Nazi propaganda play
in the beautiful open-air theatre which is near the *Schloss* over-
looking the town. It was a heavenly midsummer evening and
I regret that I was not there a week earlier when *A Midsummer
Night's Dream* had been played, I was told, to a "full house".
What I saw was a play about Scharnhorst and his part in rebuilding the Prussian army under the nose of Bonaparte. The
moral was the need for obedience to the leader and loyalty to
the national cause. Of its kind it was clever and well-constructed
and ended rather strangely with a long and eloquent speech
by the hero pointing the moral. "Deep in the German soul," it
began, "is the virtue of loyal obedience to the leader designated
by Providence," and it ended with the assertion that this virtue
preserved the German people from degeneration so that the
streets of Berlin would never be stained by the "bloody disorders of fratricidal strife". I wondered if the audience had
forgotten so soon the rise and progress of the Nazi Party and
its violence in the streets. The audience was thin and apathetic,
so perhaps it had not forgotten.

Ironically enough, when I come to the commemoration ceremony, which was the reason for my presence, I find that I remember very little. The aula of the University was well filled with senior and junior academic persons. A very competent string quartet discoursed lovely music to which I was too nervous to give attention. My address was one of three and I thought, the other two were good and was relieved that I could understand most of them. When it came to my turn, I had my script almost by heart and had been so well coached in its delivery that the audience could evidently comprehend me, for they laughed discreetly at a little academic pleasantry which I ventured to include as a specimen of Otto's conversation with foreign students. Why is my memory wiped so clean of this really memorable occasion? Because, I suppose, though I honoured and reverenced Otto and his work, all my immediate interest was on the future. What I had learned from my brief visit was hazy and confused. I wanted to sort it out. I departed from Marburg in company with my professorial guide who came with me to Cologne in the V.I.P. car. He said, "I wish you could come once a month; not only because I like you personally but because while you have been here I have had good meals and use of a car. Tomorrow I shall have to go back to austerity." When I replied that I hoped soon to see him and Marburg again I was perfectly sincere, but I have never been back. Six years later, after the war, I was within a few miles of Marburg in a car driven by an American soldier. At a crossroads a signpost pointed to the town. For a moment I had an impulse to ask the driver to go through it. But I found I really did not want to see it again and, to my shame, that I had forgotten the name of the kind Professor.

When I tried to sum up my impressions, my dominant feeling was deep alarm. Even from the small corner which I had visited, it was plain that Germany was prepared and poised for war. The machine was almost perfected. I thought, too, that the possibility of internal opposition to war on which some good judges relied was not likely to be effective. Liberal and League of Nations opinions both in Church and nation, though held secretly by many, would count for little. Hitler had the power and the popularity to carry all before him. The overwhelming majority of the young were on his side. Yet, though frightened, I did not despair, for I felt that there was no popular drive to war with Great Britain as there had been in 1912. From

Führer Hitler down to *Hitler Jugend*, the conviction that Britain's neutrality must be a condition of any hopeful attack on Europe was strong. And there was widespread belief that Hitler would avoid the mistake of embroiling Germany with Britain. At the same time, many quite civilised Germans thought that England could be bluffed into almost unlimited concessions, that Britain wanted peace at almost any price. I hoped that the catastrophe could be held off and time would give the forces of peace, which existed in many German hearts and minds, a chance to rally to the support of the League.

To round this story off, our daughter Barbara must be brought into it. She was staying with a retired professor in Bonn, studying Old High German which she would have to take as a subject in the Oxford degree examination in Modern Languages. The professor had been compulsorily retired by the Nazi authorities because he was a Liberal in politics, and so I think were all his family. As the weeks passed, the menace of war increased and I had almost given up hope. Barbara would not come home. Letters and telegrams and appeals by me to the British Consul were disregarded. The family in Bonn laughed at the idea that Britain would be involved in war. Fortunately events convinced her. On August 23rd a pact between Germany and Russia was signed. Barbara was in a café in Cologne with her Bonn hosts that evening when students rushed in and one, jumping on to a table, shouted, "Listen to the radio: great news is coming." When it came a minute later, the enthusiasm was ecstatic. People cried, "He has done it again." Barbara's friends, though not Nazis, joined in the cheers and said: "There you see you need not go home. There won't be a war. England can't stand against Germany and Russia." The wise child was not deceived. She said, "Now I am sure war is coming. I must leave tomorrow." In a sermon or some other public utterance at that time, I spoke of "Stalin's Judas-stroke", which some objected to. Calling names is usually a waste of energy, but to get the names right may be a public duty. All of us who lived through this period had the misfortune to exist at a time when two of the dominant persons were abnormally devoid of compassion and a sense of honour. To a large extent, they were instigators of the most horrible massacres and tortures in history. And the grim paradox of their careers is that both called themselves "Socialists" and were lifted into power by the votes of the toiling masses.

This chapter could be expanded indefinitely, but it shall conclude with a reference to the one attempt I made to change the course of history. When I lay awake many nights, haunted by fear of the future, a phrase used by Mr. Baldwin, when he spoke to the deputation, often came to mind. He had spoken of the Christian public opinion of Europe and added that it existed no longer. That it was not effective is only too clear, but I wondered whether it was extinct and whether it could not be aroused. That others had the same idea I knew, because I had taken part in a debate in the Oxford Union on the motion that "The only hope for civilisation is a return to religion", which was carried by a large majority. I knew that throughout the land and many other European lands people were praying for peace. A letter appeared in *The Times*, signed by the President of the Methodist Conference and other Free Church leaders, appealing for united prayer. I thought I might follow this with suggesting a dramatic and adventurous action. The letter, I can see now, was perhaps a trifle abrupt, but I had prayed over every word and, as I did so, became convinced that my temptation was not to be too "brash" but to be timid. And, for once in my life, I believed that I had a word from God to speak to some of the rulers of this world. I still think that it was a word of God and, in so far as it failed to move the leaders of Churches because I was not courageous, I bitterly repent.

Sir,

At moments we climb out of our daily preoccupations and catch a glimpse of the world as it is. At such times we forget the questions which normally are so pressing—policy, national interests, personal hopes and fears—and we understand that we are living in a world where the most civilised nations are preparing feverishly to slaughter each other's common people, and that all the resources of science are being mobilised for that end. I am no pacifist. I believe that there are causes for which it is our duty, in the last resort, to fight; but I believe that few things which we count valuable would survive a world war. Before the killing begins let us look round for the spiritual force which might save us.

Where shall we find it? The international forces seem to have faded away. The fellowship of science from which we hoped so much is made something of a mockery when the embattled nations depend on the services of rival "medicine men". The "solidarity of the workers" has turned out once more to be an illusion. We shall get no reconciliation through Labour, when the leaders of Labour in this country are not on speaking terms with the leaders of the Arbeitsfront. We are driven back on that ancient, terribly confused and widely despised international force—the Christian Church and the Christian faith.

I want to urge that now is the time for the leaders of the Christian Church to act; now, before the killing has begun. Those who can speak with authority for the Christian Church have a terrible responsibility now. For the most part they are old men; they are hemmed in by tradition and by memories of past controversies. Anything courageous which they do will offend the timid and conventional. But they can speak to the latent Christian consciousness of Europe as no others can, if they dare. If war comes without the maximum effort of the Christian Church to prevent it, our leaders will be condemned by posterity; that might not matter; they will be condemned by the Master in whose name they speak. It will be a disaster and a betrayal if any considerations of dignity, of ecclesiastical or theological punctilio or of purely national policy stand in the way of a united Christian witness for peace. If the Pope could forget for a while that he is infallible and his Church the only true one, and if the Archbishop of Canterbury could forget that he is part of the English constitution, and if they could both remember that they are ministers of Christ we might see great things. Let us hear the Word of God before the killing begins.

I am yours, etc.,

W. R. MATTHEWS.*

An encouraging result of *The Times* letter was that my friend R. C. Parsons, who was then Bishop of Southwark, got into touch with me and we found that our minds were moving in the same direction. We agreed that the only way in which Christian opinion could be aroused and concentrated sufficiently to deflect the rush into war was to bring about a startling and unexpected event which took the politicians and strategists by

* Letter printed in *The Times* of 27 April, 1939.

surprise before they could intervene. We agreed too that the most hopeful plan was to persuade the Archbishop of Canterbury to fly to Rome without any previous warning or consultation and without the knowledge of the Government. When the Archbishop arrived in Rome he would, we planned, with all the publicity possible, announce that he had come to offer to join the Pope in a supreme effort to reverse the tide which was sweeping Europe to destruction, by challenging every Christian soul to stand up for peace and justice, to insist with all possible emphasis, and with courage, that all the rulers of the nations should halt before the killing began, to think, in the presence of God, what they were about to do. Dr. Parsons had a friend who was willing to produce the aeroplane on which the Archbishop could slip away in secret to blazing publicity in Rome.

The Archbishop lost no time in summoning me to explain my letter. He was hurt by the phase about forgetting that he was a part of the constitution. "When did I ever seem to remember it?" he asked. I did not take up the point, because it would have confused the issue which was, as I saw it, whether the Archbishop was willing to risk his dignity, his good relations with the Government and even his life on an adventure which might, by the grace of God, avert war. He said, "Now prophesy to me." I repeated the arguments of my letter, and suggested in outline the plan which involved his dramatic appearance in Rome. I think at this point he began to listen carefully. Probably he had up to then taken my letter to be rhetoric, without any practical relevance. No doubt archbishops have to endure more of that kind of prose than most of us. I went on to dilate on a question which I had not touched on in the letter, What would be the consequences of failure? The opportunity came when he said, "But if I flew to Rome, as you suggest, I should only lay myself open to a public snub." This was probable enough, but in my opinion it had very little to do with the rightness or wrongness of the action. I coveted for the Anglican Church the honour of being the one Church which in the hour of crisis had put aside all pride and worldly honour and was willing to be humiliated to save the world from war after the example of her Lord, who had humiliated himself to save all men. I tried to say this, but in what words I cannot remember, except one sentence which must have been my sermon's exordium, "Suppose you are snubbed in your effort to stop a world war, who will seem the better in the judgment of history (to say nothing of the judgment of God), the snubber or the snubbed?" Perhaps if I had been brought up a "free churchman" I might have done this more effectively; but, having been conditioned from childhood to reverence fathers in God, preaching tête-à-tête to an Archbishop embarrassed me.

I had hoped, of course, that he would consent without delay, and probably that was really the only chance. Cosmo had plenty of moral courage and, I should judge, still had a vein of adventurousness in his composition. He said, "I must have time to think and to consult other bishops." William Temple was the Archbishop of York, and I thought, at the time, he would be in favour of some bold step such as Parsons and I had proposed, but, as everyone knows, we did not get the word "Go". The Pope was not troubled by an uninvited visitor, the English constitution was not disturbed by the eccentric behaviour of the Archbishop, and the war began punctually at 11 a.m. on Sunday, September 3rd, the same year.

I still think that our proposal was right and that, in the circumstances, it was the only kind of appeal which had any chance of success. I still think that failure to try it was a failure of courage and faith, but no one has a right to censure the Archbishop in a case where the pressures of political, social and military considerations must have been overwhelming. Some critics may dismiss the whole affair as an absurd fantasy based on the fallacious idea that the wills of a few individuals could hold up and change the inexorable course of history, while in fact the war was inevitable. I do not believe this fatalist doctrine. I hold that history is made by the thoughts and wills of innumerable individuals and that frequently the speaking, or silence, of individuals has made a difference between peace and war or between progress and decay.

The crisis was so acute that we dared not carry on at St. Paul's as though peace was assured and, at the Chapter meeting on Saturday, April 29th, we reviewed the measures to be taken to preserve the Cathedral. Chief among them was to settle the command. Perhaps the best thing I ever did in St. Paul's was to propose the appointment of Mr. Godfrey Allen, the Surveyor to the Fabric, to be in charge of all the protective and defensive actions in the Cathedral. He had no obligation to undertake this difficult and dangerous responsibility, but there was no one else who had such knowledge of the building or such personal authority. I was afraid that the Chapter might try to limit the powers of our commander, but I think we all saw that to attempt to carry on with normal procedure would mean putting the direction in emergencies into the hands of a committee of five elderly clergymen. Mr. Allen had already begun to recruit volunteers for the St. Paul's Watch and persuaded the President of the Royal Institute of British Architects to commend our cause to architects. We had a little group of professional architects throughout the war and they helped other recruits to learn the complex structure of the Cathedral and how to find the way on the roofs, in the dome and in the numerous galleries.

The business of working out the removal and the protective sandbagging of precious works of art and of historical value, the despatch of a large section of the Library to the National Library of Wales in Aberystwyth, occupied our attention. For my part, it was when I tried to sleep at night that the terrible anxiety and the lurid imaginations of what might happen tortured me. On August 26th, 1939, the Chapter, at my suggestion, agreed that war seemed so probable that the emergency measures should be put into force at once. On the following day, we notified all the Cathedral staff, clergy, gentlemen of the choir, works staff and virgers' staff that, to guard St. Paul's in the next few weeks before the war routine had been established, we should need volunteers to take night duties. Practically the whole of the personnel of the Cathedral responded and we had an emergency team numbering sixty-two men. The Choir School was closed and all the "Children of Pawles" were transferred to Truro together with their teachers. Every day in the lunch hour, the congregation at the service of intercession grew larger. It was almost a relief when all hope of peace was finally destroyed and the ultimatum was issued which meant war in a few hours. The "black out" began. That evening I wandered out into the darkened streets round St. Paul's and talked to a solitary policeman in Carter Lane. He was conscious of his status as a public servant and refused to express any opinion of his own; "But," he said, "I will tell you what a lot of people say to me, 'Well, this is the end of Christianity'." I wondered what they meant and if many of them had been among the hundreds praying in the Cathedral. I often think of it still.

CHAPTER 12

Days of Trial and Adventure

The second world war was for many either a terminus of their earthly lives or a turning-point in the sense that they were different persons after the war from when it began. So it certainly was with me and unless I can make this clear I shall have failed in my main concern. The difficulty is that I cannot make a coherent story of it; many things happened to me and in me, but as experiences they seemed to make no pattern, though looking back I can see that in combination they deeply disturbed the old Walter Matthews and the man who came out of the war years was in some respects a different person.

On Sunday evening, August 28th, 1939, on the eve of war, I preached to a large and anxious congregation in St. Paul's. Reading my sermon now, nearly thirty years later, I can affirm that I did my best to give as simply and forcibly as I was able the message which the crisis demanded of a faithful pastor. I warned against the temptation to despair, which is only another way of saying to lose faith in God. It seemed to me that the issue was now clear: it was no longer possible to preserve peace without betraying justice; and if war was to come, I did not believe that the Christian would stand aloof from the struggles of the nation. Rather it was his duty to make sure that, even if involved in a life-and-death struggle, we did not lose sight of the principles of justice, reason and mercy. The deepest defeat would be for us to become like what we were supposed to be fighting.

It was in the course of my sermon that I made reference to what I called Stalin's "Judas-stroke" over Poland. The sermon was printed in the church paper *Guardian* and was read by many people with agreement, but one reader objected—Mr. Bernard Shaw. In a letter to the *Manchester Guardian*, he obliquely referred to me. "Stalin took what he wanted of Poland. An eminent English Church dignitary called him Judas; but Herr Hitler quickly decided to claim Stalin as an ally and share the spoils with him." Bernard Shaw was a genius and I always read his plays and prefaces with delight, but in my opinion he was a mischievous influence in practical politics, chiefly because he was incapable of understanding the democratic ideal. Dominated by the Nietzschean idea of the Superman, he had no sympathy with the common man and was apt to mistake tyrannical dictators for the heroes of the new order. He was a socialist, but the very opposite of a democrat. His adulation of Stalin followed on an article entitled "Heil Hitler" in which he had welcomed the aggressive *Anschluss.* Along with Canon Peter Green I felt Shaw's preposterous advice needed some opposition. In a letter to *The Guardian* I did what I could, but I need hardly say it produced no change of mind in Shaw. "Since Mr. Bernard Shaw," I wrote, "in his frequent expository exercises on the policy of Russia seems invariably to refer to an alleged statement of mine that Stalin was Judas perhaps it is worth while to remark that I never said this. What I did was to speak of 'Stalin's Judas-stroke'. A careful study of the pro-Stalin dialectic has not caused me to change my opinion and I hereby repeat the phrase which has evidently stuck, in an inaccurate form, in Mr. Shaw's mind. No dialectic can alter the plain facts that the Russian Government, having promised non-aggression to Poland and indicated that it would help Poland against other aggressors, waited until that unhappy country was defending itself desperately against a superior force and then rushed in not to help but to ensure that resistance should fail. I think I know a treacherous act when I see one, and so long as this country remains free I intend to describe treacherous acts in appropriate terms. We all know that no one can say what he really thinks of Stalin in Russia, but I see no reason to conform to the convenience of tyrants unless one is compelled." Bernard Shaw in reply evaded the moral issue and pointed out that the policy of Stalin had been profitable.

I recall the times when Dr. Inge and his wife came back to stay with us in the deanery and the times when he preached again in his old pulpit. On one occasion just after the outbreak of war, he was spending the night with us. Unfortunately he was not well enough to preach his sermon on the Sunday so I volunteered to read it, knowing that he always wrote every word in his beautiful and legible script. I was amused to observe that the MSS was dated 1915 and was on the subject "Has Christianity failed?" It was a very good sermon and well worth preaching many times, though there were some places where I could not agree with him. The "gloomy dean" for once deserved the epithet, for he seemed to think that Christianity had still failed. I think he and Bernard Shaw agreed that the war could have been avoided if our government had "done a deal with Hitler". Dr. Inge was always worth listening to even when he seemed dull because an epigram or revealing sentence might reward one. A distinguished literary critic, who held this opinion, told me that he was listening to a sermon with half his mind when he heard Inge say, "Historians who have a privilege not claimed by the Almighty—that of altering the past," and from that moment looked out for similar gems.

The time was coming very soon when I would have no leisure for controversy or, alas, for serious study. This became evident to me when I tried to keep a commitment and simply could not give my mind to it. This was the Malvern Conference presided over by Archbishop William Temple and intended to be a culmination of Copec, the name given to corporate studies of Christian Sociology which had been going on for some time. The conference was addressed by many speakers to whom in normal times I should have eagerly listened—but I could not. My mind was elsewhere, wondering how the St. Paul's Watch was getting on; wondering whether the most precious books in the Cathedral Library would be transported safely to Aberystwyth, where the National Library of Wales would look after them, and a hundred other things related to my office.

Nor could I banish anxieties about my home, where my wife was concerned with organising the house for the air raids which were then expected at any time. I was fretting too over the children—all three of military age and each quite capable of going off on some warlike enterprise without consulting me. I knew that before long all three would be caught up in the war effort. The end of the conference, so far as it concerned me, came two days before its official end. I had lunched (very frugally) with Canon Marriott of Westminster Abbey who felt, I discovered, very much as I did. We decided that we would attend the afternoon session in case there might be an opportunity of saying we thought the conference might well be adjourned until peace returned to Europe. For my part, I doubted whether there would be any civilised communities left after the coming conflict. Just about tea time, I think, it was resolved that a large portion of the paper which had been read should be repeated in order that everyone should be able to grasp its meaning. I caught Marriott's eye and without a word we rose and, seizing our suitcases, made our way to the station and the next train for London.

Later, when I came to read the resolutions passed by the Malvern Conference, I was surprised at their coherence and their scope. In the last two days, after we had left, the conference must have worked very hard, because some of the subjects dealt with in the resolutions had not, so far as I remembered, been mentioned in the sessions I attended. No doubt the Archbishop and Dr. Demant had done some drastic editing.

When the night bombing began in 1940, we had to make a rule that all inhabitants of the Cathedral buildings must sleep in the crypt, because we could not spare men to deal with "incidents" in the periphery. All the Canons elected to stay, though Canon Alexander by reason of age and Canon Mozley by reason of ill-health would, I think, have been better employed in pastoral work in parishes out of the bombing area. The corner of the crypt assigned to my wife and me was also occupied by the famous effigy of Dr. John Donne, the poet and dean, dressed in his shroud. The effigy was covered with sandbags and thus hidden from view, but sometimes I dreamt that Dr. Donne was stirring in his hiding-place and I remember thinking that he might have found words to express my feelings. Mr. Allen had looked ahead; and while too many citizens of London talked of the "phoney" war and did nothing, with disastrous consequences, the Cathedral was defended night and day by trained men who knew their way about the building and how to handle hoses and ladders. Canon Cockin was concerned with the first aid which went on along with the fire-fighting exercises.

There can be no doubt that the war was an ordeal in which loss and gain accrued to me as to so many others, but it is hard to estimate or describe. In the small "mess room" which Dick Sheppard and I had persuaded the Chapter to build for the Cathedral's works staff, the St. Paul's Watch gathered at night when there was no alert. There we listened to the nine o'clock news of the B.B.C. and the voice of Winston Churchill (which always made me think of a bulldog) told of events which were often world-shaking. I may be eccentric in this, but that voice braced me not so much because it increased my hopes of victory as because it made me feel I would never give in. In that small room I heard some first-rate conversation and met some interesting men of several nations. We had professors, postmen, medical students, several architects, members of governments in exile, specially from Holland. In the quieter periods before night bombing began and later when the rocket peril took the place of the aeroplane, we lectured to each other and debated many questions—most often perhaps what we would do to the Germans when we had won the war, which seemed to me in 1940 and 1941 almost an academic question.

What caused so many men, who all had work to do and plenty to worry about, to devote so much time and labour to defending St. Paul's, for which they got no pay and no honours? Not, for the most part, primarily religion. Not a few were agnostics and others were non-conformists of various kinds. A most zealous and efficient member was a veteran architect, my friend R. P. Jones, who was a prominent layman of the Unitarian Church. I am not sure that one would have received a coherent answer if one had asked, "Why do you come when it is so dangerous and so unrewarding?" They would have said, I believe, if they had spoken their minds, "For England". St. Paul's was a part of their image of England. And that was most evident in the behaviour of the citizens who now are described by the repulsive American word "commuters"—the men and women who, day after day, through all the bombing, came to work in the City. The first thing they asked was, "Is the dome still standing?" Churchill's instinctive appreciation of popular motivation was shown by his anxiety about our dome. When it was on fire and the American press was writing off the Cathedral as lost, he telephoned to the Lord Mayor, "St. Paul's must be saved at all costs." I am sure that if the bombs had destroyed the dome of St. Paul's it would have been a blow to morale a hundred times more serious than the destruction of the Bank of England.

I learned from comradeship with the Watch too the importance of history in the national consciousness. The majority of the volunteer members of the Watch were highly educated men

who may be assumed to have an historical background in their
thinking; the members of the daytime watch, the works staff
of the Cathedral, included some men who were educated in
every sense of the word, such as the Clerk of Works, and most
of the rest were skilled and intelligent craftsmen. But I was
surprised as I came to know them better at their knowledge of
the history of London and of the Cathedral. They were proud
to be members of the foundation and were touched by the
tradition. One of the reasons, as it seems to me, to limit the
influx of men of different races is that beyond a small proportion immigrants must dilute the tradition.

The frustration of this period for anyone in my position was
hard to bear. I was meeting men who had inside knowledge and
exceptional responsibility in the war and could see clearly
enough that the war was not going well, but had no opportunity
of helping the war effort except by carrying on the work at
St. Paul's. I was therefore not sorry to be selected by the Minister
of Information to be invited to undertake a mission for his
department in some neutral countries—Sweden, Norway, Denmark and Holland. I was flattered by being told that my name
was known to theologians in those countries and excited by
the warning conveyed by my friend, R. R. Williams, then a
don in Durham University and helping the Ministry and now
the Bishop of Leicester, that there was some slight element of
danger in my assignment. What precisely that assignment was
remained somewhat vague, but in general terms it was to visit
all the Anglican chaplains in the countries and to take every
opportunity of putting our case to the neutral citizens and to
report on the state of opinion in universities and in the churches.
To this end I was to give lectures and make contact with leaders
of opinion, particularly in the theological faculties. I was dismayed to find that my mission was thought to demand that I
should dress in full decanal panoply—gaiters, apron and, on
appropriate occasions, silver buckled shoes and silk stockings.
I was not required to wear a curly decanal top hat—I suppose
because my briefers had never seen me in one. Much as I disliked this, I had to agree that to make any progress with my
propaganda I had to "put myself across", as they say, if not as
a man of note at least as something rare and strange.

The notion of propaganda had a hint of salesmanship and
of deceit which troubled me, and I was not sure what view of

the situation the Government wanted me to present. In particular, though I firmly believed that we should win the war, I could not see any rational argument to persuade other people that it was probable. I was sure I ought to clear up my mind before I committed myself and, greatly daring, I said I would not go unless I could have a private interview with Lord Halifax, who was the Foreign Secretary. I was quite sure that he would tell me the truth as he saw it.

The interview duly took place and Halifax talked freely to me, in the sense that he certainly believed every word he uttered —but I was astonished. I said my mind would be clarified if he could answer two questions: Did he himself feel confident that the Germans would be defeated? and, if so, How would the end of the conflict be brought about? Halifax said he was convinced that the end would come in the same way as the end of the first world war—by the internal break-up of Germany. To this I replied that on that morning when our meeting took place the newspapers here and elsewhere were full of rumours about the spring offensive in the west with overwhelming concentrations of troops. Halifax, however, did not believe these reports. He said he was advised that probably the Germans would be unable to mount a large-scale offensive because they had no generals with experience of commanding massive operations over wide areas, while the French and we had many who had learned this art in the previous war. This was a new idea to me and one not easily reconciled with the impression of military efficiency and confidence which my recent experience had left on my mind—that of marching youthful multitudes. But, after all, I had been only briefly in Germany and only in one corner of the land. I might well be mistaken. I will add here that my belief in the theory of German incapacity in military command did not survive more than two days when I landed in Europe. No one doubted that there would be a spring offensive; the only doubts were when and where.

I decided to go. I convinced myself that I might do some good and that I heartily desired the downfall of the Nazis and all their works. My disgust at the persecution of the Jews was intense, though at the time we did not know half of the dreadful truth. I was persuaded that on our side we were defending what was left of Christian civilisation and that I could base an effective and perfectly sincere propagandist lecture on that thesis. On the whole, the fact that we were allied with atheist Russia seemed to me a pity and, as I shall mention later, that particular logical flaw in my argument had its dangers. But along with my motives I must reckon my spirit of curiosity and adventure. I wanted to see and feel the historical catastrophe from within.

In February, 1940, I set out. The plan was to spend about a week in each country and cram as much into the time as possible by having a programme of engagements arranged partly by the M.O.I. and partly by the resident English chaplains. On the Sundays I preached in the English church. The chaplains played up magnificently and the Anglo-Dutch and the Anglo-Norwegian Societies did their part, including the Dr. Johnson Society of Oslo, an offshoot of the Johnson Club in the 18th century, which entertained me to an 18th-century dinner, but did not end by leaving me under the table. My travel was by K.L.M., which of course was "neutral", though it was alleged that some of its pilots were crypto-Nazis. The flight over the North Sea was both uncomfortable and dull. Strict black-out was imposed on passengers who were deprived of all vision beyond the interior of the plane which was compelled to fly at such a low altitude (500 feet, I believe) that bumps and jumps were alarmingly frequent. Once the North Sea was crossed, further flight was mostly at high altitudes. On my outward journey I had a wait of some hours on the Schiphol aerodrome at Amsterdam for the plane which would take me to Stockholm. I remembered that I was to be a kind of walking advertisement and selected a conspicuous table for my lunch, as I remember it, not far from the departure point of the plane to Berlin. The rich furs and the prosperous complacency of the German passengers sickened me and I wondered if they were clearing out because they knew when the offensive would be.

The quaint dress of an Anglican dean had its effects. All kinds of people took me under observation, including men who looked like detectives.

It was my good fortune to start my tour in Stockholm, where the British Minister was Victor Mallet, whose distinguished later career led him to the embassies of Madrid and Rome. He and his wife had only very recently arrived in Stockholm, which had become of course a very important diplomatic post.

The Finns, under the leadership of Marshal Mannerheim, were still resisting the Russian invaders and on the plane which took me to Stockholm were some volunteers on the way to join the Finnish army. From the moment of my arrival to the end of my mission I was disturbed by the disadvantages under which our diplomats worked, compared with their German opponents.

In the case of Sweden we had a Minister of first-rate ability and unwearying diligence. But if careful plots had been laid to frustrate him they could hardly have been more effective than the presumably accidental actual circumstances. He knew nothing of the language and had no contacts with prominent Swedes. Only one member of his staff had Swedish contacts— Commander Poland the naval attaché, who had a Swedish wife. The Polands were old friends because he was one of the major officials in the Mansion House and, during my time at St. Paul's bore many titles—the humblest being that of Mace Bearer. The German Embassy was well provided with fluent speakers of Swedish and abounded with contacts of the most valuable kind. So far as I could tell, Victor Mallet had no instructions about the policy of the British Government, but was very anxious to get information about the number of Swedish volunteers helping the Finns. Another fact which emerged was that conversation in the legation had to be most guarded, because though it was certain the staff included informers it was not certain who they were or whom they informed. My days and nights as guest of the Mallets were delightful and instructive; a happy memory. Lady Mallet is the daughter of my old friend Mrs. Andreae.

I was glad that they thought I might help in the diplomatic conflict by accepting an invitation to tea with the Crown Prince and his gracious English wife. The plot was that the Minister and his wife should accompany me to the Crown Prince's Palace and turn the conversation to the Finnish war. They were sure the Crown Prince must know the number of volunteers and adroit chatter must elicit some clue to the number. Alas, the stratagem was a failure. The Crown Prince kept the talk steadily on Chinese porcelain, on which he was an authority, and insisted that we should go round his large and valuable collection. We had a pleasant and, in a sense, enlightening visit hearing quite a lot about the Ming dynasty, but nothing about the state of Finland in 1940.

My grateful memory dwells on a kind lady whose name I
have forgotten, who saved me from blotting my copy book
socially many times over when I enjoyed the hospitality of
some of the great families. She told me when, as principal
guest, I should make a little speech of thanks, when to start
eating and when to wait and what to say when I took my leave.
I hope I left the impression that at least I was trying.

The Finnish war soon intervened in my tentative propaganda
effort. A meeting had been arranged, at a midday hour, of so-
called "Christian leaders" in Stockholm. We met in a large
room at the head of some stone steps. I remember thinking
that it would hurt to be thrown down them. The room was
packed by men of various religious allegiances but predominantly Lutheran. A tall Salvation Army major stood out from
the crowd and looked friendly. On the whole, I thought the
audience looked suspicious. It was beginning to dawn on me
that the Lutheran Swedes preferred Germans to Russians. I
gave a version of my staple propaganda speech on Christian
Civilisation which was received with courteous silence followed
by questions all fairly easy except the one I had expected: "If
you are defending Christian civilisation, why are you trying
to get allied to the atheist Bolsheviks in Russia?" Fortunately,
as I was about to reply with a long explanation, my eye caught
that of the Salvation Army man, who gave me an almost imperceptible warning shake of the head, which I interpreted as
meaning, "Drop the subject at once." I produced a fatuous
pleasantry, something about if I was being beaten up by a
murderous madman I would welcome the aid of a muscular
burglar: and I passed on to a safer subject. My Salvation Army
friend said afterwards, "If you had gone on with the question,
though this is a meeting of Christian leaders, it would have
become a rough house in five minutes and some of us would
have been thrown down the steps."

A wonderful opening was offered to me by the Archbishop
of Uppsala, who invited me to spend a night at his house and
to give a lecture in the great hall of the University. The audience
was to include professors and lecturers of Uppsala and, I was
told, probably also at least one German professor of Theology.
I did my best to produce an academic discourse which would
be both respectable from the scholarly point of view and a
subtle piece of wartime propaganda. I have lost my notes, but

I think I remember that I devoted some time to a criticism of Spengler's *Der Untergang des Abendlandes*, which was much in my mind at the time. Archbishop Eidem was a kindly and gentle pastor who was full of brotherly love and without anti-British bias. I was surprised to see the German professor in the front row of my audience and still more to find myself sitting next to him at dinner afterwards. Whether he was on the same kind of mission I never discovered. If he was, he was much better disguised than I, because his lecture was on some quite neutral topic—something like "Some Early Christian Liturgies". He was a tactful man, for when I said, "I hope my lecture did not make you uncomfortable," he replied in perfect English, "I fear I was not able to follow your argument, owing to my ignorance of the language."

From Stockholm I travelled by train to Gothenburg, which was reputed to be hostile in general to the allied cause. A curious incident happened on the journey, which I do not understand to this day. The solution to the problem: How many Swedish volunteers were in the Finnish army against Russia? was apparently handed to me on a plate. A military-looking man came into my compartment where I had been alone and began turning over typewritten sheets which appeared to contain lists of names. Soon he started a conversation by saying, "These lists are really interesting. They are the names of volunteers. I make the total . . ." What the figure was I have now forgotten; it was, I think, either forty thousand or fourteen thousand. But though I duly reported the conversation to Mr. Mallet in Stockholm, I doubted whether it was reliable, and my doubts were multiplied a hundredfold the next morning when the newspaper headlines blazoned the news of the Finnish collapse. I am sure my informative railway companion knew the war was over and probably was planting rumours that the Swedes had made great preparations to help which were frustrated by the premature surrender of Mannerheim's force.

The breakdown of the Finnish resistance was certainly unexpected by the public in Gothenburg and came as a shattering blow. People reading the news bulletins in the streets that morning looked terrified. It was not very long afterwards that I saw the people in the streets of London confronted by the surrender of the French army and the stark reality that Britain now faced the victorious Germans without an ally in the world.

My recollection is that no one looked depressed or panic-stricken nor did I hear anyone even suggest that we might lose the war. It was not surprising however that my propaganda was unacceptable in the circumstances and in fact it was in Gothenburg that I had the discouraging experience of an audience walking out halfway through my lecture. My chief effort was this lecture in the largest church to the clergy. It began badly when it was announced that the Dean of the Cathedral, who had been advertised as the chairman, did not appear but went off to a village quite a long way in the country. It was currently conjectured that he had changed his mind and did not want the British case to be heard. The audience was quite good, though it looked apprehensive. It endured my lecture for about twenty minutes and then more than half walked out. What utterance of mine triggered off this spontaneous gesture, I never discovered. Those who remained were courteous but not expansive.

There was, however, one encouraging aspect of my visit. The Consul was slaving night and day, assisted by a volunteer who was, I think, a retired officer. Between them they were coping with all kinds of problems of shipping. The chaplain and the congregation of the English church softened my sense of failure by their hospitality and appreciation of what small ministry I was able to offer.

Would Norway be equally difficult? I was afraid it might be worse, because I had been told that the Primate of Norway, Bishop Berggrav, had visited Göring in Berlin and I was therefore hoping to get a private interview with him before I spoke in public. I felt that the very first thing to do in Oslo was to ask the British Minister's advice, so that I could avoid taking the wrong line. I hoped that he might be co-operative like our Minister in Stockholm. This, however, was a total loss. The Minister was on the point of retiring and was packing up, much concerned about how to get his furniture across the North Sea. He could not help me at all even by information. He had never spoken to Bishop Berggrav and, being himself a Roman Catholic, had no interest in Lutheran bishops. This astonished me; by general consent Berggrav was one of the most popular figures in public life and the chief pastor of the Church to which the majority of the population belonged. The interview with Bishop Berggrav turned into an appearance before the whole bench of Norwegian bishops who were in session. I was a guest at a midday meal. Meals with archbishops were no new experience and the Lutheran bishops with their large pectoral crosses would have fitted well enough into Lambeth Palace. The beginning of the meal was startling to an Anglican. The Primate sounded a note and with one accord the bishops sprang to their feet and burst into song—a chorale, but the words I did not understand. I thought at the time that meals at Lambeth Palace would be improved if bishops always opened their mouths wide in sacred song.

The bishops were concerned about the possible evacuation of schoolchildren and cross-examined me on my experience in England. They were evidently considering the invasion of Norway as a real danger. I must be careful here to do justice to the bishops, and particularly Bishop Berggrav. He was a great Christian leader, and when the invasion came he stood courageously against the tyranny of the occupation, but unfortunately he was one of the principal obstructors of my propaganda. Naturally enough, he strove to keep his country and his Church out of the war and for that end he did all he could to prevent provocative speeches and movements which might give cause to the Germans, or excuse, for invasion. Like some other statesmen, he had trusted in the League of Nations and now that no help was likely to come from that quarter he hoped his nation might be saved by keeping very quiet. In pursuit of this policy, he took a definite line which he repeated on every possible occasion—he proclaimed the duty of complete neutrality. Norway, he said, must not only take no sides in action, it must take no sides in thought. He proclaimed the saving gospel of "neutrality of mind". This line of thought was precisely the opposite of that which I was advocating. I was urging that, at least in sympathy and moral judgment, my hearers ought to be for us and against our enemies. But deeper than my chagrin that my advocacy should be rejected by the Primate was my conviction that neutrality of mind was immoral. To refuse to think of right and wrong in the conflict which was likely to engulf us all seemed to me to be a failure in duty and to be a kind of moral suicide by a wilful paralysis of the conscience. That is still my opinion.

Berggrav was most kind and generous in helping me to get a hearing. I had an invitation from the University in Oslo to lecture and Berggrav took the chair, introducing me with real Christian courtesy. I could not, of course, complain that in his speech at the end he developed at some length his views on Neutrality of Mind, which effectively neutralised all that I had tried to say in my lecture. Deeply depressed by the Bishop's summing up, I went straight from the lecture hall to tea in the royal palace with H.M. King Haakon VII. He was an impressive figure of a man. I had never seen him before and did not expect that in a few weeks he would be an exile in England and a frequent visitor to St. Paul's. In a large room we were alone at a small round tea table. Haakon's first words were encouraging and bracing after a large dose of "neutrality of mind". He said, "Of course you know that Hitler is a devil." "True, Sir," I replied, "but I fear not a neutral remark." I think the King quite literally believed that Hitler was possessed by an evil spirit and, so far as I can see, that is a good description in New Testament terms. The King had heard some stories about children being poisoned by chocolates dropped from German aeroplanes, which horrified him but seemed to me almost trivial compared with the gigantic crime against whole populations which Hitler had contrived.

I met with much friendly sympathy from Norwegians and particularly from schoolmasters. I taught English for one morning in a mixed school and admired the method of teaching which, almost from the first lesson, interested the children and made them curious about the people who spoke this strange language. By the express wish of the whole form I described in detail the game of cricket. I doubt if any of my hearers was any wiser at the end and personally I should have been happier to expound the doctrine of the Holy Trinity in which a certain element of mystery would have been appropriate. I fear I left the game of cricket a profound mystery in my pupils' minds. I was pleased to hear later on of the defiant spirit of these boys and girls when the Germans occupied Oslo. Summoned by the authorities to visit an exhibition glorifying the Nazi achievements and ideals, the whole school filed through with heads turned away from the exhibits so that not a child looked at any of them.

I left Norway with mixed feelings. Somehow I felt that I should meet many of the people again, though I do not suggest that I foresaw Hitler's audacious coup. I realised that there were fascist elements in the population and was once in the same room as Quisling, but had no opportunity of talking to him. The pro-British intellectuals with whom I had converse, as at the Dr. Johnson Club, were fascinating talkers of a speculative turn of mind, some having large ideas about an Atlantic community or confederation in which Norway and Britain would play leading parts.

Denmark was less fruitful in vivid experiences. I learned much from Dean Vögelsang about the divisions in the Lutheran Church in Germany and of the extreme German Christian party which was semi-pagan. Copies of their hymnbook and liturgy opened my eyes to the extent of anti-Semitic influence within the Lutheran Church. My friends in Marburg had not told me the whole truth. Now I had to admit that the Danish dean's sardonic reply to my question, "Don't these Christians read the New Testament?" "Oh, yes, specially Romans 13, which they are always quoting," was only too true. The passage begins: "The powers that be are ordained by God." The belief that the spring offensive would open with an attack on Denmark was widespread and I was told that the British Intelligence Service had warned the Danish Government and forecast the approximate date. Neither the Danish Government, nor apparently the British Legation, did anything which would indicate that the warning was believed and, according to the British chaplain, who escaped when the blow fell, the capture of Copenhagen was effected by 800 soldiers who were concealed in ships in the harbour. Everyone knew that Denmark was almost defenceless and, in fact, only the Royal Body Guard put up any real resistance. I stayed most of the time in a hotel near the British Legation. In the next room lived a German who talked every evening on the telephone to Berlin, beginning always at midnight.

My last port of call was Holland and, when I landed in the airport there, I had a nasty shock. The programme had been carefully worked out in consultation with the secretary of the Anglo-Dutch Society. He met me with the disappointing news that the programme could not be carried out and one of the principal items would have to be changed—it was the evening lecture in the University lecture hall on "Christianity and the World Crisis". The secretary had evidently been subject to pressure from the Dutch authorities and, when I got back to England, I found that the Minister of Justice had intervened.

The secretary informed me that he had been forced to alter the title because the word "crisis" frightened people who would suspect that I was intending to refer to the war. "They would be dead right," I said. "That is what the lecture is all about." The secretary prophesied that the audience would fade away. He was not quite right, but the hall was only half full and applause rather tentative. The situation in Holland was tense. The German build-up of force just across the frontier was undeniable and just before my arrival it was known that the chief of British Intelligence had been captured by the Germans. For a night or two I stayed in an hotel and mixed with some of the guests, few of whom, I think, were precisely what they claimed to be. A curious thing which I learned was the value of an Eire passport. At that time a fortunate possessor could dispose of valuable information on both sides of the frontier.

The British Minister, Sir Nevile Bland, and his wife offered me hospitality in the Legation and very fortunate I was to have such peaceful and gracious circumstances for an agitating week. My impression was that quite a large majority of Dutchmen agreed that right was on our side and hoped we would win, but only a minority thought that we were likely to win. The military strength of Holland was of course much greater than that of Denmark and I was shown quite a large section of the defences. To my completely inexpert mind it seemed that the linked system of fortifications, dykes and canals was formidable and, if everyone did his part, an invasion could be held up for quite a long time. I wondered if the necessary co-ordination would work perfectly. So did some of my Dutch hosts. The contribution which I could make in such conditions was negligible. I took part in two public meetings connected with the Ecumenical Movement, but though I was convinced that in the long run the reuniting of Christendom was of the utmost importance, it was intolerably unreal to hold these meetings to promote and pray for peace and brotherhood and make no mention of the fact that a few miles away a vast army was being assembled. I fear that I broke a tacit convention by speaking and praying about the war.

Yet the caution was comprehensible. The Nazis had already started a reign of terror in anticipation. They let it be known that they were compiling a list of persons who would be liquidated when they walked in. Just opposite the entrance to the

British Legation they took a shop from which they photographed and recorded visitors, with the consequence that nervous individuals ceased to visit the Minister and his wife. One had the feeling sometimes that one was a character in a thriller and would be glad to escape. Two days before I left Holland I visited the British Consul's office which looked commonplace enough, but behind the façade of routine business was a secret office in which three British naval officers in uniform worked at desks, each with a loaded revolver before him. The day I left one of them was shot in the street.

No one tried to shoot me, and indeed from the German point of view it would have been a waste of ammunition, but there did appear to be some danger of a rough house in Rotterdam. By the good offices of Sir Nevile Bland, a meeting was arranged at which I was the principal speaker. Lady Bland accompanied me and sat on the platform. The hall was packed and my impression was that quite a number were turned away. It must be remembered that I was dressed all this time in decanal fancy dress—apron and gaiters—and was something of a curiosity. Also one must remember that I spoke in English. The audience did look to me glum and unresponsive, but on the whole was quiet and my speech ended to faint applause. I was surprised to hear Lady Bland heave a sigh of relief and say, "Thank God, that's over." She told me that a contingent of Dutch Nazis was in the audience and it had been feared they would attempt to take over the platform. I was glad that she waited until the end to disclose the state of affairs.

I left Holland feeling that there were many stories unfinished and that I should probably meet again some of the men who had been so friendly, which indeed was fulfilled much sooner than I expected. Not until Dr. Gebrandy, the Dutch Prime Minister of the government in exile, arrived in London in May, 1940, did I know the truth about my own story. During my brief mission Gebrandy had been the Minister of Justice and in that capacity he had on his desk every morning a list of "dangerous persons", furnished by the police. For some time, he said, my name was second on the list. I have often wondered who was number one. That I really had caused alarm was confirmed, when I returned to London, by my wife who had been awakened one night while staying in Exeter by an urgent call from the Foreign Office to say that the Dutch Ambassador had made strong representations that I should be stopped from lecturing in Holland on any subject except Shakespeare. Whether the Foreign Office feigned ignorance in order not to impede my propaganda or really had forgotten all about me, I cannot say, but I incline to the latter hypothesis.

I was back in London on March 24th and immediately re-joined the St. Paul's Watch and gave my comrades an account of my experience. Later my story was carried further before the same audience by Mr. Howard Smith, who had been British Minister in Copenhagen when the country was overrun by the German forces. In the Cathedral there had been little change except that the unremitting exercises in fire drill had immensely improved the efficiency and spirit of the Watch. I repaired to the M.O.I. to make my report to Sir John Reith and answer questions. I think we both realised that events had begun to move so rapidly that my opinions were almost irrelevant. The great offensive was at the door. No doubt Reith had knowledge which I did not possess. The only question he asked was, "If the Germans invaded Denmark and Holland, how long do you think they could resist?" To my own surprise I answered without a moment's consideration: "Holland five days and Denmark five hours," which was about right. I noticed that Norway was not included in the question. The only other recollection which remains of that interview is that I was congratulated on the modesty of my expenses, which was due to the fact that hotels cost me very little because I had so much hospitality in all four countries. On reflection, I wonder if I was not too careful in my expenditure. Perhaps if I had dined and wined some of the queer people who came to give mysterious messages from alleged sympathisers I might have learned more than I did.

The Norway story caught up with me soon enough. On April 9th Oslo was captured by about 1,100 German soldiers and the English chaplain escaped by walking to Sweden. I was more or less conscripted in a curious radio exercise. I had said a short piece on the European Service on my return and now I, along with a number of others, both Norwegian and English, were employed in putting a non-stop stream of talk over to Norway. Not a moment's interval was allowed and we stood on a staircase in Bush House, each of us alert to step into the place of the man on the step above. No one ever explained this to me and I can only suppose that there was some danger of the Germans capturing the wavelength, or perhaps putting out pseudo-British communications.

The great offensive which some thought German generals would be incompetent to launch burst upon the world, shattering the illusions of those who had trusted in the League of Nations and those who had chattered about the "phoney war". In the breath-taking onslaught which brought down so many defences, it hardly seemed to matter that three out of the four countries which I had visited had fallen into enemies' hands. Our anxiety for the freedom of England grew every day and yet, even when the French laid down their arms, I heard no one speak of surrender or compromise. Suddenly, too, the anxieties of innumerable homes were multiplied as the losses accumulated.

I come now to the great sorrow of our lives, the event after which nothing was the same again. Our eldest child, Michael Harrington Matthews, Sub-Lieutenant R.N.V.R., was killed on H.M.S. *Greyhound*, the destroyer which was the first to reach Dunkirk, on May 28th, 1940. The little boy who had clung to his mother in 1916 during a Zeppelin raid crying, "But you aren't frightened, Mummy, are you?" was shattered by a bomb from a German plane as he stood on the bridge of *Greyhound* in 1940. Margaret and he were close together. They were in many ways alike and understood each other. Her words when the telegram of death came were characteristic of both: "Well, poor boy, he can't disappoint himself now." Michael was a perfectionist so far as he himself was concerned. He could not bear to do anything in which he did not excel and his ability matched his will. After a poor start in his prep school and near failure to gain entrance to Westminster School, he entered on a spectacular school and university career. He became head of school, the first outside the circle of King's Scholars to hold that office for twenty years. He was captain of cricket and gained a scholarship to Christ Church, Oxford, where he kept wicket for Oxford. A cricket Blue and a first in "Greats"—the double triumph seemed almost incredible; but Michael had, someone said, something Elizabethan in his recklessness exemplified when he cut an optional paper in the Greats examination to play cricket for Oxford against Gloucestershire. He entered Gray's Inn with one of the top scholarships and gained a first class in Jurisprudence in Oxford. To crown it all his love of music was dominant from the day when he started piano lessons at the age of ten until his death. I treasure the memory of an essay which he wrote at his prep school on the vast subject of Music. His first words were, "Music is happiness". For him they were true.

What Michael really thought about religion I never knew, and I think he would have been hard put to it to sum up his beliefs. He joined in Christian worship and was a communicant and beyond question he had a deep sense of duty which made him a really powerful force for good when head of school. At one time I had thought he might feel a vocation to the Christian ministry, but perhaps I failed to give him the good example or a clear view of Christian truth which would have persuaded him. It has always been against my principles to urge young men to seek Holy Orders, because I believe it is wrong to bring pressure to bear on a choice of career which can be so momentous. Anyone who is thinking of becoming an ordained minister ought to be warned of the trials and hardships which may be his lot. This is true of all regular Christian ministry, but is specially applicable to the ministry of Churches which regard priesthood as being an indelible character. Michael would have been a wonderful priest, if he had recognised his calling. As it was, he was one of the young men cut off in their early prime who might have pioneered a better future for mankind. Letters from so many who shared our grief, from the Queen and Archbishop to old schoolfellows, helped us to go on, and later his name was inscribed in more than one roll of honour: Westminster School, Christ Church, Oxford, and Gray's Inn record him. Many years later I heard of one spontaneous epitaph spoken on the day of battle. I was wandering round my old cathedral in Exeter alone and saw a virger whose face was unfamiliar, so I spoke to him and, after some desultory conversation, he suddenly said, "I saw your son killed." He had been a seaman on *Greyhound* and described how Michael's body was lowered from the bridge on to the deck and, as it was lying there, another seaman went and took his dead hand, saying, "Goodbye: you were a good boy." That was Michael, always he had tried to excel, to be a good boy and, as Margaret said, he did not disappoint himself.

I conclude this chapter with the sermon which I preached on the Sunday after Michael's death. His name is not mentioned, but every word was written for him and about him. The sermon expresses what I believe to be the Christian message to parents of men and women who died in defending their country against evil tyrants. With my mind I accept it; but for years, when I thought of the waste of so much ability and the sheer stupidity of the forces which slaughtered so much brightness and hope, ungovernable rage filled my mind. Perhaps fortunately, in my rare fits of anger I become speechless and feel deathly sick. I do not curse and swear, but for a time seem paralysed by hate. One night at that time I lay in bed on my pallet in the crypt, off duty but expecting an alert at any moment, and tried to examine myself. I imagined that I could, by pressing a switch, annihilate the whole German nation, men, women and children, but could not make any selection—it must be all or none. As I felt then, would I choose to switch on destruction? I asked myself, and I was horrified to conclude that at that moment revenge and fear combined to swamp reason. I think it was not until at the end of the war I visited ruined German cities and German hospitals full of boys on the verge of death by starvation that revenge faded out of my motives. To Michael's mother, the blow was more dramatic in its effects. She had almost completed the first draft of her fourth novel when the news came and she never wrote another line. "Susan Goodyear's" pen ceased production. Margaret seemed to feel that life had ceased to be worthy of recording. For both of us, perhaps, it was a blessing in disguise that our minds were distracted from our private sorrow by the sudden outburst of night bombing and disasters in London all round.

Themselves They Could Not Save

He saved others; Himself He cannot save.

St. Matthew, XXVII: 42.

Seldom, I suppose, does a preacher find that a certain text imposes itself upon him, so that he must speak about that, or not speak at all. In these past days the words I have just read have been running in my head and forming a kind of refrain and comment on the events which have been happening with such breathless rapidity.

You remember well enough the occasion on which they

were spoken, and the speakers. They are a part of the taunts hurled at the Saviour on the Cross by "the Chief Priests with the scribes and elders". They were effective enough. They pointed out a fact which was evident, and suggested an inference which seemed inevitable. What possibility of salvation was there to be expected from one who was helpless to save Himself? "Let Him now come down from the Cross and we will believe in Him." What could be more reasonable? Show the power to help yourself and we will believe that you have power to help others.

Sometimes in great tragic dramas the poet uses the device of irony, making characters use words which have an implication of which they are unaware. I will not say that the writers of the Gospels used this device, for they were writing facts and not fiction; but they have seen the irony in some of the remarks of hostile people, how they spoke the truth, as it were, in spite of themselves.

Thus when the High Priest said, "It is expedient that one man should die for the people," he was, no doubt, expressing a cynical maxim of policy. What does the unjust death of one man matter if by it we can keep peace? But the Evangelist, and the Christian reader, see in these words a reference to the sacrifice for the salvation, not only of the Jewish people, but of all the world. So it is here. "He saved others; Himself He cannot save." There was irony in the taunt.

The words were not true in the sense which the speakers meant, but they were true in a far more profound sense. It was not true that Jesus could not have avoided the Cross. Even if we think of Him as simply a man like other men, with no more power than other men, it was not true. Without difficulty, and without any obvious dishonour, He could have left Jerusalem quietly, almost up to the moment when He was arrested. He could have evaded the excited crowds at the Passover, and remained hidden until they had dispersed. Indeed, He need never have gone to Jerusalem at all. And even when the arrest had been made, one word to His followers would have started a riot and an attempt at rescue which might well have been successful. Jesus Himself believed that powers far greater than those at the disposal of ordinary men were at His command. "Legions of angels", He said, would be sent by His heavenly Father to release Him at His request.

So also Christians have believed. Christ stayed on the Cross because He willed to stay there.

II

But in a deeper sense the taunt was true. He could not save Himself. That was indeed the one thing He could not do. The necessity which was laid down upon Him was not, as the Chief Priests and Elders supposed, one which their fraud and force had brought about; it arose from His own soul. It was an inward compulsion, not one from outside. The Cross was necessary for the fulfilment of the saving work which He had come to do. The Kingdom of God could not be established in any other way.

Suppose that, in answer to the taunts, the Crucified had come down from that Cross; suppose that some supernatural intervention had confounded His enemies; suppose that the legion of angels had appeared with flaming swords; we should have had a marvellous story, the kind of story which we all like to hear, where good triumphs without too much suffering—but we should have had no Gospel, no good news for a world of sinful and burdened and tortured men. The history of Christ would have been one more story of escape from evil, not, as it is, the history of the facing of evil right out until the bitter end. Christ would not save Himself, not because He had not the power, but because, being what He was, He could not will His own safety.

People have often argued whether God can do absolutely anything. Perhaps it is not a very profitable subject, but one interesting conclusion has been reached by most of those who have considered it. They have been led to think that there are some things which God cannot do—those which contradict His own nature and perfect holiness. That is surely true. God could not approve and bless cruelty, cowardice and treachery, nor could He condemn kindness, courage and faithfulness. He could not; because, if He did, He would cease to be God. The same is true of Christ. He could not have sought His own safety when the path of His vocation led to the Cross, for had He done so, He would not have been Christ.

III

I suppose the reason why this text has been so much with me is obvious enough. During these past days we have been following with bated breath the fortunes of the B.E.F., trapped through no fault of its own or of its commanders, in a hopeless position. We have seen the retreat and the disaster turned into a glorious page of British history, already so full of glory. We must thank God that the skill and courage of the army has been so successful, beyond our fears. But we must not forget the price which has been paid. Who has not thought of the rearguard which battled and is battling so heroically that others might escape, and of those who kept the sea, that the way might be open? Of how many is it literally true that they saved others, themselves they could not save?

Of very many of them at least it is true to say that an inner necessity brought them to the sacrifice. They might have stayed behind; they might have found safety for themselves; but they could not; being what they were, they could do no other than defend the right to the uttermost.

I touch here upon feelings so intimate that almost any word must be dangerous. This at least can be said. The loss, the tragedy, the waste, are all real enough. No words can soften them or make them different. But would we have had the men other than they were and are? We know we would not.

IV

There was another taunt flung at the Crucified. "He trusted in God that He would deliver him, let Him deliver him if He desires him." The challenge was to that faith in God which had sustained Jesus all through. Was that challenge not answered? To us, who have accepted the Christian faith, the answer is a triumphant "Yes". After the power of evil had been met to the uttermost, the cause was vindicated by the Resurrection. The most utter and irreparable waste of life which has ever been seen on this earth was not really waste and loss. The Crucified entered into the glory of the Father. This is the part of our faith to which we must cling with all our might in these dark days, when so much is being destroyed, which, so far as this world is concerned, can never be replaced. No good which has ever been is really annihilated, and no self which has been lighted by the divine spirit of sacrifice and devotion to duty has been wiped out. They are taken up into the eternal life of God. Beyond our present vision they are not frustrated but fulfilled.

We must, indeed, be careful how we apply to those who have bravely devoted themselves to a great cause all that is said of the Captain of our salvation. He was the perfect Man, the One without sin, and they were full of imperfections. But they are united with Him, at least, by the great bond of sacrifice. We mistake, I believe, very often the true values of life as God sees them. The Christian Church has laid emphasis, too much perhaps, on the sober and unadventurous virtues. It has cultivated the softer side of life, and been too much the patron of the inoffensive and quiet man. It has thought of Jesus, sometimes exclusively, as the gentle and meek Lamb of God. But that was not the way the early Church thought of Him; it is not the picture which the Gospels give. He is the "Lion of the Tribe of Judah"; the strong Son of God; the conqueror over the powers of darkness. To those who first followed Him and formed the militant Church He was the Hero. They adopted the taunt as the true description of Christ. "He saved others, Himself he could not save."

We have come in these last days to value more highly the qualities of the hero and the warrior. We have come nearer to a full understanding of the range of human goodness. In the sight of God, the soul in which there burns the fire of heroism and the capacity for devotion to the highest cause is of greater worth than the prudent and cautious soul which seeks safety as the greatest good. May the sacrifices which are being offered for us be joined with the Sacrifice of Christ, and sanctify us, filling us with an unselfish devotion to the cause of right, so that the offering may not be in vain.*

* Sermon preached at St. Paul's Cathedral on Sunday, June 2nd, 1940.

CHAPTER 13

Wartime in England and Ireland

This is not the place to tell the story of the air attack on London
and the damage suffered by St. Paul's. I have attempted to do
so in the illustrated book *St. Paul's Cathedral in Wartime:
1939-1945*. But it would give a fantastically false impression to
pretend that the bombing of London was a largely irrelevant
incident in my life. So far is that from being the case that I am
conscious of being a different person from what I was before the
war; and in reconstructing my pre-war past in imagination I do
not always understand myself. Whether the experience made
me a better man or a worse one is doubtful, but it made me
different. Of course there is nothing exceptional in that, but
the nature of the difference is interesting to anyone given to
introspection. Some people are said "not to know the meaning
of fear" and I have met persons (women as well as men) who
claim this immunity. That is not my case and I am sure it is not
the case of the majority of citizens. Two incidents marked my
progress in self-knowledge. The first I have recounted in the
book already referred to. A group of St. Paul's Watch members
were on the colonnade when the attack on the docks took place
on September 7th. I cannot improve on the words which I used
when my memory was fresh.

It was a golden, peaceful evening and, as the light faded from
the sky, the angry red glow in the east, diversified by leaping
flames, dominated the prospect, while from time to time the
peculiar thud of bursting bombs punctured the silence. We
were a silent company as we gazed upon this apocalyptic
scene, each no doubt pondering many things. We noted, without remark, the apparent absence of defence—an observation which we were to make often in the next few weeks. We

wondered how long it would be before the attack moved westwards to the heart of London. We feared that the whole port of London was being annihilated. At last someone spoke, "It is like the end of the world," and someone else replied, "It is the end of *a* world."

I wonder if it really was.

Shortly afterwards Godfrey Allen and I stood alone on the same colonnade to see the first small night attack on central London. It was a kind of trial run and possibly only one bomber engaged. But there seemed to be no opposition and the enemy plane dropped two bombs in a line which pointed at the Cathedral. We waited for the third bomb—it fell and exploded further off. We said nothing to each other, except some banality like "off the mark", but to me at least the experience was significant. I learnt, perhaps partly from Allen, that one could be frightened without being paralysed by fear and indeed might become more alert and alive when faced with the danger of death.

To overcome fear it is an advantage to occupy a position in which one is prominent. It never occurred to me that I might run away from St. Paul's, because I knew that thousands of Londoners would think that I was afraid and had lost hope of saving our Cathedral. Max Beerbohm's parable *The Happy Hypocrite* applies very aptly to the virtue of courage. In the parable a wicked man who loves a good woman puts on the mask of a wise and noble person. In course of time he becomes ashamed of his deception and tries to tear off the mask—in vain; he cannot throw off the mask, because it has become his face. How many, I wonder, of those whose courage is unquestioned started by being frightened mortals, pretending to be fearless for the sake of those whom they led. To be candid about myself, I was never so frightened of bombs as I was of height. Unfortunately, from childhood heights have made me feel quite ill and the one moment of terror I remember was in an exercise on the roof of the choir one night when the leader of the group with which I was drilling brought us to the edge of the roof where a perpendicular iron ladder stood over what seemed, in the light of "muffled" torches, to be the bottomless pit, saying cheerfully, "Quickly down the ladder." I think my heart would have failed me, but I was saved from the crime of mutiny by the sirens sounding an alert and we scattered to our action stations.

I have recorded my impression of London at the time of Dunkirk before memories were overlaid by subsequent reflections. My impression is that we in London were strangely cheerful. No doubt this was partly due to the fact that few of us really knew the full menace of our situation. Only the leaders could be in possession of all the grim facts. No account of those days, even one written from the standpoint of a single building and its defenders, could omit the influence of Mr. Churchill. Perhaps he was at his greatest in those days and his effect on the morale of the nation was incalculable. It is curious to remember now that we even gained some encouragement from the thought that we stood alone. Our greatest peril became, paradoxically, a source of hope. I have never quite understood this psychological phenomenon and I do not think it is adequately explained by the remark which I often heard, "Well, no one can let us down now except ourselves."

Some left-wing journalists, with whom in the past I had often agreed, continued their tragically mistaken activity as the war grew more fierce and those who had babbled about the "phoney war", when concentration on the coming danger was the overriding duty, now changed their tune to diatribe against "the invasion racket". Colonel Blimp was never to me an attractive character, but at any rate he was never such a fool as that. Nor indeed were most of the "intellectuals". From among them came an initiative which helped us all to hold on. Realising the imminence of attack from the air and the possible invasion which might follow, some psychologists and sociologists had the inspiration to invent a "slogan" which might sustain the morale of the innumerable individuals who would be in peril. How to prevent panic and secure disciplined defence? They avoided optimistic promises and appealed rightly to the adult sense of responsibility. Their proposal was to cover every wall with placards proclaiming, "It all depends on me." Two members of the group were kind enough to ask my opinion. Unfortunately I have now forgotten who these two representatives were, but I am sure one was a well-known psychologist, probably my friend Dr. William Brown, and the other a business man prominent in the City. When they explained their plan, I was speedily convinced that something like this ought to be done, but when I repeated the slogan, I found that it appalled me. I said, "If all depends on me, there isn't a hope." I can only accept the slogan if I add, "and I depend on God." The Archbishop of Canterbury took the same view and the "I depend on God" addition was made on placards exhibited by churches.

In passing, I may remark that in my experience most of the ordinary citizens who faced the Blitz and manned the volunteer services were believers in God. I do not mean that they were all "good churchmen", though many were, but that they held fast to a conviction that justice and mercy are at the centre of the universe and that there are evil things which one must be ready to die rather than do.

The concerted strategic air attacks in which London was perhaps the chief target began on August 8th, 1940, and ended on October 31st, the same year. The plan took the form, it seemed, of four distinct attacks. The first attack, which lasted ten days and nights, was directed against sea ports, shipping and aerodromes near the coast. Wave after wave of bombers, protected by swarms of fighters, was launched with the aim of overwhelming and putting out of action British defences. These ten days of incessant conflict were the Battle of Britain. We guessed then, and we know now, that the *Luftwaffe* had good reason for expecting victory and would have gained it but for the incredible courage, resolution and skill of "the few". The second attack followed on August 19th, 1940, and lasted until September 5th. It was primarily on inland industrial areas and was relatively ineffective. Then followed attacks three and four, both mainly aimed at London; the first phase was low-level and later, as the London ack-ack became stronger, the last phase was from high levels. Though the strain on London defences then relaxed somewhat, it would be wrong to say it was finished. Night raids spasmodically continued and new types of bomb added variety to the terror. Oil bombs started furnaces of destruction in cities, and land mines attached to parachutes fell from the sky.

For my part, I am thankful that my lot was in a place where great values, religious, national and aesthetic, were attacked by barbarian invaders and to have had such loyal and staunch comrades. Apart from the strain of daily administration and anxiety for the fabric of our Cathedral, the main difficulty was loss of sleep. At the height of the bombing we had one hundred consecutive nights filled with alerts and one became so sleepy that one drowsed on one's feet and on sitting down immediately lost consciousness. Among the relatively trivial occupations which fell to me was correspondence and negotiation with the City Corporation and the Home Office. During the war the King and Queen visited the Cathedral many times and took a lively interest in our problems. These visits were "top secret", but of course were necessarily known to many people before-hand. The traditional ceremonial for state visits by the Sovereign to the Cathedral was elaborate and conspicuous, starting with the reception of the King at Temple Bar and continuing with the procession to the Cathedral with the Lord Mayor bear-ing the pearl sword. In that ceremonial the City was represented by the Lord Mayor at the City boundary and the Dean and Chapter received the King, preceded by the Lord Mayor, at the west door of the Cathedral, thus marking the distinction between the civic authorities and the ecclesiastical. It may seem childish, but the friendly controversy with the Corporation about where the Lord Mayor should meet the King when the royal personages arrived by car at the foot of the west steps had some substance. We did not wish to concede, even in ceremonial, that the City Corporation had any authority in St. Paul's, though we always gladly accorded welcome and seats of honour. The business had its humorous side and it struck me as ludicrous that officials like virgers and masters of ceremonies should have to keep a sharp watch on the Lord Mayor and aldermen to prevent them from coming too far up the steps with the King and Queen, while we were not looking.

More serious correspondence affecting the safety of St. Paul's was called for by the failure of the water supply in the two great fire raids. Herbert Morrison, the Home Secretary, was a great Londoner whom I had always admired, and his assistant, Ellen Wilkinson, I admired too, because she was courageous and indefatigable in visiting the air raid shelters and under-ground stations at the height of the Blitz. On the evening of December 29th, 1940, the Germans launched a fire attack on London which was most successful, except that for some reason it was not followed by high explosive bombs. A large part of the City near St. Paul's was burnt out, largely because of the neglect of citizens to guard their buildings. We had not neglected this duty and were amply provided with hoses and other equipment. My wife, who was making our beds in the crypt when the attack began with the fall of twenty-eight incendiary bombs on the Cathedral roof, described the noise as like the sound of a large coal-scuttle being emptied. The attack would have been dealt with easily, but for the fact that there was no water for the hoses. All the really formidable fire attacks from the air began by putting the water mains out of action. The Cathedral that night was in dire peril when incendiary bombs penetrated the lead cover of the dome and fell on the wooden structure. The heroic old gentlemen of the Watch had no hoses which worked and could employ only stirrup pumps and pails of water. By what seemed to some a providential accident the incendiary fell from the rafter to the stone gallery where it was extinguished by sandbags. A few minutes longer would have set the dome ablaze. There was water in the river, we thought, why was it not used to save St. Paul's? That was the question which I asked and the reply that arrangements to pump water from the river had failed because of a low tide seemed inadequate. That impression was confirmed about six months later, when a similar situation occurred and the hoses once more were dry. I wrote a protest to Mr. Morrison and I think I said, "Please don't tell me about low tide in the river, because even deans know that low tides don't last twenty-four hours." I hope I did. At least it is certain that from that day to the end of the war tanks of dirty water were kept up in the City and were never needed again! But we were glad to welcome a duck which came into residence.

The Chapter met in accordance with the statutes every Saturday morning during the war, but not in the Chapter House which was gutted by the fire of December 29th, 1940. The dean's vestry was large and warmer. My recollection of Chapter meetings of the war period is that they were generally short and peaceful—not because there were no problems but because we had complete confidence in the two men who were experts in the field of the preservation of the fabric of the Cathedral—the architect Mr. Godfrey Allen and Mr. Linge the Clerk of Works. The two direct hits of 1940 and 1941 caused us continued anxiety. On October 29th, 1940, an H.E. bomb hit the roof of the choir at 5.55 a.m. and exploded between the outer roof and the inner ceiling; the falling masonry demolished the altar and the altar cross, the Victorian reredos was badly damaged but could have been restored without much trouble. The repair of the roof could not wait and was taken in hand by the Cathedral works staff. The work of restoration proceeded *pari passu* with the intensification of the destruction. From this incident a problem arose which kept us busy for years—restoration or reconstruction? A feeling existed in knowledgeable circles that the reredos was a Victorian blunder and, though in itself it was a good example of 19th-century sculpture, it was out of harmony with Christopher Wren's conception. For my part I had pious associations in memory with the altar before which I had been ordained deacon and priest, but I was sure that the obstruction of the apse and of the east windows would have horrified Wren. The day after the disaster which damaged the reredos, its fate was a subject of discussion. The general problem of the fabric was acutely urgent after the second fire raid on the night of April 16-17th, 1941. After a hectic struggle to extinguish incendiary bombs on the roof, without any hoses which worked, had been successfully concluded, the north transept had a direct hit by a heavy high explosive bomb at 2.50 a.m. My wife and I were away that night but returned early in the morning to be met by news of the latest calamity and of the ordeal of the Watch. I am sorry, in retrospect, that I missed what must have been the worst night of all. All who were there described the experience as "an earthquake", and those who were in the crypt and those who were on the roof used the same words, indicating the enormous vibration of the whole building. Of course this was good ground for anxiety. The stability of the dome was in everyone's mind and it seemed almost incredible that the blast had not shifted it—but this proved to be the case. If one wanted to use the word "miracle" in connection with the preservation of St. Paul's, I would suggest this is the point. The blast of the explosion in the building must have lifted the dome and it must have settled back again on its original situation. The immediate anxiety allayed, long-term anxiety supervened and, though we did not know it at the time, the restoration, even when it could be begun in peace and with adequate materials and craftsmen, took fourteen years. Allen and Linge once more were equal to the emergency and the Cathedral works staff responded eagerly to their call to stop the ruin which would follow unless immediate first-aid could be given. The great hole in the roof had a corresponding hole in the floor where heavy stones had crashed through into the crypt. When we looked at the scene, my wife and I noted that, had I been in my usual post at the H.Q. telephone that night when the roof crashed in, it would have buried me. I was 180 miles away at the wedding of a friend, and Mr. Tate, one of the vicars choral who had taken my place, was saved by seeing Canon Alexander wandering about and going to see if he was ill.

On the whole it would be true to say that one did not worry much. One lived in a state of admitted despair. There was so much to worry about that worrying seemed futile. One lived day by day and the words of Jesus: sufficient for the day is its own evil, seemed commonsense.

Yet I had hope and aspiration. By the ruins of the north transept I prayed that I might live to see St. Paul's restored to more than its former beauty and that I might still be dean when the restoration was completed. I thank God that this prayer was granted to me and that my Margaret was still with me to share the joy. And as I write these words I remember that we had a house companion in the difficult years—Miss Beatrice Ford. She came to us as cook in the small part of the deanery which we could inhabit. Our staff of five maids and a man had shrunk to one and the first night which she spent with us was the beginning of the night bombing. We had to take refuge in the crypt and slept hardly at all. I thought, "That's the end of Beatrice. She'll go tomorrow." But she did not, she still remains a Friend of St. Paul's and of me. She never panicked and was always cheerful. I sometimes imagined that she enjoyed air raids—but of course that was absurd. Her favourite phrase was "Well, it makes a change", and I remember saying to her on the morning of the first night when all air raid danger was finally banished, "How nice to have a really quiet night"; she replied, "It seemed rather dull." I think she is a good specimen of the Londoners who used to say in those days, when the Germans were dishing out terror, "London can take it." For a few years London was a heroic and beautiful city. When one surveys the sordid muddle that the post-war authorities have made of it, one could weep.

Broadcasting in the war years was for me only a semi-extra-mural activity, because most of it came my way only because of St. Paul's and its symbolical value. Londoners who came up to the City through the blitz looked first to see if the dome still stood. The false rumour that St. Paul's had been destroyed by fire had spread alarm and despondency in countries where the Nazis were feared; and my voice, even if it had nothing much to say, was a reassurance that the Cathedral was still in being and trying to function. But I would not admit that I had nothing to say. Never before or since have I felt so confident that I had a message which many troubled persons were in need of to carry on and to face the days ahead of them. The message was very simple and not easy to believe for some troubled minds. It was that God is and that God cares. There were moments in the experience of so many in those days of terror, when the only hope seemed to be that God was undefeatable and though violence, destruction and cruelty seemed everywhere in the ascendant, love—the kind of love which Jesus showed us on the cross—was the revelation of the supremely Real Being. For my part, in my own belief I dropped the optimism about the future of mankind in this world which had been an element in my thinking and encountered the problem of evil in a realistic manner, which made my essays in theodicy look almost trivial, though they were serious enough in intention. In my meditations and in my preaching the reality of sin and of the need for redemption came into the centre and I would have said that, unless I believed in the divinity of Christ, I could not believe in God. A tenet which I had held and defended in my book *God in Christian Thought and Experience*—that suffering is a part of God's experience—became to me an indispensable conviction. Another reason for my frequent offerings on the air was the fact that I was within walking distance of Broadcasting House and had a better chance of getting there during raids than most. More than once I walked all the way through streets littered with debris and fragments of glass and more than once when I arrived the sirens sounded and we fled down into the basement shelter.

My daughter Barbara, who sometimes, on leave from the W.A.A.F., spent a night with her parents in the crypt, expressed the opinion that we were all slightly mad and, alas, it was only too true that the strain on the wife of one of the canons led to a mental collapse, one of the innumerable secret tragedies of the war. I think perhaps I was mentally affected, remembering my conduct on one of the mornings when I was due to give the five minutes *Lift Up Your Hearts* talk. I had had no sleep that night, which had been made hideous by bomb explosions and ack-ack gunfire and had culminated in the fall of a land-

mine within a few yards of the Cathedral, burying itself, un-
exploded, in the garden at the south west corner of the building. The danger area was cordoned off and my deanery was
included in it. For some reason I dodged the police and crept
into the house without being observed, simply to get a shave
before my broadcast. I confess I was alert all the time, expecting
at any moment to hear the blast shaking the walls and bringing
down the ceiling. I got it into my head that I scored off Hitler
when I showed up at Broadcasting House shaved and washed
that day!

The broadcasters of those war years deserved well of their
country and I owed much to their kindness.

Broadcasting is like "casting bread upon the waters". Nearly
all that one says, if it has any effect at all, passes into the unknown, but some of it returns after many days. One such experience is encouraging. On one of the nights when few Londoners
had any sleep and many had horrifying adventures fighting fires,
rescuing bombed citizens from collapsing houses and searching
ruins for the dead and injured—in short one of the really bad
nights in hell—I had to "lift up hearts" (including my own). I
remember thinking, "My little address is quite inadequate and
I am on edge, because I have been scared. I must make my
voice sound calm." So I prayed that my voice would sound calm
and confident. About ten years later, I was one of the speakers
at a public meeting in Plymouth and one of the Labour M.P.s
for that part of the world was on the same platform, giving
an address on the same subject. What that was and who he was,
I have clean forgotten. I am grateful to him, because he said to
me after the meeting, "The last time I heard your voice was after
one of the worst nights in the blitz, when I was in the Fire
Service. I felt absolutely done and despairing. I switched on
for the *Lift Up Your Hearts* and heard you speak. I don't remember what you said, but your voice sounded so calm and
confident that I was quite cheered up." Well, I suppose it could
be said that, sometimes, "He also serves who only controls his
voice."

The record of my broadcasts surprises me. I wonder when I
wrote them all and surely, if I attempted to do the same amount
of work today on the wireless (supposing I could get it), I should
have to give up everything else. In those days I wrote quickly
and almost recklessly, because desperately. I thoroughly believed

that the work was real service and Christian ministry. But it was a sideline. What interested me more and exhausted me more was visiting the Army and the Air Force in England. This involved travelling, mostly by train, often in packed carriages and with long delays caused by air raids.

Conversation in trains and specially in night trains was most instructive and on the whole enhanced my admiration for the mass of British people. Possibly the fact that I wore a clerical collar had some slight influence in modifying the language of the men, but I doubt it. The idea, cherished by some of the clergy, that if they look like laymen people will confide in them is mistaken. People resent being involved in conversation with a parson without warning: they tend to imagine that a parson in disguise is either up to some scandalous conduct or is ashamed of his calling. Anyone dressed as a priest is at least unlikely to betray a confidence. Some of the conversations which I had with fellow passengers in long-distance train journeys were concerned with personal problems about which I may have been able to help. I scarcely ever learned the names of my interlocutors or what happened when the journey ended and I am certain that none of them would have consulted me unless they had known that I was a priest.

There were also conversations in which I was only a listener, but an interested one. I think one of the characteristics of Englishmen is, when the situation is alarming, to talk of something else. One night journey in raid-infested England was to my beloved old Cathedral of Exeter. I have forgotten the purpose, but remember almost everything else. It started from Waterloo and was interrupted quite soon by bomb damage to the rails. We walked in the dark a few hundred yards and embarked in another train, but that too made slow and spasmodic progress. We were diverted through Bristol, but when we arrived on the outskirts of the city an attack from the air began and the train stopped dead with all lights out. There we stayed, waiting for the all clear to sound—or alternatively, as we all knew, the crash of a bomb. I was the only passenger in my compartment not in uniform and, though I could only see the others' faces dimly, their conversation interested me as a kind of human comedy, though the subject of their talk might have claimed to be a divine comedy. They talked about Methodism and Methodists—a topic remote from bombs, yet not frivolous. The discussion was animated, but ill-informed. One or two knew some Methodists but, to my surprise, no one had any clear idea of the origin and teaching of Methodism. Some conjectures were put forward, the most bizarre being that it was a kind of Moral Rearmament and the nearest the mark that it had some connection with the Church of England. Fortunately in the dark no one noticed my clerical collar and I was saved from the embarrassment of having to correct fascinating hypotheses. On the question whether Methodism was a good thing and Methodists good people, the company appeared to be equally divided.

Time passed and the all clear sounded. The passengers subsided in their seats and went to sleep. At 2.30 a.m., the train reached Exeter, where an air raid warning was in force and every inhabitant seemed to have gone to earth, so that I had to carry my suitcase through empty streets to the house of my friend, Canon McLaren, in the Close. My adventures of the night concluded with a heartening scene. The Canon and his wife were alert and equipped. Though both septuagenarians, they wore tin hats and were armed with firefighters' axes. Perhaps I smiled a little at these old warriors as I sank to rest in my comfortable bed that morning, but not long afterwards, when the Cathedral was damaged and the daughter of another Exeter friend killed in the barbarous series of Baedeker raids, I honoured their devotion.

Opportunities of some contact with the young men who were defending us were not lacking and I seized all that could be taken without neglecting my duties at the Cathedral. Chaplains were kind enough to ask me to preach and the education officers to lecture. The conclusions to which I came as a result of these limited activities are clear and I will state them for what they are worth before they become lost in details. First, the quality of the troops. My experience is almost confined to the Air Force and I would not presume to compare one service with another in point of intelligence. I can only testify that the men who came to my lectures at the airfields which I visited were alert and intellectually alive. They wanted to be helped to think for themselves. When I lectured on a religious subject, it was always with the aim of clarifying some problem which I had reason to believe was in some minds. On reflection, I am inclined to say that the question which disturbed them most was the future of civilisation—of Christian civilisation. My readers may remember the cryptic remark of the policeman on the first night of the war: "Some say this is the end of Christianity." They meant Christian civilisation. Spengler's *Der Untergang des Abendlandes* had recently been translated and I found that his speculative interpretation of civilisation on the analogy of biological processes interested my hearers and that they were not unduly alarmed by his pessimistic conclusions. After all the "downfall of the west" looked uncommonly likely. Whether I gave an unbiassed account of Marx's theory is doubtful, because I have never been clear in my own mind on the dictatorship of the proletariat. Probably my sketch of Hegel's concept of dialectical development as the basis of Marxism was equally misleading, but at least my hearers were not bored: they argued. Of course I am generalising from a select minority and my "conclusions" are really only impressions, but one impression is worth recording. It is that the victors of the Battle of Britain were by no means unanimously in agreement with the official aims of the war. This was brought home to me when a group criticising a lecture on the causes of the war repudiated the idea that they were fighting for democracy of the "one man, one vote" type. When I asked, "What then are you fighting for?" they replied simply, "England". It may be that the dominant motive in the people of England was simply a deep-rooted objection to being pushed around by Germans.

The task of chaplains in the R.A.F. was difficult and all those whom I met were giving all they had to the job. Some, I thought, were handicapped by age; not that they were too old, but that they were too young. I may be mistaken, but I sensed a feeling among the young men who were facing death every day that the chaplain was also a young man—sometimes younger than they—who was sheltered from danger. In this he was unlike the chaplains in the Navy or the Army. The chaplains who had real influence were for the most part men who might have been the fathers, uncles or housemasters of the fighting boys. Is this an example of the "amateurness" of the Anglican ethos which is so endearing and also so maddening? Did the Salvation Army or the Roman Catholics do better? The bishops of our Church are sometimes too optimistic in their estimates of the situation. I wished I had a bishop with me (of course in disguise) when I visited a large R.A.F. station which had 5,000 personnel including 500 W.A.A.F.s. I was the only communicant at the only

celebration of Holy Communion on Sunday. The religious difficulties which harassed so many sensitive and honest believers
were not unknown in the fighting services and I know that
many priests, including many chaplains, helped men and women
to come to terms with themselves in the matter of defence and
the claim of the nation upon all citizens to protect the freedom
of their native land, and the claim of Christ upon their loyalty
to the Kingdom of God's love; but the Church as a whole had
no clear teaching to offer and the feeling that it spoke with an
uncertain voice was one of the causes of the falling away from
it.

As the war drew towards its end, the education officers increased in usefulness and influence. No one has yet appreciated
the importance of the cultural work in the forces which was
directed and served by some able and dedicated men. The swing
of the electorate after the war against Churchill and for Socialism surprised me as it did some of the Socialist leaders, but we
ought to have foreseen it as a probability, particularly if we had
known that very many service men and others thought that
Churchill would be in the Government whoever won the election.

A more dramatic extra-mural exercise was prescribed for me
by the Ministry of Information—at least I understood the
Ministry was behind an invitation which I received to address
a meeting in Dublin on the attacks on London. I was told that
the government of Eire was playing down all news which might
evoke sympathy with the sufferers from German aggression and
indignation against its agents. Dublin itself had recently had a
few German bombs dropped on it—doubtless by mistake; but
naturally some inhabitants of Eire were apprehensive. The
time was ripe, it was thought, for discreet propaganda. London
had suffered and St. Paul's was the image and symbol of London. I had often thought that I was situated not only in the
target of German bombing, but at the bull's eye. One of my
more valid qualifications was that I was not unknown in Dublin,
having been made an honorary D.D. of Trinity College, Dublin,
and given sundry lectures there. Dublin City I had loved from
the first day I saw it and two of my most valued friends, Dr.
Sowby, headmaster of St. Columba's College, and his wife offered
warm hospitality. I must not conceal a very materialistic induce-
ment which had some weight—I was told that Eire was a land

flowing with mutton chops and I had been classified by the Ministry of Food as a "non-priority adult" for the purposes of rationing. Like all other non-priority adults, I was sometimes hungry.

The tale of my incursion into neutral Eire begins in the best tradition of secret agents—"secret agent becomes known as prominent member of respectable and exclusive club". My platform was the Mothers' Union and it was at a public meeting of that society that I made my speech. What I said, beyond a description of our air raid trials, I have completely forgotten, nor do I remember who took the chair or where the meeting was held. The one impression which remains is of the audience— surely the most remarkable in the history of the Mothers' Union. It was crowded and, though undoubtedly there were not a few mothers present, the majority could never have enjoyed the privilege of motherhood. In a sense, the lecture was a suc- cess but it did not get the publicity hoped for and I should judge its value for the M.O.I. standpoint was small. The majority of Eire citizens did not want to hear about the war. Though other engagements were interesting to me, I could not claim that they were notably successful and indeed in one instance I seem to have wrecked a venerable institution, as I shall disclose.

My hopes, however, concerning mutton chops were nobly ful- filled. I was made an honorary temporary member of the Kil- dare Street Club and for a few days, whenever I had time to spare, went in and had a chop. My first duty was to call upon the President of the Irish Republic, Dr. Douglas Hyde, who was a well-known and revered Gaelic scholar and a Protestant. We had met once before, at least in the sense that we had been in the same room together, but I think did not speak to each other. Naturally enough, he was gracious but guarded as became a neutral president. His sister, who went with me downstairs when I took my leave, warmed my heart by saying: "We're doing better now, the news today is much more hopeful." She was not neutral, and I have little doubt that she prayed every day for the overthrow of Hitler. Another duty call was on the representative of the British Government Sir John Maffey, who kindly entertained me to dinner and sent his car to fetch me from St. Columba's. The approach to my host's house was through a tree-lined avenue and I noticed that men with rifles were stationed behind some of the trees. When I pointed them out to the chauffeur, he said cheerfully, "It's all right, Sir; they're on our side," but what side that was I did not discover.

A reception in the dignified lodgings of the Provost of Trinity, attended by fellows and professors as well as prominent dwellers in Dublin, was a happy glimpse of cultured society continuing in war and of some old friends and acquaintances. It was only two years before that I had lectured in Trinity. Just two minutes of embarrassment disturbed the illusion of peace. Without warning I was suddenly presented by the Provost to the German Ambassador, not in a quiet corner, but in the centre of the magnificent drawing-room and with the Provost's guests looking on. My impression is that the German was as much taken by surprise as I was. I said nothing, because I could think of nothing to say, and he too uttered no word. With stiff bows, we acknowledged each other's existence and left it at that. It was fortunate that I was tongue-tied, because as my next adventure showed there were persons who appeared to be hoping to get some words from me which could be quoted as approving Eire's neutrality.

The Mercier Society in Dublin bore the name of Cardinal Mercier, the Archbishop of Malines, who had played an important and courageous part in the first world war and had been prominent in the effort to promote understanding between the Roman Catholic and Anglican Churches. After the war the Malines Conferences, attended by Bishop Charles Gore and the Earl of Halifax with several other high church divines, made some progress towards agreement on the validity of Anglican ordination, until the conferences were stopped by the Pope. The Mercier Society was appropriately concerned with promoting interchange of ideas and consisted of "intellectuals" who, though members of different Churches, wished to continue "dialogue", as the phrase now goes. Many members of the Eire cabinet were members of the Society and of course professors and lecturers of the universities—Trinity College and the National University. I was told that the meetings were "private" and advised to avoid acutely controversial subjects, such was the policy of the Eire Government in the war. I chose a subject which I thought would be relevant without causing deep emotional reactions. The precise title I have forgotten. It was something like *The Concept of Social Justice*. After the war, I imagined, everyone would be thinking of how to reform our social organisation and our political aims in such a way as to eliminate world war. Arising out of this, I felt, the tendency to world government would be heightened and the limits of national independence become more marked. The kind of subject, one would think, which was discussed by Plato and Aristotle and turns largely on getting our terms rightly defined—terms such as "social justice".

The size of the audience astonished me. At least three hundred, I should estimate. Obviously to say that the meeting was "private" could mean little more than that its proceedings would not be reported in the press. My paper was listened to with polite attention and was to be followed by questions and discussion. I hoped to have lively and clarifying comments from the highly intelligent company. If I had had any common sense, I should have realised that under the heading of "justice" any grievance, controversy or Utopian dream can be brought into debate. The effect of this tactical error was soon plain enough. After a few relevant questions aimed at elucidating my meaning on some points, a member of the Eire Government, I think the Postmaster General, launched upon us a long speech. It was a very friendly speech, full of appreciation—perhaps too full— of things which I had attempted to do. The speaker not only had goodwill towards me, but his intention was to promote peace and goodwill in general. But he put me in a fix. He began with expressions of welcome to me personally and suggested my visit was evidence of my continued love for Dublin and the Irish people, in spite of the war. So far all was well; but he went on to dangerous ground when he said something like this, "I believe we can go further and interpret the Dean's visit here as a sign that, far from turning against us for our neutrality, he understands and sympathises with our difficult situation. I will go further and say that we hope he approves our neutrality and his visit is a token of his approval."

I was quite unprepared for this onslaught, but anyone could tell that it was intended if possible to get me to say something which could be quoted to support the neutralist policy, and would be quite contrary to my convictions and, what is more, a setback to the purpose of my mission. I am rather proud of my answer—not because it was so good, but because it was so quick. I knew I had to contradict explicitly the suggestion that I favoured Eire's neutrality, but without offending or antagonising my audience. I gained time by dwelling for a few minutes on my happy memories of Dublin and my admiration of so many Irish writers. All this flowed easily, because it was all perfectly true. The best conversation, I said, and friendly debate had often been found in Dublin. I think too I mentioned Salmon and Mchaffey as academic wits in the past. "All these wonderful traditions," I added, "are alive in the Mercier Club and long may it flourish. But really I must say quite definitely that I do not approve of your neutrality. You see, I have recently been in four neutral countries: Sweden, Norway, Denmark and Holland. Three of them have been overrun and occupied by the Germans. Unfortunately we were not able to defend their neutrality. I am glad that, so far, we have been able to defend yours." This was not just a debating point; it was a statement of the real situation; but obviously it would be unacceptable to the Eire Government and its supporters. After a brief but tense silence, during which I wondered whether I was going to be thrown out amid howls of rage, there was a round of applause! The Irish, on the whole, like a smart retort—but not on every subject, as I found out before the evening was over.

It would have been wise if I had refused to answer any more questions, but might have been considered discourteous. So it happened that I was tired when a Jesuit arose and suavely asked if I did not agree that we owed a debt of gratitude to the Pope for all his utterances and activities in the war. I do not remember why, but this question made me angry and I said what I thought with perhaps brutal frankness. I said, "If you want to know my real opinion about the Pope's activities, it is this: it is easy and safe, when evil deeds are being done, to make great sweeping general statements, but it is difficult and dangerous to speak out in condemnation of concrete outrages and wicked tyrants. If the Pope had done a little less of the first and a little more of the second, I should respect him more than I do." I do not repent what I said, but I regret the way I said it. Given time, I could have wrapped it up with smooth words, but I was not given time and I blurted out my thought undisguised. No idea crossed my mind that I might have ruined the Mercier Society, but the immediate reaction of the meeting indicated that I had offended; there was no applause and I think not even a vote of thanks to the reader of the paper. The meeting dispersed in silence. Not until I was back in London and had almost put Dublin out of my mind did I learn that the Roman Catholic

Wartime visit to St. Paul's by Mrs. Eleanor Roosevelt, their majesties King George VI and Queen Elizabeth

Dr. Jan Masaryk addresses the Anglo-Czechoslovak Christian Fellowship of which I was Chairman. Next to me is Archbishop William Temple

St. Paul's Cathedral rises above weeds and debris at the end of the war

Archbishop of Dublin had banned the Mercier Society and thereby killed it; while to crown my disgrace the Anglican Archbishop of Dublin had expressed displeasure and regret at my clumsiness. I hope that the Mercier Society was not finally snuffed out but has been revived, for it was one of the forces making towards understanding and ecumenical thinking as well as a memorial of a great Bishop.

Another personal encounter was with the Prime Minister, de Valera. It had been arranged that I should call upon him, I suppose as a matter of courtesy. He saw me in his government office and, when I arrived there, two armoured cars with soldiers were on guard. I wondered what we had to say to one another. I need not have feared that conversation would be difficult because from the first moment I found, to my surprise, that I liked him. Sometimes I have played with the fancy of testing persons whom I meet for the first time by asking myself the question, "If I knew nothing at all about this man and he asked me for help in an emergency, would I lend him five pounds on the spot?" This is not so silly as it sounds, for a Christian minister, specially if he is in a relatively public situation, is sure to have plenty of experience of dealing with persons really in need and also with expert confidence tricksters. Through trial and painful error, he acquires a kind of instinctive judgment. If I had to make a catalogue of politicians who were quite certainly not tricksters but incapable of shady conduct to serve their personal interests, of course it would be a long one and nothing would tempt me to produce it; but I will disclose that two names would be high on the list—de Valera and General Eisenhower. I do not mean that they would not be capable of deplorable actions for some impersonal cause—for their country, for example—but in personal dealings they would be inflexibly upright. In my life I have had two fairly long conversations with de Valera and neither of them had any political interest or importance. My purpose, if I had one, was I suppose to tell him about the blitz on London—a subject on which he showed little concern. In a subtle way, I think he tried to tell me why he was not particularly sympathetic with British troubles by referring to his experiences in British prisons. My recollection is that he regarded Lincoln prison as the most comfortable, but that may have been because he escaped from it. In talking to de Valera, I was conscious of a disadvantage in that I had no experience of prisons and now, I hope, it is too late to repair this defect in my education.

To round off my brief encounter with a man who always intrigued me, I will outrage chronological order and refer to my last conversation with him. My wife and I were on holiday on the west coast when one day he arrived at our hotel, having to speak at an election meeting. At breakfast the following morning, I reminded him that we had met before and I was surprised that he remembered our conversation. He asked me to sit at his table and we talked about the military defence of Eire, a subject which was currently being discussed in letters in *The Irish Times*. I am far from claiming to be an expert in military history, but I was surprised by the plan which de Valera outlined to meet threats of invasion. It was based naturally enough on the Swiss strategy—that of abandoning the lowlands and retiring to an impregnable redoubt in the mountains. Small arms could be manufactured in Eire and larger weapons supplied by Sweden. I have no doubt that the Irish would fight long and fiercely in the mountains, but would that worry the invader very much if he had control of the ports, the railways and the large towns? It is difficult to imagine a successful counter-attack on the invaders mounted from the MacGillicuddy's Reeks. On reflection, though I would lend de Valera five pounds any day, I am not absolutely certain that he was perfectly candid in his account of Eire's strategy.

As I left de Valera's room, I passed in the lobby his next visitor who was to become, though I did not know it, one of my dearest friends—Leonard Brockington, Q.C. I noticed also that the armoured cars were still there. Apparently the Prime Minister did not venture to move without their protection.

The time had come to leave and, though I was sorry to leave the mutton chops and the blessed peaceful nights of uninterrupted sleep, I was anxious to get back to Margaret who was alone in the deanery with the faithful Beatrice. The threat to St. Paul's was not much abated and the damage from the last direct hit not yet fully assessed. I still wondered, when I returned to London, whether the dome would be standing. On the same aeroplane was Leonard Brockington and we sat together in the air and on the train. The first thing one noticed about him was that he was terribly crippled by arthritis and the second that he did not allow his disability to cramp his activities. Though crippled, he was a man of amazing energy of both mind and body, and he devoted himself during the war to voluntary work of propaganda. He was a Welshman, a classical scholar who had been a schoolmaster in England. In Canada he had engaged successfully in commerce and had then become a lawyer-member of a law firm in the American style. In this too he distinguished himself by being made a Q.C. His broadcasts on the war both in Canada and England were valuable features in the war effort. I did not think that we were likely to be close friends and, perhaps but for the air raid into which we ran, we should never have been more than briefly acquainted. As the train approached London, its speed became spasmodic and at the moment when we arrived, very late, in St. Pancras station, the sirens sounded the alert and a bomb exploded not far away. The station was immediately deserted and passengers bolted for the shelter along with the crew of the train. Brockington could move only very slowly and not very far; the shelter and the Underground were full and we did not know how to get to them anyway, and Brockington would have collapsed if he had been deposited in a crowded tunnel with no chance of sitting down. We thought the German attack might be heavy and prolonged because it was evidently directed against the three railway terminuses, St. Pancras, Euston and King's Cross. We thought our best plan would be to move away from the railway as quickly as possible and make for Brockington's hotel in Russell Square which had a comfortable shelter. We did the right thing, because after a nightmarish walk through absolutely deserted streets along which Brockington gamely hobbled, we arrived at the hotel and simultaneously the all clear sounded. I continued on my way to St. Paul's and actually managed to sleep in my rocky bed in the crypt next to the sandbagged effigy of Dean Donne.

I wish I could give a true picture of the crowded and changeful life in St. Paul's during those other war years. I shut my eyes and let my memory play on the "emergent occasions" and emergent persons which swim into the mental focus. Isolated happenings and individuals whom I met only once and whose names often I never knew are vividly before me now. On July 4th, 1941, a memorial to William Fiske II, the first American volunteer who was killed on active service with the R.A.F. was unveiled by the American Ambassador. This was the first time I met General de Gaulle. The occasion was important as an indication of the probable help to be expected before long from the U.S.A. On September 16th, the coming of age of Peter, King of Yugoslavia, was celebrated in the nave by a service attended by the King and Queen of England. The Dean and Chapter presented one of the books from the Cathedral which was considered relevant. I am sure the grateful recipient never read a word of it and the whole transaction now seems to belong to a vanished world. Some time later, but still during the war, I was present at the baptism of the infant crown prince, this time in the Abbey. The ritual of the Orthodox Church seems to be capable of indefinite prolongation and at this service the officiating prelates gave us the lot, pausing now and then while they consulted the books on the next ceremony. The highlight of the proceedings came when the godfather, George VI, King of England, walked round the font bearing in his arms the baby who was stark naked and looked very slippery. Anxiety for the safety of the child was swallowed up by sympathy with the royal godparent, who was obviously dismayed by what he had let himself in for. My dear friend, Dr. Don, the then Dean of Westminster, half joking, but partly seriously too, reproved me for offending some members of the congregation by saying in a loud voice as I came out, "Well, thank God for the Reformation." I did not intend to disturb anyone, but the words expressed accurately enough my sentiments.

Real rebuke met me on October 16th, 1941, when a Salvation Army service was held in St. Paul's to commemorate the centenary of the conversion of the Founder, General Booth. Today, I believe, most Anglican laymen would say, "Well, why not?" But in those days such a service was a new thing in St. Paul's and I knew that old-fashioned high church individuals would object. But I was determined to hold the service as a kind of testimony to the spiritual unity of Christians; and I thought I had secured the path by getting agreement not only from the Bishop of London, who perhaps had the right of veto, but from the Archbishop of Canterbury, who had no right to be consulted at all. They were both heartily in favour. The Salvation Army kindly asked me to preach at the service and I agreed (though I would have preferred to hear a Salvation Army sermon), because no one, I thought, was likely to challenge the Dean's right to preach in his own cathedral. But I was wrong. The next number of *The Church Times* had an editorial paragraph on its first page—the page that everyone read—in which I was roundly accused of being "an ecclesiastical Quisling". I knew who had written this column, Dr. Prestige, and had always thought of him as a friend. I could not help being angry, because of the effect of such abuse on the reputation of the Cathedral as well as my own. I did not think Prestige had meant that I was a traitor in the ordinary sense of the word and used the word "ecclesiastical" to denote and limit the sphere of my treachery. But the reader might equally take the abusive words to mean "a traitor to king and country who happens to be a cleric". The affair ended amicably, chiefly, I think, because I was determined not to waste time with one of those tiresome quarrels between clergymen; but I wanted to indicate that I resented the attack. Having first taken quick legal advice that the word "Quisling" had been found libellous in a recent case, I telephoned to Prestige and said, "I am ringing up to tell you that I do not intend to bring any action against you for libel. Your attack on me in which you call me 'an ecclesiastical Quisling' is calculated to do me and the Cathedral harm, but I refuse to be drawn into a quarrel about words when we all have so much real work to do." It ended by our lunching together at the club. Prestige was appointed Canon of St. Paul's some years later, rather to my surprise, and we became friends until his premature death. He was a witty man and often thought of the most lovely phrases to describe his fellow creatures with a satirical slant—and when he thought of them they seemed too good to waste, so he said them, sometimes without much care whether they were true or kind. Don't we all?

Bishops were consecrated in St. Paul's even in the perilous days of 1941; but the dignity of the service was sadly diminished by being held in the crypt, because the floor of the Cathedral was unsafe—or rather the roof above the floor. In these cramped conditions we all had to sit close together. At the consecration of Dr. Cash as Bishop of Worcester, during the sermon I had to sit so near to Archbishop Cosmo Gordon Lang that I could observe every change of his expression and hear his muttered comments. A special interest in this consecration for my wife and me was that I had been strongly "tipped" for this appointment—though not by myself. I never wanted to be a bishop, for the simple reason that I never thought I was good enough or had the grace for being a real father in God; nor did I think that my teaching was orthodox enough—though I confess that now I am not so sure.

The night when the headquarters of the Salvation Army were demolished by bombs and burnt out was tense and terrible. Early the following morning, I saw the gutters in St. Andrew's Hill stained with human blood. Even more terrible was the destruction caused by a bomb which fell just outside the Mansion House and at the entrance to the Mansion House tube station. I never learned the final figure of the casualties on that night. The cause was even more shocking than the number. The bomb blasted the refugees who were sheltering on the staircase of the Underground station on to the live electric rail with results that surpass our imagination of horror. The crater stayed in the roadway for some time, but the remnants of that disaster were removed fairly soon and, so far as I know, there is no mark or monument to remind the commuters of the trials of their fathers. Nor, I think, is there any public memorial that the lord mayors of those days did not take to their heels but sweated it out with the City and its defenders. The names of Wilkinson, Lord Mayor, Herbert Morrison, Home Secretary, and of a junior Minister, Ellen Wilkinson, are among those whom I remember as sharing London's agony.

The end which had been so often deferred seemed to come suddenly at last. Earlier in the year 1944 we had rung the great peal of bells to celebrate the Liberation of Paris (August 24th) and hope grew every day that the slaughter would soon be ended, but it was nearer to Christmas that the Commanding Officer of the Western Approaches took me into his operations room and I saw the vast charts on which the positions of the U-boats were marked by Wrens. Admiral Horton had been assigned the most important command in the final stage of the European war—the place where the Germans still had a definite chance of victory. I was astounded by the number of U-boats still available to the enemy and also by the significance of their positions. They were clustered round the southern coast of Eire and the coast of Portugal. In the main, I think most people believed that the war could end before the end of 1945, but that the Germans were not finished and perhaps even a new type of missile was being prepared by the enemy which could deliver a knockout blow. What we heard from soldiers who had taken part in the Normandy landings led us to believe that, if they had been deferred for another month or two, London would have been pulverised by concentrated blows from the air. This possibility was certainly in my mind when I planned in advance the Watch Night Service in St. Paul's for midnight on December 31st, 1944. I have told this story before and I got it wrong in one important respect—I stated in my book *St. Paul's Cathedral in Wartime* that we had no choir and had to depend on congregational singing. I would have taken an oath that this was true, but I had to submit to refutation. Beyond any possible doubt not only was there a choir: there was an orchestra, too, provided by the B.B.C. This is the most remarkable instance of the fallibility of eye witness in my personal experience. If I had had no opportunity of amending my testimony, my word would have carried great weight, for was it not the testimony of the principal agent in the event, the most responsible person present who had no motive whatever for not telling the truth? I could perhaps suggest some psychological causes of my aberration, but so can anyone and I will just state the facts as I know them and assure anyone who may be interested that I tried to tell the truth both times but seem to have succeeded only once.

To resume the simple story: the Cathedral crypt was packed tight with boys and girls and men and women of all ages, mostly in uniform. About one minute before the clock told the time advertised for the service, one of the heaviest V2 bomb explosions I ever heard shook the Cathedral to its foundations and smashed one of the two or three Cathedral windows which had remained intact. Immediately there flashed into my mind a prayer, "O Lord, don't let these children panic." Silence prevailed as it seemed for minutes and then simultaneously the whole congregation burst out laughing. "The release of tension," say my psychological friends, and no doubt they are right, but what we said to one another in the congregation was something like this. "I knew Jerry would have a go tonight and it wasn't a bad shot—perhaps he'll be quiet now," and he was.

The very next day January 2nd, 1945, an event took place in St. Paul's which has meaning still for those who care for and pray for the Church of England. It was one of those events which are almost "non-events", just meaningless, though it had a dignified name—the confirmation of the election of Dr. Fisher as Archbishop of Canterbury. "Confirmations" of bishops

and archbishops are farcical—and expensive—ceremonies which
lawyers have imposed upon the archbishops and bishops of
the "Church of England as by law established". They are not
sacramental rites: they can indeed be called "religious" only
by straining words. They come down from a time when law
and order were not always duly preserved and when ingenious
highwaymen sometimes appeared in the guise of bishops. When
the dean and chapter of a cathedral were summoned to welcome
a new bishop and to elect him, they needed to be assured that
they installed the right man and not an impostor. To do this
with proper care in the case of a Primate of All England was
no trivial matter and quite a number of ecclesiastical lawyers
took part. The ecclesiastical lawyer *par éminence* in England
is the Dean of the Arches. The proceedings at confirmations
of bishops and archbishops are conducted in a special kind of
jargon. I remember that it begins by one lawyer, sitting at a
table with other bewigged barristers, saying very loud and
clear, "I porrect an instrument," meaning "I present a document." An unintelligible dialogue ensures which seems to
culminate in the presiding councillor becoming aware of the
audience: he invites anyone who wishes to object to the confirmation of the archbishop or bishop to state his reasons.
Naturally someone in the assembly takes the chance of appear-
ing for a moment on the stage of history and on both occasions
when I have been present at a confirmation in St. Paul's this
has happened. The death of William Temple had deeply
moved church people and the election of his successor occasioned
some doubt of the quality of Dr. Fisher—a doubt which was
speedily dissipated. An embarrassing moment for me followed
the invitation to object. A venerable layman with a patriarchal
white beard rose; his majestic mien commanded respect and
silence. He said that he had great admiration for the learning
and piety of the Bishop of London and had no doubt that Dr.
Fisher had many qualities which he would dedicate to the service of the Church if appointed Archbishop, but that he himself
was sure that he knew someone better qualified whom he
wished to propose. I was astounded when he went on to nominate me as his candidate. I was taken aback and speechless. But
the legal profession was on the alert. No sooner were the
words out of my proposer's mouth and long before I had breath
enough to speak, the proposal was ruled out of order and, since

no one was prepared to maintain that the Dr. Geoffrey Fisher before us was an impostor, the Church was preserved from disaster and I was content.

This seemed to me at the time very funny and I did not have time to ponder on it; but looking back I feel that we ought to have been ashamed of taking part in such a senseless rigmarole. One might be amused and even find some historical interest in the antiquated proceedings, but was there not some irreverence in mixing up what was in intention the Lord's work with time-wasting nonsense?

The end of the war, so long prayed for, came as a surprise to us in St. Paul's. We had no preparations ready for the end, though we had plenty for the next month of war. The sad occasion of the memorial service for President Roosevelt on April 17th was both a service of mourning and a prelude to the coming of victory and peace. The congregation included the King and Queen, the Lord Mayor and the members of the Government, and the ever memorable figure of Winston Churchill, weeping for the death of his American comrade in arms. On that day, many of us realised for the first time, I think, with any assurance that the war was over. For my part, I experienced the dreamlike mental condition to which the Psalmist refers as his condition when deliverance from war was granted: "When the Lord turned again the captivity of Sion then were we like unto them that dream." I will not attempt to describe those days. On May 8th, 1945, the day of the German surrender in Europe, we had nothing planned for the Cathedral; there were no placards or notices. Everyone in the City seemed to resort to St. Paul's by a kind of instinct and from morning to night services followed one another. It is estimated that no fewer than 35,000 persons were present at services on that day, beside many thousand others who spent some moments in private devotion.

The time for the final "stand down" of the St. Paul's Watch had come and we had settled that our last meeting should be a corporate act of worship in the evening of May 8th—a fortunate choice, for we had unwittingly chosen the date which came to be called "VE Day". And the following Sunday, May 13th, the national Thanksgiving for Victory in Europe was attended by the King and Queen with the whole Government. I cannot describe the dreamlike quality of those days and I end this chapter by a testimony from the book which I wrote just after the experience. My friend Miss Marguerite Verini, who was then Principal of the Women's Training College, Cambridge, wrote to me:

". . . On VE Day a woman on duty at the Mansion House station waylaid me. 'Are you going to St. Paul's?' I was. 'I'm not religious,' she continued, 'but it's meant something to us that it was there and people praying in it. It's kept us going.' The Cathedral was packed, yet even at the west end there was the stillness of worship. It focused London's heart, just as the picture later in the day on the steps—of boiling sun beating down on a blissful Cockney crowd silently swaying as it sat drinking in the brass band's joy with supreme satisfaction—seemed to focus London's smile. St. Paul's belongs to the people and they know within themselves that somehow it binds them to God."

CHAPTER 14

Thanksgiving and Recovery

When the war ended, I was sixty-five and had been Dean of St. Paul's for eleven years. If I had kept to my former occupation, that of a university professor, I would now be compulsorily retired and entitled to a pension. The war years had certainly been exhausting and I had been seriously ill with an infection of the throat of which I had been cured by the skill and devotion of my friend, F. C. Ormerod, of Westminster Hospital. Though the Cathedral had suffered grievous damage, it was still standing. My wife had endured the years of trial with me and she was with me still; our son and daughter had come through the war without injury and were happily married. Our son-in-law Captain Hebb was seriously hurt on active service in Italy, but was out of danger. The death of our firstborn, Michael, was a continuing sorrow, but also to us a sacred and uniting memory. It did not occur to me that I ought to retire and hand St. Paul's over to someone else. I was tired; but not spent. The pressure of daily events and new problems gave little leisure for thought about the future, but I could see well enough that I must get my values readjusted to the new situation.

My reflections, however, were interrupted and diverted by a summons from the Archbishop of Canterbury and the British Council of Churches to take part in an important move to open communications with the German churches. The plan was that three representatives should visit Germany and move about in the country for about a month, making contacts, observing the conditions and trying to repair the breaches in Christian fellowship. A large part of the mission's purpose was fact-finding. We simply did not know how things were. The reason why I accepted this invitation was that my friend Dr. John Baillie, Professor in Edinburgh and the outstanding

Presbyterian theologian of the time, was to be one of the three. He was, of all men that I could think of, the best equipped for the task. A fluent German speaker, on friendly terms with all the Protestant theologians and the author of many scholarly works, he could talk with students and professors in their own language and, as I knew from experience, he could be a perfect fellow-traveller. It is doubtful if our expedition did much good; and if perhaps it did, I am sure it was done by Baillie. The other pilgrim was the Rev. M. E. Aubrey, of the Baptist Church. A "bear leader", lent by the Archbishop, was Herbert Waddams, now Canon of Canterbury, who not only kept us up to our schedule, but was a delightful companion.

Few pleasant memories remain of this expedition and I shall not attempt to describe the conditions of life in Germany in the winter of 1945. We had only a superficial acquaintance with the fantastic conditions; and we went in the character of V.I.P.s, as honoured guests of the British occupying forces. Undoubtedly that constituted a barrier which hindered communication between us and the population which was controlled by the allied armies, but only with this semi-official status could we have moved about at all. As it was, we had contacts in all the zones, British, French and American. The U.S.S.R. was closed against us.

It would be unjust even in a brief account to omit reference to the military governments. So far as we could judge, the administration of the occupied territory was remarkably efficient and the officers whom we had dealings with were, for the most part, just and compassionate. It was not easy to carry on the civil administration and at the same time keep vigilant watch on possible outbreaks of violence. The need to carry on some education in the German schools was well understood by the military government in the British Zone and much effort was expended on overcoming three serious difficulties: the provision of teachers who were "safe" in the sense of being genuine anti-Nazis, the dearth of schoolbooks which were not full of Nazi propaganda, and of course the destruction in the bombing of school buildings. My brief contact with the men who were doing what they could in this particular field left me with real admiration for them.

The first night we spent at British Army headquarters in Bad Oeynhausen was disturbed by two short bursts of rifle fire. Much later, when I met my son Bryan, I discovered that we had almost met in Bad Oeynhausen; we were close to one another because he, a major in the R.A.M.C., was in charge of six hospitals full of former Russian prisoners of war and wrestling with appalling problems of communication, and while I was having respectful conference with Dr. Jaeger, the Archbishop of Paderborn, he was sharply reprimanding him for visiting hospitals without permission. We had to eat and sleep with the victorious army. We stayed at the official transit hotels and met Germans almost entirely as separated and privileged persons. I suppose that something like this was inevitable in the months after the cease-fire, but I think we all felt uncomfortable when we dined very well in the transit hotel in Hamburg to the strains of a German military band which played "God Save the King" at every meal and looked rather hungry.

Two military truths seemed to be clear from a look at German bombed cities: first that the idea of underground air-raid shelters was possibly over-emphasised in our defences, at least I saw some very large shelters above ground which looked almost intact after direct hits; and secondly when we reached Berlin it was abundantly clear that bombing from the air is much less effective than shelling. But of course the truth which transcends all other military truths is that bombing is the most inhuman and diabolical device and must be eliminated from human use if civilisation is to be saved from collapse.

Our concern was not with war but with peace and with the Church of Christ. We had not been many days in Germany before it became clear to us that, so far from the Church having been killed by the war, it was the one institution which was still alive in Germany. In the areas which had been battlegrounds and targets for air raids, many churches were destroyed and many others badly damaged. They were all full on Sunday mornings, even those which had no roofs. In the Sundays of Advent the old German custom is to hang a wreath with candles over the altar and to light a candle every Sunday from Advent to Christmas. In the cold and hunger of the first winter after the war, these ceremonies were lovingly observed. It would be difficult to analyse the religious situation. The Germans themselves were at a loss to characterise it. One obvious suggestion is that, when the structure of society had collapsed and institutions had melted away, the Church and its services were one sign of continuity. The life of the people continued in the Church when elsewhere it faltered. The German people were like persons who had lost their memories and were uncertain of their identity. The hallowed words and hymns in church gave them back some of the past and of their identity. But I am sure there was much more than nostalgia in their piety. One of the Lutheran pastors with whom we stayed was kind enough to answer our question, What did the Church hope to do for the young: what alternative was there to the *Hitler Jugend*? His reply was, "We try to gather them round the Bible." I thought at the time that the answer was insufficient and I still think so, but the earnest and prayerful study of Scripture is the source of strength in German Protestantism still. So at least it seemed to us in December, 1945, and I am inclined to think that in the weeks when we were there the revival of Christian faith in Germany took a step onward. We had nothing whatever to do with it; we just happened to be there.

Two experiences stand out in recollections as apart from the merely interesting; two experiences so deeply affected me emotionally that without exaggeration I can say they changed my outlook permanently. I must try to describe them before they get smothered by trivialities. Both are associated with German Lutheran religion. In Berlin a famous hospital and medical centre, the *Johannesstift*, is one of the charitable institutions which was not destroyed by bombs and in our programme it figured as an important engagement because we hoped to meet there some leading persons in the religious and medical worlds. No doubt we met them as arranged, but I cannot remember any of them. The experience which really shattered me was that of walking through ward after ward filled with men on the point of death by starvation. They would not all die, but every one was in danger of death, and they were not all completely "men", for the majority looked scarcely older than sixteen. "Skin and bone" was a literal description of their bodies and many were so weak that they could make no movement, except perhaps a slight inclination of the head. One human being in such a state, as many of us know, is distressing enough, but the massive impression of whole wards of starved boys was crushing. All these young victims of war had been Russian prisoners of war who had been worked by their captors so long as strength remained and then turned out to die. They were being tended by German women, deaconesses, and by German doctors who went silently about their work. To me at least they spoke no words of resentment. I could only wonder what went on in their minds. I have no doubt that many were filled with compassion, but how hard it must have been to stifle all thoughts of retribution and revenge! I had the feeling that, if not here in this most Christian place, then in many other places the hatred which might cause the next war was being built up.

The experience gave emotional support also to a thought which had troubled me as an ethical and religious problem. The justice of God, we are told, is manifested in history and the Old Testament prophets base their exhortations and warning to the people of God on his righteous judgments. So long as the concept of national righteousness is unanalysed, the belief in the justice of God in history is credible, but the catastrophe which is the retribution for the sin of the nation causes suffering to children and dependents who have no responsibility for the national sins. The boy soldiers who were dying in December, 1945, had been eleven or twelve in 1939. All this is obvious enough, but it needed a shock in my case to clear my mind of its practical application. The further consideration of this question is more difficult. A question which has troubled me is this: Does not the New Testament teaching about sin and forgiveness and about the Atonement imply collective responsibility? Can St. Paul's "As in Adam all die, even so in Christ shall all be made alive", be understood at all without bringing in some idea like corporate guilt and corporate redemption?

The second experience which I treasure out of all the experiences of this hectic month is that of the two or three days spent in Bethel, the town in Westphalia near to Bielefeld, where are located the foundations of the great modern Lutheran pastor and saint, Friederich Bodelschwingh (1831–1910). Here is a collection of institutions devoted to the relief and cure and care for victims of mental illness and specially epilepsy. Attached to this are training colleges for deaconesses and for male nurses. Bethel has also a share in the education of Lutheran clergy. I had heard of Bethel and of its importance in the work of the *Innere Mission*, but my imagination had fallen short of the magnitude and complexity of its work and of the severe disadvantages under which it had existed in the Nazi period. The ruthless "eugenical" doctrine of *Mein Kampf* had threatened the existence of Bethel's work for epileptics and the pressure to eliminate helpless epileptics who could be only a burden on the Nazi state had been constant. With great courage, and not a little cunning, Bethel had defended its patients and children. The downfall of Hitler did not mean the end of tribulation for Bethel. We visited it just after its most terrible hour. The deaconesses trained in Bethel are spread all over Germany. They are familiar and welcome figures in almost every parish. In the north perhaps they are specially numerous. As we remember, the turn of the tide so long delayed, when it happened, gathered strength and speed, so that the Russian troops overran large areas. The "liberating" Russian troops were not liberating Germans. Their liberation took the form of sack and ravage before which whole populations fled. We were told that of all the deaconesses whose *alma mater* was Bethel not one had escaped violation by the "liberators". I was for a day or two in a community which had suffered years of persecution and now was overwhelmed by rapine, yet I never heard any cry for vengeance or any expression of despair. Faith and love never failed, and the community continued quietly to serve God. It was at Bethel, I think, that I regained my deep respect for Lutheran Christianity.

I have said that our conferences with theologians were disappointing and a meeting at Stuttgart, where some anti-Nazi Christian leaders were present, was quite unmemorable. I think Niemoller was there, but if he was he said nothing which stayed in my mind unless perhaps he contributed to the complaints which were made about restrictions imposed by the military administration on the movements of German civilians. One could understand the irksomeness and feeling of indignity, but we could not do anything to alter the regulations and, for my part, I thought them reasonable enough. Some interesting points may light up the background situation at that particular point of time. When we moved into the French Zone, we found surprisingly little damage and the university life far less interrupted. In the University of Tübingen we came across signs of unrest and protest. A perplexed French Air Force officer who had charge of security wondered why a professor of theo-

Chapter meeting with Canons G. L. Prestige and Marcus Knight

At a reception after the installation of H.M. Queen Elizabeth the Queen Mother as Chancellor of London University

The Queen Mother attends a Festival of the Friends of St. Paul's

logy had audiences of over a thousand students at his lectures. He suspected subtle anti-allied propaganda. I was informed that the title of his course was *Christianity and World Crisis* or something like that, and I blushed to remember that five years earlier I had been making propaganda on the same theme. Unfortunately I could not hear what the Tübingen professor made of it.

In Tübingen Professor Baillie really came out in the top of his form and I envied him his mastery of German and his courage. For some reason, perhaps because Tübingen has both a Protestant and Catholic Faculty of Theology, the students were more vocal and critical than elsewhere. They were not docile, and they did not want to be preached to by either Scottish or English divines. Any violent outbreak of protest would of course have been suppressed by the French at once, but they were hostile. Baillie's extempore address was masterly, and he succeeded, up to a point, in getting the students to listen to the case for ecumenical Christianity. The new effort towards unity in Christ, Baillie argued, was the answer to the trend towards war. It was moving to hear a pre-eminent British Reformed theologian preaching peace and concord to the Lutherans and Catholics of Tübingen. Is it only a coincidence that, in these recent years, an eminent Catholic professor of Tübingen, Hans Küng, has published an eirenical treatise showing that the teaching of Karl Barth on Justification is in harmony with the Council of Trent and that Barth has agreed? I hope that Baillie is aware of this development.

The time to return to our homes for Christmas was near and our longest and most uncomfortable journey was the one which took us to the French Zone. I am no motorist, but any fool could see that our car, driven by a G.I. over roads deep in snow and very slippery, was often in danger. On this particular day, we were bound to Baden-Baden, where the French had their headquarters. For once our wonderful Waddams had no definite invitation to sleep in the town, which added to our gloomy feelings the note of uncertainty. To distract my mind, I began to compose the words of a Christmas hymn for travellers like ourselves. Somehow the words would not come and the lines which did form themselves tended to be apocalyptic and menacing. I gave the Christmas hymn up and listened to the rhythm of the car and the bleak noise of the wind. Lines which are just not nonsense formed themselves. I am sure they are worthless and that I can claim no part in them. They amused me on that dreary drive—perhaps they may amuse a reader:

A Bed in Baden

Lines composed in a car driving on snowy roads to
Baden-Baden in late December, 1945

Is there a bed in Baden
    To meet my pressing need?
I seek no pleasant garden,
    I care not how I feed:
If there's no bed in Baden
    Then am I lost indeed.

So fare we forth to Baden
    By dark and friendless ways.
What though the frost may harden
    What if the driver strays?
If there's a bed in Baden,
    It shall have all my praise.

Of thee, O town of Baden,
    Much have I heard and read,
Yet I must ask your pardon,
    If in my foolish head
Is one sole thought of Baden—
    Can it provide a bed?

This particular story has a happy ending. We all arrived safely in Baden and were offered regal hospitality by the delightful French C.O. We all had sumptuous beds, mine being the most sumptuous; it was indeed the largest bed I have ever slept in. We were nearly at Christmas Eve. Just before Christmas Eve we were flown from Stuttgart back to England in a Dakota designed to carry luggage rather than passengers. We went out V.I.P.s and returned V.O.P.s, which, on the whole, I find more comfortable—at any rate to the spirit. When very high over the Channel we had a glorious sunlit bird's-eye view of our native land. I was reminded by it that I had no such clear view of my life, or what remained of it.

At this point in my story I seem to myself to be passing out of recent history into the contemporary world and my aim will be more definitely to trace my own endeavours and failures and to record my own reflections. No one could doubt on New Year's Day, 1946, that we in Britain were beginning a new era. The cessation of fighting and the slow process of recovery constituted a crisis in themselves, and external events, which could not have been foreseen, emphasised the impression that we had to make a new start. To me, and to many other Christians, the sudden death of William Temple was a portent. We had taken for granted that when peace came he would be there to give a lead to the nation as well as to the Church. Though I was persuaded that Temple was the man for the hour, I did not agree with all his policies and could believe that his successor, Geoffrey Fisher of London, might have a smoother path. When Dr. Fisher was translated to Canterbury we were sure that we had a Primate of great energy and resilience who would take a realistic view of the situation.

The new Bishop of London, Dr. William Wand, was of course not so well known to us in London and unfortunately the extreme Protestants in the diocese, with the financial help of some wealthy sympathisers, organised public protests against his election. They were not serious, but they were noisy and furnished copy for the press. The evangelical clergy in the diocese had no part in this agitation and Dr. Wand's patience and good humour gained him new friends. The farcical performance called "the Election of the Bishop" by the Dean and Chapter is a necessary legal preliminary to the new bishop's enthronement and it lasts a long time. It fell to me to preside over the elections of four Bishops of London—Fisher, Wand, Montgomery Campbell and Stopford, which makes me, I think, the most experienced living authority on how to elect Bishops of London. Unfortunately perhaps, the ceremonies offer two apparent occasions when objections to the election of the bishop are invited; but, still more unfortunately, each of the occasions is illusory and any objection of substance is "out of order". This put me in embarrassing situations in the election of Dr. Wand and in the confirmation of Dr. Fisher. The election is by the votes of the Dean, the residentiary canons and the prebendaries and, though the result is predetermined, every member of Chapter is bound to attend. If anyone is absent without serious excuse, he is solemnly stigmatised as "contumacious". I am bound to add that in my experience no one who labours under this terrible imputation has ever seemed a penny the worse.

As everyone knows, the Crown has complete control of the whole exercise. Two documents are before the Dean and Chapter: first the *congé d'élire*, the permission and command to proceed to elect a bishop, and a letter from the Sovereign suggesting in the most courteous terms that Dr. A or Dr. B would be a happy choice. No hint of the Statute of Praemunire is in the documents, but the famous Reformation law is in our minds. The Dean and Chapter know that, if they do not vote as directed, they are in a state of rebellion. On this occasion, I was confronted with a procedural problem. One of the prebendaries, whose name I do not divulge, asked me if he would be in order in proposing an alternative to the Crown nominee. I have no idea why the prebendary raised the question, but I was informed that he intended to put forward my name. Of course, that would have been most disturbing, and I imagine quite illegal. I ruled that, since the Chapter was meeting in accordance with a royal command to consider a royal proposal, we must first of all put that to the vote and, if it was lost, we could then go on to consider what to do and take advice on our legal position. Dr. Wand was elected by a large majority, and the shadow of Praemunire was averted.

A bright little boy among the choristers had evidently been concerned about Praemunire, for he said, "Do you know what would have happened if you and the canons had not elected Dr. Wand? The King would have confiscated Mrs. Matthews and all the canons' wives." He was not quite right in his interpretation of the penalty attached to breaches of the Praemunire law which begins by confiscating all the culprit's "goods and chattels". The innocent child reasoned, I suppose, that even if a wife was not goods she must at least be a chattel. Only one minute reform did I succeed in securing in the election of bishops in St. Paul's. Formerly the meeting was preceded by the singing of the *Veni Creator*. I persuaded the Chapter to omit this. It was too late to invoke the Holy Spirit when the nomination was already in the hands of the Chapter clerk.

We had too a new Government, much, it seemed to everyone's surprise. Unless a very eminent member of the Labour

Party was pulling my leg when I met him at lunch with Lord Kemsley at *The Sunday Times* office, he and some of his colleagues had expected to be out of office for many years. And it seems likely that when the Labour Government was formed it had not thought out its policy in any detail. The general election was preceded by a service in St. Paul's to which we invited the leaders of all parties. Canon J. Collins (who had been appointed to St. Paul's without consultation with me at the urgent request, I believe, of Sir Stafford Cripps) had the idea with which I was heartily in agreement that a public service of intercession for a right judgment in the minds of the electors would be an expression of the Christian concern for just and compassionate government. No one was really prepared to deny the principle, but not all politicians were enthusiastic and I am sure that Winston Churchill, though he attended, was not happy. Somehow the party system, which appears to be an essential element in any free democracy, does not fit happily with united public prayer even at general elections. The suspicion that the adversaries are stealing unfair publicity, and the temptation to steal unfair publicity oneself, are disturbing. The experiment was not repeated in St. Paul's.

There is no doubt that, for a brief period immediately after the war, there were signs of a revival of religion. The "days of prayer" and the services of thanksgiving had moved people's hearts and consciences. A general resolution to build a better civilisation and to eliminate war from future history prevailed and the question was how to direct these good resolutions towards creative action. The new Bishop of London chose to begin his reign by a diocesan mission. I think it was a good decision and well-timed to catch the tide of religious questioning at the flood. Though, on the whole, my experience of organised missions has led me to think that generally the same amount of dedicated energy put into parishes as was involved in organising the mission would have had better results, this time it seemed to me the mission could have unifying effects and could encourage the parishes in the diocese to adventure in evangelism. A feature of this mission which I welcomed was that it gave due attention to the intellect and aimed at presenting the Christian religion as a creed which could claim the assent and allegiance of intelligent and educated persons. I thought then, and I think now, that the main obstacle to the spread of Christian faith and practice is that a large proportion of the population does not believe in God. After all, it is unlikely that good news about God will attract much attention from persons who think He is a myth.

Oswin Gibbs-Smith, who was appointed Archdeacon of London shortly after the mission, was very active in organising it under considerable difficulties. I was glad to be given an opportunity to take part in what may be called the "teaching" side of the mission and I contributed about half the material in a course of lectures in St. Paul's by the Bishop, Dr. Demant and myself. The general title, or text, of the mission was *Recovery Starts Within* and under that title our lectures were published. Dr. Garbett, the Archbishop of York, was encouraging enough to say that my "popular" presentation of Christianity was just what was needed and, re-reading it, I think it was at least the best I could do in that kind of composition. Perhaps it was unfortunate that the makers of a patent medicine about that time used a slogan "Inner cleanliness comes first", which gave frivolous persons materials for foolish jokes. But the mission's motto was right. Recovery starts within: we must get our thoughts and values right before we can hope to put outer circumstances right. The fact that this was not properly understood is a chief cause of the relative failure of efforts to reconstruct the Church and its worship, as I shall point out when I come to my experience on Convocation.

About this time, though not explicitly in connection with the mission, I published some of my wartime sermons under the title *Strangers and Pilgrims* (Nisbet and Co.). Without any advertising, this book has remained in print and has gained the approval of some thoughtful persons. My method of preaching has remained on the whole fairly constant. I always have a manuscript in front of me, but it may be either practically the whole sermon to be read as it stands, or a few brief notes. It is not that I fear to lack words or ideas if I speak without a note, it is rather that I should say something that I do not really mean or fall into pious jargon. The preachers whom I admired in my youth were men like Hensley Henson, R. J. Campbell, Robertson of Brighton, all men of the school of thinking Christians. To fall back on emotional rhetoric would be impossible for me. A critic of this particular book of sermons, after some appreciative comments, put his finger on

what may have been a real defect in my preaching. He pointed
out that there was no evidence in the sermons that I had read
either of the two most influential evangelical preachers of the
day, Reinhold Niebuhr, the American, and Karl Barth, the
German Swiss. My critic linked my apparent neglect of these
two writers with what seemed to him to be a defect in my
message. I did not sufficiently stress the notes of conviction of
sin and the redemption of the individual soul, nor did I dwell
enough on the idea of revelation. There is some justice in this
criticism. Though I am fully convinced that the Gospel is a
message of salvation for individuals and that Christ saves not
nations or civilisations but men and women one by one, and
no less convinced that conversion and forgiveness with the
answer of the person to Christ's call to follow him are the way
of salvation, I falter when I come to some of the words and
phrases in the New Testament which refer to the Atonement.
I am, I hope, not unmindful of the truth that Jesus Christ
died for us and for our salvation, and I can use the metaphors
of the New Testament which enlarge on the sacrifice of the
Lamb of God, but the idea that the Atonement is some kind
of transaction by which our redemption is secured means very
little to me and some of the language used in hymns about the
"precious blood" are terribly misleading, unless the word
"blood" can be accepted as meaning "the life".

The work of Karl Barth in his series of volumes on the
Christian dogmas is indeed a monument erected with immense
learning and constructive power; he was acclaimed by many,
including a Pope, as the leading theologian of the age, nor
could it be denied that in the critical days of the Hitler tyranny
his powerful influence was of the utmost value in sustaining
the morale of the Lutheran opposition. To me, however, his
method and the presuppositions in his theology were unacceptable. My old tutor, Alfred Caldecott, who wrote a book on the
various types of theism, designated one method of approach
as "the Resort to Revelation Only", and one of my predeces-
sors in St. Paul's, Dean Mansel, was a brilliant exponent of
the school. Though I would admit that the scepticism of
Mansel about philosophical explanations of the universe is
well founded, in the sense that no philosophy can be demonstrated as the final answer to the riddle of the universe, and
would agree that without a revelation our knowledge of God

would have been confused and uncertain, I cannot accept the view that I may ask no reasons for my belief in revelation. But, unless I have grievously misunderstood the views of the "Biblical Theologians", this is what they tell me. They argue that to give reasons for thinking that the Bible is a revelation of God is wrong because it implies that we, or our reason, are judging the Bible, whereas it is we who are judged by the Bible. I think, perhaps, there is still a remnant of old-fashioned Victorian rationalism in me; be that as it may, I cannot bring myself to assent to important and far-reaching statements, such as "In the Bible we have a divine revelation", without having some reason for thinking so.

In my opinion, one of the vulnerable sides of the religious recovery was that it was not able to give reasons and often saw no need for them. The apparent upsurge in religion was notable among university students and continued for a whole generation of students (three or four years). This phenomenon was most evident in Oxford and Cambridge, where the collége chapels were full, but the wave was reported too in the universities where chapels were not so abundant. This state of mind did not last long, but it faded gradually and there was a period when the Christian believers in universities were largely men out of the forces and they were opposed by a "neo-pagan" movement which enlisted the support of some of the undergraduates who had escaped the war. As after the previous war, it was noted that a kind of subconscious resentment grew up in the men straight from school as against the service men.

A humiliating experience in Cambridge made it terribly clear to me that I was out of touch with the academic youth—both Christian and pagan. The Union invited me to speak at a debate on the motion "That this House would welcome a revival of paganism". I had spoken, with some acceptance, in the Union shortly before the war, and I envisaged a similar audience after the war. I was sadly mistaken. The debate on paganism was intended as a serious trial of strength between two movements—the Christian revival and the secular humanists. My speech, which was in light-hearted vein, was disapproved by both sides. The fact was that no one ever defined the term "paganism". I took the word in the sense of a polytheistic religion, which so far from being atheist was over-rich in deities; whereas the supporters of the resolution took the word "pagan" to mean secular humanism. The height of absurdity was reached when one of the principal speakers on the side of paganism put forward Erasmus as the type of humane cultivated pagan and I ended my oration by pointing to him as the Christian humanist!

On the surface, the discussions and controversies of professional philosophers are of small importance. They often use a jargon which needs interpretation and not many men of action read their works. Yet they are important and one should not hope to understand any epoch, including our own, without some acquaintance with the current philosophies. It is often very doubtful whether the philosophies make the intellectual climate or are made by it, but in either case they are enlightening. At the end of the war, the dominant philosophy in Great Britain changed. When my eldest son, Michael, took a first in "Greats" in Oxford, the examiners were, on the whole, idealists and the logic accepted was the idealist type expounded by two writers, Bradley and Bosanquet, who were the oracles of the period. When Michael came home for a few days before the examination began I amused myself by guessing what kind of questions would be set and talking about my guesses. It happened that I touched upon several questions which appeared in the papers. One of my memories of Michael is that he said to the youth with whom he shared lodging, "If I had known how much my father knew about this stuff, I would have gone home a week earlier." If his examination for Greats had taken place after the war, my conversation would have helped very little.

Two thinkers who loomed large in the intellectual firmament were mathematicians: Bertrand Russell and Alfred North Whitehead, who collaborated in a work on the foundations of mathematics and, starting from a more or less identical standpoint, developed different theories of reality. I can claim to have conversed with both these great men, but with Russell my contacts have been pleasant and friendly though brief. He found it hard, I think, to believe that an Anglican priest could have any thoughts worth attending to. His personality has always interested me and his prose style has always had my admiration. Though he has been the most formidable critic of the Christian faith in my time, I have felt that he had the capacity for religious experience and knew something at least of what the mystics were talking about; in short, the title of one of his most important books *Mysticism and Logic* could have represented the conflict in his experience with the change of "and" into "or". The tendency of which Russell is an outstanding representative can be described with some justice as a "Back to Hume" movement and it is still powerful. The philosophical analysis of which we hear today is largely, though not altogether, based on empiricism of the type which in Hume's hands led to all-pervading scepticism.

Whitehead approached philosophy through mathematics and science, just as Russell did, but he was not sceptical. His aim was constructive and he had in the end much to say about the universe and God as well as of the meaning of religion. With Whitehead I had closer contact, though it was never my good fortune to be either his pupil or his colleague in university teaching. I met him when we were both members of the Senate of the University of London; he was a Professor in the Imperial College of Science and I was Dean of King's College. The Imperial College's relations with the University at that time were complex and controversial. Like King's College, it had existed before the University had become anything more than an examining body and, like King's, it had built up its own system of teaching and of graduating. As anyone could see, such a situation was full of complex problems affecting students past and present and the status and emolument of professors and other teachers. Whitehead used to deliver lectures to us in his silvery voice and his beautifully lucid words. My recollection is that he read these business lectures word by word from a typescript, while he talked without a written note on the subject of philosophy. When he left London to "retire" to a chair in Harvard, I began, with many other readers, to note that Whitehead was a creative thinker. I read his books as they came out and when I was in the U.S.A. the Whiteheads were most hospitable to my wife and me. A book of his "table-talk" by a former student has given the general public some taste of his wisdom and wit—just enough to deepen our regret that he had no Boswell. The specimens of his conversation which are on record are defective I think in one respect— they do not convey the religious spirit of Whitehead's thinking. Sharply critical sayings on the apparent contradictions and confusions in Christian teaching are authentic and characteristic; but, as readers of his books which touch on spiritual realities will expect, he spoke from within the fellowship of the spiritually awakened. He was a worshipper. One of the last things that he said to me was, "The older I get the more certain I am that nearly all the things that Catholics do are right, and nearly all the reasons they give are wrong." This was a parting pronouncement on which I have often pondered, but I never had an opportunity of asking him to expand it.

One other characteristic of Whitehead was his love of teaching and his interest in the development of clever young men. At an age when professors are on the brink of retirement, he went from England to America and had to adapt himself to American *mores*. He did this not only with ease but with zest and, when I asked him about the change-over, he told me that he was happier than ever in his disciples. The American young men had less "background" than English; they had more alert intelligences and responded more eagerly to intellectual challenges. I doubt whether Whitehead's influence will be lasting. He was almost the last British philosopher to come forward with anything like a system or a metaphysical theory of reality. Unfortunately his great work *Process and Reality* is written in a most difficult idiom which the reader has to acquire before he can understand the work. This is the more exasperating because Whitehead in his other writings has shown that he could have been more lucid. Whitehead's most illuminating work for the general reader is his *Adventures of Ideas*. I have always found him full of *obiter dicta*, which start one thinking sometimes by reaction against a shocking exaggeration, as for example "Most of the history of philosophy is a series of footnotes to Plato."

The years 1945–1955 were more crucial than most of us realised and, on reflection, I think the failure to go ahead was largely intellectual. The philosophers declined the duty which tradition assigned to the wise men of advising on moral and political issues. When C. E. M. Joad blamed the professional philosophers for neglecting their obligation to society in critical times, he was almost unanimously repudiated and accused of having a fundamentally mistaken idea of the nature of philosophy. The philosophy of Karl Marx was not aloof from the problems of human society—on the contrary it had a more or less coherent theory of the development of society and of the role of the individual in the movement towards the classless community. That many young people were attracted to Communism is not surprising when one remembers the vague generalities which took the place of serious thought in most Christian pronouncements.

If there had been no war and my career had proceeded along the lines I had hoped for, I might have followed up the contributions already made to philosophical theology and the re-thinking of the Christian doctrines. I had intended to write on the Doctrine of the Incarnation in the spirit and method of my *God in Christian Thought and Experience* and *The Purpose of God*. During the years when I might have been fulfilling that programme of scholarly work, I had in fact been under bombardment and distracted by the calls on my voice and my pen. In that period I constantly broadcast, wrote articles, preached sermons, was interviewed, and as I have narrated went on most interesting but exhausting tours in Scandinavia, Holland and Germany—all connected with the defence of the country and the well-being of the Church. I had no time to keep abreast of current literature. And I confess when, as it were, I got my head above water and listened to what the philosophers were arguing about, much of it seemed to me deadly dull. They had given up the great problems of "God, Freedom and Immortality" and all such profound enquiries and were engaged in "Semantics", the meaning of words, no doubt a subject of real importance and requiring patience and acute intelligence, but I was too old to start a new game. At this moment, some of my friends in the Lower House of the Convocation of Canterbury urged me to allow my name to go forward for election as prolocutor of the House. This was a move towards the centre of the administration of the Church of England. I think very likely it was a mistake and my wife was of the opinion that my notorious disability to say "No" had landed me in trouble. As I hope to show, the time and labour were not totally wasted.

CHAPTER 15

Convocation

Why so many members of the lower house of the Convocation of the Province of Canterbury wished me to be the prolocutor I simply do not know. Though I had attended the meetings with diligence, I had not taken a prominent part in its proceedings, having plenty to occupy my mind elsewhere. There was some feeling that the lower house did not "pull its weight", though what the evidence for its failure was I do not know. The fact that St. Paul's had been much in people's minds and that, by tradition, Convocation always opened its sessions in St. Paul's (though after the first day they were moved to Westminster) may have weighed with them. Perhaps they thought I could be trusted not to be overawed by bishops and, if so, they were right. I knew most of the diocesan bishops at the time and at least two of them were former pupils whose essays I had criticised. The business likely to be before the Convocations was certain to be important, because the war had not only destroyed many churches and caused shifting of population, but it had revealed some defects in the organisation which needed to be put right.

But before we go further, it may be necessary to write a few words about the Convocations for the sake of those whose history is weak. The Convocations are among the ancient and interesting institutions of our national Church—and, in some respects, the most tiresome. The chief thing to remember is that they are historically part of the English constitution. They were in ancient times the ecclesiastical parliament, and I suppose that there were periods when they represented the will of the people better than the House of Commons. The clergy had a real opportunity of making their opinions heard in their elected House. For a time the taxation of the clergy was not the business of Parliament but of Convocation. "As every schoolboy knows", Henry VIII in his reforming zeal, if that is the right word, dealt roughly with Convocation and diminished its powers. A somewhat illogical consequence of this ancient history is that no priest can be elected a member of parliament, by reason of the fact that he is "represented" in Convocation. After the civil war and the Restoration, there developed an antagonism between the two houses which was largely political. The bishops, for the most part, were Whigs appointed by Whig governments, while the "lower" clergy were predominantly Tories and had moreover to live under a muddled and senseless system which condemned many of them to poverty and to dependence. The novels of the 18th century contain much material for understanding why the Convocations were suspended and not revived until the 19th century.

The slight feeling of resentment still persisting in the lower house against the upper house, which consisted only of bishops, was a kind of tradition and without serious meaning. I am bound to add, however, that in my time as prolocutor the customs and regulations were, it seemed, designed to keep the lower clergy in their place. The Archbishop had the final word on the order of business. The upper house, presided over by the Archbishop as president, sent matter for consideration down to the lower house with an intimation that everything else should be dropped and the episcopal messages debated and accepted. When the Archbishop and bishops wished to communicate with the lower house, they did so verbally. The prolocutor would be summoned to attend His Grace and their Lordships where they were assembled. When the ostiary (doorkeeper) came with the summons, without delay I had to collect five or six members of the lower house to accompany me and to ask one of the assistant prolocutors to take the chair during my absence. The effect of this was to hold up progress in the lower house because, though they could go on debating, no motion could be put to the vote until our return from the Bishops' House.

When the ostiary ushered us into the meeting of the upper house, we found the Archbishop and bishops all in canonical dress, sitting at a long table with the Archbishop at the head. He and the bishops remained seated all the time and we remained standing. His Grace the president delivered his instructions and communicated the results of the debates in the upper house. As I was standing, dressed in cassock, doctor's gown and bands, I could not make any notes and had to trust in the memories of my companions. The instructions generally had an important bearing on the order of business. I do not remember that I was asked if I had any comments to make, though the lower house frequently submitted questions to the Archbishop through me and there was quite a lot of informal communication between the lawyers and the very able secretary of Convocation, my friend Dr. Smethurst.

I did not resent all this, because I thought that a Christian minister standing on his dignity is nearly always ridiculous, but I am ready to admit that on these occasions I was nearer to Presbyterianism than usual and to their principle "the parity of ministers". It is some years now since I attended Convocation and no doubt there have been many changes. The continuing existence of Convocation is not assured, because the Church Assembly may be empowered to take over its functions. Probably that would save much time, but I should be sorry to see this ancient institution abolished with all its dignified and scholarly customs, such as the Latin litany and the academic dress with the courtly language in which archbishop and prolocutor address one another and the assembled brethren. It is fair to add that in my time a joint meeting of the two houses was not unknown and since then they have become more frequent. Most notable of all have been the meetings of the Convocations of Canterbury and York together in London, debating together but voting separately.

One of the ancient customs in my time was that the election of the prolocutor was conducted in Latin. No doubt this was not at all embarrassing in earlier centuries when, I suppose, the majority of clerics could stammer out some sentences in Latin without much difficulty; but today Latin is not a language commonly used in daily life and moreover those who know Latin now have generally some conception of the difference between Latin and dog Latin and have a horror of howlers left over from their schooldays. I was fortunate. They forewarned me that I was almost certain to be elected and that, when the Archbishop had accepted my election in a Latin speech, I should be required to reply in Latin and to say a few words of thanks to those who had voted for me. I spent a laborious evening with Latin grammars which had lain unopened for decades and produced a piece of prose which included not only what I hoped were graceful expressions of gratitude but a very mild and obvious joke. I carried this composition about with me in the hope that, before the day came, I should meet a learned friend who would "vet" it for me. The man I met was Professor Claude Jenkins of Christ Church, Oxford, Regius Professor of Church History and the godfather of one of my children. He read it through slowly and said, "H'm, not at all bad for an impromptu speech," which was good enough for me.

That speech had a curious history. Most such utterances live only for the day when they are born; this one had a revival five years later. My successor in the chair of prolocutor, Canon R. L. Whytehead, was not so well warned and prepared as I had been. I think he was elected unexpectedly. At any rate he had no speech in his pocket and no fluent Latinist was at his elbow. With great presence of mind, he slipped into the library at Church House during the lunch interval and copied out my speech of five years earlier, leaving out the joke. Perhaps it was lack of time which stopped him short, or it may be that he thought the joke undignified. It was such a very little one; I only said that though I should try to be unbiassed in the chair I had frankly to own that I had a natural preference for those orators who cultivated the art of expressing their opinions succinctly. "Confiteor autem vobis, fratres, praejudicium meum pro oratoribus qui succincte loqui solent: sint omnes Proctores in consilio nostro, precor, sapientes qui non multa sed multum dicere volunt." This record may relieve the minds of future historians researching on ecclesiastical affairs in the 20th century and discovering that the two speeches separated in time by five years were verbally identical and prevent them from entertaining the hypothesis of miracle.

I fear that in jest I have sometimes exaggerated the severity of my ordeal as prolocutor. While the sessions were on, it was tiring to keep one's attention on debates for hours at a time and could be boring, but the general level of oratory was high compared with other assemblies. The speakers had at least a command of the English language and, even when differences were acute, were invariably courteous. They made the task of the prolocutor easy. My restlessness was due to quite a different cause—I thought we were discussing the wrong subjects. I am not sure that I formed this opinion from the start, but I became more convinced that it was true as time went on.

The reader may remember that the Report of the Archbishops' Commission on Doctrine had been published almost co-incidentally with the outbreak of war and that, before the end of the war, its chairman, William Temple, had died. The circumstances called for immediate work on the Report before memories of it had faded. The Archbishop of Canterbury did not agree, but decided that the really urgent need was a revision of the Canon Law and in this he was supported by the Convocations. No one could deny that the Canon Law was out of date, for it had not been revised since the year 1604 and was so wildly anachronistic that it was rarely cited. If it had been enforced on the clergy in the 20th century, they would have found their lives remarkably prescribed and minutely regulated. The colour of the clerical nightcap was to be black, for example, and their outdoor garb of cassock and gown regularly worn. But the Canon Law had been out of date for a long time and surely no disaster would have followed if reform of them was deferred for some years. I do not suggest that the Archbishop and those who agreed with him had not some powerful arguments on their side. Great harm was being done to the spiritual life of the people in the parishes by the apparent lawlessness of many of the clergy. The worship and the teaching varied so ostentatiously from one parish to another that a detached observer might easily be at a loss to decide whether they belonged to the same Church or even the same religion. When aggrieved parishioners, or militant Protestants, appealed to the courts of the realm against alleged illegal services in the Established Church, they sometimes won their case, but with anything but good consequences, and those clerics who were accused of breaking the law were able to reply that the law of the Church was not necessarily the law as interpreted by the secular courts. On many grounds it was much to be desired that ecclesiastical courts should be set up if the establishment of the Church by law continued. Geoffrey Fisher was a former headmaster and believed in reasonable discipline. He recognised that a pressing need in the two provinces of England was a call to order and an end to blatant defiance of discipline. One of his many merits as Primate was his unceasing and largely successful restoration of order among the clergy.

The revision of Canon Law might have been less of an

obstacle to other reforms if it had been less thorough. My own opinion, for what it is worth, is that a fatal mistake was made when the detailed legislation of 1604 was taken as a model for 1950. The kind of discipline which might have worked happily was a series of principles laying down in a broad way the purposes and ideals of the pastoral office, as understood in the Anglican branch of the Catholic Church, and beyond that almost nothing. It should be the duty of the bishops to encourage and help the parochial clergy in their immensely difficult and often depressing work. The bishops should be truly fathers in God to the clergy, and fathers on the modern pattern not the old one—experienced and wise comrades. The revised Canons tend to give more direct control and therefore responsibility. Reading through them, one constantly comes upon "with the consent of the bishop" or "shall be referred to the bishop", all expressions tending to restrict the initiative of the parish priest. When I was a vicar, I had a very pleasant suffragan the Bishop of Willesden as my immediate superior. It never occurred to me to ask him if I might ask a Non-conformist minister or a layman to speak in my church or whether he approved of an eminent woman doctor, a friend of my wife, addressing a large meeting on sex education; but we were all very pleased when he or his wife could attend and perhaps take the chair. We need freedom to experiment if we are to enlist the attention of the people. This tendency to call for the bishops must have increased their burden and occupied their time. The bishops need time to read and think. Mr. Attlee, when he was Prime Minister, referring to the nomination of clerics for bishoprics, is alleged to have said, "We want good field-officers", I suppose like Major Clement Attlee. True enough; but we need, too, leaders of armies and strategists. Compared with the bishops of the first decades of this century, our contemporary bishops carry little weight. This is partly because they have nothing worth hearing to say. We listen to them when they preach the gospel and instruct us in our duties as Christian men, but on the problems philosophical and ethical which press on thoughtful persons they have little to say. I may be quite mistaken, but my impression is that the utterances and publications of bishops in the days of Gore, Barnes, Hensley Henson and others of that period stimulated people to think and gave some guidance on how to do it; but our bishops today have no such effect—though I do not say that they actually discourage our thinking.

In Convocation the attempt to cover too many contingencies naturally took time and the notorious clerical aptitude in splitting hairs and making subtle distinctions had free play, so that by the time the end of the exercise came into sight everyone was bored with the Canon Law. For my part, the boredom was the harder to bear because I thought that the whole project was misconceived and might have consequences which had not been anticipated. It seemed likely that a clash between Convocation and Parliament might ensue, probably arising out of Canon Law, on the subject of marriage and divorce. As one who believed that, in principle, the Church ought to be disestablished, I could not regard it as a disaster in itself; but that the final decision on so great a change should be a side issue in a squabble about legal details seemed unthinkable. A great nation ought to make a fundamental alteration in its constitution only after serious and dignified debate in which the relation between Church and State, between religion and secular civilisation, was thoroughly explored.

A psychological cause can be suggested for the policy of the bishops and of Convocation. Most of us had a fear just below the level of consciousness; a vague fear but persistent. We feared that the future could not be just a gentle development of the past and present; that pre-war security could not be restored. This was a common fear, but as Christian pastors and theologians we had a more definite apprehension. We knew that there were many questions and doubts concerning our faith which had been brought home to multitudes in the war and we were only too well aware that we had no final and conclusive answers to them. In a sermon about this time, I ventured to compare the bishops to a man who occupied himself in rearranging the furniture when his house was on fire. Convocation, and the Church Assembly, and the archbishops and bishops worked hard on Canon Law, while the future of the Church became day by day more precarious and the congregations dwindled. I must not seem to claim any remarkable wisdom or courage. I ought perhaps to have resigned the office of prolocutor and protested against Convocation's proceedings but I could not say that a revision of the Canon Law was in itself bad; if it could be done wisely, it might be a lasting benefit.

My feeling that the Thirty-nine Articles should be considered first was not the view of many, and that reform should begin was the main desideratum and perhaps the question where it should begin was secondary. And, to be frank, one part of me enjoyed presiding over debates and I found many members whose friendship was precious.

Let me mention some. Dr. Barnes, the Bishop of Birmingham, was the centre of a dramatic incident in Convocation when the Archbishop of Canterbury, as president of Convocation, at a joint meeting of both houses, made a long statement on the theology of Bishop Barnes. It was not an excommunication, but it was a clear expression of the view that anyone who held the religious opinions of Dr. Barnes ought to feel that he could not continue to be a bishop in the Anglican Church. This pronouncement took me quite by surprise and embarrassed me not a little, for I had admiration and affection for the Bishop, but had often wondered that he could with a clear conscience carry on as a diocesan bishop, for his theology was more Unitarian or Quaker than Anglican. The fuss about Dr. Robinson's beliefs has surprised me and shows how soon religious quarrels are forgotten.

Nevertheless, though I think Dr. Barnes was a questionable Anglican, I maintain that he was a very good Christian. I first knew him when he was Master of the Temple and notorious for his outspoken and thoroughgoing pacifism in the first world war. In this respect, he was a Quaker. Barnes must have endured some harsh criticism from the Benchers of the Middle and Inner Temple, when he used their pulpit to advocate his Christian non-violence and anti-war opinions. I was told that, after one such sermon, the Lord Chancellor was heard to say to a fellow bencher, "If I didn't know it was legally a privileged occasion, I would have that Master of ours in gaol tomorrow." Barnes was a mathematician and an eminent one, being what in modern times is a very rare bird—a bishop who was a Fellow of the Royal Society. He wrote lectures on religion and science, which consisted of a readable conspectus of the sciences of the day, but so far as I could judge did not help much to clear up the difference between scientific knowledge and religious faith. I wrote in my copy of his lectures, "I suppose this proves that a man can know quite a lot of science and still be some kind of Christian." But it ill becomes me to criticise his lectures, for I owed him gratitude when he supported me at that crisis in my life when I was elected Dean of King's College, London, and many bishops regarded me with grave suspicion. As a bishop, his attractive personality and courtesy eased his relations with clergy who deplored what they held to be his heresies. He ceased to preach very much in his diocese towards the end, but whenever I was preaching in one of the churches in it he came to give the blessing. He did what was possible to fill the diocese with "modern churchmen" and perhaps was apt to be too hasty in his rejection of candidates for ordination. One of my students at King's College told me how he was smartly disposed of by the Bishop. He was asked two questions: "What is the date of Habakkuk?" which he got wrong, and "What church do you go to?" to which the candidate replied with the name of a well-known Anglo-Catholic parish. The Bishop summed up: "You are an ignorant man and a superstitious man. You are not wanted in this diocese." Of course, this was an invention, or an exaggeration, but it illustrated the uncertainty of the Bishop's response.

Among all my friends in that generation of "modern churchmen", I do not remember one who was in favour of disestablishment, nor one who wanted to abolish or revise the Thirty-nine Articles. Why these radicals in theology were so conservative in policy, I cannot say. I think most of them had been low churchmen and feared the Catholic type of modernism as a version of "popery". Dr. Barnes explained to me why he supported the establishment of the Church in a remarkable argument which I once had with him. I objected that his policy with regard to the Church contradicted his liberal ideals in politics. He held that the wealth of the Church Commissioners was the safeguard of liberal theology. The so-called "Free Churches", he pointed out, were not likely to support a ministry which sought the truth. The ministers, dependent as they were on the offerings of the faithful, would not be able to preach unpopular truth. The Church of England clergy, on the contrary, were largely supported by endowments and the parson's freehold, which had been the protection of the Oxford Movement and Anglo-Catholic clergy, would, he said, in the next century be the safeguard of the radical modernists.

The Archbishop pronounced his judgment on Barnes's book *The Rise of Christianity* in Convocation on October 15th, 1947.

I came in about half-way through and found all the bishops grouped together on one side of the hall and the Bishop of Birmingham isolated, sitting all by himself as though he had been sent to Coventry. On the spur of the moment, I went and sat by his side, hoping that my rank as prolocutor would excuse me for sitting in the bishops' row of chairs. Barnes was quite silent and I wondered if he was feeling an outcast. I think not, for when he saw me he said, "Well, you see I'm not deposed yet."

In this affair both men did what they had to do. The Archbishop was confronted by a majority of bishops who would have insisted on passing a vote of censure for heresy unless he spoke plainly condemning Barnes's theology and he chose the course which was least provocative, while Barnes could not retract without narrowing the permissive opinions in the Church and disheartening laymen who clung to the Church and its worship while uncertain of its theology. Barnes's reply was courteous but uncompromising.

The fact is that Barnes had no theology in the accepted sense. He had no doctrine of the Incarnation or of the Atonement. "Men saw that Jesus Christ was a very good man, so they called him Son of God" would sum up his teaching on the divinity of Christ, not inadequately. Nor was he a Biblical scholar and he exasperated other scholars who were authorities on the New Testament by his uncritical acceptance of the most negative conclusions. The book by Guignebert, *Jésus*, which maintained some very questionable views, was apparently the basis which he accepted. It was a pity that Barnes laid himself open to damaging criticism from scholars who were truly liberal in their outlook. Yet, in spite of all these criticisms, I am glad that I knew Bishop Barnes and think of him with gratitude and affection; I am sure that he contributed to the Anglican tradition by his moral courage and his simple piety.

Of Dr. Smethurst too, who was Secretary of Convocation, I must speak with gratitude. He was a scientist who had brought his attainments into the Christian ministry. His premature death was a loss to the whole Church, but he left us a book on the relation of science and religion which is a model of lucid exposition and gave us reason to hope that he would help us in this difficult field of study for many years. He was an outstanding example of the dedicated man of many talents.

A member of Convocation who was well known and regarded in some quarters as a nuisance was C. E. Douglas. I had known his brother in the University of London where J. A. Douglas was for many years the chairman of Convocation (not the ecclesiastical Convocation, but the academic one elected by graduates of the University of London). Both the Douglases were priests in the Church of England and both were eccentric. J. A. Douglas had been a good friend to me even from undergraduate days and remained so until his death. He had lived in Constantinople and was a remarkable linguist. How many languages he knew and how well he knew them, I never could be sure, but certainly I have seen him apparently in fluent conversation with many strange foreigners. He had a method of learning a new language which I never tried, but that was because I was too lazy. He would get an elementary grammar of the language and do all the exercises. Then he would get a copy of the New Testament in the language and would copy out the Gospel of St. Luke three times, writing away in any spare moments. By the time that he had finished writing the Gospel the third time, he had a good working knowledge of the language and could build up vocabulary and conversational fluency as occasion offered. I certainly had an admiration for J.A.D.'s industry. During the last war, the exiled Roumanians had occasional meetings in London and held at least one service in J. A. Douglas' church in the City. I attended the service by invitation and was deeply impressed when he took the service himself, wearing a heavy cope and singing a litany. "Why, the clever old man," I thought, "is singing a Roumanian or perhaps a Greek litany." I was quite mistaken. He was singing the Litany in the Book of Common Prayer, but pronouncing the words so badly that they were incomprehensible! Eccentric as he was, he was a public-spirited citizen and a devoted worker in good causes of a somewhat marginal character, and many of them connected with the Orthodox Churches.

His brother was on the whole interested in the same things, but he first impinged on my attention when I became a member of Convocation. He was an expert in procedure and seemed to delight in suspending business by points of order. The Archbishop of Canterbury was hard put to it to maintain his customary suavity and good humour when Douglas was on the warpath. Whether Douglas was wholly serious, I cannot tell, but he looked and sounded serious. The most exasperating thing about him was that he was almost invariably right. I do not remember that he caused me any trouble when I was prolocutor; perhaps he saved it up for the Archbishop; but I do remember his friendly encouragement and help when I began writing a Saturday article for *The Daily Telegraph*. This happened almost it seemed by accident and was not sought by me. It began in a tentative manner and I thought perhaps the arrangement might last a few months; it has gone on ever since 1946 without interruption. By the grace of God I have never failed in all those years to provide the Saturday article. Sometimes they have been written from hospital or while I was in America. I have never thought of them as a burden, but always as a wonderful opportunity.

As I have said, the beginning was apparently almost accidental. A man who was high up in *The Daily Telegraph* (I have forgotten his name) asked my advice about the Saturday article, which they thought was not then getting much attention from readers. I pointed out that there were two possible ways of organising a regular feature of a religious character; to copy *The Times* and have a list of contributors who would represent different points of view. This seemed to me the safest way. The alternative way would be, of course, to ask one man to write a series of articles in the hope that he would attract a "following" and increase the number of regular readers. I was fairly sure that they would choose the first plan and collect a team, particularly because the single writer plan had been in force when they decided to make a change. I did not think that *The Daily Telegraph* editors would have me in mind, because they had consulted me and they obviously would not expect me to recommend myself.

When they offered me the job—that is not the right word, for it was not a salaried post—when I was offered the opportunity of contributing a short religious article for some Saturdays, I was not overjoyed and wondered if I dared accept. I had to earn money beyond my stipend as Dean, which had never been sufficient to maintain my household in the deanery with its forty rooms. I reflected that a weekly article might be beyond my power and that I might be better employed in writing a large book. In the end I said, "I will try it, if you double the pay." This sounded to me mercenary and unworthy, but I regarded it as "sanctified commonsense". If I could do the articles well, they would be a way of preaching the gospel; and if the pay was enough to relieve the financial pressure which caused me anxiety, I should be more effective in all my work.

The first year of my articles was successful beyond my hopes. I tried to link the articles with the Prayer Book services for the Sundays and to state the Christian faith in a way which appealed to me and I hoped would appeal to readers. It was here that Douglas helped. He was greatly taken with my little pieces and persuaded the Faith Press, of which he was a director, to publish the whole year's contributions together with passages from Scripture on which he spent much time and thought in selecting. The Faith Press is a publishing house with an Anglo-Catholic tradition and I have no doubt its *imprimatur* did my articles some good by suggesting that I was not such a destructive modernist as some had imagined. I am grateful to Douglas, and I wish I could think that I expressed my gratitude to him adequately while he was here.

From the first, I tried to reply to letters arising out of *The Daily Telegraph,* when they asked for guidance on genuine difficulties, and this correspondence, which was sometimes heavy, helped me to know something of the minds of readers and has often suggested subjects for my pen. The short pieces which I write are a little like sonnets; the art (if that is not too dignified a word) is to say quite a lot in a very limited number of lines. The faults in them are never due to my having nothing to say, but nearly always to my trying to say too much.

Some of my literary and semi-academic activities began to fade away in this postwar period. Ever since my King's College days I had organised a short course in the long vacation, originally under the auspices of the Board of Education and later the Ministry. The subject was Religious Knowledge and the students were secondary schoolteachers who wished to be efficient in the subject. The courses were residential and lasted two weeks. They were held in universities where suitable residential colleges were available: Oxford, Cambridge, Durham and the training college in Ripon. These courses with never more than forty students, all living together, were always an exhausting experience for me, but always a great intellectual and spiritual refreshment. For many years my dear friend, Professor S. H. Hooke, was my colleague and his genius as a lecturer and

good companion always shone at its brightest. Some other constant helpers I recruited, among them Richard Hanson, who
followed me as Dean of King's College, and two headmistresses,
Miss Verini and Miss Molly Hoyle, are enshrined in my memory
as well as a science mistress, Miss Caireen Cruden, who, along
with Professor Hooke, was our bard. Alas, that their lays are
too personal to quote here.

It would be a long business if I enumerated all the valuable
lessons which these courses offered for my learning. Of one I
am bound to speak, because it altered my belief on how to spread
true religion. I could not help being struck by the number of
letters from students after every course who spoke about it as
a religious experience. One student, I remember, wrote, "We
came to a course and it turned into a retreat," and many others
used similar phrases. In a way, they rather alarmed me, because
we were certainly supposed to be imparting knowledge and not
promoting piety. And our lectures and discussion groups were
strictly academic in character. The teachers who came to the
courses were of the most various creeds and un-creeds. Not a
few, who aimed at being Scripture specialists in schools, were
agnostic in personal belief. The remarkable effect of a fortnight's
group study of the Bible and the early history of the Church,
with participants who were out to find the truth and were prepared to assume that the Bible is worth studying, was undeniable. I do not say that all became, in a week or two, good
churchmen or ardent evangelists, though some did; but I am
quite sure nearly all came nearer to God. The reader may remember the German pastor who, after the war, said he was
"gathering the young men and women round the Bible". It can
be done and it can transform people's lives when it is done,
but there is a qualification: it can only be done with great
effect when the members of the group are on approximately
the same level of culture—"speak the same language", as they
say. Professor Hooke, layman as he was and not always sure
that he believed in God, wherever he lived started a group of
educated persons to study the New Testament. When we buried
Sam Hooke early in 1968 in the country churchyard at Faring-
don, he had just published his New Testament study *The
Resurrection of Christ* and was, at the age of ninety, planning
a work on the Gospel of John. Old students all over the country
felt they had lost a friend.

A disappointment after the war was the decline in the fortunes of the Library of Constructive Theology, which had prospered exceedingly between the wars, when Dr. Wheeler Robinson was my fellow editor and Bertram Christian, of James Nisbet and Company, our publisher. Dr. Robinson's death was a heavy blow to Christian theology in this country and, for some reason, the distinguished Free Church scholar who took his place did not enlist authors for the library or contribute a volume himself. The deep cause of the decline was, I think, the wave of defeatism which carried so many theologians away. The word "constructive" which before the last war had been one of good omen was now one of suspected optimism, of wishful thinking. The up-to-date theologians were engaged in destruction. It was the era of Christian agnosticism and atheism. As one who still believed not only in God but in the validity of "natural theology" of the rational argument for the existence of God, I could not steer the barks of constructive theology into the harbour of negation. I have no doubt that constructive theology will come back. At least one Christian philosopher has signalled its return in a well argued work, Dr. F. H. Cleobury in *A Return to Natural Theology* (James Clarke).

CHAPTER 16

Reconstruction

The last time I had any conversation with King George VI was at the opening ceremony of the Festival of Britain on the steps of St. Paul's on May 2nd, 1951, and unfortunately I cannot remember anything of it except that he looked very ill and I wondered if he would be able to get through without collapsing; I remember, too, that Herbert Morrison, who was the moving spirit of the Festival, seemed to share my anxiety. This experience on the steps of St. Paul's prepared me for the news of his death early in the following year, though I had thought that he was slowly getting better, particularly because Princess Elizabeth and her husband were out of the country.

Without being in any sense close to the King or in his confidence, I had many opportunities over the years of forming a definite conception of his character. The foundation of it was the Christian faith. Of the King and Queen I would say that they were trying to follow Christ, though each had a distinctive manner of following. The Queen, when I had been Chaplain to George V and later, had often talked freely to me about religion, always with a sincere desire for truth and with a lively intelligence which asked all the questions and did not accept all the orthodox answers. The King, I think, had no taste for speculation. His dominant imperative was "duty". It was his duty to take the place vacated by his brother and to fill it as well as he could, though he had never been prepared for it, was afflicted by a disabling speech defect and heartily disliked being the centre figure in elaborate ceremonials. The picture which comes into my mind when I think of these two royal Christians is one which I saw more than once: that of the King delivering a speech and being held up by his stammer: he had come to a terrible pause, which made everyone uncomfortable, while the Queen sat where he could see her clearly, looking calmly at him with a smile and not a shadow of impatience. I like to think that I may have contributed some very minute service in bringing about the great improvement in the King's public speech, which everyone noticed in the last few years of his reign. Some expert wrote to me suggesting that the script which the King was to read should be divided up by bars, as in music, so that his pauses should come at intervals where they would be appropriate. I ventured to pass this suggestion on. No doubt it occurred to many persons who had experience of the difficulties of stammers. It was adopted, whoever thought of it, and was effective. George VI was happier perhaps in his years after the war, until disease gripped him. It is sad they were so few. He deserved the gratitude of his country.

About this time the shadow of mortality touched me and reminded me that I was getting old. I was in fact seventy in 1951, though I never thought about it and, after a rest, felt as fit or fitter than when the war started in 1939. The Festival of Britain opened with a magnificent fireworks display in London along the river. The little golden gallery which stands at the top of the dome would obviously be an excellent spot to see the fireworks. There were no sightseers in the Cathedral, because the security authorities were not able to guarantee its safety. My wife, alas, was too rheumatic to climb the 365 steps. I decided to go alone. I had no difficulty in the journey up, though I had to stop several times to get my breath. It was when I emerged on to the golden gallery that my age, as it were, rose up and stunned me. The height and the solitude combined to overwhelm me. I experienced a kind of panic and, after a few minutes, I crawled out of the gallery back on to the narrow stairs which led to it. I descended and reported that I had seen the fireworks from the golden gallery, but I added in my mind the resolve never to go there again. I had seen enough of the display to confirm my expectation that, though admirable, it could not compare with some of the Luftwaffe's set pieces, when they had lighted up the Cathedral with chandelier flares of brilliant green and red from above and with flames from burning buildings on the ground.

Still on the subject of mortality, I note that some men who had meant much to me had passed from the scene. Two who died full of years and honours were Dr. Headlam, who was active and pugnacious to an advanced age, and Sir Frederick

Maurice. Dr. Headlam used to come to the deanery after bishops' meetings in Lambeth Palace and express his views on his brother bishops with candour rather than charity. He became deaf and perhaps he stayed on in Gloucester too long, but I heard no suggestion that he ought to have resigned earlier at any time when I visited the diocese. A typical saying to my wife amused us both: "I have gone rather deaf and that prevents me from being as rude at bishops' meetings as I should like to be." His passing meant the passing out of my life of one of its chief personal influences. Perhaps I pray with more than ordinary fervour for him, "May he rest in peace."

The other senior friend, though a soldier, was not by nature pugnacious. I refer to General Sir Frederick Maurice, the noble grandson of a noble Christian scholar, Frederick Denison Maurice, who was turned out of his professorial chair in King's College, London, for heresy. When I was appointed to the same chair, I started a memorial lecture for this great teacher of piety and sound learning which has recently been enlarged beyond my hopes by the zeal of my successor, the present Dean of the College. General Frederick Maurice was the centre of a notorious conflict and dispute in the first world war, when he was accused by Lloyd George of giving wrong figures of the numbers of troops engaged on the Western Front. Too late his integrity and competence have been vindicated and history will perhaps get the record straight. The conduct of General Maurice, while the record was not straight, was that of a true Christian and a true patriot. The General was a theologian and of the school of his grandfather from whose writings, so he told me, he read some pages every day.

Two friends departed before their time—as it appeared to me. Joseph Hunkin, Bishop of Truro, died most unexpectedly and I had the sad privilege of giving an address at his funeral in Truro on November 3rd, 1950. A former Methodist, he brought some of the Methodist spirit of fellowship into the Anglican Church. A much beloved man who was a notable New Testament scholar, his early death was a loss to the whole Church and in St. Paul's we remembered his generous interest in moving our Choir School to its war refuge in his cathedral. The second untimely death was that of Harry Ireson, the Dean's Virger, whose funeral took place in St. Paul's in April, 1950. The head virgers of cathedrals are often remarkable men and

I am sure many deans would agree with me that to have a virger who is a real friend makes life easy. I think of many virgers to whom I owe gratitude: my first was Palmer in Exeter, who used to be teased by the wicked choristers about his nose. A shooting accident in youth had deprived him of his natural nose and he was said to have two artificial noses, one for every-day use and the other for Sundays and saints' days. I never dis-covered whether this was true or a legend invented by the boys, who tried to hide his spare nose. The old man was good-tempered as well as dignified. And my last virger was my friend Mr. Overington, who still I am glad to report holds office. I shall never forget his help to me in the trying weeks of my farewell to St. Paul's.

Harry Ireson was a man of great natural ability and intellec-tual acuteness. He had had hardly any formal education and was almost entirely self-educated. If he had been more fortunate in his youth, I am convinced that he would have been eminent in some learned profession. He must have been aware of his own abilities and of the careers which might have been open to him; but he had no sense of frustration. He was too interested in life to be unhappy and went on thinking and extending his knowledge. I was glad to have the opportunity at his funeral to draw attention not only to Ireson's character and ability, but also to the quality of men who can make a satisfying career as virger in one of our great cathedrals.

The Coronation of Queen Elizabeth II on June 2nd, 1953, had something of the feeling of *déja vu*, so fresh in my memory was that of her father and mother, and in a sense I was not so emotionally identified with Queen Elizabeth II as I had been with them. I was moved to express my loyal sentiments in verse which appeared on the leader page of *The Daily Telegraph* on the morning after the ceremony.

A June Day

Amid the flowers of June one flower I see
Surpassing all in grace and majesty;
It is a fair young Queen, who makes her way
To Westminster upon her crowning day,
With music and the pealing of sweet bells,
And swelling voice of multitudes, which tells,
Sweeter than all, that joy and hope and love

Rise up in many hearts, and with her move
　　Onward toward her sacring.

'Mid the rich lights of June, one gleam I see,
Distinct from all in modest gaiety.
It is the beam which shines from her young eyes,
Alight with courage, soft with mild surprise
That Providence should raise her to the throne
And set her there to reign, aloft, alone,
Yet trusting in the grace which God imparts
To all who pray with pure and humble hearts,
　　Monarch as well as subject.

Amid June's opulence three drops I see
Of holy oil, symbol of mystery,
Which on her hands, her breast, her brow are poured
That she may be anointed of the Lord.
The Spirit's fruits of love and joy and peace
Be hers and ours with ever more increase,
And may we all, the people and the State,
Be joined with her who now is consecrate,
　　Serving His greater purpose.

I do not know that one needs apologise for writing verses in honour of one's sovereign, but I will give my story. Perhaps I was simply out of date, but I must own that, though there were collections of poems on the subject, none of them seemed to me particularly inspired. I thought, "Why not write one yourself?" and the words shaped themselves in my mind. If I had been younger, perhaps I might have laid myself open to the suspicion that I was hoping to be a "court poet" and for preferment; but no one surely would imagine such things about a man who was well over seventy. My anxieties were removed by a gracious message from Her Majesty.

I will make only three comments on the Coronation Service. First, the shocking mix-up at the end of the previous Coronation in the Abbey did not happen this time and the emptying of the Abbey was rapid and orderly. And second, we shall not see another Coronation on precisely these lines. I cannot imagine the House of Lords being so prominent again, and anyway do the wives of life peers as a rule wear tiaras? I hope the liturgical experts have in mind the need for a revised form of coronation with symbolism adapted to the realities of tomorrow; I hope they are working on it and that they are consulting many wise persons who are not liturgical experts. The Coronation is a magnificent symbolical ceremony with religious overtones that can never be out of date. We must never let it decline into a quaint survival or a playground for antiquarians. My third comment is about the Queen herself. My wife and I had seats from which almost nothing could be seen of the placing of the crown on her head, but we had a close-up view of the anointing, which takes much longer and to me is the most moving and sacramental part of the service. I was sure that she was in a kind of trance and was only half-conscious of what was going on. I was quite wrong. Several years later, I ventured to ask her if my impression was correct. She indignantly replied that she was keenly aware of everything that was going on and enjoyed every moment of it!

Beneath and alongside these happenings in which I was more or less involved was the persisting preoccupation with the restoration of the Cathedral. This began early in the war when the first damage was done and went on until the last year of my time as Dean of St. Paul's. The day before I wrote this sentence, I saw in *The Times* that the Architects' Co-Partnership which designed the Choir School had received the award of the prize for the best new building of the year in the City of London, which assured me that the final stage in the restoration had been worthy to stand alongside the work of Christopher Wren.

To tell the whole story of the postwar restoration would be tedious but without some description of the process my life would be meaningless. The story begins before the end of the war and at least one decisive principle had been agreed on by the Chapter—that we would not restore the high altar, the reredos and the apse as they had been, but would attempt to rebuild in the manner which, as we believed, Wren would have chosen. This was a unanimous decision of the Dean and Chapter who had the right to make this decision: there was no legal right of appeal against it, though of course we consulted the Royal Fine Art Commission. I have always thought that the Dean and Chapter acted courageously, because we were all well aware that the easy way would be just to restore what had been there; many people had sentimental feelings about the old reredos and numbers of clergy who had been ordained in the Cathedral associated it with the most solemn moments of their lives. Visual memories are short and a large proportion of the population never saw the old reredos. No doubt some of them, when they hear that we decided to pull down an "old reredos" to make way for the existing canopy, will begin to scent "vandalism"; but they will retract when they are reminded that the old reredos was late Victorian and had never been without critics. The one argument which made up my mind was that Wren could never have wished to block up the apse of the Cathedral and cover the east window. There was no direct evidence on the subject: What would Wren have done in similar circumstances? because he never had the opportunity of similar circumstances. The obstinate Dean and Chapter in Charles II's time had forced Wren to build a screen across the choir and an organ on top of it, thus preventing any open view of the altar from under the dome. The proportions were thus completely transformed and Wren was content to have as the altar a small table which now is the altar of the Lady Chapel. Some slight evidence is perhaps to be found in Wren's papers where a sketch of a baldachino is said to show how his mind was working, but I doubt whether much weight can be given to this. I place on record the names of the members of the Chapter who reached this conclusion: S. A. Alexander, E. N. Sharpe, F. A. Cockin and V. A. Demant.

The next step was to design the new Cathedral high altar and east end. Almost by chance, the replanning of the sanctuary became linked with the idea of an American Memorial Chapel, to be given by the citizens of Great Britain in memory of the Americans who had lost their lives in the war while based on this country. The plan took shape in the mind of Lord Trenchard, who had been closely connected with the R.A.F. memorial in Westminster Abbey. I happened to meet him at some City reception and he told me of his quest for a worthy place for an American memorial. "Why not St. Paul's?" I said—too hastily I came to think when the details had to be worked out. With Lord Trenchard in this enterprise was Sir Clive Baillieu (later Lord Baillieu) who was the very energetic and tactful chairman of the committee appointed to collect funds. One advantage which the Dean and Chapter gained was that the cost of restoring the apse and its windows was partly taken off their shoulders.

A little later another partner in the enterprise was recruited. Canon Collins informed me that Sir Jocelyn Lucas and a committee were collecting money to erect a memorial to commemorate the men from the British Commonwealth who had fallen in the two great wars of this century. After a certain amount of negotiation, the Dean and Chapter agreed that the high altar itself should be the Commonwealth memorial and any visitor who looks may now read the inscription on the north side of the table. There was a symbolic value, I thought, in concentrating the memorials so closely together in such a holy place and the problem set to the architects was one which would call out their highest aspirations. In this hope I was gloriously vindicated and this is the place in which I must record my lasting gratitude that I have been associated with what I believe will be one of the artistic glories of our country for centuries Our own surveyor, Mr. Godfrey Allen, had thought out the problem and was ready with a definite suggestion—that Mr. Stephen Dykes Bower should be associated with him as consultant and together they should submit a design for the whole of the east end of the Cathedral. Without hesitation, the Chapter agreed and the Royal Fine Art Commission approved. The architects were requested to reproduce as far as possible the religious symbolism of the old reredos. With very little delay the design was submitted and an exact scale model of the new work was made which was on view in the Cathedral for some years.

I will not pretend that all these negotiations and all this committee work was perfectly easy, but it was full of interest. We had representatives of the American Ambassador on the American Memorial Committee and Lord Trenchard was a very active member. The discussions on this Committee were not always placid and I had some tough arguments about the symbolism in the American Memorial Chapel. The windows of that Chapel were the east windows of the Cathedral and stood out above the altar when seen from the choir and the dome. To have a window depicting the late war or the U.S.A. flag was obviously out of the question. I am afraid that Lord Trenchard was not happy about the picture of Christ on the cross which did not seem to him to emphasise the American theme. But we did incorporate a great deal of American symbolism. The windows in the Chapel displayed on their borders the arms of the States of the Union. To get this detail right needed some research, as some of the States did not remember what their arms were. Trenchard and Baillieu were both very able and public-spirited men. It was a privilege to work with them—but I would not have liked to have them on my Chapter!

General Eisenhower took part in the next event. On July 4th, 1951, he handed over the roll of honour of American dead who had been based in Britain, which had been inscribed in the U.S.A. to be preserved in the Memorial Chapel which was not yet completed. It was one of the most moving services in my long experience of St. Paul's and the personality of the General somehow fitted marvellously into the Cathedral and its dignity. I think it was at this service I heard the well-known passage from *The Pilgrim's Progress*, which ends with "All the trumpets sounding on the other side", for the first time in a memorial liturgy. I had met General Eisenhower before, but it was on this occasion that I decided to classify him with de Valera as a statesman who had the gift of inspiring confidence in his integrity at first meeting. He did not forget the occasion. Years later, when he was Mr. Eisenhower and on a very brief visit, he came to see the Chapel and the roll of honour. At the dedication of the Chapel and the roll of honour at which the Queen was present, the Vice President Mr. Nixon was present and made an admirable speech.

In 1953 America lured our choir away for a time and we were delighted that President Eisenhower had entertained them at the White House. To explain how they came to be there, a new character must be introduced into my story—Canon John Collins, and I intend, in parenthesis as it were, to tell the truth about our relationship. Now and then, strangers have commiserated with me on having him as a colleague and I must own that there have been times when I could wish he had not said provocative things, because so many people think that a dean is a kind of headmaster who can keep his canons on the right lines. How many times I have informed irate correspondents that, even if I wished to censor a canon's sermons, I had no power to do so! I am afraid that sometimes I have said, "If you want to accuse Canon Collins of heresy, you must write to the Bishop of the diocese and state what heresy you accuse him of." I do not suppose the bishop has ever had an accusation.

I confess that we started badly, but not by my will. I was ruffled because for the only time in my experience I was not consulted or given a real chance of expressing an opinion on the proposed appointment. The ruffled feeling was aggravated by a speech which he made at the St. Paul's Day dinner, which indicated that we were a lot of lazy "has-beens" and offended some of our guests. I still think that we had cause for apprehension and resentment. But it soon became clear to me that this was not the real John Collins and I think the visit of the choir to America was the occasion of our mutual understanding. I could not help admiring the enthusiasm and the ability which he showed in the complicated business of transporting thirty small boys and twenty adults to America and arranging a tour of large cities in the eastern parts of Canada and the U.S.A. I was overcome too by the sincere and generous invitations to me to go with the choir or to fly over to its triumphant concluding evenings. I could not go; it would have been foolish and unworthy to appear to claim any of the applause.

John and Diana Collins are Christian idealists who believe strongly that the Christian faith is the answer to the world's problems and by the Christian faith they mean primarily the beliefs that God is love and that violence and injustice must be resisted and overthrown, not by violence but by reason and love. I cannot accuse anyone who holds such beliefs and acts upon them of being unorthodox or anti-Christian. I differ from them, as I differed from Dick Sheppard, in not being able to take the Quaker line on war, nor can I lay such exclusive stress on the petition, "Thy Kingdom come *on earth*". In my understanding of Christianity, the ideas of sin and forgiveness and the life of the world to come would have more emphasis. But, just as I did when Dick Sheppard was my beloved colleague, I wish I could go with them all the way.

Collins has such a reputation for stirring up trouble because he preaches so fiercely about love. He would be magnificent as the leader of a violent revolution, *"Aux armes, citoyens"*, but he would never appeal to emotions of revenge or hate, though sometimes when listening to his denunciations of injustice I have remembered the characters in the French Revolution who, according to Carlyle, acted on the principle, "Be my brother, or I'll kill you."

A fact about Collins which I always bear in mind is that he

has renounced personal ambition. Both he and Diana are exceptionally able persons and neither of them is devoid of the natural
ambition which goes with ability; but they have never considered self-interest when it was at variance with their ideals.

To resume the story of the restoration, the happy progress
which seemed assured with Godfrey Allen in charge was not to
be and it failed for the most distressing cause, that Allen thought
we had not behaved properly to him. It has been a lasting grief
to me that the man who did so much for St. Paul's and loved it
so well should feel alienated from it. I can, I think, claim
that I was overruled by the Chapter, but I cannot escape my
share of responsibility. The crisis arose in this way: when the
town planners produced their sketch of St. Paul's as they meant
it to be in the future, it was found that they had included in
their plan the demolition of the Choir School which stood next
door to the deanery, with its entrance in Carter Lane. It soon
became evident that the planners were dominated by the traffic
problem and thought of the City not as a place to live in, but
as a channel for the flow of motor vehicles. In pursuit of this
end they decided that the ancient Carter Lane must be
widened, so that the cars could pass through. On one side of
the Lane stood the atrociously ugly building of the telephone
exchange Faraday House, and on the other our modest school.
Of course it was decided to preserve the building which ought
never to have been built at all and destroy the house which
had been carefully designed for its position and function. The
school, almost miraculously, had survived the war and we had
assumed that what our enemies had not succeeded in damaging
would not be destroyed by our friends.

Of course our friends, the Lord Mayor and Corporation of
London, did not intend to injure the Cathedral in any way and,
in my opinion, the proper method of dealing with the problem
of the school would have been to make no attempt to bargain
with the City, but to take the line: "We are in this together:
we know that you are as keen as we are to keep this ancient little
school in London. Let us do it together: after all we are losing
our school not for any reason of the Cathedral's needs, but to
make the traffic flow easier." The Chapter appointed Oswin
Gibbs-Smith the Archdeacon of London to negotiate in this
affair and naturally I did not interfere. He was well known in
the City and better acquainted than I with the technique of

such transactions. Everything was done in the most businesslike fashion, with expert advisers and lawyers. We played the game according to the rules—and so did the City.

The Cathedral surveyor was asked to submit a plan for a new school on the site of the Church of St. Augustine, Watling Street, which had been tentatively allocated for it. Godfrey Allen produced a plan without delay. It came in for criticism on some points, chiefly that it was too expensive, but also that the internal arrangement of rooms and passages was inconvenient. Looking back on the sad affair, I can see that, if we had accepted Allen's plan and persuaded him to alter the interior to meet the headmaster's criticisms, we should have saved thousands of pounds and much exasperation. What we did was to bring in advisers from the Ministry of Education and other architects who had, it was thought, special aptitude in the designing of schools. Godfrey Allen resigned. It did not surprise me, because I knew that he was the type of man who can only work happily when he is in harmonious relations with his colleagues. But I was appalled and have never ceased to wonder what I could have done, which I did not do, to avoid the break. It comforts me to know that, though he does not come to the Cathedral which he helped to preserve and to adorn so splendidly, he does not include me in his dislike. I shall always be his grateful friend. That Godfrey Allen left St. Paul's when he did may have been a fortunate event from the point of view of his career and the artistic treasures of England, for he was called upon to do much important work in Oxford and is recognised as the leading expert in the architecture of Wren and his period. He tells me fellows of a college are much more intelligent than deans and chapters!

To succeed Allen, the Dean and Chapter appointed Lord Mottistone, who had been in partnership with Paul Paget for some years in a firm which had done church building in many parts of the country. We all knew them and I had known Paget's father the Bishop of Chester and his mother one of the Hoare family.

The dealings which we had with the Royal Fine Art Commission up to the resignation of Allen had been most harmonious and, as I have related, our plans had been received with easy acceptance and indeed with enthusiastic approval. The wind had suddenly changed and plan after plan was refused. Lord

Mottistone's first design seemed to me to be good and the Council of St. Paul's Cathedral Trust agreed. But the Royal Fine Art Commission did not, though it would not tell us why. We were not compelled by law to get the Royal Fine Art Commission's approval; but we knew that the two planning authorities which we had to satisfy (the Corporation of the City of London and the London County Council) would take their advice. These deferments, these preparations of new drawings and the fee of a consultant architect consumed money and time. At last, I think for the first time in my life, I made use of something like "the old boy's network". The Permanent Under-Secretary of the Ministry of Housing was Dame Evelyn Sharp (now the Lady Sharp), whose father I had succeeded as vicar of Christ Church, Crouch End, and whose family had been at one time well known to me. I remembered Evelyn as a schoolgirl with pigtails. I gained courage from the recollection to write a really rude letter. I wish I had made a copy of it, but I dashed it off without reading it through and I can remember only one or two phrases which pleased me. It ran something like this: "What is your Ministry doing? What is it supposed to do? Here am I in the centre of London, trying for the last three years to build a little school for thirty-eight little boys and meeting with nothing but frustration, while all around buildings of overwhelming size and overwhelming ugliness are rising up without anyone making any objection. Does your department even know about this? Have they ever told you?"

The reaction to this letter was immediate. Dame Evelyn had all the information put before her (I am sure it was all quite new to her). After studying it, she called a conference at the Ministry of all the persons and offices concerned at which she presided. It was a memorable meeting. The Dean and Chapter of St. Paul's were represented by the Archdeacon of London Gibbs-Smith and myself. The Cathedral surveyor, Lord Mottistone, was present to explain his latest design. The redoubtable Royal Fine Art Commission was well to the fore. Sir Basil Spence was among them and gave me an encouraging smile—the others looked glum. The Corporation of the City of London was represented by its chief architect and so, I believe, was the London County Council.

The meeting seemed to me to be a disaster—the end of hope. The discussion of the new design dragged on and, after a boring half hour's talk round the table, it was perfectly plain that the authorities had not the slightest desire to agree. I thought it a sheer waste of time. But I think now this was the end Dame Evelyn had in view. She said to the Archdeacon and me, "You see, we are not likely to get agreement. I will suggest to the Minister that he should have a limited competition which the Ministry would run." And so it happened. A select number of architects, known to be interested in schools, including Lord Mottistone, were invited to compete. She appointed herself chairman of the adjudicators and in due course the plans of the Architects' Co-partnership were chosen and the school was built. It is generally regarded as the one truly satisfactory new building in the City. What a pity Dame Evelyn does not run the whole set-up of the country!

There is not a cathedral in England, and not a cathedral dean, who is free from anxiety about money. Readers of Trollope have pictures of deaneries which are havens of peaceful elegance and no cares but those connected with the bishop—or perhaps the bishop's wife. All this is changed now and the cause of the change is the progressive decline in the value of the pound sterling. The cathedrals, up to the middle of the 19th century, had their own endowments—some inadequate and others much more than adequate. When the reformers took matters in hand, they set up the Ecclesiastical Commissioners, the object of Sydney Smith's most amusing invective, to redistribute the resources, using some of the cathedrals' revenue to raise the remuneration of the parochial clergy. All this was on the whole right and proper; something like it should have been done long before. The negotiators on behalf of cathedrals, I suppose, had an unshakable faith in the pound sterling, for they made no provision for depreciation if it occurred. Thus every dean today must be concerned with making his cathedral's ends meet. To say then that an undue proportion of my time and thought was given to such activities is simply to say that I was like all other deans, with the addition that I had a badly damaged cathedral, an ambitious plan of interior reconstruction and the building of a new school to worry about.

I did not really worry very much, because I was sure the City of London and very many friends elsewhere would come to our aid. During the war after a somewhat painful crisis we had reorganised the office. We had appointed Mr. Floyd Ewin as receiver and registrar and separated his duties from those of our legal officer, the chapter clerk. In this reconstruction, Canon Alexander and I had collaborated. It would be hard to exaggerate the advantages of the new arrangements or the zeal and competence of Mr. Ewin. When peace came, I persuaded my old friend of King's College days, Mr. S. T. Shovelton, who had just retired from the post of secretary of the College, to advise us about investments. That again was a good move and for quite a long time, in the golden days when stocks and shares were booming, we had a loss on running the Cathedral, but made a profit in our capacity of an investment trust.

Apart from the cost of maintaining the Cathedral, we had need of capital to restore, repair and replace. But how much? Canon Alexander was of the opinion that we should need about £100,000 and that we could raise that sum by writing to firms and individuals in the City without making a public appeal at all. The matter was complicated by the need of Westminster Abbey, which had lost some of its buildings, but was not very seriously injured so far as its fabric was concerned. I had hoped that perhaps we might have a joint appeal and thus banish once for all the idea that there was some rivalry between these two Houses of God. The Abbey, however, did not agree. I think it was embarrassed by the fact that it was a "Royal Peculiar" and did not want to wait for St. Paul's to be ready to appeal to the public. So it was that we had to delay our appeal by years to give the Abbey a fair run and, though I wished it well, I hoped all the generous donors in the City would keep some for us. In the meantime a powerful committee of City men was considering our needs. Sir Christopher Chancellor was the exceedingly able and vigorous chairman and saw to it that the committee was in possession of all the facts. It soon became evident that Canon Alexander's estimate was far too low and the committee fixed on the sum of £400,000 as the target for what we agreed to call the Campaign. It was never quite clear to me whether the need for additional annual income of £20,000 was included in the target, but it is certain that we did not get it. General Sir Kenneth McLean was appointed as appeal secretary and director. He had been called back into the Army for some special duty involving his visit to South Africa and, when he was released to take over at St. Paul's, he was very tired. I had a bad fright on the day of the dinner at the Mansion House to inaugurate the Campaign when I found that our secretary had broken down through overwork. But in the end all went very well. The dinner was good and the speeches were, I thought, just right. The Lord Chancellor rose to the occasion. It gives me a warm thrill of love to remember one thing that happened on that busy evening. My friend Alan Don the Dean of Westminster pressed an envelope into my hand saying, "Don't open it until you get home." When I opened it that night, I found his cheque for £500, with the terse message, "From one beggar to another."

Some reflections on the finance of cathedrals are perhaps permissible here. Quite apart from the question whether the cathedrals have a fair deal from the church commissioners, one may wonder how long it will be possible for them to stagger along on the present system. These agonising crises and frantic appeals to save great national monuments are responded to on the whole with wonderful generosity; but with the constant rise in taxation which is slowly ruining the middle classes exhaustion point may be reached and then what happens? In the case of our appeal, by far the greater part of the subscriptions and donations came from business firms, headed by the Bank of England and the "Big Five" banks. From the nationalised industries came nothing at all, though some of the directors were our friends and well-wishers, and no doubt contributed as individuals; but if Socialism prevails on a wide scale, unless there is a change of heart or perhaps a change in management, the cathedrals will fall down. I once asked Hugh Gaitskell, when he was leader of the Labour Party, whether he had any ideas on the subject. I am not sure that he had thought it out and he may have been replying on the spur of the moment, but for what it is worth I record his answer, "Perhaps something like the Universities' Grants Commission could be set up." As one who tried, and failed, to get something out of the Universities' Grants Commission for my part of King's College, London, in the old days, my heart does not leap for joy at this prospect, but I can see that it might be the answer. It need not be administered by a Cathedrals' Grants Commission; it could include all national monuments and be concerned with the fabrics of the cathedrals as part of its wider duties.

If some way could be found to make the fabric of the ancient cathedrals a responsibility of the State, as it is in France, I do not believe there need be any fear that the freedom of the Church to use them for its worship as now would be in danger. The feeling about cathedrals among church people has changed too. Not so long ago, as I have recorded, I was ill spoken of because, with the approval of both bishop and archbishop, I held a service in St. Paul's for the Salvation Army; now no one seems to object when the Salvation Army itself conducts its own service in a cathedral. The wind has changed. There is indeed a danger that might deter me from supporting the Government care of the cathedrals. If that had been the situation when we had to decide whether or not to restore the Victorian reredos and whether or not to install in its place a quite different architectural feature, I do not believe a Government department would have considered for a moment doing something new—and if they had got so far as to consider I am sure they would talk for ever on whether they had the power.

The Campaign was the father of a vigorous body of trustees. The St. Paul's Cathedral Trust now administers the funds arising from the appeal and receives contributions for its purposes. Until I retired, I was *ex officio* chairman of the Trust Council, Lord Aldenham was the Deputy Chairman and Mr. Floyd Ewin the Secretary. The Council consists of the four canons and six or seven prominent laymen who take a keen interest in the fund and the needs which it is intended to meet.

This chapter shall end with the story of another and different body of helpers—the Friends of St. Paul's. This institution was really a child of the St. Paul's Watch. While the war was still going on, discussions had arisen about how to preserve some link with the Cathedral when peace returned. The volunteers of the Watch had joined because they loved St. Paul's and their years of service in it had deepened their love. The idea of setting up an organisation of Friends with the Watch as founder members had unanimous support and my experience in Exeter had convinced me that a well-run body of Friends could be of immense assistance to a Dean and Chapter, by undertaking work in or about the Cathedral which was beyond the Chapter's resources. Thus, in my time in Exeter, the Friends had sponsored the restoration of the colour on bosses and roof as well as tombs and wall paintings.

If the proposal had been put to the St. Paul's Chapter during the war, it would almost certainly have gone through without difficulty, but after the war the persons on the Chapter had changed and the new members did not have the experience of fellowship in serving St. Paul's, which was the motive force in the minds of the Watch. I felt myself that some of the laymen who had toiled and suffered in defending St. Paul's had more right to be heard than clerics who came on to the governing body when the stress was over. But, of course, the real situation was that the Chapter had the last word and without its good will nothing could be done. One of the recently appointed canons, Dr. Demant, was a Christian Sociologist, who had written on the philosophy and theology of social institutions. He saw the possibility of disaster in the project unless careful regulations were laid down with regard to the limits of the Friends' functions. I think the example of a very active, devoted and able lady, who dominated the Friends of Canterbury Cathedral and whose influence had been greatly exaggerated by rumour, had something to do with the difficulties in the Chapter. Some of my colleagues seemed to fear that no sooner would the Friends be in existence than they would make a "take-over bid" for the Cathedral and would oust Bishop, Dean and Chapter from their stalls.

No doubt this was partly academic argumentativeness and quite good fun in its way, but it held up any action and gave time for enthusiasm to cool, but at last the Chapter agreed to form a body of Friends with certain definitions of its purposes and its limitations. On April 29th, 1952, a meeting was held in the crypt of St. Paul's, consisting of members of St. Paul's Watch and a few other associated persons, such as Mr. S. T. Shovelton, who decided to enrol themselves as the Society of Friends of St. Paul's and to invite sympathisers to join them. The Lord Mayor of London and the Bishop of London were to be, *ex officio*, joint presidents. Sir Edward Wilshaw and Mr. Floyd Ewin were elected joint honorary treasurers. I had approached Her Majesty Queen Elizabeth the Queen Mother already and was assured that, if the Society of Friends of St. Paul's were formed, she would consent to be its royal patron. The office of secretary was not easy to fill, because we did not know at the beginning what amount of work would be required. For a time the experiment of joint secretaries was tried; but before long Miss Jennings took over the responsibility and must be regarded as the first secretary of the Friends.

The Friends made a fairly encouraging start, but nothing like what it would have done in 1946. I think our principal asset was the Queen Mother. I knew that she would not accept any office which was purely nominal and would take an interest in any society to which she had given her patronage, but she went far beyond any expectation. From the time of its foundation, the Society of Friends of St. Paul's held a Festival service in the summer, with special music and special preacher, followed by a reception in one of the city halls—generally the Stationers'. The routine soon established for these Festivals was that the Queen would have tea in the deanery with a few people, always the Lord Mayor and Lady Mayoress and the Bishop of London. Shortly before 5 p.m., the two treasurers came to the deanery to escort the Queen to the Cathedral, where she would be received by the Dean and Chapter, the Lord Mayor and Bishop. Crowds soon began to gather and the walk from the deanery to St. Paul's became one of the minor sights in the City year. In those years we were much helped in the deanery by Swiss and German au pair girls. One fine summer day, an au pair girl had an adventure. She was a very good-looking young lady and suitably dressed for the royal tea party. As the Queen with her lady-in-waiting passed through the hall of the deanery, the girl, Jutta by name, was standing by the door. The lady-in-waiting, as she swept past, picked up Jutta, saying "Come along with me, I feel nervous." The press photographers produced some charming pictures of Jutta and there was no little speculation as to which princess she was.

After the service, the Queen, attended by the officers of the Society, went all round the hall, first having a drink with the Master of the Stationers' Company. Whenever I accompanied her, I was astonished by her ability to talk to one or two persons in a crowd and give the impression to a dozen people that they had been included in the conversation. She has always been kind to me and she was thoughtful for me when I had retired and the Friends' Festival was being held without me. My wife was dead, the deanery was no longer my home, I could not even attend the service and sit unrecognised in an obscure corner of the Cathedral. The Queen had thought of that and invited me to lunch on the day of the Festival, where I met many eminent and pleasant persons who were also just retired. And, when I returned to my flat, I found she had sent me a signed photograph of herself, which reminds me of her kindness.

The course of the Friends was not always smooth. I was disappointed that the clerical members of St. Paul's were not always enthusiastic helpers. I think the canons did what they could and were concerned about the Society and one at least of the minor canons was interested. Now the prospects are better, because Canon Hood has seen the possibilities of the Friends and gives constant thought to developments. Among those that offer thrilling prospects is that a branch of the Friends of St. Paul's has been started in the U.S.A. and is visited every year by Canon Hood.

The Friends I hope may remember me for a few years. I wrote a hymn for them and Dr. John Dykes Bower composed the tune.

Hymn for the Friends of St. Paul's

Behold us gathered on this hallowed ground,
  Where generations of our fathers prayed,
To praise thee, Lord, for all the grace they found
  And all the riches of thy love, displayed
    In sins forgiv'n, in lives renewed,
    And souls sustained by heavenly food.

Thou dwellest not in temples made by man,
  Yet thou didst bless the building of this shrine
The work of him whose mind conceived the plan,
  The gifts of those who loved this house of thine,
    The artist's and the craftsman's skill,
    This glory on a city's hill.

Bless now thy children of a later day,
  Who hold this heritage of beauty dear
Lift up our hearts upon our earthly way;
  True be our worship and our love sincere;
    And all the splendour and the fame
    Be to the honour of thy Name.

So shall this soaring majesty of stone
  Be symbol to us of thy temple pure,
Made of the souls adopted as thine own,
  Thy Christ its builder and foundation sure;
    Newly created by thy grace,
    Grant us therein to have a place.

CHAPTER 17

Some Opinions

The years immediately following the war were times of scarcity and rationing, but the City of London was not shaken out of its pleasant habit of dining in company and dining well. Gradually the dinners and lunches in the Mansion House, Guildhall and the halls of those guilds which still possessed them were resumed. Nearly all of those badly damaged by bombs were restored or rebuilt. One which was not rebuilt was the hall of the Barber Surgeons, which used to stand in a court off Aldersgate Street. I mourned its loss, because it was a charming little building, which had escaped the Great Fire of 1666 and had a mulberry tree in its garden which was perhaps as old as the hall. In its day it had played a part in the development of medicine, for it had been the father of the Royal College of Surgeons, who have risen in the world since and do not parade the virtues of their humble ancestors. But one does not have to be romantic to think it interesting that the dining table at which one has eaten so well was the table on which the clever barbers cut customers for the stone without anaesthetics. But the little hall was annihilated by a direct hit and could not be restored. A new building would have lost most of its tradition.

I must touch lightly on the hospitality of the City, not because I am not grateful nor because I did not enjoy it; but because I do not want to produce the same impression on readers as was produced by my revered predecessor's *Diary of a Dean* on my dear and generous friend Dudley Sommer, the author of a valuable life of Lord Haldane. When the *Diary of a Dean* came out, Sommer was a Baptist who had been brought up in the Puritan tradition but was beginning to be attracted by the Anglican type of worship. When he read of the dinings out of the dean so zestfully chronicled, he was disappointed and at about the same time he read Bishop Hensley Henson's autobiography with much the same result. "I didn't know that bishops and deans were like that," he said. And, after all, a running commentary on other people's dinners can be tedious. Let me say I tried to moderate my dining out because it took time when I ought to be reading or writing. I felt that by accepting these attractive invitations in moderation I was getting into touch with many people who had important and influential positions and whose opinions counted in the world. In the postwar City dinners, I profited, too, by my articles in *The Daily Telegraph*. So often I would sit next to a man who had read my piece on Saturday and either wanted to discuss the subject or possibly to register his disagreement. Very often such conversations gave me the subject of my next article.

Speeches after dinner are rather like sermons in one respect: we constantly complain that they are a bore and when they are not provided we complain that something valuable was missing. The one place where I have dined with some regularity and without having to listen to speeches is Gray's Inn—but of course barristers talking at length in public to other barristers without being paid for it is almost a contradiction in terms. Really accomplished after-dinner speeches can be an intellectual delight. The skilled practitioner is a master of English speech and of the nuance of vocabulary. Though he may be saying nothing of any moment and be an entertainer rather than an orator, he must speak to educated men in the form of rational discourse.

My education was continued after the war by the contacts which became, as it seemed, more and more varied and I finally lost the shyness which had clung to me right up to the war. At last I could stand alone in a public place with people all around and think about something else. My experience before the war, however, had not been so happy. Being self-conscious, I was apt either to be struck dumb with nothing to say or to be clumsy and rude. One of my failures in my early days in St. Paul's in social *savoir faire* was at a dinner in Vintners' Hall. I began by arriving late, without having carefully read the invitation. When I entered the hall, the reception was apparently over; but I saw a man whose face seemed familiar and I went up to him and said, "I am sure we have met before, your face is familiar, but for the life of me I can't remember who you are." He was the Earl of Athlone, the husband of Princess Alice, whom I had met several times. He was moreover the Chancellor of the University of London who had recently conferred the degree of D.Lit. upon me. Fortunately he took this in good part and laughed at my mistake—perhaps he thought I was drunk. The Earl that night had quite a startling evening for, unless I have mixed up two evenings with the Vintners, it was the day when a wonderful conjuror did all kinds of things with the Earl's watch, including pounding it in a mortar, and at the end presented the watch intact on a silver salver, tastefully surrounded by the Earl's braces. I have always been content, like my old virger, to suppose that these things are done by magic; but if you insist on asking how the braces were included in the act, I can only suggest that, in spite of his expressions of surprise and incredulity, the Earl of Athlone was an accomplice before the act.

Public speaking and public eating are two activities which the City of London demands from its Lord Mayors in extreme measure. On occasion I have been asked to suggest material for speeches, and almost invariably the Lord Mayor consulted me on the speech which he made at the annual banquet for the archbishops and bishops when, as host, he proposed the toast of the Anglican hierarchy in England. I am amazed at my moderation when I think of the criticisms which I might have put into the Lord Mayor's mouth—but Lord Mayors have not reached the chair without acquiring a certain caution about what they say in public, and even if I had been deceitful enough to try, I should never have escaped detection. As it was, I do not remember a single speech at the bishops' dinner which was not appropriate and sincere.

It can be embarrassing to hear a speaker who has asked one's advice making a muddle and missing the point. The instance which comes to mind was a speech at the dinner of the Musicians' Company. An elderly alderman, whom I had known and liked when he was Lord Mayor, had been asked to propose the toast of the Company and he asked me if I knew of an amusing story relating to musicians. I thought at once of the story about the great G. F. Handel who was a hearty eater and, being hungry, he went to a coffee house and ordered dinner for two. After an interval, when no guest appeared, the waiter asked Handel, "Will the other gentleman be coming soon?" to which Handel replied, "I am der oder gentleman." The alderman thought this would do well, so we ran through it again and even paid some attention to the German accent in the dialogue. I was at the dinner. All went well and my alderman friend made a good start with his speech. I could see that he was working up to the story. Imagine my dismay when he began in a firm and audible voice, "Hamlet was a hearty eater", and told the whole story with Hamlet as its hero. I never knew what had happened, or what confusion of mind had overtaken him. I did not even know that he was aware of his mistake. And, in the end, it was quite all right. Everyone roared with laughter at the joke which had missed fire and much more probably than they would have done if the joke had been perfectly phrased.

In 1947 I acquired two "baubles" to add to my orders when dining at the Mansion House and received the King's permission to wear them in this country. In fact I never did wear either, because the one which came from Czechoslovakia fell apart into two pieces when I handled it and the other, which came from Norway, seemed not to fit in with British decorations. I mean I could not find an appropriate place on my chest. But, all the same, these two foreign orders had emotional associations for me. The Norwegian Freedom Cross of King Haakon VII I am proud to have. It recalls the hectic days in Oslo just before the German invasion. It also recalls the days when the King and his government were refugees in London and the moving services which he attended when the Church of Norway used its own language and sang its own songs of praise. Two "amens" for men's voices we adopted in St. Paul's for regular use. I hope they are sung there still. It was rumoured that, when the Norwegian government fled to England, some of its members wished to flee further, to Canada; but the idea was quashed by King Haakon who said, "So long as the King of England stays in England, I stay too." When the war was over, I was delighted to visit Norway and to meet some of the hosts who entertained me on my first visit and to give an English lesson in the school where I had been before. I am not sure, but I think the class was still reading that part of *David Copperfield* where we are told so much about Mr. Peggotty, his house and Ham's trousers.

The Order of the White Lion of Czechoslovakia, 3rd Class, was conferred upon me, I suppose, because I had been, during the war, joint president of the Anglo-Czechoslovakian Religious Fellowship. My fellow president was Dr. Hnik, a theological professor and an energetic colleague. He had managed to bring his family with him and was in close touch with Dr. Beneš. In those days both Beneš and Hnik were optimists and liberals in the tradition of Masaryk. Jan Masaryk was also liberal and optimistic. My contacts with the Czechoslovak clergy were limited by language difficulties and by the calls of other duties, but I saw enough to gather that there were divisions even among the ministers of religion, some of whom were not altogether opposed to Communism. In my talks with Beneš, he made it clear to me that, in his opinion, Czechoslovakia was so situated geographically that she must depend either on Germany or Russia, so that her independence which he ardently supported must always be a relative one, within the sphere either of German or of Russian influence. After the war I kept for a time in touch with Hnik, because he came to London at intervals to buy books for one of the university libraries in Prague. He was still optimistic. But one day he came to see me looking deeply depressed. He told me that he had seen Jan Masaryk the day before and, for the first time, Jan had been apprehensive. The day after I received my order of the White Lion from the Czech embassy, Jan Masaryk was murdered, or committed suicide, and communications ceased. I was sad at the death of Masaryk, who had been so cheerful and courageous in the darkest period of the war. I cannot believe that he killed himself. He would have fought to the end.

After that Hnik faded into the background and I made no effort to find out how he was. But strange pieces of information drifted my way. I was told that he had become a bishop, but in what Church I could not tell. Then a cutting from a newspaper was sent to me because it had a picture of Hnik presiding at a rally of the Communist Party. The final communication was a stout book in Czech, of which I am completely ignorant, but I was furnished with English summaries and translations of I suppose the most pungent passages. If I had known then all that I know now of the conditions of life, and specially of religious life, in Czechoslovakia, I think I might have responded differently to Hnik's book; but when it came it seemed to me so full of the Communist Party line propaganda and so self-righteous in tone that I was repelled by it and I fear wrote that I could not read such spiteful nonsense. Probably I was wrong, and I wish now that I had not judged so hastily and I wonder how much pride was behind my resentment of the book.

I have some reason to fear that he did not live long after sending the book.

To Margaret and me, after six years of strain and tribulation, ten years of comparative happiness were granted during which we had, once more, weeks of holiday in Switzerland and opportunities to pursue some of our interests which we had been compelled to drop during the war. In this chapter I try to recall both the happy days of vacation and the various controversies in which I became involved. But in these years the inevitable penalty of old age began to overtake us—the deaths of old friends. One of these, Sir Roderic Hill, Principal of the Imperial College of Science and Vice Chancellor of the University of London, was a personal friend of my old age. This friendship, which did not begin until the end of the war, was cut short by his death in 1954. Roderic Hill had done wonderful things in the R.A.F. and was the model of a scientific warrior but what specially attracted me was the fact that he was pre-eminently the model of the Christian warrior. Had he lived, I believe he would have been a powerful influence for good among the students and the scientific dons. I did not get close enough to him to be able to speak confidently about his inner thoughts, but our minds certainly had much in common and I was both cheered and alarmed to find that he believed I had a message for scientific students. Now I am happy that his widow is still among my friends.

Before we broach more serious matters, let me touch briefly on our holidays. They were made delightful by grandchildren and most of all by one granddaughter Gillian, my daughter Barbara's elder child. The stress of war had caused her to be close to us for years and I often had to reproach myself for thinking of her as my daughter. From a very early age, she accompanied us on our visits to Switzerland. One year, when I had a scare about my throat, I was forbidden by doctors to utter a sound except occasionally a whisper. Pontresina in June was the setting and the story was being invented by a little girl and a man who spoke only in a hoarse whisper. We wandered about and Gillian not only kept me amused, but suppressed any ordinary speech from me. One of our exercises was the composition of "songs" which were actually intoned poems. Turning over my papers, I came upon a song about a cow. It was modern in style in that it had no rhyme and very little reason, but somehow it did seem to have some relation to "cow". The reader shall be spared this composition, but I must add that it was the first of many and a little later I was spurred into activity by making the acquaintance of a remarkable lady, Mrs. Amy Greif, who was well known in Baltimore and in Lucerne, where she was accustomed to spend August at the Schweizerhof. She was the regular poet of *The Baltimore Sun*, to which she contributed two verses every week. How she managed to keep this unbroken stream of poesy running, I never understood. The only hint she ever gave me was that she never travelled without her rhyming dictionary. She has published several volumes of light verse and, though she laughs at the idea that they are in any literary sense admirable, some of her efforts in my opinion are both funny and charming. When we met in Lucerne, we always had friendly little contests in verse-making. Once, when the last day of the holiday was near, we agreed to have a kind of minstrels' contest and I think Gillian insisted on competing too. So far as I was concerned, the contest was a débâcle, because I had composed some cheerful lines playing on Mrs. Greif's name which I thought was Ada, but was in fact Amy. I did not allow myself to be entirely silenced however by this error. More or less spontaneously, I coined an epigram which pleased me and her too.

> Inconstant Muse, coquettish days are o'er,
> You clock in twice a week in Baltimore.

If the reader will permit me to be so frivolous, I will add another copy of verses which were called forth by an incident in our hotel: not a real grievance, because Mrs. Meyer did not incommode anyone and the "I" who speaks in the last stanza is not the real I of the author, but a conceivable human being.

Meditation in an Hotel

> Where'er I go in this hotel,
> I seem to fall beneath a spell,
>   The spell of Mrs. Meyer.
> I choose a table to my mind,
> With chair that flatters my behind
> Only, alas, too soon to find,
>   Reserved for Mrs. Meyer.

And that is life; for in my day
I've struggled hard upon my way
 In hopes of rising higher;
But when I think I've won the race,
With smile of triumph on my face,
Some other chap has got the place,
 Pushed by some Mrs. Meyer.

Produce this all-pervasive dame,
So potent to damp down the flame
 Of those who would aspire;
That I may, with my utmost art,
Attempt to move her woman's heart
To me some corner to impart
 Reserved for Mrs. Meyer.

I pass on to some serious questions which I tried to think about. The first was no new question but one which has haunted me from when I first became fully self-conscious until today—death and the hope of immortality. As I have said already one of my earliest recollections is of myself lying in bed one early morning and wondering what made me to be me. That sounds silly, but it is not really silly, because it is a childhood way of stating the problem of individuality which of course is closely connected with the hope of immortality or with any belief in the survival of bodily death. I cannot say why death was so much in my mind. I do not think that I talked about it, but it certainly was a subject on which I reflected. I am inclined to think that many children do and my own children did, but they may have been exceptional as having a parson for their father. My eldest child, I know, had fantastic ideas about death when he was still a baby. I had been teaching him the Lord's Prayer and trying to get into his little head some idea of the Father in heaven. I was interrupted by an objection: "If He was very kind, He wouldn't cut off people's heads." "But when does God cut off people's heads?" I asked. "When they die," was the shattering answer. I found after some research that the nursery looked over the churchyard and that the nurse had told him about the boxes, the coffins, and that when people died their bodies were put into the ground and God took their souls in heaven. The child had evidently thought about death and, like many philosophers, could not attach any meaning to the word "soul", except that it was different from the body, and concluded that it must be the head. If Plato is right when he suggests that philosophy is a meditation on death, many young children I believe are already on the philosophical road.

However that may be, I was worried about death when I was young and the death of my brother Hubert must have affected my thought. The worry about death at first was identi-fied in my mind with the worry about the resurrection of Christ. I suppose that sermons had led me to the opinion that everything turned on the accuracy of the Gospels in their narratives of Christ's appearances after the crucifixion. But quite soon I became aware that the appearances themselves presented prob-lems and that belief in the bodily resurrection of Christ was not a necessary part of the hope of immortality. Quite early in life, before I left school, I had read about psychical research and either at school or soon after I went into the Westminster Bank I read F. W. Myers' pioneer work *Human Personality and its Survival of Bodily Death*. It happened too that, when I went into the Bank, one of the clerks in the head office named Pod-more was the brother of a man who was among the group which pushed ahead in research. Strangely, I do not remember at this time meeting anyone who had been to a séance or claimed to be a medium. My knowledge was derived from books, but the evidence impressed me.

When I had left the Bank and was working hard at King's College, I had no time to pursue this subject, but when the strain of "finals" was over the Society for Psychical Research fascinated me and, when I could afford it, I became a member. Here I want just to sum up the development of my opinions on this subject. About thirty years ago, I remember writing somewhere that I expected the next great scientific "break-through" would be in the sphere of mind. I think I meant that the nature of mind would be elucidated in a manner compar-able with the scientific advances in the knowledge of matter. I was confident that any such advance would make it easier to believe in the immortality of the soul. I had the honour of giving the Myers Lecture to the Society on *Theology and Psychical Research*, in which I advocated the study of psychical research as an adjunct to the study of religion. I had too the advantage of the friendship of Miss Longridge, my volunteer helper as secretary, who had the gift of automatic writing. In the course of years, I met and sat with mediums of various types, though I had not the time to undertake systematic research. The most I could claim is that for many years I was in touch with the activities of the researchers. When I wrote the Maurice Lectures on *The Problem of Christ in the Twentieth Century*, I did not hesitate to refer to what I believed to be more or less assured results as considerations which would illuminate our thinking on the Person of Christ by indicating some powers and aspects of human personality which are overlooked by commonsense and academic psychology. I still think that in the main I was right, but I have to admit that I was too optimistic about the actual state of knowledge.

It is necessary for me to state this in order to avoid misunderstanding. I am a "patron" and supporter of the Churches' Fellowship for Psychic and Spiritual Study and I believe that the idea of such an organisation was mooted in something I wrote. My suggestion was that psychical phenomena were relevant to any study of religion and that their interpretation must depend to some extent on our presuppositions, so that what a believer in Christianity would find credible might often differ from what an agnostic would regard as likely and of course an orthodox believer would start with the concept of spirits, whereas an agnostic would probably reject them out of hand. I hold this view still. But I see a danger that the believer in God may be too easily persuaded to relax the standard of evidence. And this is happening. We shall profit nothing if our Churches' Fellowship gains a reputation for credulity.

Sad as it must seem on reviewing my own lifetime's experience, I can only say that in respect of evidence for personal survival after death I am in about the same situation as I was sixty years ago. I think there is quite a lot of evidence of various kinds which would fit in with the hypothesis that some persons in some sense continue to exist after the death of their bodies. This evidence consists of alleged communications from the dead by various means such as trance mediums and automatic writing and the principal difficulty is how to prove beyond doubt the identity of the alleged communicator from beyond the grave. Mediums I have known have been mixed. I mean of some one would not be surprised if they were guilty of fraud; but others appear to be incapable of conscious deceit. But experience shows that the most unlikely persons are sometimes guilty of trickery in these matters. Some most disturbing disclosures occurred in the controversies about Borley Rectory and one is driven to admit not only that some most respected individuals are capable of fraud, but also that genuine mediums may cheat—possibly unconsciously.

I have to admit too that my opinion about the spiritual peril of playing about with psychic phenomena has changed. I believe now that concentration on "spiritual" beings can be dangerous; whatever causes we may assign to them, examples of decline in moral standard and even in sanity are known. I do not want to support superstition about being possessed by evil spirits, but it would be foolish to pretend that cases are not known where the hypothesis is suggested by the facts. Some years back, I asked my friend Dr. Graham Howe if he thought possession was a reality and if so how to guard against it when researching on spiritual phenomena. He replied that possession by evil power seemed all too possible but if one was pure in heart nothing could touch one. Evidently he thought that my chance of meeting that test was slender, for he went on to tell me of some deplorable magical precautions which I have completely forgotten. It was when I was at a direct voice séance, which I was pretty sure was an elaborate conjuring trick, that it came upon me as a kind of revelation—"What kind of show is this? You are like a group of savages gathered round a medicine man who is playing on your affections and your fears just to make money out of you."

The work of Professor Rhine and many others on extrasensory perception (E.S.P.) was until recently the centre of active research and seemed to open up new avenues. As everyone knows, it was claimed that some individuals had the power of perceiving objects such as playing cards without employing the normal senses. This was said to be demonstrated by using a small number of cards, say five, so that the chances against accurate random guesses could be calculated and, when an individual's score frequently topped the chance figure, the chances against the successful guesses reached astronomical figures. The mathematics of chance are not so simple as one might suppose; but to me it seemed, and still seems, that unless the scores reported by the experimenters can be questioned, or some kind of conspiracy can be suspected, there is a high

probability that some factor that must be psychical is involved.
Of course, a serious objection may be made on the ground that
whatever this factor may be we cannot predict that it will work,
nor have we any clue to the special conditions in which it
functions. Another cause for hesitation is the fact that the
number of individuals who possess this strange capability has
dwindled and the really striking examples are those reported
some time ago. It is conceivable that the earlier experimenters
were mistaken or deceived and also it can be argued that the
calculation of odds has been muddled. I do not believe this
sceptical hypothesis can be sustained and I do believe that the
"Psi" factor is no myth, but there is no knockdown answer to
the doubter.

There is a trap in psychical research: to confuse the psychical with the spiritual. The "gift of God is eternal life", not an
indefinite extension of our temporal lives, but a quality of
life which transcends time. Anyone who has this faith and even
the dimmest insight into its meaning will think of his personal
survival of bodily death as of secondary importance, but nevertheless as probably implied in the idea of eternal life. The
question whether an individual person is conceivable without
a body is difficult, and one of the fascinations for me in the
psychical research literature is the data which may be noted
as bearing on the words of St. Paul about the "spiritual body"
of the redeemed in the world to come. The Theosophists have
the concept of the "etheric" body, which may be akin to the
"spiritual body" in St. Paul. In either case, the name seems
to indicate a synthesis of elements in themselves incompatible
with each other. In spite of disappointments and the apparent
stagnation of research, I still hold that psychic phenomena are
genuine and that they have an important bearing on the powers
of the human personality. I would add that, while the attempt
to make a religion out of these phenomena (which seems to be
a fair description of the extreme type of spiritualism) is a
dangerous heresy, it is entirely rational and necessary to study
the psychical phenomena in the context of religion and to
consider whether the needs which are met by spiritualism
cannot be met by a deeper understanding of the communion
of saints. I fully admit that the fear of opening the way to
superstition is justified; but is it fantastic to suggest that the
Feast of All Souls could be given a wider reference than has

been customary and express a wider hope? I have often felt that the "souls of the faithful" will rest in peace whether we pray for them or not; it is the souls of the unfaithful who need our prayers. When I met an archbishop who agreed with me, I was encouraged, for is it not rather a queer kind of worship to keep on imploring God to be himself and to forgive those who repent?

In the post-war period, some dissenting opinions of mine obtained public notice and the Archbishop of Canterbury, on being asked what he thought of them, coined a phrase: "It is not the teaching of the Church of England", which he used on all occasions. It did not annoy me, because I never claimed that my opinions were part of the teaching of the Church— not even that they ought to be. It fell to me to propose the health of the Archbishop at a Mansion House dinner and I was rather pleased to have such an obvious opening. "It has seemed to me of late that whenever I express an opinion the Archbishop hastens to announce that it is not the teaching of the Church of England; but this evening I am confident that my speech will express the feelings not only of the Church of England but of vast numbers of well-wishers of all creeds and of none—it is to propose the toast of the health and happiness of the Primate of All England."

I know not why I was selected by the Archbishop to serve on his Commission, appointed in December, 1945, "To consider the practice of human artificial insemination with special reference to its theological, moral, social, psychological and legal implications and to report to the Archbishop." The terms of reference were so worded as to give the Archbishop the decision whether or not the report should be published. Dr. Wand, the new Bishop of London, was nominated by the Archbishop as Chairman, and my fellow members included Professors E. O. James and R. C. Mortimer, now Bishop of Exeter. Medicine and psychotherapy were well represented and we had Mr. Justice Vaisey and H. U. Willink, K.C., to advise us on the important legal aspects of our study. The secretary of the commission was a priest who was also a medical man, the Rev. G. L. Russell, M.B., Ch.B. The subject had no special attraction for me and it was only when I began to understand the large possibilities for good and evil of artificial insemination through the writings of Julian Huxley and others that I became deeply

interested. As it happened, I was concerned with the subject
for some years, because I was a member of the working party
of the British Council of Churches on Human Production,
which published its findings in 1962, and, after giving the
Herbert Gray Lecture for the Marriage Guidance Council in
1961, became an honorary Fellow of the Eugenics Society. I
learned a lot from my colleagues on both these committees.
With regard to the British Council Group the question of
agreement or disagreement did not arise, because our task
was to report on the facts and on the new techniques and also
the questions which seemed to arise for the Christian conscience
without pretending to make authoritative judgments. In the
earlier Commission, that which had to report to the Archbishop,
we were expected to give authoritative guidance.

I felt unable to sign the report, because it gave a final judgment on a subject which seemed to me not ripe for anything
more than interim counsel. The short, and most decent, way of
describing my dissent is to quote from the "Findings" which
were presented to the Archbishop:

Artificial insemination with donated semen involves a breach
of the marriage. It violates the exclusive union set up between
husband and wife. It defrauds the child begotten and deceives
both his putative kinsmen and society at large. For both
donor and recipient the sexual act loses its personal character
and becomes a mere transaction. For the child, there must
always be the risk of disclosure, deliberate or unintended,
of the circumstances of his conception. We therefore judge
artificial insemination with donated semen to be wrong in
principle and contrary to Christian standards.

(*Artificial Human Insemination,*
S.P.C.K., 1948, p. 58.)

With the view that A.I.D. has many dangers and should
be carefully regulated, I cordially agreed; but I could not agree
that A.I.D. was always inherently evil. The argument that it
was a kind of adultery I thought was unsound. In actual fact,
women who resorted to A.I.D. were often childless married
women who refused to take the adulterous way out. I did not
submit a minority report, but I was permitted to append a
note to the Report, explaining why I could not sign it. I quote:

I wish to record, not violent disagreement with my colleagues, but a perplexity of mind which has not been cleared up by the evidence or the reasoning which I have heard. If I ventured to criticise the Commission, I should say that it has been, very naturally, too eager to reach final and absolute judgments on a matter which is as yet very imperfectly understood. I believe we should have done better if we had been content to state what we believe to be the proper attitude of Christians to A.I.D. in the present circumstances, while reserving the question of its absolute condemnation in all circumstances for further study. After all, one should be cautious in adding to the list of deadly sins.

In 1961 I was involved in discussion of the same problems at a somewhat more advanced stage. *Eugenics and the Family* was the subject of my Herbert Gray Lecture and the theories of some eugenists involved the technique of A.I.D. on a large scale. In this lecture, I tried to convince my audience that we are in a situation with regard to the possible future of the human race which has no parallel in the past, because man is now able to take a decisive part in the evolution of the human race and "plan" the generations which will come after him; we are, in fact, confronted with the possibility that a new stage in the evolution of man is now beginning in which human intelligence and co-operation may help to produce a higher type of human being. Throughout this lecture, I had in mind the idea of crisis for humanity and the menace of the "population explosion". Political controversy had to be avoided, but I hope that I left in the minds of my hearers the uncomfortable suspicion that the welfare state might be ruined by causes which politicians rarely mention. "One suspects," I said cautiously, "that many parents who ought to have many children have only one or two; while very many whose contribution to the upgrading of the human race is likely to be negative have all too many."

The American biologist Dr. Hermann J. Muller's paper on *The Guidance of Human Evolution* furnished a text for comments on the perils and the possibilities which startled me. From it I deduced the conclusion that it was high time Christians began to think seriously on the moral aspects of probable drastic proposals from eugenists. The most startling to me was the contention that A.I.D. should be the normal mode of pro-creation. Julian Huxley, unless I am mistaken, agreed in principle with Muller. The claim was made that by A.I.D. the process of evolution might be accelerated and controlled. By the A.I. technique for example (if it had been known while he was alive) thousands of children of William Shakespeare could have been born and indeed could have continued to be born after his death. A slight acquaintance with the achievements of A.I. in the breeding of cattle is enough to convince any reasonable man that, given the right conditions and powers, biological experts could probably breed human beings of quite exceptional powers, including intellectual powers.

I returned to this subject in the Charles Gore Lecture which I gave in Westminster Abbey and also in a lecture in Carlisle. The American and British authorities whom I quoted were all good liberals and explicitly stated that their eugenic pro-posals were submitted under the understanding that no legal compulsion should be employed and everything should be voluntary. There can be no doubt of the sincerity of these pro-fessions and we may be perfectly sure that our experts are not conspiring against our personal liberty. Yet can one predict the minds of a century hence? In his clumsy way, Hitler was interested in eugenics and, as I had seen in Bethel, was not likely to be deterred by ideals of freedom from experiments in breeding masters and leaders of the chosen race. Scientific humanism is as yet very imperfectly defined and I do not know that eugenics are a part of its accepted programme, but it would be surprising if the humanists were indifferent to the challenge of biologists to act creatively in the crisis of human evolution. It seems that both humanism and Christianity ought to define their positions.

The question of the family and its future is central. Unless he has changed his mind recently, Julian Huxley holds that the family is a valuable institution and that it can be preserved, and even improved, even if all children are born by A.I.D.; in short that the social and spiritual value of the family could easily be preserved when its biological foundation had been destroyed. I simply cannot believe this. To imagine a com-munity of families in which no child knew who was his father is too much. Plato at least provided the children in his Utopia with a myth.

I cannot improve on the words which I wrote in 1961 as the conclusion of my lecture. After referring to St. Paul as a man of great quality and weak body, I proceeded:

> Paul was certainly not the kind of being whom eugenics would have looked upon as a success. His frame was evidently not impressive or attractive and he suffered from some permanent disability which he calls "a thorn in the flesh"; some scholars have thought that he was epileptic. In any view, however, he was a man who played an outstanding part in history and made a unique contribution to the cultural tradition of the western world, while in the Christian view he was much more; he was a vehicle of divine revelation and the greatest of the Apostles.

This introduced the last point which I wished to make:

> He too was concerned with the making of improved men, or rather, he would say, with making new men. His own experience led him to this, for he felt himself to have been transformed from within by a creative spiritual experience, and he believed that this same experience was possible for all. This is not the occasion to dwell on the significance of the conversion of St. Paul or on conversion in general; but the chairman's address at the conference in which Dr. Muller developed his ideas for the future included a reference to "the divine spark which reminds us that there is another factor in the development of human beings". The fascinating study of heredity and environment is certainly of the highest importance and it would be folly to ignore the great benefits which may be derived from the science of eugenics, but it is a dangerous fallacy to suppose that we are completely determined by heredity and environment or that we are and can be nothing but what they make us. Our heredity is given and we cannot alter it, nor for the most part can we choose our environment, but we may make something good and valuable out of the given material or something worthless and mean. Which we shall do depends on our spiritual nature, on the "divine spark" within us.

The subject which these lectures dealt with is of the greatest moment, though my contribution to its understanding is little enough. But every intelligent believer must have it in mind, for Christian faith is "eschatological", concerned with last things and with man's destiny and future. Scientific humanism has its own interpretation of eschatology, which depends not on alleged revelation or divine intervention but on man's directing intelligence intervening in the process of evolution. How many of our bishops or other religious leaders have anything coherent to say on the conflict between the two eschatologies? How many show any sign that they have given an hour's serious thinking on it?

On May 2nd, 1950, I involved myself in a controversy about death. Dr. Killick Millard had invited me to speak at the annual meeting of the Society for the Legalisation of Voluntary Euthanasia and I accepted. I knew that voluntary euthanasia was a hotly debated subject, but I did not anticipate the chorus of contending voices which would follow my short and modest paper. The audience at the meeting, as I remember it, was fewer than a hundred and there were no discordant utterances when I sat down, but *The Daily Mirror* took up the topic and linked it with cases of "mercy-killing" which had been in the news. My address contained nothing which had not often been said before and the only remarkable thing about it was that it was given by an Anglican clergyman who happened to be Prolocutor of the Convocation of Canterbury. And I was not the first clerical advocate of euthanasia. Dr. Major, the editor of *The Modern Churchman*, and Dr. Leslie D. Weatherhead, Minister of the City Temple, were on record as supporters of voluntary euthanasia. Perhaps some of the Christians who were indignant at our stand were alarmed by the company we joined in this controversy, which included Bertrand Russell and Bernard Shaw.

The Society for the Legalisation of Euthanasia is not fighting for a general relaxation of legal measures against suicide or murder; it aims at getting Parliament to pass a law which would legalise the actions of doctors and others in providing a painless passage out of this world for hopelessly ill patients who of their own free will ask for it. Those who have drafted the bill have, as it seems to me, guarded against the possibility of criminal use of its suggested procedure. This is not the place to argue the issue in detail; I am sure that anyone who will examine the bill will agree that charges of murder and suicide are beside the point if the words are given their normal meaning.

In my paper, I began by admitting that Christian history ought to make us shrink from euthanasia in any form, because in its struggle against paganism the Christian Church had stood for the sacredness of human life against the exposure of unwanted children and gladiatorial shows. It is right that a Christian's first thought, when he hears of the proposal to legalise any kind of euthanasia, should be that it is dangerous because it seems to contradict the fundamental principle of the sacredness of human personality. The argument for voluntary euthanasia must begin then by showing that there are cases where this principle must be modified by the all-sufficient principle of *agape*. I said:

> It is plain to me that the principle of the sacredness of human personality cannot be stretched to cover the case of those whom the proposed legislation has in mind. We have to present to ourselves the condition of a man who is incurably ill and destined to a period of agonising suffering, relieved only by the administration of narcotic drugs. The situation then, in many instances, is that a disintegration of the personality occurs. Nothing could be more distressing than to observe the gradual degeneration of a fine and firm character into something which we hardly recognise as our friend, as a result of physical causes and of the means adopted to assuage intolerable pain. It is contended that the endurance of suffering may be a means of grace and no Christian would deny this, but I would urge that, in the case of a man whose existence is a continuous drugged dream, this cannot be alleged.

The theological objection to voluntary euthanasia was based on a doctrine of divine Providence which had surprising power in the minds of religious persons, as I knew very well. That remarkable woman and evangelist, the wife of General Booth, was convinced that her last illness and every torture which it inflicted on her was decreed by the God who is revealed in Christ. She endured to the end of a slow cancer death without any alleviation by drugs, in the firm belief that this was the will of God for her. She was more logical than many others who professed the same doctrine of Providence; i.e. that to each one of us is allotted a definite span of life, a "number of days" and that any attempt to shorten that span is impious. To be perfectly consistent, one would suppose a believer would have to condemn any attempt to lengthen the allotted term. Obviously this conception of Providence, when worked out in detail, leads to conclusions which no sane person could accept; but it is even now currently accepted as Christian doctrine, and reaction against it is one cause of the spread of humanism. In a sentence or two I tried to state an alternative doctrine which still seems to me acceptable:

I suggest that a truer view of the providential order is as follows: The Creator has given man reason, freedom of choice and conscience and has left him with the possibility of ordering his own life, within limits. He is to do the best he can with the material presented to him, and this means that it is the will of God we should use our reason, conscience and freedom of choice when we are faced with evils that have a remedy. My view of Providence then leads me to suppose that we are required by our belief in God to give the most earnest consideration to the proposal to legalise voluntary euthanasia.

I should not put forward this statement as a complete account of the doctrine of Providence, because I would add words to cover the belief that for the child of God there is always a course of action which is the will of God for him and that his prayer must always be that he may be shown what it is. I put this better in that little prayer which I once composed for a book on the Seven Words from the Cross: I quote it again.

Thou hast a work for me to do; O Lord,
show it to me; Thou hast a place for me
to fill; help me to fill it to Thy glory;
Thou hast given me a soul to make; make
Thou it for me and build me into Thy
spiritual temple: for Jesus' sake.

The Daily Mirror weighed in with an article headed, in

overbearing type, *The Right to Die*, and the floodgates were open. The letters in the press and the letters in the post were so numerous that I could not read them all. So far as I could tell, the religious feeling was, on the whole, against euthanasia and, in spite of arguments to the contrary, favoured the charges of murder and suicide. As I expected, *The Modern Churchman* published my speech in full and gave editorial support and so did the more liberal of the Free Church ministers, including Leslie Weatherhead. The surprise was that there was so feeble support from the medical profession. The doctors did not accuse us of being propagandists for murder, but they took refuge in the principle that their vocation was to preserve life, not to destroy it. In my opinion, this was an evasion of the issue. The quietus to this discussion was given by my honoured friend Lord Horder in a long letter to *The Sunday Times*. I have never understood his arguments against the legalisation of voluntary euthanasia, so I will not attempt to refute them; of one thing I am certain—that he believed the patients for whom we advocated this legal reform would be better off in the hands of really competent physicians than they would be with legal safeguards.

Since then the question has, I suppose, been slightly affected by the controversy about transplanting of organs and the related controversy about the tests of death. Vistas of fantastic grimness open before the imagination; but I am too old to pick up the trail again and leave this subject with the remark that the Society for the Legalisation of Euthanasia still soldiers on in spite of the fact that its bill has once more been rejected by Parliament.

1957 saw the publication of *A History of St. Paul's*, edited by W. M. Atkins and me. The book was planned by Mr. W. S. Shears, who was actively associated with its preparation which lasted more than ten years. The original idea was that the editor should be Sir Ernest Barker and that I should be associated with him. As the work proceeded, however, it became clear that the preparation would take longer than had been anticipated and that Sir Ernest could not give time and attention to detailed editing. He kept in touch, however, with the progress of the work and contributed a characteristic foreword to the volume. I had the great good fortune to enlist Mr. W. M. Atkins' co-operation in editing the history. A former minor canon and librarian of St. Paul's, he had a wide and scholarly knowledge of its history and was acquainted with most of the authorities on the subject. It is the simple truth to say that without the help of Mr. Atkins the book would have taken twice as long to produce, if it had ever seen the light at all.

I was disappointed that my friend of King's College days, Norman Sykes, did not write a section of the history. His untoward death soon after leaving Cambridge to be Dean of Winchester removed a notable Church historian and scholar. The final misfortune was the death of Dr. G. L. Prestige, Canon of St. Paul's, who had been working, as was supposed, on the chapter on the Victorian period. He had published a book *St. Paul's in Its Glory* on the period and we supposed that his material for the chapter had been expanded into a volume. But no draft of the chapter could be found among his papers and we were confronted with the problem how to fill the gap without postponing the publication date for a year at least. Atkins was equal to the occasion. He wrote the section entitled *The Age of Reform: 1831–1934*, dividing it into three chapters: 1831–1868, 1868–1911, 1911–1934. This is one of the longer and in a sense more difficult chapters in the book, not because of the absence of facts, but because of their overwhelming number. The intricate story which leads on to the period when I was Dean is told fully and clearly. It would be unfitting for me to review the history. Returning to it after an interval, I find it deeply interesting and am struck again by the research which lies behind Professor C. N. L. Brooke's chapter on *The Earliest Times* to 1485.

This chapter may not end, however, on a note of complacency, for in 1960 the volume of *The Cambridge Modern History* which covered the first half of the 20th century was published under the title of *The Age of Violence* and was received by reviewers with violent disapproval. I was involved, because I had rashly accepted an invitation from the editors to write a chapter on *Literature, Philosophy and Religious Thought*. I have never argued with reviewers and I made no reply to the strictures on my contribution, partly because I agreed with some of them. To have undertaken a summary account in 5,000 words of literature during the half century— not only in Britain and the U.S.A. but in the whole civilised world—was absurd and not only for me but for anyone. I suppose the way to deal with such an assignment (if one was foolish enough to accept it) would be to write about trends and movements in abstract terms, but I could not do that and I was loth to refer to books which I had never read. Inevitably my offering was too personal and eccentric to pass as history. One critic blamed me for not mentioning the name of Tolstoy, whose works were all written and published in the 19th century. I think he must have been looking carefully for points of attack.

The section of my chapter which dealt with philosophy I would defend as an objective account of schools of thought prominent in the west during the half century. The confusion of tongues was unprecedented, and one of the chief subjects of contention was the nature and method of philosophical thought. To illustrate the confusion, one might point out the difference which geography would make to the standpoint of the historian of thought. The important developments of philosophy in India were radically different from those in the west and even there the prevailing philosophy in England was not the same as that in Scotland and even less in Germany or France—to say nothing about the position in America. An attempt can be made to by-pass this awkward situation by the idea of dialogue and by trying to regard dialogue as the essence of philosophy. But dialogue for the sake of dialogue is difficult to accept as the rational aim of thought—dialogue about what and with what end? Perhaps truth?

CHAPTER 18

Mixed Activities

In 1951 I attained the age of seventy, but the fifties were an active period of my life and I do not remember being tired beyond measure. Nor was my activity confined to London or the British Isles; I visited Germany, Holland and America and in each had a full schedule of lectures and preaching. I used to say that my knowledge of foreign parts was confined to those countries whose inhabitants were foolish enough to pay me to lecture, and it was not far from the truth, because when I was young and eager to travel I had to take "locums" in the long vacation for the sake of my wife and children. I do not complain, because I am sure that to keep in touch with them was better than anything else I could do.

Up to the war, where I went Margaret went too; but she could not accompany me in my travels in 1940, nor could she be with me when I went to Germany in 1945, because the military government of the British Zone would not give her a pass. And unfortunately she was not so fit as she had been. Though she had come through the bombing of London without showing any sign of distress, the death of Michael had been a shattering blow from which she never completely recovered and I am sure that she found life less worth living, though she was delighted with her grandchildren and from them gained some peace and joy. But nothing would persuade her to resume writing novels. She was rheumatic, and the crypt of St. Paul's, where we had slept during the bombardments, was not so dry as one might expect. Another infirmity reduced her activity— she became deaf in spite of all that our friend Professor Ormerod could do and that deprived her of her pleasure in conversation. She was a brilliant talker, not of the type which "holds the floor" and monopolises the talk; but of the more civilised type which makes conversation a pleasant game in which two or three minds are communicating with one another and lightly exploring, not only each other, but themselves. Margaret rejoiced in dialogue and developed a technique which loosened the tongues of most men who had the good fortune to sit next her at dinners. Hearing aids were a palliative, but she had not the patience to master their manipulation or use them to the best advantage. I think she would still have said that the only advantage of London over the country, so far as she was concerned, was that it offered more opportunities for intelligent conversation. The old cottage which she had bought (largely out of the royalties on her novels) had been a way of escape from urban life in the war, but when peace came we could not afford to keep it up and it was sold to an officer in the R.A.F. stationed at a nearby aerodrome.

She encouraged me to accept invitations, and understood well enough that if I had anything of value to contribute to the study of religion and the Christian faith not many years were left to me for this. The six or seven years that the war and its consequences had stolen from me could never be restored, but some fragments perhaps could be gathered before the day ended. My first impulse, when an invitation came to me to spend two months in Canada, was to decline on the ground that I had plenty to do at home, but reflection changed my mind. The invitation was primarily to attend the meeting of the General Synod of the Church of Canada, which takes place once in three years, and to preach the Synodal Sermon. There were other invitations too. I was asked to lecture at Trinity College, Toronto, and to give three lectures in McGill University in Montreal. On my way back, so to say, I was asked to Harvard to preach and to stay with my old friend Willard Sperry; when I left Harvard I was enticed to New York for twenty-four hours, during which I would preach in the Cathedral of St. John the Divine in the morning, lecture in the Chapter House in the afternoon and visit the choir school before I took the 'plane back to Toronto. All this, though attractive, was formidable and I reminded myself that I was over seventy, but the persuasion of my old friends Dr. and Mrs. Sowby and their invitation to make their house a kind of headquarters while I was in Canada removed my hesitations.

I had known the Sowbys for a long time. When he was a master in St. Edward's School, Oxford, when he was headmaster in St. Columba's School, Dublin, and, at the time when the invitation came, when he was the Warden of Upper Canada College, Toronto, one of the most famous boys' schools in America. Mary Sowby is an expert theologian as well as a highly intelligent woman and author. In moments of depression, I cheer myself up by thinking that it was my book *Studies in Christian Philosophy* which drew her to the study of theology. Though she was more high church than I in her worship, we talked the same language and laughed at the same jokes. Cedric Sowby was a valued friend who cherished the flattering illusion that I was a great scholar and to whom I owed many pleasant contacts in Eire. I always wondered what part he took in the gracious act of Trinity College, Dublin, in bestowing on me the honorary degree of D.D., which I am proud to hold.

On August 26th, 1952, I embarked at Liverpool on the Canadian Pacific boat *Empress of Scotland* for Ontario. The kind official who arranged my travel was clearly of opinion that I should be letting down the dignity of my office and that of the Canadian Pacific if I did not go first-class and I am glad that once in my life I had the experience of travel at its easiest. I think that if I had plenty of money and no responsibilities I would go round the world by sea in a moderately sized liner. I had known first-class comfort on the *Bremen* just before the war, but then all comfort was clouded by apprehension; now I was indeed a little apprehensive, but only that I might fall below the expectations of my hosts and, after all, it would not be a disaster, or even an unusual occurrence, that an aged cleric should make a fool of himself. The euphoria of the voyage was shattered at Montreal, or at any rate as we were going up the St. Lawrence River, by representatives of the Canadian Broadcasting authority who suddenly appeared on board and, without warning or time for reflection, presented me with a microphone and with the demand that I should give a message to the people of Canada. I stammered out a few unpremeditated words which must have convinced anyone who listened to them that the Dean of St. Paul's who was about to land was, in fact, an aged cleric making a fool of himself. This incident soon ceased to trouble me, but one omission of mine on landing always shames me when I think of it. The man who looked at me so reproachfully as I left the ship was the man who had cleaned my boots and had not been tipped.

From the moment when I landed to that when I departed, I was surrounded by hospitable friends and carried through fresh experiences. Of some I must say little, because though delightful they were not part of my mission. For example, I stayed with the minister of a "company town" in the forest lands near to the Great Lakes. The inhabitants were all connected with the industry of growing trees, looking after them, felling them and cutting them up so that they could be turned into wood pulp and into newspapers. A large pyramid of wood blocks dominated the view—a fit emblem of the town's activity. A minor purpose of my journey was to present fragments of St. Paul's, taken from the marble of the bombed Cathedral, to churches which had asked for relics to build into their own fabrics. I had one for my hosts, but the question where it should be placed in the little church was not easily settled and the constitution of the congregation was peculiar. My good host, the Rev. Owen Barrow, seemed to serve two masters quite happily. He was a duly ordained priest in the Church of Canada and thus also in the Anglican communion; as such his obedience to the bishop had been promised; but he was also a recognised minister of the United Church, which was an amalgamation of non-conformist Churches and thus, I suppose, under some other authorities. When I was there, Mr. Barrow was an Anglican on Sunday morning and some kind of Presbyterian on Sunday evening. Though the congregation was poised between Episcopal and Presbyterian, they were, anyway, delightful people and it was a privilege to be allowed to minister to them. Through Mr. and Mrs. Barrow, I had thrilling experiences in the small aeroplane which was used by the surveyor of the area and the doctor. The danger of forest fires was evident enough when from the air one could see more than one incipient fire which would have spread indefinitely but for the action of the fire wardens. One camp of these forest guards I visited, situated on the shore of a small lake and furnished with a watch tower which was always manned. When the snow covered the trees the guards packed up for the winter.

My days at Upper Canada College were instructive in many ways and I learned many new things from my learned hosts, but one thing I did not learn, though I tried, was how to follow Canadian football. I spent happy hours watching the boys playing and winning enthusiastic applause, but the scoring and the strategy eluded me.

The General Synod assembled at London, Ontario, on September 12th, and opened with a service at which I was the preacher. Strangely enough I have only a dim memory of this really historic occasion. There remains the confused picture of a large and varied assembly of clergy and laity and of the Primate as the president. I have the printed copy of my discourse before me and it brings back to me some of the fear and trembling with which I delivered it. In 1952 the world was not without cause for Christian concern and even apprehension, but the hope for greater unity of Christians was brighter than it had been for some time and the ecumenical spirit was well represented in the Synod. In duty bound, I devoted most of my sermon to this topic. The text was St. Paul's exhortation to the Ephesians to "redeem the time" or rather to "buy up the opportunity" (Ephes. V). I do not flatter myself that I added anything of value to the literature of the ecumenical movement, but I thought that perhaps I might do some good by referring to the intellectual aspect of the crisis for faith. I quote part of the conclusion of the sermon; it still expresses my convictions:

I do not question for one moment that the truths of our religion are eternal and independent of the changes of human thought, but I urge that the situation demands that we should try to understand and meet it. We cannot dispense with the work of Christian scholars and philosophers who are equipped to grapple with the problem. The battle for the allegiance of mankind, the battle for the Christian future of civilisation is to a larger extent than we often recognise an intellectual conflict. We shall be judged indeed by our faithfulness and our loyalty to Christ, but included in that faithfulness is the question whether we have served Our Lord fully with our minds and thought courageously enough, and deeply enough, at this time of opportunity. Have we been sufficiently careful to show our generation that Christ is the truth—the answer not only to the needs of their hearts but to the questions of their minds? St. Paul, we may observe, links the making use of opportunity to redeem the evil days with knowledge—"knowing what the will of the Lord is".

I had no more business in London, Ontario, except to present to the Cathedral of St. Paul in that city a slab of marble from the ruins of the choir in the Cathedral of St. Paul in London, England, and to give the cordial greetings of my Chapter to the Dean. I attended some sessions of the Synod and tried to gain some insight into the working of synodical government in a Church which was not trammelled by establishment. I learnt practically nothing, partly no doubt because I was stupid, but chiefly, I think because I was hot. The heat was quite intolerable and seemed to drain away all my energy and boil my brains so that I could exert neither mind nor body. I felt that I might collapse. Fortunately the Provost of Trinity College, Toronto, Dr. R. S. Seeley, was present and was straining at the leash to get back to his college. He took me back in his car at a terrifying speed in record time and I had a few days respite. It is sad to relate that shortly afterwards he was killed in a motor accident which deprived the University of one of its outstanding administrators.

And now for the lectures: I had prepared them in such a form that I thought they would all centre upon one theme and each set would expound a different aspect of it. Apart from single addresses and lectures, I had engaged to give three courses of three or four lectures each in Toronto, Montreal and Winnipeg. The main theme I described as *Faith, Myth and Reason*. This was a subject on which I had been reflecting for some years and later I gave three lectures on Faith in Lichfield Cathedral under the appointment of the Dean and Chapter. In the Cathedral the lectures went well—at least the audience was not driven away nor did it fall asleep, but when I came to write out the lectures for publication I failed in self-confidence. Was it Augustine who said, when asked to explain some point of doctrine, "If I was in the pulpit I could do it easily, but not in conversation"? I had that experience.

I could not help thinking that there was a touch of irony in the fact that, when I was a boy, I had been distressed—I could almost write "agonised"—about the meaning of "saving faith" and now, when a doctor of divinity several times over and a former professor of theology I was as perplexed as ever. I had hoped that the exercise of putting together three related courses of lectures would lead to clarification of the problem of faith and, up to a point, it was a help that some of the discussions were useful, but the book remains to be written.

In Toronto, I was given the Hon. D.D. in Trinity College. The occasion was made memorable to me by two of its "accidents": one that a fellow honorary doctor was Mrs. Reinhold Niebuhr, the wife of the well-known American theologian whom I had met before the war in New York; she was in anxiety about her husband who was seriously ill: the other "accident" was that the lot fell upon me to make a speech of thanks for all the honorary graduates—a task which was far beyond my powers.

The flight from Toronto to Winnipeg was unforgettable. We flew into the sunset over the Great Lakes. When I arrived at Winnipeg, I found that I was billed not only to preach, as I had expected, but to be the principal speaker at a town meeting. It was never quite clear to me what the purpose of the meeting was. It somehow combined presenting the prize for the most public-spirited family of the year and a welcome to the Standard Revised Version of the Old Testament which had just been published. In spite of its mixed purposes, I found the meeting inspiring. The winning family, consisting of father, mother and, I think, four children, were Ukrainians only recently added to the citizens of Winnipeg. They were quite obviously a welcome addition. Healthy, lively, keen and happy, they listened modestly to the recital of the virtues which had won for them this civic crown. I wondered what miseries in their native land had driven them out. One other memorable side-show enlivened my stay in Montreal, when I was lecturing at McGill University: the Catholic University, which happened to be celebrating some anniversary, most kindly invited me to a wonderful banquet over which the Cardinal Archbishop presided as Chancellor. The speeches were in French and most instructive to me. The Canadian type of speech was to me easier to follow than the Parisian type, of which we had an eloquent speaker in a professor from Paris. On October 17th, just as the fall was at its colourful peak, I left for Liverpool on the *Empress of Scotland*, carrying with me many happy memories and, owing to the hospitality of the Sowbys and other friends, a modest financial gain.

On Shrove Tuesday, 1954, I flew to Amsterdam to begin a series of lectures under the auspices of the Anglo-Dutch Society. In contrast with my previous visit during the war, this one was not only peaceful but delightful and, when joined in memory with the 1940 visit, took on something of the appearance of a happy ending. But not altogether, for there were some wounds which would never heal. Among the continuities were the kind reception at the British Embassy and the Embassy chauffeur who was the same as the one who had driven me in 1940. He had lain hidden in the cellar throughout the war. I met, too, one of the university dons who had helped me in my propagandist talks. He had taken part in the Dutch resistance during the German occupation. From him I had first-hand information of the works of the tyrants and the sufferings of the conquered. One incident above others shocked me, because I had visited the house where the victims lived. It was a Jewish orphanage. One evening, vans drove up to the door and, with the efficiency of men well practised in the art, every inhabitant including the staff, nurses and matrons, were bundled into the vans and driven away—not one of them was heard of again. The underground members were taken by surprise and able only to rescue one matron in the dark as the vans drove away. The Dutch people do not forget such events and are, I would suppose, the most constant friends, along with the Norwegians, we have in Europe.

The subjects of the lectures were chosen by the branches which I visited out of a list of subjects on which I thought I might be able to speak intelligently for an hour. It is surprising how few there are when one is faced with the demand for a list. The majority of the branches chose *The Church of England*. The fact is that to most Europeans the C. of E. is a fascinating riddle. Most of the church historians in Germany, Scandinavia and Holland adopt as guide Macaulay's epigram: the Church of England is a Church with a Catholic liturgy and a Calvinist theology. In 1912, I attended lectures in Marburg by the Professor of Church History in which he adopted Macaulay's view and demonstrated to the satisfaction of his audience that the C. of E., being an artificial combination of two contradictions and not a synthesis, could not possibly exist much longer.

Younger ministers of the Dutch Calvinist Church came to hear my discourses on the C. of E. and I think one or two Roman Catholic priests. I could sense the feeling of disquiet in the younger ministers and their interest in the worship in

Anglican churches, but I did not foresee the length to which revolt and demand for reform from within would go. Unless the change in outlook has gone very much further than I expect, the line of thought in lay circles is apt to be very different from the thinking of the theologians. I was told during my tour that the latest schism in the Calvinist Church was on the question whether Adam and Eve talked to each other in Hebrew!

Preaching in the Anglican churches in Amsterdam and The Hague, I noticed once again how many of the communicants were Dutch people who had been confirmed as converts in spite of small encouragement by the Anglican authorities. The policy of the Anglican episcopate about conversion of Roman Catholics to Anglicanism seems to me quite unrealistic. Reluctance to "set up altar against altar" might make sense if there was any real prospect of reunion with Rome; but, as things are, the needs of many good Christians who worship God in the Catholic manner but totally reject Papalism are not met. I would say to the bishops: Give up the fatuous idea that union with Rome is possible, unless the Papacy disappears, and invite all who want to join us in fellowship and worship to enter. Why not in Holland have regular services in Dutch as well as English?

The subject on which I learned most from this lecture tour was not theology, but English literature. Rashly enough, I had set down Modern English Poetry as one of my themes. I aimed in the lecture to give some idea of the poetry being written in England in the 1950s by commenting on and reading from two poets whom I knew personally but not intimately. The two poets were Walter de la Mare and T. S. Eliot and, since it was near the beginning of Lent, I chose a long passage from *Ash Wednesday* and from de la Mare two of his lyrics including *Fare Well* and *The Listeners*. My expectation was that de la Mare would be an instant success with my Dutch audience, while Eliot would be difficult to put across. I was quite wrong. De la Mare's rhythms did not enchant my hearers and I doubt if they were "tuned in" to his imagination. When I read Eliot's *Ash Wednesday*, I was aware that I had a different problem, because I had never found him easy to understand myself. I read very slowly and was all the time consciously trying to convey something of the poet's meaning, almost as if I were speaking to a group which was a little hard of hearing and not very intelligent. I could feel from the first line that the hearers were responding, but what astonished me most was that I was caught up myself by the poem as never before. Its meaning, which had not been clear to me before, seemed obvious and really, for the first time, the verse was fascinating and beautiful. I learned that one ought to read modern poetry very slowly and out loud before rejecting it. Even then quite a lot of it will probably still fail to move us and in that case we had better put it aside as uncongenial to us, or to our mood at the moment. I have a grandson now who writes very modern poetry and I have resolved to express no opinion on any of his poems until he has read it through three times in a loud voice and very slowly and distinctly. Unfortunately one cannot apply this test to poets outside the family circle or to those who are dead. There are some lines in *Paradise Lost*, for example, which are difficult to scan, but no doubt Milton's reading of them would reconcile us to them.

My happy and peaceful tour was far from idle. I lectured in all the principal cities and towns of Holland. I visited the churches, large and bare inside, which are the masterpieces of brick Gothic. I saw all the pictures which I could not see in 1940. I met many learned and charming persons and before I left I dined with a distinguished fellow Bencher of Gray's Inn, Sir Arnold McNair, the President of the International Court at The Hague where he resided in solitary state, as it appeared, to avoid all possible suspicion of being "got at". I was back in London a few days before the memorial service in St. Paul's for my predecessor, Dr. Inge, which was attended by the Lord Mayor and many eminent citizens. My address at the service caused me some anxiety, because I felt Inge himself would have wished nothing but the truth to be said. I quote the more important passage which I can now repeat with complete sincerity:

I do not know whether he should be called a prophet, but he had at least one quality of the prophet—he never prophesied smooth things. He did not gain the public ear by repeating soothing platitudes or by offering superfluous support to popular causes. He was a severe critic of democracy; he thought the belief in inevitable progress a superstition. Nor did he spare the religious beliefs of his fellow-countrymen

Return of St. Paul's choristers from their tour of the United States

Dedication service and laying the foundation stone of the new building of my publishers, Hodder & Stoughton

With H.M. Queen Elizabeth at the dedication of the Chapel of the Order of the British Empire in St. Paul's

and fellow-churchmen. He called us to the painful task of examining our presuppositions. The reason why so many attended to what he said, even when they disagreed, was that they recognised the force of his intelligence and his candour. . . . I do not suppose that anyone, even among his most fervent admirers, agreed with all his views, and some who loved him had their moments of exasperation when he seemed unduly provocative, but he did us all the greatest service when he made us think out the presuppositions of our beliefs. Dr. Inge was a true philosopher—a lover of wisdom. His life was devoted to the search for truth and reality, to the great problems which concern us all—God and the human soul, the meaning of human life and human destiny. He did not claim that he had found the final answer to these eternal questions. He did not seek to found a school of thought or set up a party of disciples. His aim was to help others to find their way in the perplexities of our age.

To those who did not know him, he may have appeared an austere and aloof person wrapped in abstruse contemplation, but those who had the privilege of personal contact with him knew a different man. He had a delightful wit and deep affection for his family and his friends. He would take much trouble to help those who were in distress of mind and, as I have good reason to know, he was generous with encouragement to younger men who were trying in their feebler way to follow the path of religious philosophy which he trod so confidently.

On Low Sunday, April 28th in this restless year, I flew to Germany to visit Berlin in a vaguely official capacity. Ernst Reuther, the Mayor of West Berlin, invited me to be the guest of the municipality for a few days after Easter and I was told that my name had been privately suggested, by the British Government to Berlin, as someone who might be worth entertaining in order that he could have first-hand knowledge of the situation. It was a pleasant situation for me, because I could easily convince myself that it was my duty to undertake this service to international understanding and I was full of curiosity to see again the Teutonic cities and the life on the border of the land behind the Iron Curtain. One brief stay on my journey out I contrived in Hanover, which I still vividly remembered as reduced to rubble in 1945 and where dwelt the Lutheran Bishop Lilje, who seemed to me the wisest of the leaders of German religion. He had been imprisoned by the Nazis and chained in his prison cell in Berlin during the bombardment of Berlin from air and land. He had visited us in London soon after the end of the war and attended the Cathedral service as a member of the congregation—the time had not yet come when it was safe to ask any eminent German divine, however little he had supported Hitler, to preach in London's Cathedral. This short stay in Hanover was symbolic of the change which had brought optimism back as a plausible attitude to the future. The Bishop's cheerful hospitality and his involvement in the ecumenical movement were in sharp contrast to the hard times of 1945 and a material symbol of the new spirit was the rebuilt city and, at its centre, the restored Markt Kirche which, I was reminded, was taken in hand by the restorers before the factories. When I was persuaded to write an account of "Germany Revisited" for *The Church of England Newspaper*, I felt bound to put this wonderful recovery in the first place chiefly because it was the best reply to the many "good haters" in Britain who could still carry on the war mentality which was so hard to throw away and so dangerous to preserve, and also because one could not help contrasting the organised diligence and endeavour of the Germans with the slackness and disunion in England.

There was no wall then dividing the western section of Berlin from the Soviet territory; like the equator, the dividing line was imaginary, but very effective. The courteous guide, who showed me the city and explained the wonderful progress which it had made in great difficulties, had to hand me over to an English guide provided by the C.O. of the British Army when I crossed the invisible line. The employee of the German municipality was forbidden to enter the Russian sector for fear that he might be kidnapped. The eastern part of Berlin then consisted of one magnificent street and a lot of dilapidated and untidy lanes, plus one staggering monument. There was one similarity with the pre-war Germany which I had known—the personality cult. Formerly the gigantic propaganda posters called for gratitude to Hitler for all the alleged boons which the people enjoyed—now the name was changed to Stalin. The people in the streets looked tired and depressed compared with those in West Berlin who on the whole were astonishingly cheerful. I remember noting that Nazis and Communists seemed to have the same taste in architecture—they liked the emphatic, rather ponderous, inflated style and I wondered whether totalitarian states all tended to admire this. Could the Roman Empire be said to show the same characteristics in its buildings? Of one thing the tour of the Russian part of Berlin convinced me: the Russians intended never to leave it.

The memory of the air lift to supply the blockaded city of Berlin was fresh in our minds and I met several men who had taken part in it. We had been far nearer to war than most of us had suspected. An accident or a loss of temper or a momentary impatience might have precipitated world war III and, at the date of my visit, the situation seemed so fantastic that one felt the whole set-up might collapse any day. When I was there the weekly influx of refugees from the Communist area fluctuated between 2,000 and 3,000 a week, the numbers depending on the activity of the Communist police. Most of the refugees came by Underground or on foot, having left almost all their possessions behind. Of those I talked to, some physicians and surgeons left the deepest impression on my memory, because they revolted against the attempt of the Communist tyrants to compel them to make false statements on public health. The Berlin municipality made really heroic efforts to deal with the influx. I spent a day at the reception centre and followed the routine through which refugees had to pass; first the security officers had to sift out the spies who came in refugee disguise, (no easy task), then a medical inspection, after which came the problem of how to dispose of the persons admitted. This was really impossible. West Berlin was surrounded by Soviet-controlled territory and to transport refugees by train or road would be equivalent to handing them back to the tyrants from whom they had fled. The only way was by air and the resources there were so limited that refugee camps in Berlin were building up dangerously. The problem was not solved but removed by the building of the wall ostensibly to keep enemies of East Germany out, but really to keep the East Germans in the prison that Stalin built.

It was no surprise to find that the churches were foremost in the refugee work. Both the Roman Catholics and the Lutherans were alert to welcome fellow Christians in the name of the Lord and to see that the strangers were incorporated in the worshipping community. The Lutheran Church certainly atoned for some weakness in the Hitler period by its strength in the Stalin emergency. Dr. Dibelius, the Bishop of Berlin, was a fine and dauntless leader; through him I was able to meet some pastors from the Russian Zone and some theological students who were preparing themselves to work there. On my return to England, I wrote the following note of my impression:

One salient fact is that though Germany is divided the Church is not. There is not much active persecution in the Russian Zone. So long as the pastor keeps to his church and does not touch on politics, he can carry on without much difficulty. All organisations and particularly youth organisations are suppressed and the propagation of the gospel is prohibited. The attitude of the Communist government is that you may worship God if you are foolish enough to believe in Him, but you must not persuade others to do so. The younger generation was the prize for which the Communists were fighting the Church and its weapon was compulsory anti-religious education in all schools. When I asked how far this was effective, my informants agreed that it was less effective than might have been expected, largely because the children knew the teachers were compelled to give the lessons on pain of losing their jobs. Probably perfunctory anti-religious instruction is as ineffective as perfunctory religious instruction. The most significant memory of my visit to Berlin is a private meeting with the men who were training young pastors for work in the Russian Zone. In true German style the principal of the little college summed up the matter in two theological phrases. He said, "We realise that we are in an 'eschatological situation' and in a 'confessional situation'." In my English untheological way, I tried to get him to interpret these phrases in terms of conduct and practical policy and I think I know what he meant. They knew that in witnessing to Christ in a Communist and atheist dictatorship they had come to an end (an *eskaton*) in the sense that human foresight and strategy were of no avail and they were thrown back on God. The only policy was to do His will in proclaiming the gospel as the days passed, hoping that their obedience would have some good effect. And they were in a confessional situation because the primary duty of the Christian and perhaps the most costly was to make clear without any compromise or evasion that he stood for Christ and His Church.

In my notes written immediately after my visit, I moralised a little on the resemblance of the Christian situation in Communist East Germany to that of the primitive Christian Church in the pagan Roman Empire. Perhaps the resemblance is not quite so obvious today because some contemporary theologians have more or less abandoned the theistic creed of traditional faith and we hear not only of Christian agnostics but even of theologians who would not reject the idea of a Christian atheism and can adopt the cry "God is dead" as a part of their gospel. No doubt dialogue between Communists and Christians can have some useful purpose in clearing up misunderstandings, but on reflection I still hold that Marxism is essentially an atheistic creed and Christianity essentially theistic. "Synthesis of opposites" can be a cover for intellectual confusion and moral compromise.

A cause which had my support for many years was the challenge of anti-semitism and, arising out of that, the relations of Jews and Christians in this country. During my fourteen years as Dean of King's College, London, the problem did not trouble me much because there was practically no anti-semitic feeling. Jewish students were not numerous and such members of the staff as were known to be Jews were distinguished and well liked. I have cheerful and happy memories of Israel Gollancz, the Professor of English Literature, whose flamboyant personality enlivened the College and did not conceal the fact that he loved the English language. His edition of the poem *Pearl* which he gave me recalls him as he was in the full tide of life. G. K. Chesterton and Hilaire Belloc were writers high on my list of contemporary authors, but the anti-semitic tone of some of their writings did not attract me, though I sympathised with their radical non-socialist politics. It seemed to me that the rich people whom they attacked were far from being all Jewish.

When I became a member of the London Society for the Study of Religion, I met Jewish scholars and heard them contribute to our discussions; above all I came to know Claude Montefiore, one of the salt of the earth. Like most other English people, I was slow to grasp the enormity of the persecution of Jews in Germany, though I was not altogether deceived. The experience which my wife and I had in a Bavarian hotel was significant. Matthews in English is very like Matheus in German and, though no one molested us and the chambermaid sympathised with us, we could not help feeling that we were not liked and not welcome because we were thought to be Jews. After a day or two of discomfort, we went to Austria where the atmosphere was less oppressive.

On the brink of war I became involved in attempts to get individual Jews out of Germany: among those who were rescued were two old ladies with whom my daughter stayed in Darmstadt when learning German. Another Jew who came out was an eminent psychologist from Vienna, Dr. Oswald Schwarz, Privatdozent in the university, to whom I was able to give some slight help in acquiring British nationality just in time. Dr. Schwarz was able to throw some light on a problem which troubled me not a little. Growing suspicions about the German menace led to belated movements to oppose anti-semitism. William Temple was deeply concerned and I became associated with a scheme to start a powerful Anglo-Jewish society. This began in a very small way, because the imminence of war distracted attention. The movement, however, arranged to start with a semi-public lunch at which known sympathisers would be invited to speak. I was to make an opening speech, stressing the need for some society of Christians and Jews. To prepare for this I collected as many expressions of opinion as I could personally. The result of this astounded me. I asked a perfectly fortuitous collection of persons: people I met in trains, barbers, tradesmen, in short anyone I happened to meet who did not look like a Jew. How many opinions I collected, I cannot remember; but the salient fact was that out of between twenty-five and thirty-five separate opinions, not one was in favour of the Jews and three or four, so far from being shocked by Hitler's anti-semitic acts, were heartily in favour of them.

More light on the problem, however, came from Dr. Schwarz. He practised medicine in England and kindly replied to my question whether his experience of taking up work in a new environment might help us to understand anti-semitism. He said that he had been surprised at the difficulty of adjusting himself; he confessed indeed that he had carried through the most arduous psychological adaptation of himself that he had ever undertaken. "I had so many advantages," he said, "I speak English fluently; I have read a lot of English literature; I have known many English people; as a physician I speak much the same language as English physicians and have much the same standards as they, but I was conscious that I could not integrate myself into British ways of life and the British medical profession without a determined and well thought out conscious effort." He went on to point the moral by comparing his task of self-adaptation with that which faced Jewish immigrants from Poland or Russia—or from any ghetto. They did not know that there was a problem and, if it could have been explained to them, they would not wish to be "integrated". In his opinion, three generations under favourable conditions were the minimum required. All this appears to be relevant to the racial problems which threaten the peace of Britain today. Unfortunately we are not likely to have three generations to solve them in.

Of all the good causes which I had some part in, I am inclined to think that the counter-blast to anti-semitism in Britain has been one of the most successful. The Council of Christians and Jews is now a highly respected institution under the patronage of the leaders of the Churches: the Archbishop of Canterbury, the Cardinal Archbishop of Westminster, the Moderator of the Church of Scotland and the Chief Rabbi. It was not easy to persuade all these eminent persons to co-operate and when they had begun it was not always easy to keep them together. Both the Roman Catholics and the Orthodox Jews had qualms about the possible effects of intercourse with heretics on the faithful. Now, however, those fears are at rest and the Council stands for tolerance and understanding between Jews and Christians, a positive ideal beyond the negative one of resisting persecution. This has been achieved because some highly intelligent persons, both Jews and Christians, have put in some good thinking on the problems of co-existence and have worked hard at the job of putting principles into practice. W. W. Simpson, the Methodist minister well known in all denominations for his ecumenical work, is an outstanding member of the band of Jewish and Christian workers who made the Council of Christians and Jews. As I grew older, my interest in this field became concentrated on the attempts on both sides to promote understanding of our religions, of their agreements and their differences.

The London Society of Jews and Christians, affiliated to the Council of Christians and Jews, was founded to pursue mutual understanding and one of my most cherished titles was President of the London Society. In this capacity I met many European Jewish scholars, but only one shall be mentioned here— Rabbi Leo Baeck, the heroic Rabbi of Berlin who lived his last years, worn out by privations, in England. Two "reformed" rabbis were among my friends, Rabbi Mattuck, and his successor, Rabbi Edgar. I could claim to have had some small part in Edgar's education, because he was for a term or two a member of a seminar on the Philosophy of Religion, which I presided over in King's College, London. There is no lack of learning among the members of the London Society of Jews and Christians, but unfortunately very few orthodox Jews join it and, I think, no orthodox rabbis.

In September 1953 I had the good fortune to engage Miss Ann Edmonds as my secretary. I almost lost her because she had been ill, as a result of overwork in the Foreign Office, and would not be allowed by the doctor to do a full day's work. She looked delicate and I almost decided that I could not take the risk. On this occasion I prayed about my choice before I went to bed and woke up the next morning to find that my mind was made up and I was certain that I should make an effort to get her to come. I was suddenly afraid that I had lost an opportunity by my hesitation. That calamity did not happen and for the rest of my time at St. Paul's I had her loyal and expert help—she was a true friend. Her health rapidly improved and I now thank her for assisting in the compilation of these reminiscences. Any coherence that they may have is largely due to her.

In my domestic annals, the years 1947 to 1963 can be described as the *au pair* girl period. We continued to live in a corner of our forty-roomed deanery with the aid of two charladies and a long succession of Swiss, German or French young women who came to learn English. On the whole we were most fortunate. We aimed at treating the girl as a daughter of the house and felt responsible for her study of English. The Swiss girls mostly came from the city of Burgdorf and that part of the country, so that we sometimes had one girl suggesting as her successor a girl from the same school. My impression of Swiss education is that the schools are very efficient and the teaching of languages incomparably superior to anything we have in English schools of the same grade. All the girls who came to us from Switzerland had three languages and some had four: Swiss-German, High German, French and English; some also knew Italian up to a simple conversational standard. Some of them were in a way temporary daughters to us and both Margaret and I enjoyed teaching them. Towards the end of the *au pair* era, I read *Macbeth* and some other English poetry with a clever German girl and certainly educated myself by trying to answer her questions. I am not without hope too that I contributed a little to her education. I think I must be the only employer of *au pair* girls who included composition of English verse in his instruction. My theory is that rhythm and rhyme stay in the memory and I used to start by teaching my pupils to say and chant English nursery rhymes. From that, I went on to translating songs of Heine and Goethe into English prose. But why not English verse? That too we tried, but only one of our efforts survived and perhaps the reader may think it a pity that it should. We translated Heine's well known poem *Wo?*, one of his melodious complaints about his exile. I suppose every schoolgirl has done it, it is so simple in sense and rhythm that it almost translates itself.

Where?
translated from the German of Heine*

In the end, O wandering spirit,
　　What last resting place is thine?
Under palms in southern regions,
　　Under lime trees by the Rhine?

Shall I lie in some void desert,
　　Buried by a stranger's hand?
Shall I lie on some far sea coast
　　Covered by the drifting sand?

Here or there alike, encompassed
　　By God's heaven I shall be,
And, as death lamps for my burial,
　　Stars will glimmer over me.

* Christmas 1962.

I have wondered whether the influence of St. Paul's on our *au pair* guests was wholly good. Nearly all were fascinated by the building and the music. When they had overcome their suspicion that we were really Roman Catholics, they worshipped in the Cathedral with understanding and were sorry to leave it when their year ended. I could discern little affection for the worship of the Swiss Evangelical Church. One girl who wept at departing said, "I loved St. Paul's; I don't suppose I shall ever go to church again." As she was catching the boat train, I never replied and to this day I do not know how to reply.

Towards the end of this period, an incident occurred which struck everyone who heard of it as funny; to me it was also significant. I was in a bus passing St. Paul's and moving towards Liverpool Street station. I sat next to an elderly countrified-looking man. "Ah," he said, "there's St. Paul's. What's happened to old Inge (pronounced to rhyme with 'hinge')?"

"I'm afraid he's dead," I answered.

"Poor old Inge," he said, "used to write some spicy articles in *The Evening Standard*: every Thursday, I think. Who's there now?"

"A man named Matthews, I think," I replied.

"Ah, don't hear much about him, do we?" he said.

"No," I answered. "Rather a dim type if you ask me." This remarkable and enigmatic person got out at the next stop, leaving me to my reflections. They were humiliating: Here have I been Dean of St. Paul's for nearly thirty years, writing and speaking all the time, and there are intelligent people who are under the impression that Dr. Inge had no successor.

CHAPTER 19

The Curtain Falls

Very early in the morning of October 11th, 1963, my wife Margaret died in St. Bartholomew's Hospital, London. In this chapter I shall be writing about the final years of my tenure of the office of Dean of St. Paul's and shall mention events which preceded her death in time, but in my recollection the year 1962 is part of the overshadowed period. When death came it was, in one meaning of the word "sudden", but we had both faced the fact that we were in the end time of our lives. Depressing circumstances in 1963 reduced our vitality. A short holiday in Swiss mountains had so often given us new energy that we were bitterly disappointed when our stay in Engelberg was spoiled by unending rain and mist with the consequence that Margaret hardly left the hotel at all. Our granddaughters Gillian and Anthea Hebb provided nearly all the sunshine we had and I hope they were not too bored by our efforts to amuse ourselves by instructing them. Margaret, I think, told them tales of the time when her mother was a child and I improved my Latin, and possibly theirs, by reading with them the Latin version of *Winnie the Pooh*. We returned from that holiday to difficulties in running the vast deanery, but in the autumn I took Margaret to Droitwich for three weeks' treatment in the famous baths; I too tried them. That autumn was golden and I am thankful now that we had those weeks alone together, for in the hotel garden and under the October sun we were perhaps closer together in mind than ever before. We thanked God for our children: one, the most ambitious of the three, killed on H.M.S. *Greyhound* at Dunkirk and the other two, after serving in the war, established in life with children of their own. It distressed me that Margaret in these exchanges of ideas reproached herself for not being the right kind of wife for me. If by that she meant she was not like the typical clerical wife, she was right, but she was the right wife for me. Though I have done quite a lot of work in my time, I am by nature lazy and begin to function effectively only when challenged and criticised. To have had a "yes woman" as my wife would have been exceedingly bad for me. Margaret was an acute critic on two levels. She knew good writing when she read it and good preaching when she heard it and was never sparing in her criticism from the literary angle. She was no less excellent as a judge of thinking. I am afraid it has to be admitted that she never really moved far from the position with regard to the Christian faith which she held when we were married. She was precisely what was meant by the words "reverent agnostic". She never laughed at or ridiculed sincere belief and had no sympathy with militant atheism. That she truly worshipped God and was a person of real integrity there could be no doubt. She had far more influence on our children when they were very young than I and the qualities of truth seeking and truth speaking, together with a sense of social responsibility which I note so thankfully in them and their children, are due largely to her. The question which I ask myself is whether I was the right husband for her. A real man of prayer would have shown her the way to develop the mystical longings which she had. To "pray without ceasing" has always been a difficulty and a problem to me and it lies heavily on my conscience that I was in this respect the blind leading the blind. Now, as I see her life and mine in the perspective of some years' elapse, I feel that her great talent for writing ought to have been evident to me much earlier than it was and that she could have done more and better work in literature if I had been more alert to the importance of her writing and less absorbed in my own.

Margaret had an alarming heart attack at night on, I think, October 8-9th. She was hurried to hospital by ambulance and emergency treatment given. The events of that night are not clear in my mind, but I know that after what seemed hours of anxious waiting I was told that she was through the attack and asleep. I staggered home and slept. She was almost her old self on the next day and I was told that probably I would be able to take her back to the deanery on the morrow. That night I went to bed looking forward to our reunion. As I was shaving the next morning and thinking of her, Bishop Wand came and very quietly and gently told me she was dead. I shall always be grateful to him for his loving understanding and to the matron at the hospital who had the kind thought to enlist his help. What happened then in my mind and spirit I cannot tell. I felt confused and at the end of my life. The Bishop must have had an intuitive understanding of my state, for the one thing I remember that he said to me was an earnest word of advice to make no decisions or plans for some time—to wait until the shock had passed and I could see more clearly what I ought to do. My impulse was to go out of my office as Dean and leave the house which was full of memories for me—to give up my hope that I might see the conclusion of the restoration and reconstruction of St. Paul's. In the days of reflection which followed, I came to the conclusion that there was no reason why the Choir School should not be built in a year or two and my departure before that happened would certainly not expedite the completion and might delay it. Reflection on Margaret's death brought consolation, because her departure was after the manner she would have chosen. The nursing sister who was with her when she died had been talking to her and she made a cheerful and joking reply, then quite suddenly she sat up in bed and died apparently without pain. She had dreaded disabling old age.

One question had to be answered at once—the location of funeral and burial. I had hoped that I might be thought worthy of some memorial in St. Paul's and, though my body could not be buried in the Cathedral, my ashes might rest there. I was determined, however, that Margaret and I should be side by side. A considerate Chapter, in my absence, resolved that, when the time came, our ashes should be kept in the Cathedral under one stone. To hope that our ashes might rest in St. Paul's was not presumptuous, perhaps the reader will agree, when he remembers that our years at St. Paul's were not only exceptionally numerous, but also the most dangerous and troubled in modern times.

Margaret's funeral was sad but beautiful. Her body was brought into the crypt chapel after evensong on the day before. Somehow I felt quite unable to conduct any service or give any address to my family that evening. I wanted to be silent and so, I think, did they. So the family alone that night sat or knelt round her coffin for an hour. That fellowship of silence was to me, and I think to my family, a spiritual experience which we

shall never forget. Michael, our eldest son who had preceded
her into the next world seemed to me to be present with us in
the silence. The funeral service at noon on October 16th, 1963,
was attended by all the members of the Chapter and the Bishop
of London with the suffragan bishops. The service at the crema-
torium was taken by my friend, Canon John Collins. I have a
confused memory of these rites, but it is a beautiful and consol-
ing memory. Margaret would be glad that the Cathedral choir
and specially the singing boys, the "Children of Pawles", took
part in her funeral.

After a few days in my lonely deanery, during which I tried
to deal with the letters of sympathy from so many friends, I
escaped from London and went to Exeter to stay with Dean
Marcus Knight and his wife, who were now occupying the
wonderful deanery which we had left to go to St. Paul's. We
had been so happy there and our friends were so kind that I
gained some peace of mind and courage. Not all the memories
were cheerful, for I could not forget how bitterly Margaret
had regretted leaving Exeter and I was still not certain that
I had done well to leave it; but my judgment was still that I
could not have refused to face the challenge of opportunity.
After a week of peace during which I haunted the Cathedral,
meditated and prayed in it and talked to some more or less
chance acquaintances, I returned to London just in time to do
my duty as Dean of the Order of the British Empire, of which
the Duke of Edinburgh was installed as Grand Master, but of
that I have little to record, except that I almost tripped over
my robes when descending the steps into the crypt in order to
perform part of the ceremonies in the chapel of the Order. I need
not add that I was proud to be Dean of the Order and regard
the establishment of its chapel and spiritual centre in St.
Paul's as one of the happiest events of my period in office.

Two events in 1962 were important enough to come through
with clarity in my clouded recollection—the consecration of
Coventry Cathedral and the re-dedication of the restored north
transept of St. Paul's. Though it was no business of mine, I
had my own views on Coventry. At first, I was opposed to the
erection of a new cathedral. As everyone knows, alongside Coventry Cathedral stood another spacious and majestic mediaeval
building—the parish church—and I thought it could well have
been adapted as the Cathedral, the war damage grant being

devoted to more urgent repairs. That opinion did not prevail and I could understand the motives, religious and patriotic, which led to a determination to rebuild. Another debatable question arose when the plan which had been outlined by Giles Scott (the architect of the great Cathedral in Liverpool) was rejected and Sir Basil Spence was commissioned to design the church. Sir Basil told me that, when he knew he would be the architect of a new cathedral, he went into St. Paul's and remained there for more than an hour meditating. His impulse was natural and laudable from the merely human point of view, and from the artistic point of view it showed his comprehension of the nature of the task. Christopher Wren had been an innovator: he built a new kind of church: he set the pattern for a new architectural epoch. Basil Spence would not say that he was revolting against Wren and his tradition; rather that he was carrying forward and adapting it to contemporary conditions. I looked forward to the hallowing of the new Cathedral.

My hopes were frustrated by a set of trivial accidents which in retrospect are humorous, but in fact were agitating and humiliating. The deans of all the English and Welsh cathedrals were invited guests and had the singular honour of processing through Coventry to the Cathedral, dressed in academic gowns and hoods over their cassocks. I set out happily walking with my friend the Dean of Liverpool. He shattered my peace of mind by asking, "Have you brought your envelope?" His words revealed the dreadful truth to me. I had clean forgotten that the Coventry brethren had sent to every dean an envelope in which to convey his offering and that of his chapter and present it ceremoniously in the service. I had no envelope and, what was worse, no offering at all, for I found that I was so swathed in doctor's robes that I could not get a sixpence out of my pocket. My dismay was increased when I found that the offerings were to be placed by the deans one by one in a vast silver dish. There was little chance of passing the alms dish unobserved. The public disgrace was averted by events which at the time seemed to me almost providential (though I would not defend the proposition that they were). Just as the silver dish was about to be put before me, someone dropped another silver dish at the feet of the Queen with a startling clang, notes and coins strewed the floor and, to crown the distraction, almost simultaneously, the Lord

Mayor of Coventry fainted and I think was carried out. I had the frivolous thought that the distractions, welcome as they were to me in my predicament, were slightly overdone.

I joked about this incident, but it really was disturbing. Was my grip on things weakening or was my mind so full of anxieties that I was inefficient? I was sad too because I had formed no opinion on the new Cathedral. On the whole I felt that I would be unsettled if I worshipped in it regularly. I am glad that I avoided any serious criticism when I knew so little about the subject, for some time later, when I had left St. Paul's, I changed my mind about Coventry. I was preaching in the Cathedral on Whitsunday, a day of spring sunshine. In the morning there was a large confirmation of boys and girls, after which came the First Communion, celebrated by the Bishop. The Cathedral revealed its character to me then. It is perfectly adapted to use as a place of community worship. It is a place where a crowd easily becomes a fellowship. In the evening I opened a discussion in the crypt, which is a favourable environment for dialogue. This is not a dissertation on the Cathedral; it is an expression of my feeling of happiness that it exists and that Basil Spence has given a masterpiece to God. Having said that, I will add a personal complaint which is probably due to my own matter-of-fact philistinism. I wish there was not so much symbolism! It worries me to think that whatever I look at in the building is symbolical of something.

Perhaps this is the place to record an opinion on modern cathedrals. I do not accept the view that the Middle Ages were the time when cathedrals were at their supreme point. As former Dean of what I consider to be the greatest modern Cathedral, St. Paul's, I maintain that in their different styles the modern cathedrals in England are worthy to stand beside the work of the mediaeval builders: Truro, Liverpool, Coventry, Guildford are witnesses among us to the beauty of holiness.

On June 11th, 1962, the north transept of St. Paul's which had been devastated in the blitz, was re-dedicated by the Bishop of London. The bishops suffragan and the prebendaries were present in full force: I preached a sermon and we entertained the bishops and prebendaries to lunch in the Chapter House. This ought to have been an occasion of great joy and thankfulness, for we had known anxious moments when the first bomb fell and fourteen years of careful planning and build-

Handing over the key of the new Choir School to the Lord Mayor of London, Sir Robert Bellinger

Relaxing on the Tillingham Estate (dating from A.D. 604) with Canon Hood, Mr. E. Floyd Ewin, Registrar, Mr. Fuller, Librarian, together with tenant farmers and estate agents

Returning to the Deanery for the last time as Dean

ing when the delicate operation of pushing back the walls into their proper alignment, the restoration of the roof and simultaneously the unfailing support of the dome was proceeding; but in fact the service was decorous rather than ecstatic and only a handful of people constituted the congregation. The war in those fourteen years had become history and no one wanted to be reminded of the evil days. Perhaps it was on June 11th, 1962, that I first understood I belonged to a previous generation and was in danger of becoming a more or less interesting survival from the past.

I have refrained from burdening the reader with lists of my lectures, sermons, reviews and pamphlets, but I must at least mention the fact that my pen was rarely still and my voice rarely silent and some of these utterances had a certain influence on public opinion. As my time became shorter, the stream of exhortation and argument seemed to grow in volume. I will not contest the judgment that if I had said less and thought more I should have served the cause of religion better; but I do not repent that I supported wrong causes. I make no retractions. The year 1959-60 may be a specimen. In 1959 I was "select preacher" in the University of Cambridge. A sermon on the relations between the Church of England and the Church of Scotland was reported in *The Expository Times*. The 250th anniversary of the birth of Dr. Samuel Johnson was celebrated by a service in the Cathedral at Lichfield, his birthplace, and, as President of the Johnson Society of London, I found myself unable to avoid preaching on the occasion. The same year I discoursed at the 40th anniversary of the Save the Children Fund and, shortly after, at the St. Cecilia's festival in St. Sepulchre's. A week or two later, I talked at large to Friends of St. Paul's on twenty-five years at the Cathedral. In that year I seem to have reviewed an incredible number of books.

At Gray's Inn, the fourth centenary of the birth of Francis Bacon was commemorated by a dinner on February 17th, 1961, in which members of the Bacon Society were associated with the benchers of the Inn. Gray's Inn could boast of only two Lord Chancellors, but they were illustrious—Francis Bacon and Lord Birkenhead (F. E. Smith). When I had been preacher at Gray's Inn the question which of the two shed the greater lustre on the Inn was debated; but it was not raised at the dinner, perhaps because of the presence of the Baconians. I was asked to be one of the speakers at the dinner and was really delighted to have the opportunity to work off, in slightly disguised form, an old lecture on Bacon's scientific method, which I had in stock from the days when I taught philosophy. Unfortunately the Baconians at the dinner turned out to be mostly believers in the theory that Bacon wrote the works of Shakespeare and were naturally not interested in logic. The one really first-rate speech on that occasion was made by a French professor, in English.

Even more alarming was the celebration of the Tercentenary of the Royal Society of London, which included a service in St. Paul's (or rather the attendance of Fellows of the Royal Society at the Cathedral morning service) on Sunday, July 24th, 1960. The historical association of St. Paul's with the Royal Society through Christopher Wren was a tempting subject to enlarge upon, but I had sense enough to see that my brief opportunity of saying something which would possibly be relevant to scientific work was to try to speak to the need of intellectuals who were afraid of religious experience. Who can tell whether words spoken and remembered have lasting effect? I was at least encouraged by observing that the congregation stayed awake and by receiving interesting letters from some Fellows. In the records of the Royal Society of London, my sermon will be handed down to posterity and I wonder how it will appear to anyone who is invited to preach a hundred years hence and, indeed, whether I shall have a successor then. Relevant to this reflection is a consideration which interested some of my hearers. I said:

> It is certain that all the scientific textbooks now current will be out of date and unread long before the next centenary; it is equally certain that the first chapter of St. John's Gospel and the first chapter of Genesis will still be read. If we could answer the question, Why? we would have a clue to the difference between science and religion.

The resignation of Dr. Geoffrey Fisher from the Archbishopric of Canterbury took me quite by surprise in 1961 and I saw no sign that he was losing grip. His qualities of toughness and resilience seemed to me unimpaired and, in my opinion, his leadership on the whole was a great asset to Church and nation.

On May 2nd, owing, I suppose, to my seniority in age, I was asked to speak briefly in his praise at a meeting of Convocation. My speech, which is on record in the *Chronicle of Convocation*, was a sincere statement of my feelings, but I would stress now, more than I did in the speech, his human sympathy and his ability to get on with all kinds of human beings. I had many opportunities of hearing him speak after dinner in the City, just as I had previously heard his predecessor, Cosmo Gordon Lang. They were both first-rate, but in different ways. Lang had the kind of eloquence which Asquith displayed—the easy flow of well-turned sentences and the graceful comments on affairs passing easily from grave to gay. Fisher was more collo-quial and spontaneous and less orderly in the presentation of ideas. One never forgot for a moment when listening to Lang that he was Archbishop and a great prelate; that could not be said of Fisher. Which style is to be preferred is a matter of opinion and I claim no infallibility when I record my own preference for the Asquith type of oratory—at any rate for archbishops.

As I have already said, my chief criticism of the policy of the Archbishop since 1945 is that, under his guidance, the Con-vocations concentrated on the revision of Canon Law, when the most urgent need was to reconsider and reform the official teaching of the Church of England as set forth in the Thirty-nine Articles of Religion. A lecture on them at Sion College was considerably enlarged and published as a pamphlet by Hodder and Stoughton. I gave some pains to the composition and I think it is probably the best piece of prose which I ever wrote, but being argumentative and controversial it is not the most attractive. The aim of the lecture and the pamphlet was to force the intelligent churchman to understand what the Articles really mean when they are put together and to ask him, "Do you believe this, and can you reconcile it with the faith that God is love?" The ethics of subscription have been freely debated and some explanations have been put forth of the limits of the obligation implied by assent to the Articles; recently partly inspired by my pamphlet, further modifications of the authority of the Articles have been suggested but the Articles retain their place in the Prayer Book and incumbents are still re-quired to read them publicly and assent to them. In my opinion the problem of subscription to the Articles will not be solved so long as the Church is "by law established".

On November 21st, 1962, one of the most happy and at the same time embarrassing events in my life took place at the St. Ermin's Hotel, Westminster, where my friends gave me a dinner. I think they had just discovered that I was over eighty and the idea of celebrating my age was advanced by my young friend Ralph Stevens, who was active in promoting meetings of liberal-minded clerics. The new Archbishop of Canterbury, Dr. Ramsey most generously presided and his wife attended with him. What I am most thankful about when I recall that evening is that my wife was there and able to follow the speeches. I think it was the last public dinner that we went to. My daughter and her husband Martin Hebb and my son and his wife Margaret were present; also my sister, my brother and sister-in-law, together with a surprising number of friends. A list of others who were not able to be present but wished me well by letter and telegram caused me to wonder and be glad.

The Archbishop began with a shattering statement, "We have met to honour a great man" and elaborated the text so generously that I did not recognise myself. I have sometimes suspected that I was rather clever in some respects, though stupid in others, and I have, I think, a certain obstinacy beneath a gentle and conciliatory manner which sometimes surprises people who are misled into the belief that I am easily over-ridden when principles are involved; but the epithet "great" is not for me. To listen to speeches about oneself is an ordeal even when the speakers are kind friends and there were moments when I felt that nothing but a public confession of sins and failures on the lines of Moral Rearmament could get the record straight. Victor Gollancz proposed my health in a characteristic speech which did not make me blush, because he told a Hebrew story which he alleged was a kind of parable relevant to my career, but I was baffled by its subtlety and, though some guests appeared to see the point, no one explained it to me. He liked to speak in dark sayings. At the end of his life he called himself sometimes a "non-practising Jewish Christian" and at other times a "non-practising Christian Jew". He never told me the difference, if any, between the two doctrines, nor did he elucidate his parable. On November 24th, 1966, I saw him for the last time, when he was grievously stricken and at the point of death. The seconder of the toast, if that expression is allowed, was Mollie Sharp, whom I had known when she was a school-girl and lived in the vicarage of Crouch End; she had now become a distinguished headmistress. Her father had played a part in my life for which I am still grateful after many years.

My own speech was rambling, I fear. Somehow I was impelled to dwell on my early years. I think I was trying to say "thank you" to the teachers who had helped me and I may have dwelt too long on my schoolmaster T. P. Nunn, afterwards Sir Percy Nunn, who I believe was one of the most salutary influences in my life which would have taken quite a different course if Providence had not brought us together. My friend H. D. Ziman, then literary editor of *The Daily Telegraph*, who was at the dinner, quoted the lines, "I fought with none, for none was worth my strife"; but his pun stood reality on its head. It would never have occurred to me as possible to contend with Percy Nunn.

One of my former pupils at King's College who talked with me on old times referred to my "wonderful health". The words in the '6os reminded me of the blessing which I had taken too much for granted. Apart from the malformation of my feet, which was not crippling, I had been seriously ill only once and had come through that apparently very well. The trouble in my throat had set me back just before the war and prevented me from saying that I was perfectly well. Old people generally show the advance of old age by falling down. I had always been unsteady and used to fall about without damage to myself. Two falls, however, now caused me to take more care. The first was really nothing to do with age. I fell down by slipping on black ice one Sunday afternoon on my way to evensong in the Cathedral. I had a hard fall on the edge of the pavement and broke my left arm. And then one Christmas Day I fell on the marble floor of the sanctuary after celebrating the Holy Communion. I almost knocked myself out, but soon recovered and preached at the 10.30 a.m. service. Hearers were kind enough to say that the sermon was no worse than usual. I was not seriously displeased when two minor canons slipped and fell in the same place and the Chapter took measures to make sure that the feet of the priests were not set in slippery places.

Of all the Cathedral events of these years, naturally the state funeral of Sir Winston Churchill on Saturday, January 30th, 1965, stands out in memory. I shall not attempt to describe the service, which was seen by millions on television and can be heard on two excellent records. I suppose that Churchill's funeral is the most completely recorded event in history. Here I shall try to record my own experience and thoughts.

The funeral had been in our thoughts for about eight years, from the day when it was known that the Queen had decided there should be a state funeral. When a state service is ordered, the responsibility for it does not rest entirely on the Dean and Chapter. The Earl Marshal, who is the Duke of Norfolk, has important duties and with him the College of Arms and the Heralds join in. All the preparations had to be made in private. Everyone will understand that it would be unsuitable to announce that the obsequies of a famous man were being planned in detail while he was still very much alive. With infinite tact Winston's wishes were ascertained, chiefly through the help I believe of Lady Churchill. Death does not wait on the convenience of mourners and, though some changes in the choice of hymns were made, almost from the day when we knew there would be a state funeral service, we could have carried it through with only two days' notice. A foolish detail comes to mind, the many persons who worked secretly to prepare the hero's funeral invented a word for it—"Operation Hope Not". I never discovered if the Duke of Norfolk knew of this title; I never heard him use it. My own feeling was one of hearty approval of a state funeral service in St. Paul's and of disappointment that the tomb of the great leader was not to be in the Cathedral; surely Winston Churchill's place was with Nelson and Wellington. He surpassed them both in that heroic quality, magnanimity.

The procession arrived at St. Paul's exactly according to schedule, setting the pattern of all the succeeding movements. The complicated arrangements through the whole day worked with amazing smoothness and, as it happened, I witnessed the one slight miscalculation which might have thrown the proceedings into confusion. I went into the pulpit while the procession was moving up the Cathedral and the choir were singing the opening sentences in the burial service. From that vantage I saw clearly the heavy labouring of the stalwart bearers of the coffin. I am sure that there was real danger of their collapse and I believe that the weight had actually been underestimated. I had some minutes before the bidding to prayer was to be said. I noticed with admiration and sympathy among the pall-bearers the bent figure of Earl Attlee, who must have suffered agony to mark his respect for his rival and companion in arms. When I turned my head to look across the dome, I saw a row of representatives of allied and friendly states; no doubt all distinguished, but only one impressive, Charles de Gaulle. Standing in a row of statesmen, he seemed to obliterate all but himself. Physically he towered above his fellows, but at that moment I felt what I had never felt before that he was a spiritual force—which does not mean necessarily a "good" force; perhaps the word "numinous" is applicable. Though incomparably more civilised and humane, as well as more intelligent, he was in this single respect in the same category as Hitler.

None of these thoughts was pursued in those minutes. I was impressed by the idea of the millions of people who in a moment would hear my voice. Millions would not only hear my voice but hear my words, because I had composed the "bidding" and it was the only part of the service written specially for this occasion. No sermon was offered to listeners to direct their thoughts. In two sentences I must, by God's help, strike a Christian note. I spent much thought on the words, but I asked no one's advice. The words are not perfect either in rhythm or sense, but I think they are Christian and not humanist, because they presuppose the need for mercy and forgiveness of sins, the hope of eternal life and the communion of saints.

A Bidding to Prayer

Brethren, we are assembled here, as representing the people of this land and of the British Commonwealth, to join in prayer on the occasion of the burial of a great man who has rendered memorable service to his country and to the cause of freedom. We shall think of him with thanksgiving that he was raised up in days of desperate need to be a leader and inspirer of the nation, for his dauntless resolution and untiring vigilance and for his example of courage and endurance. We shall commit his soul into the hands of God, the merciful Judge of all men and the giver of eternal life, praying that the memory of his virtues and his achievements may remain as a part of our national heritage, inspiring generations to come to emulate his magnanimity and patriotic devotion. And, since all men are subject to temptation and error, we pray that we, together with him, may be numbered among those whose sins are forgiven and have a place in the Kingdom of Heaven, to which may God by his grace bring us all.

The reading of this Bidding was followed by my saying, as the Book of Common Prayer directs:

> I heard a voice from heaven, saying unto me,
> Write, from henceforth blessed are the dead,
> which die in the Lord: Even so, saith the Spirit,
> for they rest from their labours.

I did not strictly follow the service paper, which planned for silence at the end of the Bidding, but carried on, feeling that the silence should be after the words "rest from their labours".

On the following day, Sunday, January 31st, at the evening service we had a Churchill Commemoration for all who were able to come. There was no publicity, but the Cathedral was full and, as I stood again in the pulpit to preach, I could see that the congregation was like those who came at the end of the war. An uncomfortable thought somewhat disturbed me. At the funeral I was, for a brief interval, presented with a vast unseen body of hearers and I duly spoke the words set down for me, careful words, quite sincere words, but coldly formal. If St. Paul had been in my place, would he have acted so? Would he not have given his message, his "gospel" to a listening world, regardless of protocol and decorum? The possibility of such an action had not come into my conscious mind until the opportunity had gone for ever.

In these years, my world seemed to be both expanding and contracting. The perils of the population explosion became ever clearer and the incapacity of politicians to meet them more obvious. Yet for me the world was emptying. One by one, the friends and companions of my youth and middle age stole away; not always through the gate of death. Some like my friend and colleague George Appleton, Archdeacon of London, took up work far away. He was consecrated Archbishop of Perth, Australia, in St. Paul's on June 24th, 1963. I could not question that he had a vocation to this important sphere but I and, I think, he grieved at the parting. Of those removed by death, one or two must be mentioned. On June 1st, 1966, I attended the memorial service for Alan Don, Dean of Westminster and for many years my opposite number. He had only recently retired and one hoped that he would leave a record of his experiences, which would have been both fascinating and instructive. Perhaps historians may edit his papers with profit. On August 30th, Mrs. Wand's funeral service was held in the Cathedral and on October 1st a memorial service which was attended by many of us who knew and loved her. On November 24th, I saw Victor Gollancz for the last time. Professor S. H. Hooke, my dear companion in many "short courses" and my inspired guide through the Bible was taken from us, "full of years and honours" and much beloved. Another learned layman was snatched away suddenly—Dudley Sommer, the author of a life of Lord Haldane and a friend for many years. How often I had cause to thank him for easing my life. For instance he paid all my taxi fares for some years, a thoughtful succour to an ageing Dean. I had the privilege of speaking about him at a commemorative service in the Savoy Chapel.

As the laying of the foundation stone indicated, the Choir School was beginning to rise from the ground. I was proud that my name was inscribed on it and that I was given the office of placing the stone ceremonially. Other historic occasions came over my horizon and had their interest, particularly the Commemoration of the signing of Magna Carta: the 750th anniversary was marked by a service on June 10th, 1965. The Lord Chancellor was the outstanding figure in these ceremonies and the Inns of Court showed their traditional hospitality to guests. Lincoln's Inn on this occasion entertained my daughter and me to luncheon and conversation—both admirable.

Of all the events of these years, from one point of view, one which had very little publicity was the most important. It is recorded in my desk diary that on June 21st, 1965, Sir James Harman, Alderman and former Lord Mayor intended to hold a press conference in the Chapter House on the subject of cleaning the exterior of St. Paul's Cathedral. My friend Sir James had pondered this project for some time and he knew that the Dean and Chapter had raised so much money for St. Paul's that they could not make another appeal when their original appeal for post-war restoration had included no mention of external cleaning. He knew also that opinion was divided on the desirability of such an expensive operation. Sir James offered to raise the money himself. This munificent proposal forced the Chapter to take the project very seriously. There were two kinds of objection; aesthetic and structural. There were authorities who admired the black and white appearance of St. Paul's and found the dark patches caused by centuries of soot attractive, as it were like beauty patches on the faces of the great ladies of Wren's time. Others dwelt on the possible results of washing and scraping the stones and foretold the crumbling of the fabric in the near future. Buildings in Paris of about the same age were being cleaned at the time and Lord Mottistone and his partner, Paul Paget, consulted the French experts who co-operated by advising out of their experience. Once more the Dean and Chapter had to make a decision without clear and united guidance from the experts and I believe that once more they made the courageous and right decision—but I suppose we cannot yet be quite sure and there are still objectors who deplore the removal of the soot. And what encrustations of soot were washed away! No one who has not seen the Cathedral closely, both before and after the cleaning, can have any idea of the changes produced by streams of cold water. Cherub faces in clusters, like that of the "weeping cherub", have been brought to light and the enrichment of the walls by delicate and charming patterns is now visible to the public.

The elaborate scaffolding required for cleaning could be used in the last war damage operation, which consisted of the repair of the leaden dome. The large holes had been covered up, but there were hundreds of small holes, most of them caused by ack-ack shrapnel. There was no need to replace Wren's lead; it was taken down, melted and restored. It remained a question in my mind whether I should see the dome free from scaffolding before I ceased to be Dean. It would have been a pleasant coincidence if my departure and that of the scaffolding had been simultaneous, but it beat me by nearly a year. A less fanciful reason for wishing the speedy disappearance of the scaffolding was the temptation it offered to boys who evaded guards and appeared from time to time at hair-raising altitudes. This story of a generous gift and how it was accepted and used ends happily with a feast given by the contractors, Szerelmy, to the chief representatives of the Cathedral at which we told each other what good fellows we were and what a good job we had done. How good we shall have to wait to know. Who can tell how long the cleaning will last? Already the enchanting honey colour which followed on the washing is fading and the colour is near white. The optimists think St. Paul's will need no washing again for 250 years. It will last my time.

Sir James's benefaction improved enormously the outward appearance of St. Paul's, but in my opinion the town planners were at the same time spoiling the City's skyline by building massive towers which interrupted the views of St. Paul's and finally ruined Christopher Wren's conception of London gathered round the Cathedral. Though on the whole the rebuilding of the City of London is to me a bitter disappointment, I would not deny that there are some welcome improvements. Speaking now only of the "square mile" of the City, the only almost unqualified improvement is Cheapside and it may be that when the new buildings on the south side of St. Paul's are completed we shall be able to acclaim a masterpiece of planning. I will also admit that the buildings on the north side of St. Paul's are not so bad as I had feared. Yet to speak frankly, the impression which I have is that, when the opportunity came to build London's "waste places" we had not the men who could rise to it.

Could it be that it came when the art of architecture was in decline? Not altogether, I think. Perhaps the fault is not so much in the architects as in the citizens who employed them. The problem of the future of St. Paul's in the changing City was not caused by the war; it existed in 1935 and at that time we were concerned with the deteriorating position of St. Paul's owing to the height of new buildings in Fleet Street. Sir Edwin Lutyens helped to keep the view from Fleet Street open. When the bombing started, Lutyens was thrilled by the possible developments if the buildings in the vicinity of the Cathedral were destroyed. He produced a plan which embodied Wren's ideal adapted to modern conditions. When he was kind enough to comment for our benefit on his designs, I confess I had a feeling that they were too good to be true, or at least to be practical politics, by which I meant likely to be accepted by business men who were concerned with rents and rates. I did think, however, that they would accept a modified version which would keep the main features of Lutyens' dream—particularly the open sweep from the south portico of the Cathedral down to the river. As I write these words, it seems probable that something like this on a smaller scale will be done.

We did what we could, at considerable expense, to oppose the more glaring violences done to the Cathedral precincts, including the intrusive Juxon House, but with almost no effect. We and our descendants will have to live with these buildings and must make the best of them. The Cathedral Square is the most successful part of the new work and could be dignified, but I think it has changed the weather (so to speak) of St. Paul's in unforeseen ways. When there is any wind the west steps of St. Paul's are its playground—that has always been so, but now the high buildings channel the gusts so that children and old people can be blown down by a sudden burst, while in strong winds the Cathedral Square is a kind of cave of Aeolus round which dust and waste paper are chased by breezes. No doubt a way will be found to mitigate these inconveniences.

I am impatient to finish this chapter and I was impatient when I lived it—at least for three years. Not that I looked forward to leaving St. Paul's, but I knew that it had become a part of myself and, when it was taken away, I would have to remake my life. The Cathedral was not idle; the national and ecclesiastical services were more numerous than ever, but they ceased to thrill me. I would wonder how much religion was behind them and how much pride, search for prestige and personal ambition were mixed with it. Of the daily services and what my predecessor Dr. Inge described as the "constant serenading" of the Almighty, I never tired and to have them as part of one's daily work was a priceless benefit. For ten years I had suffered from that great trial of the aged—the drifting away of old friends into the next world and, what was often harder to bear, their drifting away into mental eclipse and imbecility.

When the building of the Choir School had sufficiently advanced, the date for its opening and consecration was fixed for May 4th, 1967, and I at once announced the date of my resignation as eight days later, May 12th.

In recording the last phase of the office of Dean of St. Paul's, I ought to have mentioned much earlier the gracious action of The Queen in bestowing on me the Companion of Honour (C.H.) in 1962. I am glad that my wife lived to rejoice in this new honour which we both associated with our memories of Dick Sheppard, who always wore his C.H. decoration in St. Paul's. The honour is limited in number and is a kind of junior O.M.; the Sovereign is said to have special interest in choosing members and each has a special investiture to himself. I decided to adopt Dick's custom.

Musing in the deanery when the date of my retirement was fixed was not unmixed sadness, though I did not hide from myself that much which had become a part of my life must fade out, and that I had still to face the judgment on my stewardship. My huge and dignified house was part white elephant but also wonderfully spacious and full of memories. I thought of its front façade and of its front door with Grinling Gibbons' carvings of lions and leaves and of the elegant stone steps which led to it. I thought of the entrance hall, with its fireplace and logs, the portraits of former deans and the bench on which the lackeys used to sit outside the dining-room. In the thirty years of my occupation of the deanery, what a variety of persons had entered by that door! With that quirk towards the bizarre which my memory seems to show, the first picture which came to mind was of a man whom I prevented from entering by the door. It was in the beginning of my deanship when we were quite new to the place. One day a message came from the police that a man had escaped from a mental hospital who was dangerous and had a grudge against me. He had a scar, I was told, on his right cheek and would be wearing a brown coat. Shortly before we had received an anonymous letter telling me how to administer St. Paul's and ending with the warning "to disobey means death". That same morning while dealing with correspondence my secretary answered the door and there stood before her a man wearing a brown coat and what she took to be a scar on his right cheek, who demanded to see me on urgent business. She reported to me and I immediately rang the police who said they would come at once and asked us to keep our visitor in conversation without letting him enter the house. In a few minutes while we were talking to the man two policemen walked stealthily through the courtyard and, springing up the stone steps, clutched him on both sides and hurried him out of our sight. We never saw him again—but he was the wrong man anyway! He had come to ask me a question on religion. I left it to the police to explain the error.

In the pre-war years, too, the greater part of the Oxford University Eleven once slept scattered about in the attics and corridors during the Universities cricket match. Our son Michael kept wicket for Oxford. It was the year when he got a first in "Greats" and the culminating year of his youth. How high were our hopes for him and his future and how happy we were in that summer weather. The threat of war to us then was only a "cloud no bigger than a man's hand".

In those days when domestic help was available we could afford some modest lunches and dinners. An exceptional one was for all the rural deans in the diocese of London, together with the archdeacons and suffragan bishops. Margaret had a cold on the night and our daughter Barbara found herself playing the part of hostess at a very tender age; she did so with admirable composure. An argument arose in the family circle about the proper collective noun. I did not accept one member's suggestion; a "gaggle of rural deans".

The war years had left the old house still standing but minus one half of its roof and most of its windows. When it was habitable again on the upper storey, our son, Bryan, with his wife, Margaret, his small son, Paul, and daughter, Celia, moved in and occupied it. Bryan had spent profitable years in Oxford, after demobilisation, where he obtained the D.M. He came to live in the deanery in the last stage of his climb to consultant's rank and we were glad indeed to have the whole family so near at hand. Bryan's reputation in the sphere of neurology rapidly grew and it was my pride to read his writings and attempt to understand them. When he was elected a member of the Athenaeum Club I was thrilled to be his proposer. Bryan is a scientific researcher in his field and at the same time one who carries on the tradition of English medicine—the alliance of science, compassion and culture.

The deanery seemed empty when Bryan and his family moved to Derby on his appointment as consultant in the Royal Derby Infirmary, but that was partly remedied when my friend W. M. Atkins, at one time minor canon and librarian of St. Paul's and later rector of St. George's, Hanover Square, occupied some of the rooms. He had no vicarage or rectory and it seemed to us we might lend him our spare rooms, particularly as he and I were engaged at the time in editing the *History of St. Paul's*.

But musing does not allow itself to be confined and my musing went on to embrace the whole Cathedral. The word "family" is sometimes used of church groups. I did not employ it often, because I was wary of sentimental language, but in these last months of my deanship, I really felt like the father of a large, clever and good-tempered family. The spirit of fellowship pervaded the group. The Works Staff were friends and Mr. Harvey, the clerk of works, set an example of devotion to the Cathedral. I think the building and its history had an influence on all who worked in it. Among so many friends it is hard to single out individuals but two surveyors and architects must be mentioned. Lord Mottistone, whose sudden death grieved so many, did not live to see the Choir School and the tower of St. Augustine completed, but the Cathedral has a memorial of him in the pulpit, which he designed. Paul Paget, his partner, who succeeded him, retired in 1969, after me. His skill and integrity are known widely and he has friends in many places but nowhere more than in St. Paul's.

Among the minor canons, Joseph Robinson steps forward in my musing. I had resolved to do what I could to help poor and struggling scholars, among whom I had been one. Robinson is a real scholar and a real theologian. I rejoiced that he was appointed canon of Canterbury, with a delightful little house in the Close, where his children can play in a garden.

The receiver and registrar, David Floyd Ewin, had been so close to me day by day for so many years that I could hardly imagine a time when he would not be just over the road to be consulted on every kind of business and of the virgers, Mr. Overington and Mr. Morrison, I felt they were part of the order of things.

Mr. Rogers, voluntary Cathedral chorister and expert physiotherapist, who had helped me to keep active for many years, most generously continued to treat me.

An idea dawned upon me. How thankful I ought to be that so much of my life had been lived in the context of such beauty. Two Cathedrals had been my homes and places of business, Exeter and St. Paul's, so different from one another but each of surpassing beauty. In each I had worshipped with the loveliness of sound. Gratitude to the musicians who had made the music flooded my mind, as I thought of Sir Thomas Armstrong, Sir Stanley Marchant, Sir John Dykes Bower, Dr. Douglas Hopkins, Mr. Harry Gabb and so many other music makers, choristers and organists, men and boys. The headmasters of the Choir School and their wives had been good neighbours: Jessop Price and his artistic wife, who evacuated the school and brought it back at the war's end, and John Llewellyn and his wife, Audrey, to whom I owe so much for their help in my wife's illness and in my desolation after her death. All these are indelibly inscribed in my memory.

Perhaps it was only natural that among my musings thoughts about my own future should occur. I was indeed fortunate that others were thinking and acting for me. I feel that in these chronicles I have written too little about Barbara and her husband, Martin Hebb. He has always been a model son-in-law and in the operation "abandon deanery and set up elsewhere" he played a leading part. He looked after my financial prospects, which were complicated by the fact that I was not eligible for any pension. He was concerned with the distribution of furniture which I had to discard. In those last months my granddaughter, Celia Matthews, stayed with me and made me feel that, after all, I was not quite out of touch with youth.

I ought to have pulled myself together, I suppose, and taken a more active part, but I had not yet said farewell, in my imagination, to the past; it was on the past that I mused. And in these final days as Dean, the sound of music from the Choir School next door really wrung my heart. I could not bear to think that I had heard for the last time the boys singing their morning hymn or rehearsing the anthems. It hurt me to remember that no one would hear those delightful sounds in the deanery again.

The singing boys had always been my joy, not only because of the lovely sounds they made but because they were so happy and lively. Walter de la Mare, an old chorister, was a benefactor to the school and used to give a prize for English poetical composition. In fact he put one or two poems, written by choristers, in his charming book *Early one morning*. When he died I took over the prize and had much fun and some enlightenment from the discussion of poems submitted. It saddened me that I should never again take the whole school to the theatre to celebrate the feast of the Conversion of St. Paul. In a thousand ways I should miss them and, though all thirty-eight now knew me well, in a year's time the lowest form would never have heard my name.

We approach the final scene. On Ascension Day, May 4th, 1967, I preached for ten minutes at the sung Eucharist. I then enjoyed the hospitality of the Goldsmiths' Company at lunch: the Lord Mayor and the Bishop of London attended Evensong at 3.15 p.m. and then proceeded, in torrents of rain, to the opening and blessing of the new Choir School, when I handed over, with due solemnity, the key of the school to the Lord Mayor. A week later I ceased to be Dean of St. Paul's.

But I did not cease to have a link with my loved Cathedral. The Bishop of London had a surprise in store for me. At the dinner in Fulham Palace which Mrs. Stopford and he gave for me, he announced that he was appointing me Dean Emeritus. I value this title greatly, partly because it reminds me of the unvarying kindness and friendship which Mrs. Stopford and he have always shown—I wonder how such busy persons find time to be so thoughtful for their multitudes of friends. Another and less respectable reason for gratitude is that I can still claim to be "Very Reverend"; the day never came when I declined to the simple status of "Reverend".

Two magnificent arm chairs were presented to me at a party in the Chapter House by my friends and colleagues in St. Paul's. God bless them all.

The play is over. How shall we bring down the curtain? I preached no farewell sermon, but my sermon on Easter Day was to me a kind of last testimony of faith. Let us end with that.

The Moment of Truth

I Corinthians XV 13, 14: "If there be no resurrection, then Christ was not raised . . . then our gospel is null and void, and so is your faith." (New English Bible)

St. Paul is writing about some self-styled Christians who did not believe that there was any hope of resurrection and he challenges them to say what they believed about Christ. Did Christ rise? Do you deny that? If you do, then there is no gospel and no basis for faith.

In spite of many profound differences in respect of belief in the Resurrection there is a resemblance between St. Paul's situation and ours. We are often rightly urged to be "realistic" and we had better start by looking facts in the face with regard to the extent of unbelief in the present generation. We don't need statistical research to prove what is obvious to any man who listens to the talk of his fellow citizens, that a large proportion of the population either are indifferent to the question of Christ's Resurrection or are definitely negative in their reaction to the message of Easter. They deny the Resurrection both as an historical event and as an eternal truth—in both senses, a large number believe today the Resurrection is not true.

We who are here today to celebrate the glorious Resurrection of the Son of God have a duty to witness to the truth of the message, "He is risen". It is a duty which today is exceptionally urgent and exceptionally difficult. Are we willing to witness, and are we competent to witness? Even the simplest and most unlearned Christian may have a part in the most vital and convincing kind of witness—that of showing forth the life of the Risen Christ in himself; but the intellect has its rights and an indispensable aspect of the Christian witness is the attempt to show that belief in the Resurrection of Christ is not a superstition but one which can be held by thoughtful and reasonable people. What then do we say when confronted by aggressive unbelievers? What kind of reason can we give for our hope and faith? It would be absurd to try to cover all this ground in one sermon; all that I can do is to suggest ways of thinking about it.

As a preliminary, I think it is very important to get things in the right proportion; we need to understand precisely what it is we are defending or presenting as the Christian gospel. Confusion and misunderstanding have been caused by failure to distinguish between convictions which are vital and those which are secondary. And again, it is important to realise what a large weight we should give to presuppositions. For example, we may be talking to a materialist who holds that the reality of everything is matter and motion and the universe is one infinite machine. He could not possibly believe in the Resurrection without completely contradicting his basic principles: but we may be talking to a man who believes in God as creative Mind; the task of defending our faith to him is already half accomplished.

But I must compress what I have to say and avoid losing direction in the vast fields of speculation and argument which lie all around my subject. Let me try to tell you quite simply where I start and where I end. In between these points are questions, difficulties, conjectures on which we shall find ample food for reflection if we are really interested in the eternal destiny of ourselves and those we love.

Where do I begin? I begin with the Christian Church which

exists beyond all doubt and has existed for a long time. The Christian Church tells me about Jesus Christ. I should never have heard about Him but for the Church. It puts into my hands the Bible and draws my special attention to the New Testament which purports to tell me who He is and what He does. So far we have mentioned only things which no reasonable person could doubt. Still keeping in the same cautious line of enquiry we can add that Jesus of Nazareth was a religious teacher who had disciples and spoke about the Kingdom of God. The fact that He was crucified is not really open to question, though the causes of the crucifixion and the allocation of responsibility between Jews and Romans are not free from difficulties. That He was crucified, however, is practically certain and the natural consequence was that His cause was ruined and His followers were dispersed. The surprising thing is not that this happened but that the defeat lasted for so short a time. We do not have to rely only on the Acts of the Apostles for evidence that there was a rapid recovery of confidence in the followers of the crucified Jesus. After a time to be reckoned in weeks the Christian Church emerged. At first it had no notable or influential leader though the conversion of Paul who had been a prominent persecutor brought into the Church a man of genius and a leader of heroic mould. The Church spread with gathering momentum and in thirty years from the Crucifixion had become a social and political factor in Rome and other large cities such as Corinth, Antioch, Ephesus and Alexandria. In A.D. 64 the Church was sufficiently prominent and numerous to be the victim of a large scale persecution by the Emperor Nero. But neither Nero's burning of Christian martyrs nor the contempt of the educated classes stopped the onward march of the cross and 300 years after the birth of Christ the persecuted and despised Church was victorious and paganism vanquished.

Our great sceptical historian Edward Gibbon saw clearly that this remarkable and true story demanded an explanation and in his famous 15th chapter of the *Decline and Fall of the Roman Empire* he has given us a list of purely historical causes which he argues account for the survival and triumph of the Church and exclude any supernatural influence. Though I think Gibbon wrong I would never dissuade anyone from reading this chapter because it is a masterly piece of writing and all the causes he suggests had some effect, but when you have read it I would ask you to look again at what the Church itself believed about its victory. It is all in the New Testament. As Gibbon said, their belief in the Resurrection of Christ was a cause, but of course in his view a mistake; the Church believed that the Resurrection was both an historical fact and an eternal truth; it believed that it was the earthly body of the Risen Christ and that the evidence of personal experience from the first Easter day onwards was available to all those who were redeemed members of His body, that is of the Church.

The later chapters of the history of the Church are confused and often disappointing and indeed I often think that it could be represented by critics as a standing objection to the Christian gospel. But this at least can be said even at the worst times: the promise, "I am with you always even unto the end of the world" has never been wholly forgotten and there have always been groups and individuals who lived by the power of the Resurrection.

We began with the earliest Church—the Church as it was on the day of Pentecost when the Holy Spirit was poured out upon it; we will end with the contemporary Church—our Church. A momentous difference separates us from the first century. I need not dwell upon the obvious. Sufficient to say that we are in the middle of a scientific and technological leap forward which has radically changed not only our idea of the Universe but the very manner of our thinking. Can it be wondered that the Church—the "ark of salvation"—rocks in the storm? I am very glad that I managed to persuade the artist to change the picture of the Ark in our beautiful East window. He had represented the Ark as floating on a perfectly calm sea but I protested that the true Church of Christ never has been and never will be, in this world, becalmed. It will always be battling with the waves. The really wonderful thing is that in all these changes not only the teaching but the person of Christ is a powerful motive force. New Testament scholars warn us that the material for a biography or character study of Christ is not to be found in the New Testament. Yet all the time men and women, and children too, continue to live, as they say, "in Christ", in harmony with Him and by the power that He gives them. I will go further: illogically, as it seems, some of those who as scholars deny that we can have any certain knowledge of the historical

Jesus—men like Albert Schweitzer—are among those who in daily life walk most fruitfully in His steps and as it were restore the waste places they have made in their critical study of the New Testament by the witness of their obedient lives to the Risen Christ.

You see, as we pursue our course of reflection on belief in the Resurrection the discussion becomes personal and embarrassing. We can't go on in the detached and objective manner as if we were not involved. The question is not simply, can I believe the testimony of others to the Resurrection? It faces us with another question, can I hesitate any longer to be myself a witness to the Resurrection by allowing the Risen Christ to shine in me?

Have you noticed one rather strange thing about the appearances of the Risen Christ to individuals? The two disciples on the road to Emmaus; the solitary figure in the mist by the lake; Mary Magdalen's impression of the gardener by the tomb; at first sight the Lord Jesus is not recognised, but soon there comes the "moment of truth" and the cry, "It is the Lord". It is as if the Master is disguised and is waiting for the disguise to be penetrated by the disciple. "The moment of truth": I don't know who first used this phrase; I came across it in an American story about a bull fight where it was used to describe the feeling of a bull when he dimly realised that he was about to be slaughtered—to make a sadists' holiday. But "moment of truth" is better used to describe experiences of sudden revelation and sudden joy. Have you never had one when the eyes of your spirit were opened? I am talking, for example, to a person who seems quite commonplace and ordinary and then something he says or does, some gesture or even some silence reveals to me that he is quite an extraordinary person; Christ is living in him, he is a living witness to the Risen Christ; and because the Christ in me responds we have our moment of truth and joy. I am strengthened and confirmed in my faith that Christ is risen and I am risen with Him to eternal life.

·   ·   ·

On May 13th I finally shut the deanery door and without looking back left for Derby to be with my son Bryan and Margaret his wife.

Many kind and eulogistic words were spoken about me, which I dare not quote, lest it should be supposed that I believed them all. I venture to quote a very short poem by a very young poet which appeared in the *Choristers' Magazine*. It was written by Master Robert Clark (age 11 years) and appeals to me by its succinct statement of what I would like to believe I tried to do, linking me with the movement of the school from Carter Lane to New Change:

For Dean Matthews on his Retirement

> Author, scholar, preacher, poet,
> Words of comfort,
> Words of peace;
> Thirty-four to sixty-seven,
> All will remember you.
>
> Through the war you kept the watch,
> And as a Phoenix from the ashes
> Wren's great work rose up again
> From the desolation round it,
> It will remember you.
>
> Carter Lane saw you come,
> New Change sees you go,
> Thirty-four to sixty-seven,
> Retire in peace, our Dean.
> We will remember you.

Thank you, Robert!

Index